Creating Community Anywhere

Creating Community Anywhere

Finding Support and Connection in a Fragmented World

Carolyn R. Shaffer
and Kristin Anundsen

Foreword by M. Scott Peck, M.D.

A Jeremy P. Tarcher/Putnam Book
published by
G. P. PUTNAM'S SONS
New York

Kristin:
To my family of friends, who sustain me daily, and members of my biological family, who are with me despite geographical distance.

Carolyn:
To my husband, Sypko Andreae, and my extended Shenoa family, from whom I have learned the deeper meaning of partnership and community.

Jeremy P. Tarcher/Perigee Books
are published by
The Putnam Publishing Group
200 Madison Avenue
New York, NY 10016

Library of Congress Cataloging-in-Publication Data

Shaffer, Carolyn, date.
Creating community anywhere : finding support and connection in a fragmented world / by Carolyn R. Shaffer and Kristin Anundsen : foreword by M. Scott Peck.
p. cm.
Includes bibliographical references.
ISBN 0-87477-746-1 (alk. paper)
1. Community. 2. Social groups. 3. Community development.
I. Anundsen, Kristin. II. Title.
HM131.S437 1993 93-14895 CIP
307—dc20

Photographs reprinted with permission of Don Armfield, page 288; Kathleen Thormod Carr, pages 34, 70; courtesy of Chattanooga Venture/Finn Bille, pages 90, 250; The CoHousing Co., page 152; Heather Hafleigh, pages 170, 270; Jeff Holland, page 20; Jones & Resikos (courtesy of Herman Miller, Inc.), page 112; © James Konwinski, page 222; Stephen Mangold, page 304, Jennifer Leigh Sauer, page 2; Jane Scherr, page 206; Marvin W. Schwartz, page 52; courtesy of Sirius Community, page 186; © Jane Standerfer, page 130.

Cartoons reprinted courtesy of Kirk Anderson, Madison, WI, pages 30, 139, 311.

Design by Mauna Eichner
Cover design by Lee Fukui
Cover illustration © by Robert de Michiell
Printed in the United States of America
5 6 7 8 9 10

This book is printed on acid-free paper.

Contents

Foreword

THERE IS SOMETHING AFOOT. Social scientists might label it "the community movement." From an ivory tower, they also might hedge their bets, leaving wide open the possibility that it is but a fleeting phenomenon on the social scene.

I cannot be quite so objective. Almost a decade ago, I first penned the words, "In and through community lies the salvation of the world." Last year, after nine long years of working together with hundreds of others in the context of the Foundation for Community Encouragement (FCE), I publicly reaffirmed that grandiose-sounding statement. In regard to the community movement, I am not an onlooker; I am a dedicated participant. In the long run, I do not believe that such participation is an option. There is no viable alternative—no other way out for survival.

In this book, Carolyn Shaffer and Kristin Anundsen wisely present community, for the time being, as a choice. They are very gentle. And gentleness is needed in this time of transition. Over and over again, they say, "If this is the way you would like to live, here are some of the ways you might go about it." And in doing so, they have written the most comprehensive book I know about the community movement in all its variety, complete with helpful, up-to-date resources.

On one level, the social scientists would be correct to hedge their bets. The requirements of real community—such as personal commitment, honesty, and vulnerability—are so alien to our twentieth-century culture of rugged individualism that it is utterly unclear whether the citizenry as a whole will be willing to meet them. As a species, we may not choose survival.

So if you do choose to explore the "less traveled road" of community, you will be embarking on a true cultural adventure. As the book says, communities are "the research and development centers for society."

Among the reasons I feel privileged to introduce this book is that its authors portray community with integrity. They clearly identify it as a current social frontier. With integrity, they do not attempt to make life on the frontier sound easy or even particularly glamorous. It is hard work. But they also make it clear that you will not be alone; there are many human resources to call upon if you are humble enough to ask for help in your group life. Group or community consultants are analogous to psychotherapists for individuals: the healthiest and wisest are the most likely to seek their services; the most blind and unhealthy are the most likely to stay away.

I believe the authors have been wise to restrict their research to the United States. But it should also be made clear that the community movement is international. No example is more successful than the L'Arche communities, which work with the retarded. Originating in France, these communities now number close to one hundred around the globe. FCE itself already has performed services in the United States, Canada, Wales, Scotland, England, South Africa, Australia, and Russia.

Why this movement now? Very simply, our organizations and institutions, reflecting the prevailing "ethic" of rugged individualism, are no longer working. Look around. The old society is dying. If you join the community movement, your existence may not be any easier, but it will be more alive.

M. Scott Peck

Acknowledgments

IN WRITING THIS BOOK, we deepened and broadened our own community and experienced support beyond any that we could have imagined. Our friends and colleagues also lovingly challenged us—to clarify our ideas, be true to ourselves, persevere through difficulties—as only partners in true community do. At times, we wished we did not have to live every chapter as we wrote it, especially when we came to the shadow and conflict chapters. But, at every turn, we found support, sometimes in unexpected places.

So many people made this book possible that we cannot hope to mention each by name and stay within the limits of the standard acknowledgment format. We thank all who took time from their busy schedules to provide interviews, contacts for interviews, resource material, photos, guidance, critiques, and listening ears.

We especially wish to thank Sypko Andreae, our computer wizard, electronic community expert, schedule manager, Macintosh formatter, and unpaid all-around assistant, without whom we never would have finished this book on time. Thanks to Sypko's technical support, the two of us were able to stay in electronic contact throughout the years of writing this book, shuttling versions of chapters back and forth as quickly as if we were in the same room instead of across San Francisco Bay from one another. In the last few weeks of our producing a final draft, Sypko devoted himself virtually full-time to the project despite an uncooperative body that sent him to the emergency room at one point. I (Carolyn) am profoundly grateful to my generous-hearted friend and husband for believing in me and this book and supporting me emotionally and spiritually, as well as practically, through the ups and downs of the last few years. He knew when to bring tea and give a hug and when to call a planning meeting to set new deadlines.

Also crucial to delivering this book on time—and with its concepts and its resource lists in order—was Tom Atlee, social change philosopher, editor, research assistant, and word processor (among other things). In the final weeks of producing the final draft, Tom worked mostly as a volunteer and, like Sypko, almost around the clock. Throughout the writing of the book, Tom provided invaluable insights, editing suggestions, and resources for almost every chapter.

Others who shared professional and philosophical insights as well as their personal stories include Claude Whitmyer, John Helie, Peter Gibb, Shoshana Alexander, Sandra Lewis, Susan Tieger, David Johnston, Eleanor Cooper, Jim Autry, Marc Kasky, Tova Green, and Corinne McLaughlin and Gordon Davidson and other members of the Sirius Community.

Our community study group helped us clarify our ideas, practice community-building skills, and resolve our shared-authorship issues. Its long-term members included Sypko, Susan, Celest Powell, Carolyn North, and Roger Harrison.

Founding members of the study group met through mutual participation in the Shenoa Retreat and Learning Center. Shenoa served as an informal laboratory in which the two of us refined many of our notions about community building. Carolyn—deeply involved, with Sypko, in major aspects of this multi-layered community—is especially grateful for the love and support she has received here and the learning she has experienced. Like any true community, Shenoa serves as both cradle and cauldron, providing a safe container in which its members and their evolving vision can grow and be tested. We appreciate the time and thought Stephan Brown, Mary Anna Maloney, and other Shenoa staff and Land Stewards gave to the various chapters featuring Shenoa stories. We also thank former (and, we hope, future) Shenoans Rennie and Hope Innis, Jane Harris, and M. L. Mackie for their insights.

We both thank Suzanne Arms Wimberley, Rosalind Diamond, and Dori Gombold, our process consultants, whose professional guidance helped keep us in partnership. Carolyn acknowledges, with gratitude, the circle of women (plus Sypko) who gathered on short notice to create a ritual of empowerment during the darkest days: Sandra, Susan, Shoshana, Ruth Eckland, Laurinda Gilmore, Caite Mathis, and Mary Jean Haley. Carolyn appreciates the many times these and other friends provided support and encouragement.

Others who helped in myriad ways, from finding margin quotes and photos to reviewing chapters and providing resources, include: Stacy Horn and others in the ECHO network, the staff of Chattanooga Venture, Carl Moore, Joan McIntosh, Michael Doyle, Margaret Harmon, Geoph Kozeny, Don Lindemann, Bonnie Fish, Kathryn McCamant, Ken Norwood, Kay Tift, Frances Moore Lappé, Paul M. Du Bois, Arlene Skolnick, Nancy Lon, David and Alexandra McNamara, Kay Lynne Sherman, Garth Alley, Eleanor Vincent, Betty Didcoct, David Goff, William Lonsdale, Kay McClure, Suse Moyal, Terry Mollner, Fred Olsen, Julia Ketcham and Richard Hawkins of the Rapha Community, and Lynell Arnott, Hollis Ryan, and Nan Kreckner of the Goodenough Community.

Jeremy Tarcher, our publisher, recognized the value of a book on community and believed we could produce one. And Connie Zweig, our editor, and Felicia Eth, our agent, encouraged us and gave us the confidence to continue. Allen Mikaelian, assistant editor at Tarcher, guided us calmly and competently through many of the myriad details and challenges of the editing process. We also wish to acknowledge Peter Beren, who introduced us to Jeremy P. Tarcher, Inc., and Claude Whitmyer, who introduced us to Peter. At Putnam, Coral Tysliava was especially helpful at the copyediting and galley stages. Ron Jones suggested an excellent modification of our book title, Rose Boché provided the title for Chapter Ten, and Lynne dal Poggetto provided invaluable assistance researching photos and obtaining permissions.

We salute, as well, our many support groups, friends, colleagues, family members, and the others who make up our communities.

Authors' Note

SOME OF THE PEOPLE we interviewed agreed to let us use their full names in recounting their personal stories. Others have preferred that we talk about their experiences without revealing their identities. We have honored these preferences—in fact, in a few cases we decided to protect the privacy of sources who did not explicitly ask us to.

When you read a full name in these pages, you can be sure that this is the person's actual name. A first name, by itself, may be a pseudonym. To further protect the privacy of certain sources, we have changed certain details in a few stories.

Introduction

As we interviewed women and men across the United States in researching this book, we discovered how deeply people yearn for community. We also learned that most don't know how to begin creating the kind of community they long for. Some wax nostalgic about the extended families and closely knit neighborhoods of their own or their parents' youth, yet hold little hope of reconstructing anything resembling this in their own lives. Others have fled from their childhood homes to escape family and community they considered stifling, abusive, or hypocritical. They long for a web of connection and support but have no models of healthy community. Still others easily can imagine the details of their ideal community but their dream of it remains just a dream. They believe they have to live without community until they have saved enough money to construct their ideal version and have met the right people to join in the project.

If you yearn for community, this book tells how you can begin creating it in your life now, whether you live in the city or the country, are single or partnered, and reside near or far from your relatives. You don't have to uproot yourself or your family and move to the country to experience the kind of mutual support and connection people often associate with small-town life. Using the models and skills we offer here, you can begin to create satisfying community wherever you live and work. While *Creating Community Anywhere* doesn't pretend to be a complete manual for building community, it can help you get started. Each chapter refers you to resources that provide specific guidance for whatever form of community appeals to you.

Too often, people postpone creating community because they consider the process an all-or-nothing endeavor that requires a major commitment of time and resources. Some identify community with living together and regretfully give up on the idea as incompatible with their current life circumstances. We want you to know that you do not have to move in with other people to enjoy mutually supportive community. In *Creating Community Anywhere,* you will meet groups of people who play, work, learn, and celebrate together with the same level of commitment that folks in small towns and closely knit neighborhoods did generations ago; yet many of these contemporary community builders live in ordinary apartments or single-family homes scattered across a large metropolitan region. For example, members of the Goodenough Community, who live in and around Seattle, have created a contemporary equivalent of old-fashioned barn-raising. When a member needs to move to a new house or paint a garage, the others throw a work party to help. The members also support each other's psychological and spiritual growth through community-sponsored workshops, retreats, and celebrations.

Many forms of community are simpler and require less commitment than Goodenough. Members choose to work, play, and live together as they pursue a shared vision. If you're not sure what type you're ready for, this book will help you sort out your options. It also tells you how you can test the waters. By trying some of the partial and temporary forms of community we describe here, such as peer support groups and wilderness adventure trips, you can learn important community-building skills and meet people you might want to include in a more committed, long-term community.

Creating Community Anywhere introduces you to people successfully creating webs of mutual connection and support in traditional and nontraditional settings. You will meet an urban professional, tired of associating with others like himself, who joined an amateur league hardball team and discovered the kind of heterogeneous community he had enjoyed in his hometown. For an older woman, recovering from her husband's death, an electronic community of seniors, linked by telephone lines and home computers, provided company through the long nights of grieving and continues to offer support and conversation. Several families you will meet in these pages either have created a residential urban neighborhood together or joined a well-established rural community.

By providing a wide range of models, we help you assess the forms and levels of commitment that will work best for you. We also supply you with tools, tips, and other resources to begin your own custom community-building endeavor. You'll learn how to create community agreements, run effective meetings, choose appropriate decision-making processes, and resolve conflicts. We also guide you through the phases of community, warning of the pitfalls and pointing out the opportunities that each provides.

But *Creating Community Anywhere* is more than a how-to book. We found that many who yearn for community have only a vague idea of what it means. We also have noticed that for all of the talk about community today, few politicians, pundits, and trend-watchers have shed much light on this subject. One of our primary reasons for writing this book is to offer a fresh perspective on the nature of community. The kind of community that works for the end of the twentieth century and the beginning of a new millennium is quite different from what worked for your grandparents and your ancestors before them. Unless you understand how community needs to be different today, you may flounder among a variety of forms, unable to determine which work for you and which do not. Your community also could blame itself for failures, such as interpersonal conflicts, that are not failures at all but essential parts of the process of community building. If your attempts at connecting with others in the past have left you dissatisfied, you might be measuring them against a faulty, outdated standard. In Chapter One, we offer a vision of a new kind of community, one that builds on the best of the traditional forms and takes into account the enormous psychological, sociological, and demographic changes of the past century.

While we believe that creating community is a lot simpler than most people think, we don't pretend that it's easy. Letting go of centuries of tradition- and role-bound models of relating is no easier for a group than it is for a couple or a family attempting to break out of outdated relationship patterns.

The two of us, as coauthors, had to practice many of the community-building skills we describe in the book as we wrote it. Twice we faced interpersonal crises that threatened to split apart our community of two. At one point, we met with a conflict resolution mediator. Now that we have completed our joint project, we can appreciate more than ever the value of our staying committed to it despite enormous differences in style, pacing, and perspective. We both agree that the book is stronger, deeper, and clearer than a version either of us might have written alone. To bring this strength, depth, and clarity to the book, both of us had to assert ourselves with honesty and passion, hear one another with an open mind and a loving heart, listen to the book itself and what it required, and recommit, again and again, to our common vision. These are the same simple but not necessarily easy attitudes and skills that can enable you to create the kind of community that nurtures and endures.

In this book, we focus on creating small-scale, primarily personal community. Yet the very attitudes and skills that we suggest you bring to this personal community—the ones that enabled the two of us to complete this book without sacrificing our individuality or our partnership—are the same ones that cities, nations, and the global community desperately need to survive into the twenty-first century. Increasing eruptions of hate, crime, racial and ethnic wars, and economic and ecological violence threaten to shred irreparably the fabric of our natural and social systems. Strategies of denial, attack, and control no longer work, whether practiced by governments or by social change groups. We can no longer afford the luxury of taking sides or ignoring our interdependence. We share a common sphere, the earth, which has no sides.

The only way we will turn the tide of polarization and destruction is by becoming willing to listen to one another across the barriers with open minds and hearts, and to respect each other's differences while affirming a common purpose. Frances Moore Lappe calls this "living democracy" and describes its essence as building relationships—a radically different approach to political change from forming a faction and selling your own agenda.

Developing such skills as healthy communication, fair conflict resolution, and inclusive decision making will not only bring intrinsic rewards to your personal life but will also help you contribute to turning the global tide one person or small group at a time. You don't need to feel powerless in the face of the many social and planetary threats, or retreat into private community as an escape from the dangers of the wider world. Listening and speaking openly across the barriers to your friend, mate, neighbor, or co-worker are excellent ways to model—and, we believe, to effect—the changes you yearn for in the wider world. For those of you who wish to build community and initiate social change beyond your immediate circles of family and friends, practicing at home and in your neighborhood can give you the confidence and skill to become a more effective social change agent. The community you create close to home also will provide the warmth and support you need to take on larger groups and issues.

As we worked on this book, we kept reading and hearing that people's awareness of interdependence is becoming more and more pervasive. Certainly, a systems orientation appears to be on the rise in fields ranging from business to psychology to subatomic physics. This is a perspective that takes relationships into account, and considers each thing a whole in itself and a part in relation to ever-larger wholes. Since interdependence is the essence of community, this increasing awareness is an encouraging sign.

We believe that the time is ripe for community-building—that sincere efforts to create supportive webs of relationship are likely to be met with greater understanding, enthusiasm, and participation than in the three or four previous decades.

In using this book to help you create community in your life and beyond, you might approach each chapter the way we suggest you approach community itself. Get a sense of what's there, notice what appeals to you and seems workable, and focus on that. Your intuitive responses will prove useful guides. Then, keep the book as a reference and a companion as you explore different forms of community and various levels of commitment. You may find some sections more relevant and helpful in the years to come.

Part One

What Community Is and Why We Need It

ONE

A Return to Community—But Not the Kind Our Grandparents Knew

Many of us under fifty years old have never known the feeling of a small town, the camaraderie around a "pot-belly stove," or even friends and neighbors we can know and trust.

BILL KAUTH

CHARITA ALLEN GREW UP in a neighborhood filled with aunts, uncles, cousins, and grandparents. "It was absolutely wonderful," she recalls. "If you got spanked at one house, you knew you could go somewhere else and immediately be accepted because they didn't know what had just happened, and it didn't matter anyway." Charita's mother was the oldest of nine, all of whom were born and grew up in the same mid-sized city in the South, and most of whom continued living in the same neighborhood even after they married and began producing children of their own.

Charita, one of the oldest of the third generation, remembers going from house to house to find not only affection but also the best menu for dinner. "If I didn't like what my mother was cooking, I could call an aunt or an uncle and ask 'What are you having?' If I didn't like that, I could call the next one and go right down the line."

Today, single and twenty-eight years old, Charita resides in an apartment complex where, even after two years, she has only a waving, hello-there acquaintance with her neighbors. She considers this an odd, disconnected way to live. Charita yearns for the closeness and easy camaraderie with neighbors, both kin and non-kin, that made her childhood so pleasant and secure. "The nurturing was shared then," she remembers, "as well as the pain."

Still, Charita considers herself lucky. She not only remains on good terms with her large, closely knit extended family, but she also lives within driving distance of most of them. Few American adults today enjoy such strong bonds with aunts, uncles, grandparents, and cousins. Many have become distanced from their families, emotionally or geographically or both. And their other relationships—with neighbors, friends, lovers, and colleagues—seem too incomplete or unstable to make up for the lack of old-style family cohesiveness.

Clearly this nation, though steeped in the severe individualism of the frontier notion of freedom, has a yearning for the community feeling that comes from collective undertakings. . . . The question is whether any enterprise other than war can tap that yearning.

GEORGE WILL

It seems that we have lost hold of our communities. It seems as though our country is pulling apart into separate peoples who do not know each other.

EDWARD M. KENNEDY

COMMUNITY IN TRANSITION

Only two or three generations ago, community was a fact of life for most people. Neighbors left their doors open, helped each other build things, and kept an eye out for one another's well-being. In 1930, less than eight percent of American households consisted of a single person, and many families occupied the same home for generations.

Today, almost a quarter of U.S. households consist of people living alone. Doors, literally and figuratively, are closed and locked to keep out crime and strangers. Americans move so frequently that direct mail marketers consider a two-year-old mailing list hopelessly out of date; more than thirty percent of the addresses will have changed in that time. More and more women, who used to be the caretakers of community while the men pursued opportunities in the larger world, now find it necessary to work outside the home as well. Neither women nor men feel they have much time to maintain the ties of mutual support. It is commonplace for families as well as singles to have little or no contact with others who live only a door or two away.

Earlier generations relied upon family and community for different functions than people do today. Not that many decades ago, relatives and neighbors helped each other give birth at homes and eventually die there. They nursed one another to health, took in the orphaned children of brothers and sisters who died young, and gave up personal ambitions to carry on the family business or to care for an aging parent. Today, institutions and professionals have taken over many of these roles. People go to hospitals, schools, and nursing homes to receive health care and education. Most are born and die in institutions. If they need a loan, they visit a bank before asking Uncle Joe or a neighbor. If they lose their job or their home, they go to a governmental agency for assistance. If they become depressed, they call a therapist.

As the old forms of community have unraveled, so have many marriages, families, and neighborhoods. Some individuals have fallen apart too, drifting into loneliness and isolation. As more and more people have lost the sense of inclusion and belonging, they have ceased to identify with their fellow humans and with the piece of the planet they all share. Crime, violence, addiction, depression, teen suicide, and other personal and social ills have mushroomed.

[America is a place] where men and even houses are easily moved about, and no one, almost, lives where he was born or believes what he has been taught.

George Santayana

The American dream used to mean owning your own home, taking care of problems by yourself, preserving your privacy, and placing top priority on improving your earning potential. But after decades of focusing on individual achievement and fulfillment, Americans are realizing that acquisition has not brought happiness and rugged individualism is inadequate. Even those who have settled down to raise families, and have managed to stay in touch with a large network of friends, feel that something is missing. They yearn for a deeper sense of belonging, kinship, and connection to some kind of larger, shared purpose. Some seek a child-friendly community, which allows a return to the easy informality of earlier times when friends and relatives lived nearby and were able and willing to take turns with child care. Most, whether single or partnered, long for continuity: a stable circle of family members—or friends who feel like family—that they can count on through good times and bad. But community is no longer a given, and the old forms do not fit current realities. If people want community today, they have to find new ways to create it for themselves.

In one way or another, we must find a place in a social network. It is not given for us to nearly the degree it was in prior times.

Paul L. Wachtel

The Legacy of Rootlessness

American culture has savored the freedom associated with autonomy and rootlessness. Its members have delighted in finding their own way and in not having to answer to anybody. Americans have defined themselves in terms of individual freedom: a people breaking away from old, limiting structures, dogmas, and attitudes and pushing forward to new frontiers.

But with every gain there is a loss, as director-writer Barry Levinson revealed so poignantly in his semi-autobiographical movie *Avalon*. Levinson traced the lives of three generations of a Jewish family that immigrated to the United States in the early 1900s. As the members of the second-generation became successful in business and moved out of the old, tightly knit neighborhood into the fast-growing, single-family-dwelling suburbs, their family lives turned drab and lonely. No longer were three generations laughing and arguing around the kitchen table of a cramped, multi-family flat. The second-generation wives were cooking alone in their modern kitchens while watching game shows on television. The increasingly successful husbands were working late at the store or the office, and the children—with no grandparents or cousins around to play with—were amusing themselves in silent living rooms or bedrooms. By movie's end, one of these children watches helplessly as his grandfather, who in earlier years always had been surrounded by family, lives out his days in a tiny room in a nursing home with his only companion a television set.

In place of materialism, many Americans are embracing simpler pleasures and homier values. They've been thinking hard about what really matters in their lives, and they've decided to make some changes. What matters is having time for family and friends, rest and recreation, good deeds and spirituality.

JANICE CASTRO

Even if they had wanted to, however, members of this family could not have turned back the clock. No matter how nostalgic people become for a familiar kind of cohesiveness, going "back home" rarely provides the answer. Few people can uproot themselves and their children and return to the old neighborhood. Most have no home to return to—divorces have fragmented the family, the friendly street has become a shopping mall, old friends have relocated thousands of miles away. Even those who return to what looks like home do not find the kind of community in which they grew up. Not only have specific towns, neighborhoods, and people changed, but the entire culture has shifted as well.

We are faced with having to learn again about interdependency and the need for rootedness after several centuries of having systematically—and proudly—dismantled our roots, ties, and traditions. We had grown so tall we thought we could afford to cut the roots that held us down, only to discover that the tallest trees need the most elaborate roots of all.

PAUL L. WACHTEL

New Forms for New Realities

This change is not a complete tragedy. As tightly knit and stable as most old-style communities were, they were also homogeneous, suspicious of outsiders, socially and economically stratified, emotionally stifling, and limited in opportunities for personal and professional development. So long as members belonged to the right ethnic, religious, or racial groups—or stayed in their place if they did not—and behaved within a narrowly defined set of parameters, they could count on strong communal support. But if they strayed too far outside the lines, their fellow community members might well shun or harass them. For example, sons and daughters who married outside their clan, class, or religion, or chose not to marry at all, risked being ostracized. Some in this stratified society transcended the boundaries of race, ethnicity, and class to help each other out professionally in time of need or to engage in socially acceptable recreational activities. For example, a white doctor and an African-American plumber

The Couples Connection

To better understand the profound shift going on in the way people view community, you need look no farther than the revolution that has been taking place in couple relationships. In earlier times, family and society determined the form and function of such partnerings, just as these two forces dictated community relationships. The quality of the personal relationships took second place. "If a marriage was unhappy," notes John Welwood in *Journey of the Heart: Intimate Relationship and the Path of Love*, "community pressure would hold it together." Only recently has this situation changed. The binding of family and community ties on individuals has loosened and fewer people feel compelled to conform to a common set of values.

Today, with few convincing extrinsic reasons to stay together, intrinsic rewards provide the primary glue for couples and communities. "Now, for the first time in history," proclaims Welwood, "every couple [and, we would add, every community] is on their own—to discover how to build a healthy relationship, and to forge their own vision of how and why to be together. *It is important to appreciate just how new this situation is. We are all pioneers in this unexplored territory.*" [Italics his.]

Fewer marital partners today are willing to be one half of a whole, or to let gender determine their roles. Part of the intrinsic reward they seek in their relationship is the opportunity to become whole by exploring whatever roles attract them. Both partners want to learn how to lead and how to serve, how to think and how to feel, how to speak the truth from the heart and how to listen to the truth with love.

Just as with the emerging conscious communities, the evolution of such conscious couple relationships is not necessarily smooth, especially when the partners' dreams appear to vary in significant ways. One partner may want several children and a home in the country, while the other may have city living in mind and, at the most, one child. A community of ten or twenty members multiplies the potential for such differences. Yet, the approaches that couples have been developing to deal with their differences and forge a satisfying life together can work as well for communities. The good news for those of you desiring to create conscious community is that you do not have to break totally new ground; couples have been doing the spadework for decades.

The traditional community was homogeneous . . . experienced relatively little change from one decade to the next and resented the little that it did experience . . . demanded a high degree of conformity . . . [and] was often unwelcoming to strangers and all too ready to reduce its communication with the external world.

JOHN W. GARDNER

might well have laughed and shared fishing stories at their sons' Little League games. But they likely would not have visited in each other's neighborhoods, shared personal secrets, or challenged the cultural arrangements that kept them from functioning as peers.

Today, Americans are not content simply to follow tradition or the expectations of others. People of different genders, races, income levels, sexual preferences, physical abilities, and so on are no longer staying in their places, geographically or socially. Couples and families also have begun to redefine relationships. Fewer and fewer partners are willing to be one half of a whole, defined by gender-based roles. In wider communities as well, people want to share leadership and try out new roles.

Although the West is known for its individualists, most of the West's history is one of cooperation. Westerners today are rediscovering cooperation as the "myth" for our times.

NORTH DAKOTA GOVERNOR
GEORGE SINNER

We believe that the demise of old-style communities, defined primarily by blood ties, place, and necessity, offers an unprecedented opportunity to create new models of community that incorporate the best qualities of the traditional forms without their limitations. People today are intentionally joining together to create communities based on shared intrinsic values rather than common external threats and obligations. These communities, whether composed of kin, non-kin, or a combination of both, are choosing to honor diversity, encourage change, and support individual expression within flexible, evolving structures that the members reexamine regularly.

As befits today's mobile society, community does not need to be defined entirely by where you live. You can choose to pursue community anywhere. Your work team, with whom you spend the largest part of your week, may provide more opportunities for kinship and inclusion than your residential neighborhood. You may feel closer to members of your men's or women's group, who commute to the meeting place from different towns, than you do to family members. You may even feel strongly connected to people you have never seen; growing numbers of personal-computer users around the globe share intimate conversations by way of electronically linked terminals. Any of these circles of relationship can provide fertile soil for community. You can even overlap your circles by introducing members of one group to those of another. If some of your communities fail to satisfy you, you can create new ones or change the existing ones through new group process techniques.

Choice is an important distinction between today's community and that of yesteryear. The first-generation family in *Avalon* created a tight community upon their arrival in Baltimore because they had no choice but to share houses, food, and income. Charita Allen's African-American ancestors originally stayed together in one area because Jim Crow laws forbade them to live in white neighborhoods and use white facilities. But like the subsequent generations in *Avalon,* Charita and other members of her family have now begun to leave the old neighborhood and spread across the city and into other states. Some are taking advantage of career opportunities; others simply are choosing to live in more convenient or attractive areas. "We feel more secure living in different places now than my grandparents and parents did when they were growing up," she says. "Back then, it didn't make sense to move away from the family into a white neighborhood because people wouldn't like you there and your children would most likely not be able to play with the neighbor kids." If Charita decided to move back to her grandparents' neighborhood, she would not be doing so because her family expected her to or because she needed their material support or protection. She would be making a conscious choice, knowing she could live in any number of neighborhoods, alone or with others.

We are not just another country. We have always been a special kind of community, linked by a web of rights and responsibilities, and bound together not by bloodlines, but by beliefs.

BILL CLINTON

For now, Charita has chosen to develop her own custom-made community of kin and non-kin who live in different parts of the city. In many ways, this community echoes the relational patterns of her extended family. For example, when one friend, a single mother, goes out of town on business trips, Charita takes care of her house and two school-age children. Not only does this offer the friend the practical kind of support people used to count on extended families to give, it also provides Charita with a chance to connect with children and take a break from apartment living.

Charita's kin-based extended family has developed a new tradition that helps members stay in touch, have fun, and improve their fitness at the same time. They have proclaimed the last Friday of every month Family Night. Relatives come from miles around to the gym of the middle school where Charita's mother serves as principal. They play basketball, jump rope, enjoy a potluck dinner, and otherwise enjoy each other's company.

Opportunities for community today are limited only by your imagination and the degree of your intention. Many individuals and groups, as you will discover in this book, are finding new ways to enrich their webs of relationship. They are taking some risks and doing so with excitement, some trepidation, and a great deal of that traditional American quality: individual initiative.

What Community Means

People today use the word "community" almost as loosely as the word "love." As a result, its meaning, like that of the "love," has become extremely fuzzy. People refer to their neighborhoods, towns, and cities as communities whether or not they know the people down the street. Journalists dub virtually every collection of people who share a salient characteristic or profession a community—referring, for example, to the gay community, the Hispanic community, and the medical community. When some hear us speak of creating community, they immediately picture an updated version of the 1960s idealistic commune in the country.

If there are vast numbers of a selfish, narcissistic "me generation" in America, we did not find them, but we certainly did find that the language of individualism, the primary American language of self-understanding, limits the ways in which people think.

ROBERT N. BELLAH AND COAUTHORS

One of the things a community is not is a simple geographical aggregate of people.

M. SCOTT PECK

Because community today can take so many different forms, it resists being pinned down by definition. But after much research and interviewing, we did develop a context for talking about it. The basic five-point definition we have arrived at is both strong and inclusive. It contains a time factor and encompasses both traditional forms and the newer ones that social pioneers are now forging.

Community is a dynamic whole that emerges when a group of people:

- participate in common practices;
- depend upon one another;
- make decisions together;
- identify themselves as part of something larger than the sum of their individual relationships; and
- commit themselves for the long term to their own, one another's, and the group's well-being.

Certain timeless qualities epitomize every type of community, whether traditional or newly emerging. Chief among these is commitment. Commitment as a group—whether to family, place, clear communication, or the healthy working out of conflict—requires that community members embody such other timeless values as trust, honesty, compassion, and respect.

Evolution toward Wholeness

Communities in the past that fit our definition tended to be what we call *functional communities.* In these, members support the physical and social well-being of the group and its participants, making sure all members are sheltered, clothed, fed, educated, and fit so that they can be productive and maintain the social order. However, its members do not spend much time examining the community's internal dynamics or questioning whether the individuals within it are feeling personally fulfilled by their participation. Many families, small towns, and urban neighborhoods prior to the 1960s exemplified such functional community, and some continue to do so today.

The emerging affiliations that we call *conscious community* incorporate many social and survival aspects of functional community, but also emphasize members' needs for personal expression, growth, and transformation. Conscious community nurtures in each of its members the unfolding from within that allows them to become more fully who they are—and it nurtures its own unfolding as well. Its members trust that what best serves the community's collective evolution also will best serve the individual evolution of its members, and vice versa—provided the members speak their truth with love and hold both their individual needs and the group's needs in their awareness.

This is the mystery of synergy, the ancient and new truth that characterizes the emerging communities. Individuals gain rather than give up power and freedom when they participate in communities such as these. The more individuals speak their minds and hearts in a group context, the greater the collective wisdom of the group and the wiser and stronger each individual becomes. Conscious community honors the individual as well as the group, knowing that the well-being of one cannot be bought at the expense of the other. It requires strong, healthy individuals who feel secure enough to speak truthfully, to listen to the truths of others, and to attune to the needs of the whole.

In such conscious community, members not only help each other take care of business together—the external task—but also reflect together on their common purpose, internal processes, and group dynamics. Who are we? Why have we come together? How are we doing in our relationships with one another? What might help us improve? How might we better walk our talk? Members may discover painful truths, but by staying committed to each other and the group as they work through their issues, they build a community so firmly rooted in learning, honesty, and love that it can handle any trial that may come its way.

Such a community renews itself regularly, celebrating individual and group passages and revising and recommitting to its vision and mission. In doing so, it challenges its members and itself to move beyond roles to wholeness.

Conscious community implies a systems understanding of reality. Each individual and group functions as a whole system within a larger whole. Each is complete in itself, yet is dependent upon the systems within it and beyond it. In this sense, community is like a living body, in which the brain, heart, and other organs are interdependent. Like such a body, community thrives on the diversity of its members. While occasionally even the healthiest community must ask a member to leave, rejecting all members

The Hopis say that we all began together; that each race went on a journey to learn its own road to power, and changed; that now is the time for us to return, to put the pieces of the puzzle back together, to make the circle whole.

STARHAWK (ON WHAT SHE LEARNED FROM BUCK GHOSTHORSE)

Community is like pornography, to paraphrase Justice Brennan: I don't know how to define it, but I sure as hell know it when I see it.

A FEDERAL JUDGE ATTENDING A COMMUNITY BUILDING WORKSHOP

who challenge the group by acting or thinking differently—being more emotional than the others, for instance, or more mental—would pose a serious threat. The resulting likemindedness may feel comfortable for a time but would eventually lead to a lack of vitality and wisdom.

Imagine a brain deciding to sever its connection with the body because it did not like the way the heart operated. All the heart did was dumbly pump blood day in and day out in the same old boring rhythm while the brain had to continuously make rapid-fire decisions regarding many different areas of behavior based on an overwhelming amount of information that never stopped coming. Why should two such different organs exist in the same body? the brain might ask. If the body were a typical human group, this question might seem reasonable. (How many people have been tempted to leave their families, neighborhoods, jobs, or social circles because certain members of the group were just too different from them?) But since the body is a living system, such a question is obviously self-deluding. Although the brain and the heart are each whole, separate organs, they are interdependent with each other and with the other organs and systems in the body. The body as a whole is not a completely autonomous entity either; it requires a dynamic relationship with a larger system that includes air, water, food, warmth, and much more to stay alive and healthy.

A true community is inclusive, and its greatest enemy is exclusivity. Groups who exclude others because of religious, ethnic, or more subtle differences are not communities.

FOUNDATION FOR COMMUNITY ENCOURAGEMENT

We live with heterogeneity and must design communities to handle it.

JOHN W. GARDNER

A community is no different. It is also an interdependent system. And if it isolates itself from the human and natural systems of which it is a part, both the individuals and the group become weaker. Conscious communities continually ask themselves whether the group is serving the greater community and what it may need from the greater community to perform its functions better.

This interdependent perspective prevents communities, from small families to nations, from becoming worlds unto themselves or worlds primarily in opposition to others. It keeps them open, flexible, and willing to embrace new people and ideas rather than becoming closed, controlling, and cultlike. Individuals in conscious communities also are willing to open themselves up. They share what lies beneath the surface, risk being vulnerable, and honor the feelings of others. As M. Scott Peck declares in *The Different Drum: Community Making and Peace,* "There is an 'allness' to community. It is not merely a matter of including different sexes, races, and creeds. It is also inclusive of the full range of human emotions. Tears are as welcome as laughter, fear as well as faith."

Most communities today cannot be categorized as either simply functional or totally conscious. They appear somewhere along a spectrum and can even move back and forth along that spectrum. Over the long term, the movement tends to be toward greater consciousness. However, to shift from a functional, survival-driven mode to a conscious, choice-driven one, a group needs to learn new attitudes and skills, just as certain couples have done as they have made the shift to conscious relationship. Conscious communities develop tools for maintaining and improving their internal processes—communication, conflict management, governance—and regularly monitor how well they are doing, internally and externally. They may need to develop specific organizational procedures to ensure that the group keeps its internal dynamics healthy while it takes care of external business.

Because the systems view of mind is not limited to individual organisms but can be extended to social and ecological systems, we may say that groups of people, societies, and cultures have a collective mind, and therefore also possess a collective consciousness.

FRITJOF CAPRA

As communities move toward the "conscious" end of the spectrum, they approach what we call *deep community*: a state in which the new attitudes and behaviors have become so internalized that they are second nature. As the partners in certain conscious couple relationships have discovered, what seemed such an effort in the beginning—communicating clearly, fighting fairly—has become simply the normal way they talk, argue, and resolve their differences. In deep community, members easily and naturally attune to what is best for themselves and the group. When they sense an imbalance, they give immediate and clear feedback to the others—just as the brain, heart, and other organs do within the body—enabling each to make whatever adjustments are needed to bring the system back into balance. Every member knows how to lead, follow, listen, speak from the heart, and mediate conflicts, and performs these functions spontaneously whenever a situation calls for them. Such deep community remains rare at this time, but it is something to aspire to as you struggle to master your group's new toolbox of community-building skills.

Proto-Community: A Chance to Practice for the Real Thing

Many experiences that feel like community do not quite match our strong definition, yet they provide great opportunities for experiencing mutual support and connection and for practicing community-building skills. In a study group discussion of community, one member, Sypko Andreae, recalled a week-long men's workshop in which the participants in his small group, instead of relating on a "What do you do for a living?" basis, looked deeply into each other's hearts and experienced great closeness as they stripped away pretense and allowed themselves to be vulnerable. But after the workshop was over, none of these men kept in touch with each other.

Synergy is everywhere in nature. If you plant two plants close together, the roots comingle and improve the quality of the soil so that both plants will grow better than if they were separated. If you put two pieces of wood together, they will hold much more than the total of the weight held by each separately. The whole is greater than the sum of its parts. One plus one equals three or more.

STEPHEN R. COVEY

The Three Dimensions of Community

If you want to determine whether your group qualifies as proto- or full community, check its dimensions. According to Tom Atlee, the editor of *Thinkpeace* who conceived the following three-dimensional perspective on community, an affiliation that has developed significantly in all three directions will feel like a real community, while one that is missing any one dimension, or only has slightly developed along one plane, will feel flat and leave you longing for more. Tom describes the dimensions as follows:

- *Length:* How long your group has shared experience and how committed you are to continue that sharing.
- *Breadth:* How many facets of your life you share, and how wide a range of people and experiences you include.
- *Depth:* How deeply, thoroughly, or intimately you share.

Imagine families in a small farming community who have lived as neighbors for generations and who fully intend to do so for the foreseeable future. They have raised their children together, helped bury each other's parents, and survived droughts and floods. The town includes young and old, rich and poor, liberals and conservatives, but no people of color and few artists and intellectuals. While the townspeople support each other on a practical level through personal and communal crises, they rarely talk about their feelings and keep their shameful family stories secret.

If you pictured this community as a solid object, it would look extremely long, quite broad, but deep at only one end.

A different kind of an affiliation, a three-day community-building intensive held at a downtown hotel, might look quite deep, moderately broad, and extremely short. In a very brief time span compared to the farming community, the participants in this intensive express a full range of emotions and reveal secrets from their personal lives that, in a traditional small-town setting, could disrupt the social fabric.

A member of the farming community yearning for emotional honesty might envy the intensive participants' commitment to this, while several of these participants could long for the commitment to continuity demonstrated by the farming community.

Sypko was not at all sure whether the workshop experience could be called community, although it certainly bore several of the hallmarks of conscious community.

In *Urban Neighborhoods, Networks, and Families: New Forms for Old Values*, Peggy Wireman of the Department of Housing and Urban Development analyzes the relationships generated within neighborhood organizations. In these relationships, she says, there can be intense involvement, bonding, and even the kind of conflict one finds in a family. However, sharing of personal information is not considered central to the relationship. She cites an instance in which the chairwoman of a neighborhood council suffered from epilepsy—a fact that others on the council never knew until she had a seizure and could not chair the annual meeting. While this council resembled community in many ways, its members related to one another in too limited a fashion to be considered full community.

To those groups and activities that approximate community in many aspects, but are not complete communities in themselves, we give the term proto-community. (The prefix "proto-" often refers to an early stage of development in which an entity is not yet fully formed.) Proto-communities either do not serve as wide a range of functions or do not last as long as the groups that fit our definition of community. We have discovered examples of both functional and conscious proto-communities.

An example of a functional proto-community might be a civic organization like those Wireman studied. Another might be a group of strangers who help one another cope with an accident or a natural disaster. Such proto-communities formed after the Oakland hills fire destroyed 3,000 households in northern California in 1991 and after Hurricane Andrew devastated parts of southern Florida in 1992. Volunteers helping with these crises relied on each other, developed teamwork, and reported a strong sense of oneness. Although most dispersed once the crisis was over, they still remember the heartwarming connections they made during the dark moments.

Conscious proto-communities look more like the men's group in which Sypko participated. These proto-communities usually consist of a brief but intense group experience in which participants focus more on interpersonal process than on the performance of an external task. Such community often develops among groups of people attending workshops on relationship or community-building skills. Support groups, such as twelve-step meetings, can also serve as conscious proto-communities. Although they may be narrow in their functions and restricted to a small time slot,

The community stagnates without the impulse of the individual. The impulse dies away without the sympathy of the community.

William James

If there is radiance in the soul
it will abound in the family.
If there is radiance in the
family it will be abundant
in the community.
If there is radiance in the
community it will grow in
the nation.
If there is radiance in the
nation the universe will
flourish.

Lao Tsu

they allow their members to practice the arts of community building and to experience the intimacy and mutual support that are key features of community. As members of support and affinity-based groups become more confident in themselves and their group skills, they can better participate in full communities that are more diverse in composition and serve a broader range of functions.

The individual, if left alone from birth, would remain primitive and beastlike in his thoughts and feelings to a degree that we can hardly conceive. The individual is what he is and has the significance that he has not so much in virtue of this individuality, but rather as a member of a great human community, which directs his material and spiritual existence from the cradle to the grave.

ALBERT EINSTEIN

The kinds of community that are emerging today tend to be more fluid than those of the past. They consist of systems of evolving relationships that may or may not have a geographical base or a clear organizational structure. Members may leave, and new members may join, without destroying the group. Since these emerging communities are identified more by their process than by their form, they can shift form and function and move from one level of consciousness to another. For example, a neighborhood association that begins by focusing strictly on business can flower into a deeply personal, even highly conscious community for whom business meetings represent just a small part of its life together.

A series of temporary community-like experiences can evolve into a full-fledged community over time. For example, Sypko describes a river-rafting cooperative he belongs to whose members enjoy rafting trips together that last anywhere from one day to almost a month. Each trip constitutes a temporary experience in functional community: people depending on each other to do everything safely and make the right decisions, allocating and sharing tasks, facing risks and dangers together, developing skills as a group, interacting in various social patterns. They engage in candid talks around the campfire and rituals for facing fears. The group itself, which has been taking trips together every season since 1976, holds two "patch parties" each year to repair the rafts, plus an annual business meeting. A number of the members socialize outside the scheduled events and help each other with such practical tasks as repairing cars and painting houses.

THE CHALLENGE FOR COMMUNITY SEEKERS

For more and more people today, functional community of the type our ancestors experienced is unavailable or inadequate. But that does not mean that we have to settle for a life devoid of continuity and connectedness. As the many stories in this book illustrate, we can create new forms of community that more closely fit a mobile, ever-changing society. These new

COMMUNITY SPECTRUM

	Functional	Conscious	Deep
Community	Focuses on external task: supports physical, social well-being of members. Traditionally, slow to change and structured according to a hierarchy of fixed roles. Pays little or no attention to group process.	Focuses on internal dynamics and external task. Attends to whole system: individual and group development, process as well as task, interaction with larger communities. Characterized by openness, fluidity, diversity, role sharing, use of group skills, regular renewal.	Conscious group skills/processes and systems orientation are so ingrained they are part of natural everyday behavior.
Examples	Traditional extended families, closely knit neighborhoods, small towns.	Certain systems-oriented organizations, group households, intentional families; long-term neighborhood or peer groups that interact on several levels.	Some visionary residential communities.
Proto-community	Similar to functional community but with narrower range of functions and/or shorter or sporadic time span.	Similar to conscious community but with narrower range of relationships, little task-orientation, and/or shorter or sporadic time span.	Similar to conscious proto-community but members are experienced enough to achieve trust quickly.
Examples	Neighborhood councils, strangers helping each other in crisis, group wilderness adventures.	Certain twelve-step groups, men's and women's groups, other process-oriented peer groups.	Certain process-oriented and community-building intensive workshops.

forms, which honor individual as well as group needs, promise a depth and wholeness that members of old-style communities could scarcely have imagined.

The challenge lies in infusing today's fluid, more process-oriented communities with as much commitment and caring as marked the best of the traditional communities that were bonded by blood ties, necessity, and a deep affection for place. These traditional communities, despite their limitations, provided benefits to their members that few people today comprehend. What is more, these benefits depended upon a level of commitment that many contemporary Americans would be hard-pressed to emulate. Members of traditional communities, supported by these strong webs of connection, could rest assured that others recognized them and would be there in case of need, even when these others did not particularly like them. Everyone participated in a common group rhythm, working, playing, and celebrating together. The sense of security this brought produced a well-being that extended to the physical health and longevity of the individual community members. When the emerging, more conscious communities can generate the same kinds of benefits, American culture can congratulate itself on having met the challenge.

They [the people we interviewed] realize that, though the processes of separation and individuation were necessary to free us from the tyrannical structures of the past, they must be balanced by a renewal of commitment and community if they are not to end in self-destruction or turn into their opposites. Such a renewal is indeed a world waiting to be born if we only had the courage to see it.

ROBERT N. BELLAH AND COAUTHORS

RESOURCES

Recommended books and articles

In the Company of Others: Making Community in the Modern World edited by Claude Whitmyer (Tarcher/Perigee, 1993)

The Different Drum: Community-Making and Peace by M. Scott Peck, M.D. (Simon & Schuster, 1987)

A World Waiting to Be Born: Civility Rediscovered by M. Scott Peck, M.D. (Bantam, 1993)

The Spirit of Community: Rights, Responsibilities and the Communitarian Agenda by Amitai Etzioni (Simon & Schuster, 1993)

Habits of the Heart: Individualism and Commitment in American Life by Robert N. Bellah, et al. (Harper & Row, 1985)

Community in America: The Challenge of Habits of the Heart edited by Charles H. Reynolds and Ralph V. Norman (University of California Press, 1988)

The Poverty of Affluence: A Psychological Portrait of the American Way of Life by Paul L. Wachtel (New Society Publishers, 1989)

From Power to Partnership: Creating the Future of Love, Work and Community by Alphonso Montuori and Isabella Conti (HarperSanFrancisco, 1993)

The Hunger for More: Searching for Values in an Age of Greed by Laurence Shames (Times Books, 1986)

No Contest: The Case Against Competition by Alfie Kohn (Houghton Mifflin, 1986)

The Small Community: Foundation of Democratic Life by Arthur Morgan (Harper, 1942)

"Building Community" by John Gardner in *Kettering Review,* Fall 1989

Periodical

Thinkpeace, edited by Tom Atlee ($15 for six issues), 6622 Tremont, Oakland, California, 94609; (510) 654-0349. In-depth essays on the conscious evolution of community, democracy, peacemaking, and collective intelligence.

The towering moral problem of the age [is] the problem of community lost and community regained.

ROBERT A. NISBET

TWO

How Creating Community Can Enrich—Even Prolong—Your Life

The obvious subjective benefits that follow feelings of connectedness to other humans are but the tip of the iceberg in evaluating the benefits of caring relationships. There is now a mass of evidence to indicate that such support may be one of the critical factors distinguishing those who remain healthy from those who fall ill.

MARC PILISUK AND SUSAN HILLER PARKS

IN THE EARLY 1960S, a small town in Pennsylvania became the focus of attention for scores of medical researchers. The community of Roseto appeared unremarkable in every way except one: its inhabitants were among the healthiest in the United States. The rate at which they died of heart disease was significantly lower than the national average, and they exhibited greater resistance to peptic ulcers and senility than other Americans.

When researchers searched for clues to the Rosetans' health and longevity among the usual array of factors, they came up empty-handed. The folks in Roseto smoked as much, exercised as little, and faced the same stressful situations as other Americans. The residents of this closely knit Italian-American community practiced no better health habits than their neighbors. So why were they so healthy?

The answer surprised the researchers. After extensive testing, they learned that the Rosetans' remarkable health was linked to their strong sense of community and camaraderie. The town was not so ordinary after all. "More than any other town we studied, Roseto's social structure reflected old-world values and traditions," says Dr. Stewart Wolf in a booklet summarizing the study that he directed. "There was a remarkable cohesiveness and sense of unconditional support within the community. Family ties were very strong."

Developments since the initial study underscored this conclusion. As young Rosetans began to marry outside the clan, move away from the town's traditions, and sever emotional and physical ties with the community, the healthy edge Roseto held over neighboring towns began to lessen until, by the mid-1970s, its mortality rates had climbed as high as the national average.

The most important factors in health are the intangibles—things like trust, honesty, loyalty, team spirit.

DR. STEWART WOLF

We do not have *truth. We have a relationship to it.*

MAURICE FRIEDMAN

Community Is Good for Your Health

While you cannot, and for many reasons would not want to, recreate the patriarchal, religion-bound, old-world traditions that helped keep Rosetans healthy, you can discern the positive qualities of social interaction that contributed to their health and take steps to nourish these qualities in various areas of your life.

An important reason to seek functional or conscious community, even proto-community, is that it can keep you healthier in many respects. The Roseto findings are far from unique. Contemporary medical, psychological, and sociological literature overflows with studies that point to the life-prolonging, even life-saving qualities of interpersonal support. For example:

- Dr. Dean Ornish, a California specialist in coronary heart disease, developed a treatment program with support groups that surprised even him and his colleagues with its positive results: chest pains diminished or went away entirely, severe blockages in coronary arteries reversed, and patients became more energetic. In Ornish's study, which was partially funded by the National Institutes of Health, patients lived together for a week in a retreat, then met two evenings every week for four hours.

  "At first," Ornish writes in *Dr. Dean Ornish's Program for Reversing Heart Disease*, "I viewed our support groups simply as a way to motivate patients to stay on the other aspects of the program that I considered most important: the diet, exercise, stress management training, stopping smoking, and so on. Over time, I began to realize that the group support itself was one of the most powerful interventions, as it addressed what I am beginning to believe is a more fundamental cause of why we feel stressed and, in turn, why we get illnesses like heart disease: the perception of isolation.

"In short, anything that promotes a sense of isolation leads to chronic stress and, often, to illnesses like heart disease. Conversely, anything that leads to real intimacy and feelings of connection can be healing in the real sense of the word: to bring together, to make whole. The ability to be intimate has long been seen as a key to emotional health; I believe it is essential to the health of our hearts as well."

The factors most toxic to the heart are self-involvement, hostility, and cynicism.

DR. DEAN ORNISH

- The University of Michigan's Dr. James House and two fellow sociologists concluded, from their own studies and those of others, that there is a clear link between poor social relationships and poor health. "It's the 10 to 20 percent of people who say they have nobody with whom they can share their private feelings, or who have close contact with others less than once a week, who are most at risk," the researchers declared. This risk extends to life itself. In fact, House reports, the people with the weakest social ties have significantly higher death rates—100 percent to 300 percent for men, 50 percent to 150 percent for women—than their counterparts who are more socially integrated in terms of marital and family status, contacts with friends, church memberships, and other group affiliations.
- A study at St. Luke's-Roosevelt Hospital and Columbia University in New York City revealed that, for people with heart disease, living alone is a major independent risk factor comparable to such factors as previous heart damage and heart rhythm disturbances. The data indicate that heart attack patients living alone are twice as likely as others to suffer another heart attack, and more likely to die of an attack, within six months.

  "What's particularly significant is the magnitude of the effect," said clinical psychologist Nan Case, coauthor of the study. "We know that emotions and [social] integration have an effect, but we never knew it could come close to the physiological factors in heart disease."
- A team of Stanford Medical School psychiatrists, led by Dr. David Spiegel, found that metastatic breast cancer patients who joined support groups lived nearly twice as long as those receiving only medical care.
- At Ohio State University, psychologist Janice Kiecolt-Glaser and her colleagues discovered, in comparing thirty-eight married women with thirty-eight separated or divorced women, that the married women had better immune functions than the unmarried.

- A research team headed by K. B. Nuckolls studied 170 pregnant women and found that the rate of complications, including threatened miscarriages and stillbirths, was significantly higher among women who perceived themselves as receiving less support from their families and friends.

Whether we look at heart disease, cancer, depression, tuberculosis, arthritis, or problems during pregnancy, the occurrence of disease is higher in those with weakened social connectedness.

ROBERT ORNSTEIN AND DAVID SOBEL

Several studies suggest that it is not the number of personal contacts that affects people's health, but the degree to which people perceive that they have someone they can turn to. Social networks do not always feel like community. Unhappy marriages, alcoholic families, and other dysfunctional relationships can actually damage a person's health. Psychologists at the University of Washington concluded that even supportive actions and words do not necessarily translate into perceived support. "It all depends on whether your social support comes from someone you believe truly loves, values, and respects you," concluded one of the researchers, Dr. Gregory Pierce.

Psychologist Robert Ornstein and physician David Sobel believe that human beings evolved as social animals, and that our brains are programmed to connect us with others in order to improve our chances of survival. When the brain detects signals of isolation or emotional imbalance, it transmits these signals to other parts of the body. The way you interact with family members, co-workers, and others in your social sphere are translated by brain mechanisms into changes in hormone levels and in neurotransmitters.

"People need people," the researchers conclude in *The Healing Brain*. "Not only for the practical benefits which derive from group life, but for our very health and survival. Somehow interaction with the larger social world of others draws our attention outside of ourselves, enlarges our focus, enhances our ability to cope, and seems to make the brain reactions more stable and the person less vulnerable to disease."

Giving to others is a way to enhance your own health, a number of researchers have found. One team, led by the above-mentioned James House, found that doing regular volunteer work—more than any other activity—dramatically increased life expectancy. Not only does volunteerism provide you an opportunity for contact with others; by enabling you to do good for these others it warms your heart, increases your self-esteem, and contributes to your vitality and zest, as a woman named Betty in Cincinnati discovered. After suffering a serious stroke in her sixties, Betty began volunteering at her neighborhood senior center. The more hours she spent volunteering, the better she felt. When, at the age of seventy-five, she received an award for putting in 7,500 hours during the past year, she exulted, "I want to get a ten thousand hours this year!"

Allan Luks and Eileen Rockefeller Growald of New York's Institute for the Advancement of Health argue that the "feeling of warmth from doing good may well come from endorphins—the brain's natural opiates, which have also been linked to the highs we feel from running and meditation."

Community Is Key to Recovering from Addiction

One of the reasons twelve-step groups, such as Alcoholics Anonymous, work so well is that they build a context of community for their participants. Rev. Carter Hayward, a theologian at the Episcopal Divinity School in Cambridge, Massachusetts, tells a story about the link between community and recovery. "Bonnie, the friend who accompanied me to my first [twelve-step] meeting, told me that during her whole first year in the program she had missed the entire point of AA by failing actually to hear the first step: We admit that we were powerless over alcohol, that our lives have become unmanageable. She had not heard the 'we' but rather had held onto her misperception that she, as an individual, had a problem which she individually could solve. . . . In our disconnection and isolation, we are indeed powerless—over alcohol, over food, over our lives. With one another, however, we become empowered, empowering brothers and sisters, friends of the spirit." She adds that "this radical relational process takes root in the community of peers who share stories of vulnerability, pain, fear, loss, hope, dreams, and accomplishment."

As she has become confident in her own connectedness, Carter has been able to implement practices and beliefs important to recovery. She has learned to slow down a bit, to know that she can only do what she can do, one day at a time, and to know that this is good enough. "There will always be others," she now acknowledges, "in this and in generations to come, to carry the load with me—or for me, if I have gone as far as I can go."

Harry, a printer at a college in Tennessee, also learned about the link between community and recovery through Alcoholics Anonymous. A small incident between him and his sponsor, the person he checks in with between meetings, brought the meaning of mutual support home. Harry and his sponsor were driving about sixty-five miles per hour down a highway, when Harry, at the wheel, began reaching into the back seat for a Coca-Cola. As he fumbled in the cooler with one hand while steering with the other, his sponsor chided him, "Now Harry, what was the first thing I told you? When you need help, ask for it."

Harry has been asking for help ever since, and giving plenty of it in

The . . . national epidemic of drug use and alcoholism is the product, I think, of a culture that offers so few sustainable, non-drug opportunities for interconnection, self-expression, and spiritual meaning.

Lilly Collett

The most profound feelings come from being connected to another human being. People who are involved with others live longer.

Allan Luks

return. The loving community of AA has kept him sober for ten years, taught him self-acceptance, and given him the courage and openness to develop satisfying relationships outside the meetings. The missing element in Harry's previous attempts at community, through everything from church groups to drinking buddies, was acceptance. "In AA," he quips, "they don't care whether you came from Yale or from jail." When Harry began attending meetings, he had long hair that fell to the middle of his back, but he felt completely accepted by the others, including men in crew cuts. "We'll love you until you can love yourself," they told him. Within this nonjudgmental community, Harry—who today sports short hair—has learned to love himself and is now better able to build honest, loving community beyond AA.

Stress and loneliness may have as much to do with healing as the latest drugs and expensive procedures. . . . Human beings aren't intricate mechanisms whose fuel injection systems can be dispassionately adjusted by medical mechanics. . . . The need for contact, communication and compassion has been programmed into the functioning of the cells in our immune system, the walls of our coronary arteries, and our very will to live.

PETER ALESHIRE

COMMUNITY CAN SAVE YOUR LIFE

"Community is not just something that is nice to have," notes psychotherapist Susan Tieger. "It's one of the keys to survival." Susan has personal reasons for saying so. A few years ago she suffered serious complications arising from treatment of an auto-immune disease and was unable to work for months. "I lost all my money and I couldn't do anything about it," she recalls. "I was really in dire straits." Her mate at the time, Bob, and nine others formed a Susan Tieger Support Group. They took turns shopping, cooking, and cleaning for her, and provided company when she wanted it. When they realized they could not raise enough money among themselves to help her pay her staggering and mounting expenses, they sent out a letter on her behalf to a larger circle of friends and associates, requesting contributions to a fund established for Susan's support. The letter expressed, in closing, the hope that the recipients "will feel freer in the future to seek the help of others in our community if your own need should arise."

The outpouring of love in response to the letter boosted Susan's spirits and strength as much as the flow of money helped pay her debts. Now recovered, she acknowledges that her community effectively saved her life. "I did feel a little funny about that letter," she admits. "But I realized that what happened to me could happen to anyone. Community is all about helping each other."

Many of the contributors expressed their gratitude for the opportunity to be part of a network of love and support. "We are grateful and honored to be able to help," wrote one couple, adding thanks to Susan "for being such a good model to us all by letting your people be of support to you."

This communal support in response to a letter from friends is not unique to Susan's situation. We know of at least three other such efforts among our combined social circles. These spontaneously formed support networks—functional proto-communities—are emerging as a crucial expression of community. They function as temporary family in an era in which many adults are either geographically separated or emotionally estranged from their families of origin. And they fill the gap left by shrinking government and other institutional services.

There are simpler ways for sure. But community is the path of greatest challenge; community presents the opportunity for the most growth; community provides the means for work of the deepest impact. Is it worth it? For me, yes.

PETER GIBB

"I, like many others," says one recipient of such communal support, "fell into the cracks between welfare and other social services assistance." Dulcie Wright, a single mother of three who had to quit work when her youngest daughter contracted leukemia, was not poor enough or old enough for the government to help. Her private medical plan did not cover household and other nonmedical expenses, and her family and grants from the Leukemia Society could not completely fill the gap. So her friends came through.

The kinds of crises that struck Susan and Dulcie could undermine anyone's financial and emotional security. While institutional safety nets can help, they may not be nearly as reliable and are certainly not as emotionally satisfying as a strong network of friends. Taking the time to build this kind of network community now may save your life and your sanity in the future.

Among those who have had to generate such networks quickly are people directly affected by the AIDS crisis. In the process of learning how to do it, these people created models of mutual support that can serve us all. Thousands of informal circles and networks have sprung up in addition to the hundreds of organized support groups and services for people with AIDS and their caretakers. The informal groups operate much like the networks that carried Susan and Dulcie through their crises, although the emotional challenges of these groups are often greater. Members can be almost certain that the friend they are supporting is dying.

Learning how to be comfortable with the dying process, says one member of such a support group, was one of several gifts he received through his participation. Duncan Campbell, an HIV-positive landscape gardener and musician, also credits the experience with teaching him much about intimacy and about the healthiness of cultivating a diverse community of friends.

COMMUNITY CAN BE A SAFE PLACE TO GROW

Besides improving health and longevity and providing support when you are in need, community steps into other roles once filled by family—sometimes even doing a better job of it. It gives you a sense of belonging, an identity that takes in more than just the self. It turns on the lights in areas of your life that you may not even have realized were in need of illumination. Rather than interfering with your personal development and goals, it can enable you to grow psychologically and can make possible your full flowering as an individual. Community can fill your life with enriching discoveries and surprises.

We know that where community exists it confers upon its members identity, a sense of belonging, and a measure of security. It is in communities that the attributes that distinguish humans as social creatures are nourished. Communities are the ground-level generators and preservers of values and ethical systems. The ideals of justice and compassion are nurtured in communities.

JOHN W. GARDNER

Cat Austin had known Nan and Jerry Meek for eleven years. All three friends were successful professionals who enjoyed their independent careers and interests. Never had it occurred to them that they might one day be joined in a kind of interdependent family. But a combination of health and economic factors changed their way of life. Cat became aware that she suffered from severe environmental illness and needed to get away from the city into smog-free air. Nan and Jerry had bought a large, gracious house in an upscale San Francisco suburb called Portola Valley, where they were surrounded by decks, hills, and spectacular views. Unfortunately, they found themselves financially strapped when they were unable to sell two other properties they owned.

When Cat asked Nan and Jerry if she could move in with them for a short time while she recovered her health, the two agreed immediately. Two years later the three friends were still living together happily. They had even been joined by a fourth roommate, Don Paulhus, a horse trainer whom Nan had met at her riding stable. So cohesive was their unplanned, unsought community that, when Nan and Jerry had an opportunity to buy a large horse ranch in Sonoma County, Cat moved with them. Don had planned to join them, but decided to stay in the old place at the request of the new owner, thereby planting new community seeds. However, he kept his ties to his first informal "family."

Those outside that community of four were certain that the living arrangement would be a recipe for broken friendships and possibly a disrupted marriage. But all four insist that their lives became much richer and more pleasurable than they were before. Nan and Jerry feel that the economic advantages are insignificant compared to the social and psychological advantages. Rather than putting a strain on their marriage, they say, "it helps to have a focus outside ourselves." To Cat, it's "like being brothers and sisters but without the hassle. Nan and I have a deeper friendship than ever." She helped Nan move furniture around, Don and Jerry worked on cars and motorcycles in the garage, Cat and Don discussed their mutual interest in psychic phenomena, and Nan and Don shared their passion for horses. As an unexpected extra benefit, Cat's health improved.

Patch Adams, M.D., belongs to a group that lives together and operates a free hospital called Gesundheit Institute. To him, community has been an incredible boon both to his family and to his business. "I have been with my wife sixteen years," he writes in the *Directory of Intentional Communities*, "and we have known only the communal lifestyle. I am sure that living in community is the major reason we still have a rich, vibrant love for each other. We are always surrounded by men and women friends. When one of us wants some space from the other we can simply go elsewhere in the house and play with someone else. When a project ties one of us up, the other need not feel neglected and without companionship. . . . And child-rearing . . . Oh, this may be the best! Our child has had such magical input from each member."

He adds, "Gesundheit was not the quest of one man but the living by-product of committed friends. . . . Nothing can encourage your dreams more outrageously than chums in mutual support."

It is not necessary to live together to experience the benefits of community. Just having others involved in your life, commenting on what is going on with you, and reacting to your decisions helps to keep your life in perspective. You have probably noticed that you make better choices when you can check out your thoughts and feelings with others who are honest with you, and when you take advantage of group wisdom. True community, like genuine family, provides a safe place to grow without worrying about rejection. It also serves as a mirror, showing you parts of yourself that you may not have noticed before. And, as Susan Tieger and others attest, community can save your life.

[The] notion of dynamic balance is a useful concept for defining health.

FRITJOF CAPRA

My argument, stated generally and briefly, is that the driving force in nature, on this kind of planet with this sort of biosphere, is cooperation. . . . The most inventive and novel of all schemes in nature, and perhaps the most significant in determining the great landmark events in evolution, is symbiosis, which is simply cooperative behavior carried to its extreme.

LEWIS THOMAS

YOU CAN HAVE COMMUNITY AND YOUR INDIVIDUALITY, TOO

Despite the clear benefits of community, many people are hesitant to pursue it. So they go on feeling isolated even though they yearn for greater support and a stronger sense of connection. In talking with people about their hesitation, we have discovered several reasons for it. The primary reason, expressed in a variety of ways, is fear of having to give up too much. "My privacy is important to me, and the idea of others encroaching on it is uncomfortable." "I might have to make too many compromises and I might have to share possessions or resources that I would rather keep to myself." "Creating community will take more time and energy than I have to offer." "I won't be able to keep my independence and my uniqueness."

A movement of enlightenment and liberation that was to have freed us from superstition and tyranny has led in the twentieth century to a world in which ideological fanaticism and political oppression have reached extremes unknown in previous history. Science, which was to have unlocked the bounties of nature, has given us the power to destroy all life on the earth. Progress, modernity's master idea, seems less compelling when it appears that it may be progress into the abyss.

ROBERT N. BELLAH AND COAUTHORS

To cooperate is not to sacrifice either an achievement orientation or a strong sense of self. On the contrary, success will more likely be the result of working with other people, and the same might be said for healthy self-esteem.

ALFIE KOHN

These are not foolish or frivolous fears. America's long cultural tradition of individualism keeps people wary of groups. They fear they will have to sacrifice too many personal desires to the group's demands. In couple relationships, the greatest stumbling block is fear of intimacy and commitment—a loss of one's separate self in fusion with the other. This fear extends to relationships with more than one other person. These fears arise, in part, from painful personal experiences in couples and in families and from dominance by state and religious organizations. The groups most people have participated in or been influenced by have been dysfunctional, leaving community seekers few examples of healthy affiliation.

Fears of groups also arise from a deeper source, the illusion that humans are separate by nature. Corollary to this is the belief that community is a social construct that people can choose or reject.

Forgive yourself if you have fallen into either of these illusions. The prevailing culture has drummed them into the American psyche for centuries, and their roots reach back to the Enlightenment era in Europe and the cultural and scientific currents that preceded this era. Newtonian physics, the description of reality that shaped European and American thinking for centuries, tells people that they, like all other particles of matter, are separate. Only in the last few decades have physicists, biologists, and systems thinkers discovered what mystics and ancient religious traditions have been telling people for millennia: everything is connected to—and both influences and is influenced by—everything else. The insight that rocked the scientific world in the early twentieth century and led to the development of quantum physics is that the nature of reality is dynamic relationship, not isolated units of matter. No one thing, not even an electron, is fully knowable in isolation.

If a primary quality of community is connectedness, then you are in community intrinsically, down to your electrons, protons, and neutrinos. You are more interdependent than independent. Systems thinker Joanna Macy likes to say that we humans have insider knowledge of community because we embody it: in the communities of bacteria in our guts and mitochondria in our cells. In a sense, you merely have to discover the community that already exists, bring it out, and give it context. Of course, this is not as simple as it sounds, since the old, recognizable forms are dissolving.

These old forms of community assumed that individuals had to sacrifice themselves to the demands of the group or the leader for the social fabric to remain intact. They did not take into account the phenomenon of synergy: the experience of individuals and groups existing in a dynamic balance and contributing to one another's full expression rather than detracting from it. Individuals exist only in the context of the larger whole, embedded in and defined by a nurturing web of relationship. The stronger and healthier the community, the stronger and healthier is the individual, and vice versa. You do not need to decide whether you are an individual first and in community second, or whether the rights of the community come first and your individual rights second. Both are essential to the system. The key to keeping this system—whether a family, a circle of friends, a neighborhood, or a business—healthy lies in maintaining a dynamic balance between individual expression and cooperation with the larger whole.

Imagine an improvisational jazz ensemble, a good example of a human system in dynamic balance. No one directs, the musicians simply jam, and they are so tuned into themselves and the group that they intuitively know when to play solo and when to play together. Their differences contribute to, rather than interfere with, the musical message. Each brings a unique sound to the group, yet the overall sound is much more than a collection of separate notes. Relationship is crucial—the musicians' subtle signals, their deference to one another, their weaving of melodies and rhythms—and so is individual expression. Without soaring or soulful solos, the music would be reduced to a bland, spiceless stew. The best jazz ensemble musicians are both assertive and cooperative—and they are not known to com-

Communities are places or entities where each member can give something, where they can contribute something that they feel especially able to give, something that they are good at. The gift from each member is valued by the whole community and all gifts are unique and individual. The gift that community gives back to each member is that of a role and a connection.

ED MARGASON

The one thing we do know for sure about our bacterial ancestors is that they learned, very early on, to live in communities.

LEWIS THOMAS

plain about a lack of freedom. The dynamism between individual and group encourages spontaneous expression, resulting in an organic, ever-changing flow of music. Each rendition of the same piece is recognizable, yet fresh and new.

From a systems point of view, absolute individualism is an illusion. People are connected to others in an ever more complex web whose strands encircle the globe. This relational web is not a form of bondage, because freedom and spontaneity exist within the system. Humans and their environment—families, neighborhoods, cities, ecological systems—are not machines that operate according to a linear sequence of cause and effect. Everything is connected to, and both influences and is influenced by, everything else. We are all open systems continuously exchanging energy with other systems, and every movement in the web causes vibrations in other parts of the web, whether we realize it or not.

An elementary particle is not an independently existing unanalyzable entity. It is, in essence, a set of relationships that reach outward to other things.

HENRY STAPP

As man advances in civilization, and small tribes are united into larger communities, the simplest reason would tell each individual that he ought to extend his social instincts and sympathies to all the members of the same nation, though personally unknown to him. This point being once reached, there is only an artificial barrier to prevent his sympathies extending to the men of all nations and races.

CHARLES DARWIN

Functional communities as well as conscious communities need to be in balance. If your life is out of balance, you will not be an effective contributor to any type of community. Ask yourself, "Where in my life do I sense an imbalance?" Perhaps you are too wrapped up in your work or too focused on your inner life (your relationship with yourself) to give much attention to a group. Or perhaps you are too devoted to others, such as family members, to the detriment of your work or your inner life. If you already belong to a conscious community, you may be so focused on the group that you neglect your personal needs. Ignoring any part of the system is not good for the community or for the physical and emotional health of its members.

As long as you keep balance in mind, the time and commitment you devote to creating community in your life will not result in a sense of sacrifice or lack. Giving and receiving support within webs of caring that you can count on not only feels good but also reduces your stress, strengthens your body, and gives you the courage and confidence to give and receive even more. A healthy community will help you return to balance if you become stressed or ill and will remind you of your innate strength and loveableness. As an empowered, well-loved individual, you, in turn, will be better able to contribute to the rebalancing of the larger society.

You will need to exercise some initiative and creativity in developing forms that work for you. Community is like a self-tending garden, in which you are both the plants and the gardener, the seed and the sower. As the sower, you can determine what type of community suits you best. Community is not an all-or-nothing proposition. It comes in a wide variety of forms, from informal circles of friends to highly structured residential enclaves. Levels of commitment can vary in terms of time, energy, money, and intimacy. And experiences of sharing and interdependence can range from temporary proto-community to long-term conscious community. You can create a custom community to meet your current needs in whatever area of your life you desire: your workplace, your neighborhood, your family, your group of friends, your international computer network. This may require learning new skills to deepen your current relationships or build new ones. The following chapters are designed to help you clarify your personal dreams of community and learn how to make them come true.

In the midst of crisis people often break through to intimacy, an empathetic, mindful relationship that arises naturally out of who we are. Being who we are calls forth respect and love and wanting the best for one another and for ourselves. This "right relationship" . . . is as essential to the continuity of human life as is the air we breathe.

ROSALIND DIAMOND

RESOURCES

Recommended books and articles

The Healing Brain: Breakthrough Discoveries about How the Brain Keeps Us Healthy by Robert Ornstein and David Sobel (Simon & Schuster, 1987)

Dr. Dean Ornish's Program for Reversing Heart Disease by Dean Ornish (Random House, 1990)

The Roseto Story: An Anatomy of Health by John G. Bruhn and Stewart Wolf (Harper & Row, 1979)

Leadership and the New Science: Learning about Organization from an Orderly Universe by Margaret J. Wheatley (Berrett-Koehler, San Francisco, 1992). An excellent introduction to systems theory and its applications.

The Turning Point: Science, Society and the Rising Culture by Fritjof Capra (Simon & Schuster, 1982)

The Healing Web: Social Networks and Human Survival by Mark Pilisuk and Susan Parks Hillier (University Press of New England, 1986)

The Brighter Side of Human Nature: Altruism and Empathy in Everyday Life by Alfie Kohn (Basic Books, 1990)

The Healing Power of Doing Good: The Health and Spiritual Benefits of Helping Others by Allan Luks and Peggy Payne (Fawcett-Columbine, 1991)

The 7 Habits of Highly Effective People: Restoring the Character Ethic by Stephen R. Covey (Fireside/Simon & Schuster, 1990). Clear discussions of how individuals and groups can reap the benefits of synergy.

Gesundheit! Bringing Good Health to You, the Medical System, and Society through Physician Service, Complementary Therapies, Humor, and Joy by Patch Adams, M.D., with Maureen Mylander (Healing Arts, 1993)

THREE

Getting Started:

Simpler Than You Think

Community is the only real basis of security.

STARHAWK

AFTER HER DIVORCE, JENNY, a thirty-year-old office manager in Kansas City, suddenly found herself cut off from her former social circle, which consisted entirely of couples and families. What do single people do on Saturday nights? she wondered. How do they build networks of friends? After depending on her marriage to provide a social life for so many years, Jenny feared she had lost the knack for building personal support systems.

Roger, a California-based consultant in his fifties, already had a network of friends. Moreover, he was living with a woman he loved. But he too felt the need for something more: closer relationships with other men, in which they could explore their common experiences. Although he did have male friends he could talk to about subjects deeper than Monday night football, they were scattered around the country. Roger wanted an ongoing form of local support and closeness.

Despite the busyness of their two-career, two-child family life, Anthony and Maggie, a young couple in New York City, yearned for a sense of connection beyond their immediate family. They lived thousands of miles away from most of their relatives, so they could not rely on kin to provide the close-knit community they sought. And their current network of friends, more a collection of separate relationships than a weaving of interdependent ones, seemed too fragmented to serve the purpose.

Ted and his wife Cynthia, whose adult children had flown the Los Angeles nest, found themselves facing their sixties with some anxiety. How could they create a form of community for themselves that would be as satisfying as family and that would help them keep on learning and growing throughout their golden years?

Whether single, married, raising a family, or nearing retirement, many men and women in today's fragmented world long for community. Even if they have plenty of friends and opportunities to socialize, they want something deeper. And, although they feel competent at getting what they want or need in most situations, developing community baffles them. We often hear the refrain, "Of course, I want more community in my life. I just don't know how to get started." This is not surprising given our fears about community, the hectic nature of our lives, and the number of options available. It is easy to become confused, to hesitate, to put off taking the first steps.

My insurance policy is my friends.

JAN THOMAS

If you think of community as a grand vision for the future, you can get stuck in the imagining. Psychologist Arthur Gladstone used to have such a vision. "At first I imagined a special place with special people," he wrote us, "where I'd feel safe and comfortable and completely at home. It would be far away from all the people and things I didn't like, maybe on an island or in a remote valley. We would have the best possible rules and structure, designed to keep us secure, creative, free from worry and conflict.

"I still have this fantasy sometimes, but I can see that it really is a fantasy, unrelated to the realities of community. . . . I no longer see community as a safe place, or as a specific structure. I think of it as an attitude and a process. It is understanding and practicing interdependence, recognizing that we need one another for everything that makes life worthwhile and even for survival itself. Community as a process means commitment to mutual aid, open and full communication, resolving conflict, and making decisions by care-full consensus. This can involve sharing a house or a piece of land, but it can also take many other forms."

The following steps are designed to help you identify the qualities and processes of community that most appeal to you, and then to begin pursuing the forms that suit you best. You can complete the exercises by yourself or use them to stimulate group discussion and action.

STEP ONE: TAKING STOCK—YOUR PERSONAL RESOURCES

Before embarking on your search, take an inventory of the resources you have: your reservoir of past community experiences and your current web of social connections and personal support. As you do this, you will begin to view community as an actuality, something to build on, rather than an impossible dream.

Community Memories

Scan your past for positive experiences. Remember times when you felt connected and supported, although you may not have labeled the situation "community." Allow yourself to sense fully each remembered experience, and jot down what appeals to you about each memory. You will begin to get a feeling for the qualities you desire in community, and with the knowledge that you have experienced these in the past, you will realize that you are not starting from scratch.

It is one of the most beautiful compensations of this life that no man can sincerely try to help another without helping himself . . .

RALPH WALDO EMERSON

When our community study group conducted this exercise, memories arose that were surprisingly comforting and encouraging. One of my (Kristin's) favorite community experiences was my college dormitory in Iowa, particularly the third floor, which I shared with twenty-one other women. We were from different cities and different backgrounds, and many of us would never have picked each other as roommates. At this college there were no sororities—we were thrown together by fate—and we were amazed by fate's wisdom. We were always there for each other, in small groups or one to one, and we shared our deepest feelings as well as our differing philosophies. We developed our own jargon and our own rituals, lent each other clothes, shared disappointments in love and in academic struggles. We overcame interpersonal disputes and small rivalries. It is hard to imagine a biological family as close as the third-floor residents of our dorm.

The unexpected memories that arose in my (Carolyn's) mind were of the annual holiday gatherings at my maternal grandmother's home: my grandma's aproned lap and down-to-earth love, my uncles' jokes and games, the foibles of certain aunts and cousins. I was choked with emotion as I described to our group an experience of connectedness that I had not recalled for decades and had never before considered community.

After conducting the above exercise for two or three memories, notice any patterns that emerge. You might want to go beyond jotting down a few notes to telling a full-blown story. Consider inviting a few friends over for an evening of storytelling about memories of community. This could be the beginning of your own informal community.

Your Current Social Web

1. On a blank sheet of paper, draw a circle in the center and label it with your name.

2. Now contemplate those people in your life with whom you interact personally. They may include co-workers or professional colleagues whom you also consider friends.
3. Draw circles around the center circle for each of these persons or groups of persons. Position the circles closer or farther away from the center one, depending upon how close or distant you perceive the relationship. To help determine how close and supportive people are, ask yourself, Whom can I ask to drive me to the airport or to help me cart boxes when I move? From whom can I borrow money? To whom can I reveal my fears and doubts—and who trusts me enough to reveal theirs? Whom can I depend on to follow through on personal commitments? Some of the circles may overlap.
4. Label the circles either with generic names such as "spouse" or "work group" or with specific names such as "Terry" or "Computer Systems Group." Other examples of categories you might include are family, housemates, close friends, church group, neighborhood, not-so-close friends, and professional association.

We are all Holy sparks, dulled by separation
But when we meet and talk and eat and make love
When we work and play and disagree
With holiness in our eyes
Then our brokenness will end.

FROM "TIKKUN OLAM,"
A KABBALISTIC STORY ADAPTED
BY NAOMI NEWMAN

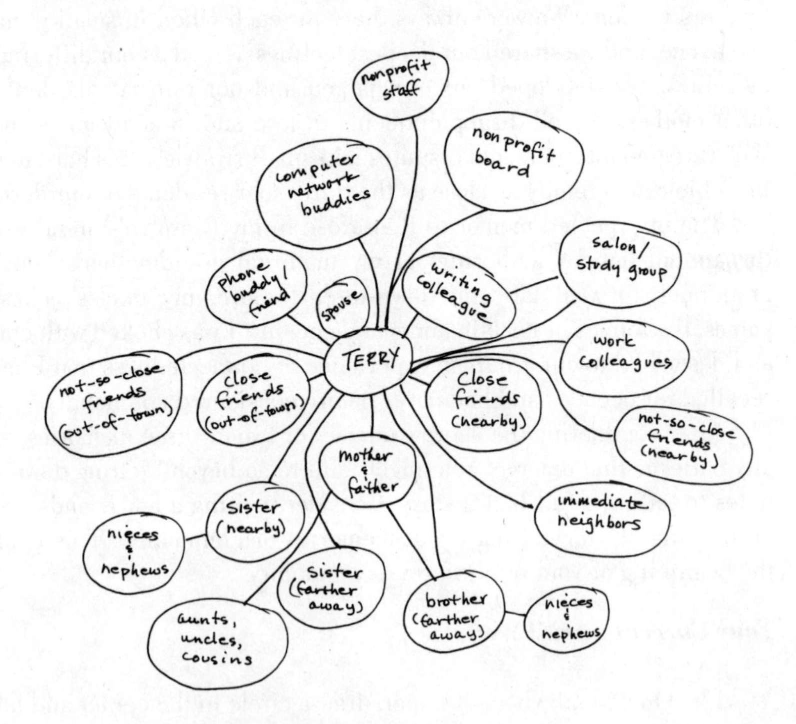

Social Web Exercise

5. Indicate which people you see or talk with frequently and which only occasionally. You might outline each circle in the first category with a red marker and each in the second category with a blue marker.
6. Show which individuals or groups are linked with each other by drawing lines between circles. You might use solid lines to indicate close links and dotted ones to indicate not-so-close links.

Individuality doesn't just mean individualism—standing alone. It means developing one's unique gifts, and being able to share them for the enjoyment of oneself and others.

FRANCES MOORE LAPPÉ

Keep this diagram for use in the steps below. These members of your social network are often the easiest to start with when you begin moving toward community. The diagram can help you start making decisions about whether to rejuvenate your current support network, create a new one, or combine old and new. Try repeating this diagramming exercise six months or a year from now to notice how—or whether—this network has changed.

Step Two: What Type of Community Do You Want?

Community comes in a plethora of shapes, sizes, and levels of commitment. To avoid false starts and disappointments, it is important to think about what you want to get out of it and what you want to put in, including how much time you are willing to spend. Saying "I want community" is not specific enough. What kind of community are you looking for? The following checklist can help you map the path you choose to follow.

Which of the Following Statements Are True for You?

- ☐ I want more emotional closeness in my life. I would like to gather around me a group of people who are always there for me, as I am for them, and with whom I can be completely honest.
- ☐ I want to develop relationships with a network of others who share my interests, values, background, profession, spiritual or religious orientation, or political views.
- ☐ I want to broaden my perspectives by forming relationships with people from different backgrounds and with different interests and ideas.
- ☐ I feel that my mission is to create a better world, and the kind of community I'm looking for has to be dedicated to a specific purpose related to this goal.

- ☐ Although I support the creation of a better world, I believe I need to heal myself first, so I'm looking for a community that focuses on mutual support and assistance.
- ☐ I would like to share living space with people beyond my immediate family.
- ☐ I want to create a nurturing environment for my children, where they will have plenty of interaction with other adults and kids.
- ☐ I don't have much time to develop or participate in community building, and would like to start with a small commitment.
- ☐ I want a low-cost living situation that is based on mutual assistance and support.
- ☐ I want an ongoing, committed community that I can grow old with.
- ☐ I would like to start my own community.
- ☐ I prefer to join a group that already exists.
- ☐ I don't want to join a group at all—just deepen the relationships I already have and build them into a support network.

If you think you can't change the world by yourself, join some people who agree.

MOTTO OF BUSINESS PARTNERSHIP FOR PEACE

Add your own "I want"s here, followed by "I don't want"s:

By now you should have a clearer idea of what you mean when you say you are searching for community. After you have finished reading this book, you may want to look at this checklist again to see whether, and how, your attitudes and perceived needs have changed.

STEP THREE: PERSONAL REQUIREMENTS FOR SUCCESSFUL COMMUNITY

Community begins with one-to-one relationships. The most basic of these is your relationship to yourself. Look back at the circle diagram, with yourself in the center. To be successful in creating community, you need to start here. You may find that before—or while—you reach out to others, you need to develop certain personal qualities that are necessary for successfully participating in functional and conscious community:

- *A healthy sense of self.* This means self-esteem and self-awareness, not the kind of self-absorption that is antithetical to community. Although you do not have to achieve perfect self-confidence and centeredness before moving toward community, it is helpful to know what you want, what your strengths and limitations are, and how you plan to grow. You will need to be secure enough not to have to defend, protect, or prove yourself constantly.
- *Openness and flexibility.* This means not only tolerating diversity, but welcoming it. Community includes other people, who have different ways of viewing and approaching things. If others tell you only what you want to hear, you miss the true richness of community.
- *A sincere interest in others.* We heard a person say, not entirely in jest, "I love community—I just wish I didn't have to do it with people." Folks like this will have difficulty getting started until they deal with the anger and hurt that lie beneath such comments.
- *Willingness to abide by community agreements.* For people who rely on a distorted version of autonomy that views interdependence as a threat, this can be a real sticking point. Once they realize that who they are, in essence, is not defined by any group, they can relax and uphold agreements, knowing that their inner integrity can never be threatened. They can move from "I" to "we" without losing "I."
- *Willingness to pursue group goals.* This may entail placing group goals ahead of certain individual ones for a time, trusting that eventually individual needs will be served in the context of community.
- *Willingness to risk asserting yourself.* Taking initiative and, when necessary, disagreeing are as essential to healthy community as the willingness to get along with others. To become closer, it may be necessary to risk some painful interactions.
- *Willingness to practice the skills that enhance community.* These include the communication, conflict resolution, and decision-making skills discussed in Part Four.
- *Desire to see yourself and others as you really are.*
- *Willingness to give and to receive,* to take care of others and have them take care of you.

Definition of "self-esteem" developed by the California Legislative Task Force on Self Esteem (1990): Appreciating my own worth and importance and having the character to be accountable for myself and to act responsibly toward others.

- *Commitment to see it through.* If you want community to last, you must be determined to stay with the group despite conflict, changing individual needs, and other demands on your time.

There is a yearning in the heart for peace. Because of the wounds—the rejections—we have received in past relationships, we are frightened by the risks. In our fear, we discount the dream of authentic community as merely visionary. But there are rules by which people can come back together, by which the old wounds are healed.

FOUNDATION FOR COMMUNITY ENCOURAGEMENT

Because we are social beings, self-love and love for others are actually facets of one nature. Self-love is a product of lives lived with others. We develop self-esteem only in community. We love ourselves in great measure based on how well we love others and as we believe ourselves worthy of the esteem of others.

FRANCES MOORE LAPPÉ

STEP FOUR: OVERCOMING RESISTANCE

Besides the fear of giving up too much time, individuality, or independence, many people experience anxiety about rejection or failure when they think about creating community. "If I try to join an established group," an internal voice might whisper, "I won't be accepted. If I ask family or friends to form deeper bonds with me, they'll think I'm foolish or they'll be threatened by my desire for greater intimacy and commitment." Another message might be: "I'll put in lots of time and energy and others won't follow through. Or, even if they do, we'll bungle our attempt. Then I'll end up feeling more disillusioned and lonely than I do now."

If you have experienced any of these fears, you may be unconsciously erecting barriers to achieving community, even if you truly desire a deeper sense of kinship or connectedness. Facing and exploring your fears can help you release such obstacles. Here is an exercise that can help.

What's in the Way?

Find a quiet, comfortable place where you know you will not be disturbed. Think about a specific action you might take to reach out to others to create or deepen community. Imagine taking this step. Be specific about the individual or group you are contacting. Notice how you are feeling as you are about to pick up the telephone, enter the room, or otherwise start the conversation. Do you sense anxiety, doubt, judgment, or any other kind of resistance? Write down what you are feeling or thinking, or, if you prefer, draw a picture.

Perhaps you experienced nothing but eagerness and joy at the prospect of initiating a fresh community-building endeavor. If you are like most people, however, you discovered a few parts of yourself that are not quite ready for this attempt. It might be that little kid in you who recoils at the thought of reaching out to make a new friend only to be rejected again, or the teenage rebel who says, "Who needs other people? They'll just try to tell me what to do." You may have found a seen-it-all cynic inside who is convinced that all idealistic efforts toward bringing people together in harmony are bound to fail; always have, always will. Or you may have met the judge, a cruel, stern fellow or woman who reminds you of your father, your mother, or your least-favorite teacher. This character is reminding you that you are no good at this sort of thing, just as you are no good at so many other things.

Congratulate yourself. You have met the enemy within and are now better able to disarm him or her—or them, if you encountered more than one. These inner characters—personality aspects formed, or deformed, by past emotional trauma—tend to act like children. The more you ignore them or push them away, the more they act out. But if you acknowledge them and allow them to express themselves while you listen with loving awareness, you will notice that they soon play out their drama and return to a normal, uncharged state. They may rise up fearing or fuming in a different circumstance but that is because, like children, they are insecure and need more reassurance from your conscious, aware self that they will be seen and heard. As with children, that does not require your caving in to them.

Almost every problem of the community, state, and nation is met with on a small scale in our relations with people closest to us. Unless we can be successful in those relationships we have not yet mastered the art of building a community. We need not wait for great programs. Each person in his day-to-day relationships can be mastering the art of community.

ARTHUR E. MORGAN

Uncovering your fears is an important step in creating healthy community. How you begin to release these fears is up to you. There are dozens of ways to do so, from emotional clearing on your own to seeing a therapist. You certainly do not have to cleanse yourself of every fear, doubt, and judgment before connecting with others to generate community. You simply need to be aware of your resistances and willing to begin releasing them.

Step Five: Reaching Out

From Friendship and Network to Community

Start with people you know. When you are ready to reach out to others, to go public, as it were, with your intention to generate more community in your life, look again at the diagram of your current social network. Jot down the names of those in this web of connections you would like to know better, those who might enjoy meeting one another, and those you feel might wish to join you in creating a community, at whatever formal or informal level you desire.

Now assess the possibility of generating such a community from within your network of family and friends. You may not want to start here. Perhaps you have changed and grown in directions that do not interest the rest of your current social circle. Before writing these people off completely, however, you might check with one or two. Perhaps they have been yearning for community also but have not known how to talk about it.

If you find one or more people within your current social network with whom you would like to begin building community, start doing so. You can begin with something as simple as a telephone buddy system, requiring nothing more than a commitment to call a friend once a week. I (Carolyn) have cultivated a telephone buddy friendship for more than two years and been surprised by the strong bonding that has resulted. Although, happily, I see my buddy Sandra now and then, our friendship grew and continues to be maintained through our telephone conversations. We have found it helpful to take turns going first, devoting at least fifteen minutes to the initial speaker before shifting the focus to the other for another fifteen minutes or so. Given our highly scheduled lives and the fact that we live on opposite sides of the San Francisco Bay, our phone talks make up for the neighborhood café conversations we would love to share but do not have time for.

Working together to create change in the world and to relieve the suffering of others can be bonding and refreshing to a family. It can be more rewarding than the usual pastimes. In a busy family, it can be the impetus that gets family members to commit time to doing something together.

RAM DASS AND MIRABAI BUSH

If you are ready and have time for face-to-face community, invite one or two of your friends over to explore the subject. Your friends may know of others looking for the same thing. Together, you might call a simple gathering at one of your homes during which you each take a turn talking about the kind of community you seek.

When Roger decided that he wanted to get to know other men better, he sought out a male colleague whom he thought might want the same. They decided to call a meeting of other male friends and colleagues they felt would be interested. Roger and his colleague each invited about five others to attend. Most of those who attended the first meeting chose to continue. Together, they formed a personal and professional support group that met regularly for years.

Benefits of Proto-Communities

Although most people are seeking some form of lasting community, there are plenty of ways in which you can experience the process of community and cultivate your community-building skills without making a permanent commitment. Some have learned a great deal—and found satisfaction for several months to several years at a time—in proto-communities: men's or women's groups, church projects, and professional or personal support groups. Helping organize neighborhood activities such as street fairs and block parties also gives you an opportunity to form new bonds with others without making an ongoing commitment. Workshops that involve a high level of interaction allow you to develop your interpersonal skills, discover personal barriers to community, and make new friends with common interests.

One limitation of many such personal growth workshops and interactive trainings is that the intense connections made during the week or weekend usually end when participants pack their bags and go home. But this is not always the case. Certain organizations and teachers attract students who keep coming back, either to review the experience or to advance to a new level. The community formed then becomes not so much temporary as intermittent. For those who do not want more day-in-and-day-out community in their lives, this can be a satisfying alternative.

Social support connotes all we mean by caring relationships among people. Our embeddedness in a continuing network of such relationships is perhaps what counts most. This secure place in a network has a profound effect upon how we think and how we feel about our surroundings, and particularly about how we affirm the value of ourselves.

MARC PILISUK AND SUSAN HILLER PARKS

Ted and Cynthia, the couple who wanted to generate a form of social connectedness that would continue to work for them after retirement, are creating yet another kind of intermittent community. They and two other couples have developed a tradition of vacationing together. The relaxed and profound nature of their sharing during these weeks proves much more satisfying than the surface conversations—over dinner or at a party—they ordinarily have with friends during the rest of the year. Their deepening commitment to each other and to the tradition itself feels like the seed of the community they all desire as they grow older.

Community can arise naturally when people come together for the purpose of helping others. For example, a Berkeley-based volunteer organization called Daily Bread and a similar one in San Francisco called Food Runners—both part of a nationwide network of such organizations—collect surplus food, which might otherwise be thrown out from bakeries, markets, and restaurants, and take it to local free-food kitchens and shelters. So many volunteers are involved that even people with busy lives are not overwhelmed. Carolyn North, who started Daily Bread, comments, "We're creating a sense of community among participants as diverse as hunger activists, food professionals, students, housewives, and retirees." Food deliverers make connections not only with each other, but also with people in the restaurants, bakeries, and free food programs. One family began holding its birthday parties and other family celebrations in a Berkeley shelter for the homeless, inviting the residents to join them. A couple of retired women who make food runs to a family shelter started sticking around to play with the kids and provide a grandmotherly lap.

In 1985 Edgar Cahn, a professor at the District of Columbia Law School, launched a nationwide chain of volunteer organizations in which the volunteers and the recipients are the same people. Called "Time Dollars," the program is based on service credits: each hour you give to someone else in the program, or to the community at large, is credited to your computerized account, for you to draw on when *you* need help. About three-quarters of the participants are older people, who tend to have more time than money to contribute and who may need the companionship that working with others can provide. Groups of people have pooled their time dollars by joining in a large service project, such as distributing food, clothing, and water to victims of Florida's Hurricane Andrew.

In his book *Compassion in Action,* Ram Dass describes the powerful sense of community he found when he became involved with Seva Foundation, a nonprofit organization dedicated to the alleviation of suffering in the world. He became immersed in the problems, processes, discoveries, and joys inherent in an increasingly conscious and very diverse community, grappling with his commitment fears and working out conflicts with others on the board of directors. Of his Seva group, he writes:

Genuine trust is . . . a readiness to go forth on this occasion with such resources as you have, and if you do not receive any response, to be ready another time to go out to the meeting.

MAURICE FRIEDMAN

"We spend time with the many children the group has spawned and with our Nepalese, East Indian, Guatemalan, and Native American friends who come to our meetings. We travel together, bumping along in jeeps in remote corners of the globe or work together on one project or another. Finally, I have come to appreciate living among peers. We are so different, yet over the years our mutual love and respect have become strong. We listen to one another, we bust one another when we get too phony, and we enjoy one another. No one misses meetings if she or he possibly can help it." For him, what had started out as proto-community burgeoned into something deeper and more lasting.

Step Six: If at First You Don't Succeed, Try Again

Do not be discouraged if your first attempts at creating community fizzle, or if you find yourself carrying the ball alone for a while. Remember that you are blazing new cultural trails. Also, recognize that what you get may not last in exactly the form you had in mind. Community today is more flexible and fluid than that of yesteryear. While Roger enjoyed the men's group he helped start, he eventually dropped out of it. The members were not delving as deeply as Roger had hoped and tended to smooth over interpersonal issues. Roger joined a monthly community study group. Later, he moved into a residential spiritual community that meets needs he did not even know he had when he initiated the men's group.

Of course, your efforts at building community might click on the first try. Our culture is increasingly hungry for meaningful connection, so do not be surprised if the reception you receive when you initiate a move in that direction is more enthusiastic than you had anticipated. Some time ago the editors of *Utne Reader* decided to offer their subscribers a chance to get to know each other through starting neighborhood salons: "Send us your name and address," a notice in the magazine suggested. "We'll send back a list of your neighboring *Utne Reader* readers, who've indicated they'd like to meet too." The editors expected that maybe a thousand readers would respond—and were overwhelmed by a deluge of more than eight thousand. All over the country, enthusiastic groups of Utne-inspired neighbors began deciding what kind of joint activities to pursue—exchange of ideas, co-learning, poetry readings, neighborhood action . . . the possibilities are legion.

The more realistically one construes self-interest, the more one is involved in relationships with others.

BERNARD CRICK

Salon coordinator Griff Wigley figures that, given the fast pace of people's lives today, neighbors seldom get to know each other gradually through frequenting local hangouts, and long for "a structure that makes it easier to do more than chitchat." Although salon discussions are a form of socializing, they involve the whole group at once and are focused on issues that matter to the participants. Salons can easily be started by individuals who put up notices in neighborhood cafés and retail stores, or who simply round up a few friends with similar interests.

Susan Ovington decided she wanted a support group where members could share techniques for working through emotional problems. So she called ten people she had come to know through a personal development workshop a decade earlier and invited them to a potluck at her house. As it turned out, most of the people who showed up at Susan's wanted a salon for idea exchange and celebration of community rather than a process-oriented emotional healing group. Susan went along with the prevailing interest and is glad she did, especially since she was able to resolve her emotional issues with a therapist.

The salon, which includes both couples and singles, now meets bimonthly on Sunday, from 10 A.M. to 4 P.M., to discuss such varied topics as education, management, and gender roles. By agreement, there is no "awfulizing" about politics or the ozone layer, but there is plenty of support and encouragement for each other's endeavors. The continuity as well as the meaningful exchange of ideas appeals to Susan. "It's nice to be seeing these people regularly," she comments. "The older I get, the more people I know, and it's hard to keep in touch with all of them."

As the above stories show, one person—you?—can initiate community. Sometimes it is as simple as discussing what you want with the next person. Who could you call right now to share your ideas and visions for community?

Community is where you find it. Whether you want to deepen existing associations or begin venturing further into new forms of interdependence, you will feel more empowered, more connected, the minute you take the first small steps.

Community is a safe place precisely because no one is attempting to heal or convert you, to fix you, to change you. Instead the members accept you as you are. You are free to be you. And being so free, you are free to discard defenses, masks, disguises: free to seek your own psychological and spiritual health.

M. Scott Peck

Resources

Recommended books, articles, and periodicals

Revolution from Within: A Book of Self-Esteem by Gloria Steinem (Little, Brown, 1992). "Intended," writes Steinem, "for everyone—women, men, children, and even nations—whose power has been limited by a lack of self-esteem." She places this personal issue in a larger context.

Keeping Us Going: A Manual on Support Groups for Social Change Activists by Sara Conn et al. (Interhelp, P.O. Box 86, Cambridge, Massachusetts, 02140; (617) 776-8186; 1986)

Going Nowhere Fast: Step Off Life's Treadmills and Find Peace of Mind by Melvyn Kinder (Prentice-Hall, 1990). How people can be—and are—reconnecting with themselves, simplifying their lives, and developing deeper, more satisfying relationships with others.

Embracing Your Inner Critic: Turning Self-Criticism into a Creative Asset by Hal Stone and Sidra Winkelman (HarperSanFrancisco, 1993). The sections on how to keep from sabotaging your relationships readily apply to community building.

The Truth Option: A Practical Technology for Human Affairs by Will Schutz (Ten Speed Press, 1984). Includes exercises that help you assess yourself, your relating behaviors, and your compatibilities with others.

Community Building Exercises, a thirty-page booklet published by the Sirius Community, P.O. Box 388, Amherst, Massachusetts, 01004. Experiential games and exercises for warming up a group and deepening the bonds among members.

Time Dollars by Edgar Cahn and Jonathan Rowe (Rodale, 1982). Describes service credit programs.

Compassion in Action: Setting Out on the Path of Service by Ram Dass and Mirabai Bush (Bell Tower, 1992). Describes many aspects of the type of community generated by working together to create change in the world.

"Helping Ourselves to Revolution" by Gloria Steinem in *Ms.,* November/December 1992. Includes practical information on starting your own mutual support and action groups.

Utne Reader #44, March/April 1991. Theme: Salons. Contact the magazine at 1624 Harmon Place, Minneapolis, Minnesota, 55403; (612) 338-5040.

Organizations and networks

Neighborhood Salon Association, c/o *Utne Reader,* 1624 Harmon Place, Minneapolis, Minnesota, 55403; (612) 338-5040. For $12, membership in NSA links you with others for regular informal get-togethers and provides a guide for various group processes.

Study Circles Resource Center, P.O. Box 203, Rt. 169, Pomfret, Connecticut, 06258; (203) 928-2616

Time Dollar Network, P.O. Box 42160, Washington, D.C., 20015

Part Two

Community without Cohabitation:

You Don't Have to Move in Together to Enjoy Mutual Support

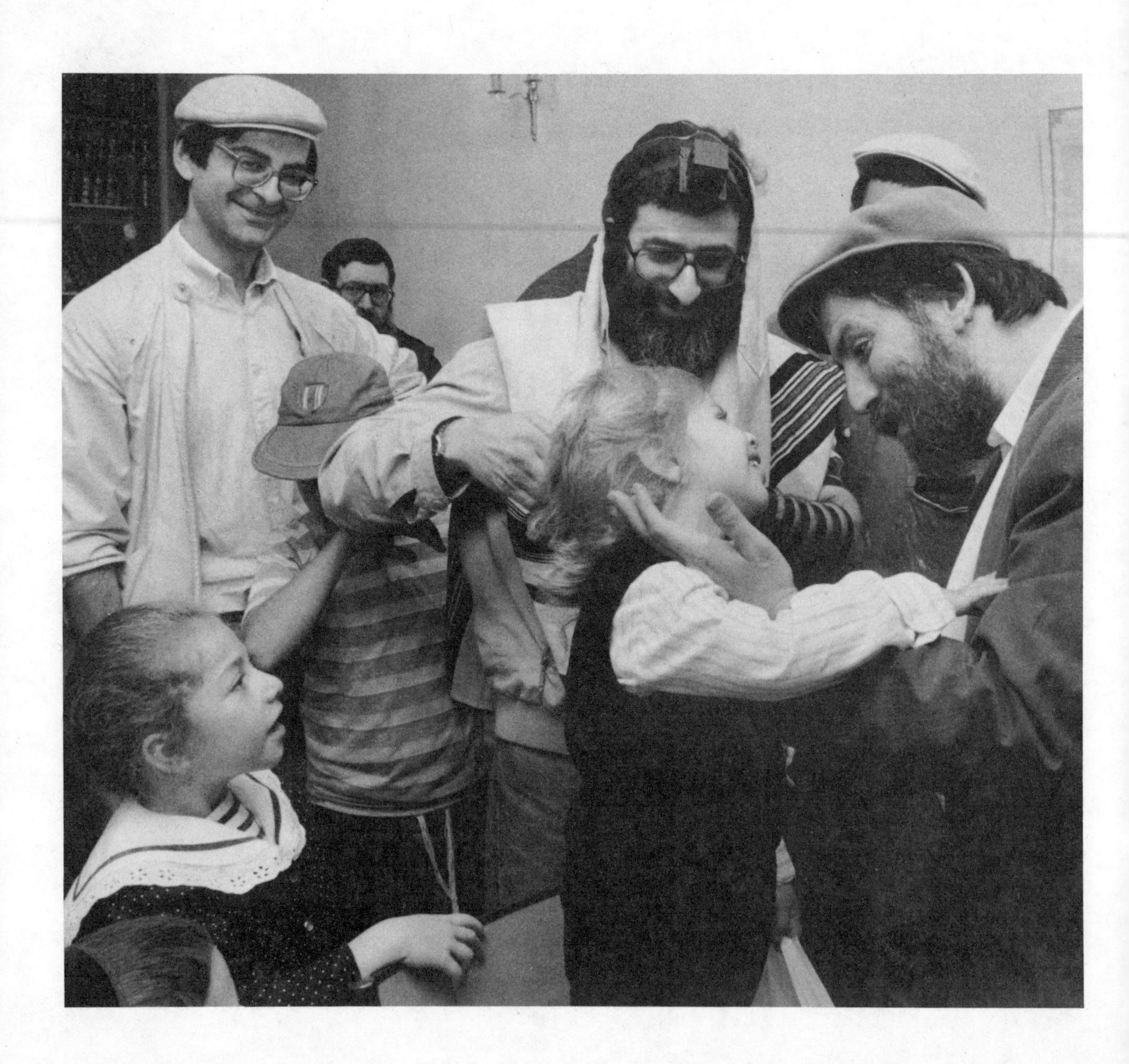

FOUR

Creating Community Among Family and Friends

What we're seeing is an attempt to balance things. Work is not the only source [of satisfaction]. We need kids too. We need friends too.

SUSAN HAYWARD

FOR VIRGINIA KING, a financial planner with a husband and two teenagers, developing friendships has never posed a problem. The challenge lay in melding these friends into a community. "Since my friends didn't know one another," she says, "it was as if I were part of thirty different communities. I felt scattered."

Throughout most of the last two decades, Virginia and her husband simply accepted that, in Virginia's words, "We don't have community anymore. That's contemporary life." But recently they began to feel a desire for a deeper sense of belonging and connectedness. For Virginia, this means more than just getting together with other couples for an occasional dinner on Saturday night. It means "a community of friends that has continuity and that includes children."

Like Virginia, many people in midlife, whether raising children or not, lack the time, energy, and desire to join an intentional residential community or participate in formal group meetings. Yet they yearn for connection with others that goes beyond the occasional lunch date or party. For some, a supportive but loosely woven circle of friends is enough. Others want the commitment and closeness of an extended family. As Virginia and the others you will meet in this chapter attest, you can generate this circle of friends and sense of family in many different ways, whether you are single, divorced, married, or with or without children of your own. And in doing so, you do not need to be bound by place or by blood relationships.

I remember hearing Margaret Mead say that for 99 percent of the time that humans have been on the planet, they have lived in tribes of 12 to 36 people. Only in times of war, or the psychological equivalent of war, do we have the nuclear family, because the advantage of the nuclear family is its mobility, which is good for survival.

ERIC UTNE

We have just begun to admit that exchanging old-fashioned family values for independence and self-expression may exact a price.

JERROLD K. FOOTLICK

THE FAMILY IS ALIVE—IT JUST LOOKS DIFFERENT

One pitfall in creating an intentional family—or any kind of community—lies in becoming wedded to a particular form. In this sense, the process is not so different from that of looking for the ideal mate. When you search for the ideal community or intentional family, you can miss any number of community-generating opportunities because they do not match your imagined form, even though they may provide the deeper emotional satisfaction you seek.

Preachers, politicans, and television series that idealize the 1950s breadwinner-homemaker model of the nuclear family have delivered a message to Americans that if their families do not look like this, something is wrong with them and the nation. This fixation on one form of family has led some experts to lament the rise in divorces, single-parent families, and unmarried mothers as signs that the family is breaking down, perhaps irreparably. For example, they predict, in tones of alarm, that with the high rate of divorce, forty-five percent of all children born in 1990 will live in a single-parent family or a stepfamily by the time they are eighteen.

Although such statistics are based on documented demographic trends, they do not necessarily indicate that the family is doomed. The conventional structures of family and community in America are shifting, dissolving, and re-forming as you read this. The form that works for you may not have existed in the past. Given the profound demographic, economic, and social changes since the 1960s—a "cultural earthquake," according to Arlene Skolnick, author of *Embattled Paradise: The American Family in an Age of Uncertainty*—"family arrangements that made sense in 1800 or 1900 or even 1950, have little relevance for how we live today."

Despite doleful messages from the media, we can make a case that the family is as strong or stronger than ever, especially if we define this social configuration by its functions and the quality of relationships among its members rather than as a specific form.

When Massachusetts Mutual Life Insurance Company polled Americans on their views about the family in 1989, almost three-quarters chose as a definition of family "a group of people who love and care for each other." Less than a quarter chose the standard legal definition: "a group of people related by blood, marriage, or adoption." Most respondents apparently viewed the family in functional and emotional terms—what it does and how it feels—rather than legal and biological ones. Yet, perhaps because of what they read in the papers and see on television, the majority perceived the family and family values as declining. When Massachusetts Mutual conducted a second family values survey in 1991, the company discovered that the majority held to this perception even though their commitment to "core family values," which was strong to begin with, had increased significantly over the intervening two years.

Families have always been in flux and often in crisis; they have never lived up to nostalgic notions about "the way things used to be." But that doesn't mean the malaise and anxiety people feel about modern families are delusions, that everything would be fine if we would only realize that the past was not all it's cracked up to be.

STEPHANIE COONTZ

Surprisingly, the model of the family idealized in such 1950s television shows as *Leave It to Beaver* and *Father Knows Best* was never universal and had little to do with lived reality even in the past. "The distinctive feature of American family life," reports Skolnick, "has always been its diversity." She notes that one researcher, seeking the "normal American family" in the late 1950s, found, in his words, "the most astonishing variance in its structure and function." This and other studies reveal that the so-called traditional nuclear family, in which Dad worked outside the home and Mom took care of the children, is a historical aberration, practical only in limited circumstances—and, moreover, a distinctly white middle-class phenomenon. According to a *Newsweek* special edition on the family, this model, which "never applied widely among blacks or new immigrants, who could rarely afford to have only a single earner in the family . . . thrived roughly from 1860 to 1920, peaking, as far as demographers can measure, about 1890." The much-proclaimed breakdown of the family may simply be a transition to more workable forms, made painful by the refusal of governmental agencies and certain segments of the population to acknowledge and support such variations.

Our expectations of what a family ought to be will shape the kinds of social policies we want. Webster's offers 22 definitions.

JERROLD K. FOOTLICK

CREATING INTENTIONAL FAMILIES

For Barbara Sachs, the nuclear family model stopped working when her marriage dissolved in 1970, leaving her to raise a three-year-old daughter and an eighteen-month-old son while working full time. She could not afford a nanny, and day care covered only a fraction of her child-rearing needs, so she set about getting help by creating an intentional extended family composed of friends.

"I chose my friends as much by how willing they were to get involved with my children as by how interesting I found them," Barbara recalls. "If my kids didn't like them, or my friends weren't willing to spend time giving me practical or emotional support around child-rearing, I didn't have time in my life for them." While Barbara found it difficult at first to ask for help, she soon realized "that the worst that could happen is that someone would think badly of me. My good friends learned to say no when they weren't available."

A friend is someone who leaves you with all your freedom intact, but who obliges you to be fully what you are . . .

JOHN L'HEUREUX

At first, Barbara thought she was creating this extended family for her children's sake. Soon she learned that she needed support as much as they did. "I was starving emotionally," she says, "and I needed input from others on how to deal with my kids." When a family problem arose that Barbara did not know how to handle, she would pick up the phone and ask, "If you had a kid who was doing such-and-such, what would you do?" Her friends gave other kinds of support as well. One drove Barbara's daughter, Deborah, to her Scholastic Aptitude Test on a Saturday when Barbara had to work. Another provided companionship and practical help on a family camping trip across the United States.

In some ways, Barbara's children, Deborah and Bradley, led lives richer than those of their friends raised in nuclear families. The "adopted" aunts and uncles in their intentional extended family taught them skills, both practical and relational, that Barbara was unable to teach. One such uncle gardened with the children, another showed them how to shingle a shed, and an adopted aunt gave Deborah informal sewing lessons. What's more, each adult related to the children differently. "You have to be you with the kids," Barbara told her friends. When problems arose, she insisted that the friends work these out in their own fashion directly with her son and daughter. "I wouldn't let them go through me." As a result, her children relate well with many different kinds of people. Her friends have benefited also. Several have told Barbara how much they appreciate the communication skills they learned through the experience.

As a testament to the high quality of relating in this unorthodox family, several of the adults who signed on as uncles and aunts fifteen or twenty years ago remain active in these functions even though some live hundreds of miles away. They often join the family for holidays and continue to enjoy occasional heart-to-heart talks not just with Barbara but with Bradley and Deborah as well. "The friendships are two-way and don't depend on me," Barbara reports with satisfaction.

One of the adopted uncles, Gary Linker, has come close to serving as a second father to Bradley. The two became buddies when Bradley was three and Gary a twenty-four-year-old graduate student at the University of California at Santa Barbara. Barbara had hired Gary to help with the garden-

Creating an Intentional Family or a Community of Friends

Decide what kind of social network you want. Do you desire a sense of family—not necessarily your own kin but a mix of adults and children who feel comfortable with one another and are willing to work, listen, cry, and play together? Or do you respond more to the peer community model, a loose network of other adults? Consider talking with a friend or family member who will understand. This could be your first step in generating a circle of friends that feels like community.

Your next step involves clearing time in your life to nurture your growing friendships. Conscious community takes time and continuity as well as openness to personal sharing. Take a moment or two to review how you spend your time or, better yet, keep a log for a week or two. Are there some solitary, passive, or consumption-oriented activities you would prefer replacing with social, active, participatory ones? Ask yourself, "How essential are the items on my to-do list compared to weaving a web that feels like family?" Also consider how you can convert routine tasks and errands—such as cleaning house, grocery shopping, or gardening—into community-generating encounters with friends or family members.

Remember to acknowledge and honor whatever needs you have for solitude, recognizing that alone time can contribute significantly to the quality of community in your life.

A family liberation movement is being born. To be effective, this movement, by defining family *in the broadest possible way, will enlist the commitment of people who are not parents; it will be both personal and political; it will define* liberation *not as the act of breaking off from one another, but as the individual's ability, particularly the child's ability, to live to the fullest potential. . . .*

Richard Louv

ing, then discovered that he and she had just entered the same graduate program. While the two adults became fast friends, so did Gary and Bradley. Gary gave the young boy the rough-housing he longed for and which Barbara did not feel comfortable providing, and also bonded with him through sports, playing ball with Bradley and occasionally taking him to professional games. After Barbara and her children moved north to the San Francisco Bay Area, Gary visited them two or three times a year and even made a special trip to watch Bradley play in a championship baseball game. When Bradley entered college, he chose Santa Barbara and lived with Gary during his first year. He continues to seek Gary's counsel on such issues as career and relationships.

Their familial roles have come full circle. Bradley now delights in playing uncle to Gary's little girl, Danielle.

This quasi-family relationship has not always been easy. "At times I came down hard on Barbara about what I thought she was neglecting," says Gary. He and Barbara had rows, for instance, about how regularly she should be providing home-cooked meals for her kids. His role became especially unclear during those times when Barbara was living with a man who took a fatherly interest in Bradley. Although Gary's relationship with Barbara has always been non-sexual, he admits to feeling twinges of jealousy toward potential competing father figures for Bradley.

By the end of the century it will be conventional wisdom to invest in our children.

SHEILA B. KAMERMAN

Let us put our heads together and see what life we will make for our children.

SITTING BULL, LAKOTA LEADER

Despite such complications, the rewards of developing long-term, family-like relationships have outweighed the challenges. Gary now credits Barbara with modeling excellent parenting skills. "She gave me confidence to be a father to my own child," he says. Over two decades of friendship, Gary and Barbara have become friends with each other's parents and siblings, weaving a broad web of connection they never dreamed of when they met.

Barbara and her intentional family took a situation labeled by many as a double-pronged problem—a broken home and a single parent—and turned it to their advantage. All involved experienced, and continue to enjoy, the kind of close-knit, extended family that for most people remains a nostalgic dream. They learned that you no longer have to restrict yourself to the relationship and geography cards life dealt you at birth.

Unlike most people, especially women, just a few generations ago, today you can leave home, marry whom you choose, stay single if you wish, divorce your mate if your marriage is not working, and, whatever your marital status, remain childless or raise children. You can also—with sufficient intention, time, and energy—create whatever kinds of support networks you desire. Your survival no longer depends on your blood relatives or your kin-based clan. In earlier times, before government agencies took over most of the functions of community life, blood- and marriage-related kin felt bound by duty to educate and care for one another and protect each other from attack by outsiders. Few traveled far from their village and most entered marriages arranged for economic and political purposes. Today, women and men—together and separately—are pioneering radically new approaches to relationship. They are creating partnerships and families bound by intrinsic rewards rather than external pressures.

Yet even pioneers borrow from the past, taking what works and leaving the rest. Barbara knew how to build an intentional extended family, in part, because she grew up among grandparents, aunts, uncles, and cousins in a lively kin-based extended family that lived first in Chicago and later moved en masse to Los Angeles. These traditional forms can serve as models not just for single parents like Barbara but for anyone, including unattached adults without children.

Charita Allen, the single twenty-eight-year-old southerner you met in Chapter One, is creating a multi-generational network of mutual support inspired, in part, by her own closely knit African-American extended family. Although Charita has made some friends through the usual singles venues—apartment complex parties and after-work happy hours—she says that "most of my networking and community-building happens through the volunteer work I do." She tutors at-risk children at a local elementary school and serves on the board of the Catholic high school she attended. She sometimes brings students with her when she visits an older couple who have spent their lives traveling the world as missionaries. She likes to expose these students to the stories and artifacts of other cultures. As a kid, she remembers, she enjoyed listening to the tales of an aunt who came from Thailand.

While families provide primarily emotional protection, friendships usually involve mysterious novelty. When people are asked about their warmest memories, they usually remember holidays and vacations spent with relatives. Friends are mentioned more often in contexts of excitement, discovery, and adventure.

MIHALY CSIKSZENTMIHALYI

Charita faces the challenge of developing a social network that bridges black and white cultures without diluting her culture of origin. In the past, if she and her African-American friends wanted to immerse themselves in their own culture, they would drive to the nearest big city where more of the shops and clubs are African-American–owned. Recently, she says, "I've made a concerted effort not to do that because all my ties were being established in another city."

While Charita stays in touch with many of her relatives, she has chosen to reach out especially to her eight-year-old cousin and the cousin's "sister," a best friend aged ten. Charita recalls that when she grew up surrounded by relatives, she "learned a little bit from everybody" and, given how busy and geographically separated people are these days, she does not see that happening with the children in her family now. So she invites her two young friends to stay with her one weekend a month. "We will go to the museum, and I'll ask them to tell me which paintings are their favorites and what they like about them—little things that they may not get in school or from their parents or other relatives. People tell me I'm so good to do this. But why am I good? This is family."

In Charita's case, the family is at least partially blood-related, but Gary Linker could give the same response to those who tell him how good he is for spending time with Barbara's children. The functions he serves in their lives and the commitment he has made to them are as family-like and family-strengthening as those Charita provides for her young cousin. So long as people like Charita, Gary, Barbara, and their children and "adopted" children continue to reach out to one another, the prevalence of divorce, the increase in working mothers, and the proliferation of single-parent and stepfamilies need not signal the disintegration of the family. Instead, they can lead to the creation of a healthy and practical diversity of family forms—"a breakthrough rather than a breakdown," as Shoshana Alexander, author of *In Praise of Single Parents,* puts it. Through her own experience as a single parent and through interviews with dozens of other such parents, Alexander discovered that those who succeed in meeting this challenge do so in large part by reaching out to create extended family and community. "No one *can* be a single parent," she claims. "Raising children taxes the resources of even the two-parent family."

People need help in defining the family as a place of shelter *from the incessant demands of the consumer culture. . . . But the next step is to help people find their way to* noncommercial, *preferably inexpensive, sources of pleasure and satisfaction with their families.*

BARBARA EHRENREICH

The single-parent extended family represents one of several new and not-so-new forms of family on the rise today. Others include blended families in which the husband and wife bring children from previous marriages; three-generational families in which married sons or daughters with children of their own rejoin a parent or parents; families in which the adult children choose to stay home with mom and dad; multi-racial families; and families with same-sex parents. One lesbian couple we know successfully blended children from their previous marriages, including two adopted Vietnamese girls and an adopted African-American boy, into a lively family more loving and stable than many of the so-called standard nuclear variety. Variations on the family also include nuclear families who unofficially adopt older men and women as grandparents, as well as childless singles and couples who commit themselves to active involvement with their friends' children.

African-Americans offer positive models of extended family for a culture in transition. For centuries, they have been improvising family as slavery and other forms of economic and social oppression have torn apart their nuclear families. African-American families often treat unrelated adults as kin, calling them aunt or uncle or referring to them as sisters or brothers. Both close and distant relatives also frequently raise children who have lost or been separated from their parents. Recently, African-American families have been adopting black children, including crack babies, in record numbers. In California, black adoptions increased thirty-nine percent from 1989 to 1991, a much steeper rate of increase than for non-black adoptions.

While women always have helped support each other emotionally, we consider it likely that as the men's movement matures and men take increasing responsibility for the relationship side of life, more men, following the example of Gary Linker, will participate in such mutual-support communities.

Some intentional families are temporary ones, coalescing around a crisis and returning, once the crisis has passed, to the looser weave of a network of friends. An example is the ad-hoc community you met in Chapter Two that supported Susan Tieger through months of serious illness.

Nurturing Spontaneous Community among Friends

The primary purpose of an intimate group is being*: being a group, creating community, forming long-term, ongoing relationships. . . . Families are intimate groups, as are households that aspire to familylike bonds. Task groups and healing groups sometimes develop into intimate groups. All intimate groups take a long time—years, not weeks or months—to develop.*

STARHAWK

You may not want more family in your life. You may even be wary of intentionally seeking community for fear this will raise expectations that others cannot meet. Or, intentionally building community may seem artificial to you. If you are the kind who views attending gatherings to create community as on a par with joining singles clubs to meet a mate, and you do not like either activity, read on. As the men and women featured in this section demonstrate, mutual support need not be manufactured. In the right kind of environment, it arises naturally.

Many people develop satisfying, mutually supportive networks of friends without purposely setting out to create community. These spontaneous communities occur when people come together for a purpose other than creating community and, in the process, form supportive, ongoing affiliations. Women traditionally have created community this way through quilting bees and other cooperative task-oriented groups. In many urban parks in ethnic neighborhoods, you can see men building such community—around the bocce ball courts if they are Italian, or the Go tables if they are Chinese.

Volunteers and activists often develop spontaneous communities when they meet repeatedly to plan fundraisers or organize political campaigns. Any activity that is ongoing, requires peer participation, and allows time for conversation can generate this type of community. The stories of successful spontaneous communities that follow can help you recognize and nourish this kind of mutual support in your life. While such communities emerge naturally and in their own time, they can be encouraged. You can deepen them by the quality of relating you practice and the types of interactions you support.

Bonding through Baseball

"My baseball team turned into the equivalent of a men's support group without our ever intending it," reports Marc Kasky, executive director of a West Coast community cultural center. "It was a nice surprise during our

The test of friendship is assistance in adversity, and that, too, unconditional assistance. Cooperation which needs consideration is a commercial contract and not friendship. Conditional cooperation is like adulterated cement which does not bind.

MOHANDAS GANDHI

third year together. No one pushed for it." Marc, a member of a formal men's support group for the past nine years, marvels at the similarities. In both groups, the men talk openly about relationships, families, health, and work. They call each other between meetings if they need advice and help each other through crises. When one team member's marriage broke up and another's engagement fizzled, "we were there for them, calling and offering support," says Marc. Team members also engage in classical business networking, helping each other find jobs and clients. "When one member opened a restaurant, we all patronized it," says Marc, "and five of us are participating in a local television show that a couple of our teammates developed."

Except for Marc, the members of this amateur hardball league team are not likely to join a men's group devoted primarily to mutual support. They signed onto the team for the task—playing competitive ball as best they can—not the relationships. If this ethnically and racially diverse group—which includes a banker, a cabbie, a tile worker, and a nurse—had not joined the same team, they probably would never have met.

Keys to the group's success as an informal yet deeply bonded community include their fierce commitment to the team—"I never miss a game unless I'm injured," Marc insists—and their ritual of meeting for a meal after every weekly practice and game. This combination provides a natural balance of task and process. Marc was attracted by the excitement of the task. "We're the regional champions right now," he notes, "and I love that sense of tangible accomplishment. If I didn't get it through baseball, I'd probably take up a musical instrument and join a rock band." It is the kind of reward his men's group is not designed to give.

Reclaiming the Sewing Bee

One unlikely virtuoso of community building calls herself a hermit at heart. Augusta Lucas-Andreae has lived alone, by choice, for thirty years. In many ways, she fits the prescription for loneliness in America: she is sixty-three years old and resides in a small studio apartment in a major metropolitan area. But this artist and teacher has never lacked community. One of the ways she has nurtured a mutually supportive circle of friends is by hosting intimate gatherings that focus on creative expression and allow free rein to conversation.

Years ago, Augusta and several women friends decided to meet once a week to do handwork. All of them liked to knit, weave, or sew, but none enjoyed doing these activities alone. As these women—homemakers and professionals, married and single—worked together, they talked, much as their sisters in previous centuries did as they quilted. "We came to know one another very deeply," says Augusta. "The group became so important to us that we didn't want to miss a session." The handworkers met for four years, helping each other—much as Marc's baseball team does—through divorces, career transitions, and family quarrels. For Augusta, childless and long-divorced, the group offered a chance to feel connected to the dynamics of couples and of family life. Although the women no longer meet regularly, they often reconnect at other intimate gatherings. Some have taken part in the craft-oriented sessions that Augusta held for many years in her home. As in the weekly handwork group, participants in these occasional gatherings quite spontaneously fell to telling personal stories and sharing feelings and dreams as they painted Easter eggs or made Christmas cards by hand. Those who returned regularly began to form a loose network of friends.

Friendship is, strictly speaking, reciprocal benevolence, which inclines each party to be as solicitous for the welfare of the other as for his own.

PLATO

As Augusta's professional identity has evolved from artist and craftswoman to art therapist, her gatherings have changed in nature and so has the level of community they generate. Augusta now includes meditation and intentional personal sharing in the groups that she hosts. "The friends and friends of friends who come now," reports Augusta, "share more deeply about their personal and professional lives, and the community-making that occurs goes deeper as well."

As much as she loves her groups, for Augusta, spending time alone is as important to building community as gathering with friends. "I need 'alone time' to deepen my sense of who I am," she explains. "The more I make space for this in my life, the more easily I can join in a group without fearing that I'll lose my individuality. I have more fun and express myself more when I maintain this balance."

Building Trust

In spontaneous communities like Marc's and Augusta's, the intimate sharing emerges naturally, and only when the individuals and the group are ready. Marc reports that it took two years of practices and games before he and his teammates began to openly express their hopes and fears. "We had to check one another out first," he says, "to see if it was safe."

Self-disclosure in such groups can be simple and unfussy. Yet this willingness to reveal the soft underside can deepen the level of intimacy profoundly. "At a dinner party the other night," wrote columnist Adair Lara in the *San Francisco Chronicle*, "a friend told us that he doesn't mind being single, but that he feels lonely in the morning, when he first wakes up. I thought what a gift he has, to tell us such things. It was as if someone had lit the logs in the fireplace, and we had all gathered around, warmed, suddenly a community of close friends."

A friend is one
To whom one may pour
Out all the contents
Of one's heart,
Chaff and grain together,
Knowing that the
Gentlest of hands
Will take and sift it,
Keep what is worth keeping
And with a breath of kindness
Blow the rest away.

ARABIAN PROVERB

Virginia, the mother of two teenagers who had almost given up on finding community amid contemporary life, discovered one form in which such personal sharing can deepen the bonds in a group. Her family's spontaneous community emerged from among a dozen or so people who, by happenstance, traveled to Moscow together to attend a Jewish film festival. En route they became fast friends and vowed to continue meeting, not just at an occasional reunion but for regular potlucks that their whole families could attend. Others in the group, it turned out, shared Virginia's and her husband's desire for a non-residential community that had continuity and included children.

"One evening," Virginia recalls, "when someone new had joined, we decided to go around the circle introducing ourselves to one another. Each of us talked for about twenty minutes about how the trip to Moscow had changed our lives and how we were feeling about the Persian Gulf war, which the United States had just entered. We became much closer through this simple process. Our reunions after that have been warmer and more wonderful than before, and we have stayed later and later, often past midnight. Although we haven't needed to use this structured circle-sharing form again, it served to deepen our trust."

Their potlucks—held on Friday evenings to honor the Jewish Sabbath, or Shabbat—resemble the baseball team's after-game dinners and the handwork group's regular circles: all provide a safe container, without any self-disclosure expectations or obligations, in which community blooms effortlessly in its own time, like a meadow of wildflowers. If you prefer this kind of indirect, spontaneous community building, imagine ways you can nurture it with others of similar bent, perhaps in gatherings and organizations in which you already participate. Just being with people, say in a traditional classroom setting, is not enough. Figure out ways you can interact, one to one or in small groups. Then practice patience.

Creating Intentional Communities of Friends

You may not want to wait for a loose network of friends to develop spontaneously into community. Maybe you are ready to turn your network into a community intentionally; you simply need to find an approach that works for you. Putting out the word to friends and inviting those interested in community-building to a potluck can be an excellent start. Once a core group has formed, you might choose to meet weekly or monthly or spend longer periods of time together one or more times a year.

A group of friends in Portland, Oregon, coalesced into an informal community when they began vacationing together at a beach house every summer. During the rainy winter months, they often met for soup and storytelling around the hearth of one couple's home. Another network of friends—about fifty adults and twenty-five children—in the Boston area holds weekend gatherings several times a year and has developed a set of group processes designed to deepen bonds, keep communication clear, and deal with conflict.

The two models that we describe in more detail below are formally structured but at opposite ends of the commitment spectrum. If neither matches your needs exactly, note which elements you find attractive and incorporate them into your custom-made, non-residential peer community.

Real friendship is exchanging secrets, taking hostages, rolling over like a dog and exposing the soft throat. You tell your friend things you wouldn't tell just anyone, that you wouldn't want the people at the next table to overhear, and you feel the friendship growing, like a bank account, with each story you tell, with every story you hear.

ADAIR LARA

Publishing a Personal Newsletter

If your friends are spread across the country and you cannot find the time to stay in touch with them individually, consider turning these connections into an informal community through a personal newsletter. The advantage of a newsletter with multiple contributors over the standard single-author letter is its networking capability. Not only do you, the publisher, stay in touch with your friends scattered over a wide geographical area, but, through the publication, your friends also communicate with one another. And you do not need fancy equipment to do the job; a no-frills personal computer or a simple typewriter will work quite well. You might call the personal newsletter a low-maintenance approach to community building.

One such newsletter publisher writes and edits *Claude's Family Scanner* and distributes it to about 150 friends and family members around the United States. Producing the newsletter with the aid of his home computer takes Claude Whitmyer about a day, including printing and mailing. "It's a lot less labor-intensive than writing individual letters," he points out. With every mailing, he includes a postcard on which Scanner people can write their own messages to be included in the next newsletter. About ten percent do contribute to every issue.

While not a replacement for face-to-face community, personal newsletters like the *Scanner* help friends and family in a mobile culture feel connected to one another and to the important events in each other's lives. When Claude married, many in his network lived too far away to attend the wedding. A recap of the ceremony, including readings by friends, printed in the *Scanner* touched network members' hearts and helped them feel a part of the celebration. Other contributors help one another by recommending books and travel opportunities, suggesting publishers for manuscripts, and simply responding with warmth and understanding to each other's accomplishments and predicaments.

The Goodenough community has rediscovered the ancient concept of discernment *to assist people in making major life decisions. . . . Friends are selected to help look at all aspects of a decision. They do not make the decision, but help you become aware of elements you had not considered before.*

JOHN HOFF

A print medium like this can facilitate face-to-face friendships as well. Three or four times a year Claude and his wife, Gail, host potlucks to which they invite those on the *Scanner* list. When a guest encounters another at one of these events, he or she is likely to say, "Oh, I read your letter in the *Scanner*. How's your new project going?" or "I liked the way you described your feelings about finding work that you love." Conversations tend to move quickly from small talk to substantial, heartfelt communication.

Making a Formal Commitment to Friend-Based Community

The Goodenough Community, clustered in and around Seattle, consists of several hundred individuals who consider friendship, and the community that follows from it, a high art and have decided to make it a priority in their lives. They organize moving parties when a member needs to relocate, support each other through life crises, learn from one another in structured and unstructured settings, and play and celebrate together.

When a member couple with an eighteen-month-old child gave birth to a premature infant, the community instantly mobilized, using a well-established telephone tree to coordinate the daily delivery of meals for an entire month. No member had to take responsibility for more than a single meal.

When several households of friends in eastern Washington chose to move west, Goodenough organized moving parties, complete with full crews and plentiful food at both the eastern source point and the western terminus. A subgroup formed spontaneously to travel to eastern Washington to help a member convert her apple orchards to organic growing methods. They enjoyed themselves so much they plan to return each summer.

Besides celebrating birthdays, weddings, and even divorces, members help each other professionally. One community member successfully made a transition from corporate employment to private practice with the help of a short series of meetings she arranged with her Goodenough friends. She later asked several to become members of an ongoing council of advisers.

Sometimes, in the spirit of true friendship, a group will initiate a meeting with an individual they perceive as needing help through a challenging time. One longtime member, Lynell Arnott, recalls with appreciation the personal transformation she experienced when several of her friends asked her to be the focus of such a group. "They told me I was increasingly difficult to be around, and that they loved me," she recalls. "Until then, I didn't believe the two could go together. The experience was terrible and wonderful at the same time." The group helped her solve a problem involving a stressful business partnership, the source of her "difficult" behavior.

Goodenough is not defined by place, bloodline, or activity, but by covenant. Each member becomes accountable to the others by agreeing to a common covenant that spells out the community's primary values regarding relationships and personal growth. While the form and activities of the community have changed over the years, sometimes dramatically, the convenant has remained. Goodenough began in the late 1960s as a series of casual social reunions for people who participated each summer in a pro-

I dream'd in a dream I saw
a city
invincible to the attacks
of the whole rest of the
earth.
I dream'd that was the new city
of Friends.

Walt Whitman

The Covenant of the Goodenough Community

The purpose of the Goodenough Community is to create a way of life through the relationship we share.

By entering into this covenant, we define the Goodenough Community and shape the relationship between and among us.

We agree to be accountable to each other for upholding the covenant.

As part of the Goodenough Community, I commit:

To make and keep agreements with great care;

To remain constant through conflict;

To trust the good intentions of each of us;

To relate with acceptance and respect;

To enter fully into life's experiences;

To acknowledge the inner connectedness of all creation;

To awaken my awareness to my unique role in the universe.

fessional training program, the Human Relations Laboratory. "The week-long Lab wasn't enough," explains Lynell. "Participants wanted more opportunities for growth and connection and a system of support to keep this growth alive." In 1981, the community formally incorporated as a nonprofit educational organization, named, for the record, the American Association for the Furtherance of Community. For years, it governed itself according to a structured system that included, at its core, a council of seventeen members. Goodenough members developed related organizations including a school for adults that focuses on human development and a spiritual community. In 1989, when the council dissolved itself to "take a break," the community continued to thrive as an informal network of dedicated friends and of these linked and overlapping organizations and projects. Two years later, the community chose to return to its formal structure and engaged in an in-depth renewal process.

As the Goodenough Community demonstrates, a new kind of non-place-based community, suited to the realities of contemporary life, is possible. Goodenough incorporates the security and long-term commitment of traditional community—members take care of each other's practical needs through good times and bad—yet also embodies the flexibility and psychological sophistication characteristic of contemporary American culture. It functions like a healthy living system:

- It grows and changes spontaneously in response to feedback from within and without.
- It possesses identifiable boundaries yet remains open to fresh energies (its members live and work in diverse settings, and new people can join easily).
- It consists of a whole made up of parts (organizations and individual members) that are themselves wholes.

Unlike traditional communities and organizations, Goodenough does not rely on dogma, rigidly enforced rules, a hierarchical bureaucracy, or a strong authority figure at the top to maintain its activities and identity. It functions primarily as a voluntary, peer-based community.

Creating such community—whether formal like Goodenough or informal like the circle of friends that meets for Shabbat—requires time and effort. It also gives you the kind of security, support, and personal satisfaction that no amount of money can buy or insurance policy can offer. And none of the examples described here require that you quit your job, uproot yourself or your family, or invest large sums of money in real estate. You do not have to wait for the ideal rural retreat or urban or suburban shared living arrangement to become available or affordable. You can create community—or nurture the seeds of it that are sprouting naturally—right now, where you live and work.

Resources

Recommended books and articles

The Way We Never Were: American Families and the Nostalgia Trap by Stephanie Coontz (HarperCollins, 1992)

The Family by John Bradshaw (Health Communications, 1987)

Embattled Paradise: The American Family in an Age of Uncertainty by Arlene Skolnick (Basic Books/HarperCollins, 1991)

Childhood's Future by Richard Louv (Houghton Mifflin, 1990). Insightful critique of family and society with practical suggestions for improving family life and the lives of children.

Journey of the Heart: Intimate Relationship and the Path of Love by John Welwood (HarperCollins, 1990). Insightfully explores the cultural changes that have so profoundly affected couple, family, and—by extension—community relationships.

Home Fires: An Intimate Portrait of One Middle-Class Family in Postwar America by Donald Katz (Aaron Asher Books/HarperCollins, 1992)

In Praise of Single Parents: Mothers and Fathers Embracing the Challenge by Shoshana Alexander (Houghton Mifflin, forthcoming)

What to Do after You Turn Off the T.V.: Fresh Ideas for Enjoying Family Time by Frances Moore Lappé and family (Ballantine Books, 1985)

In Context #21, Spring 1989. Theme: "Caring for Families: Nurturing the Root of Culture"

"The Return of the Extended Family" by Katherine Boo in *The Washington Monthly*, April 1992, reprinted in *Utne Reader*, July/Aug 1992

"What Happened to the Family?" by Jerrold K. Footlick in *Newsweek*'s special issue on the family, Winter/Spring 1990

FIVE

When Family and Friends Are Not Enough:

Finding a Support Group

EXTENDED FAMILIES AND COMMUNITIES of friends, even when loving and helpful, may not be able to provide all the support you need as you face your life's challenges. You may prefer talking about certain problems to people you do not see every day or meet at social events. Or you may think your mate, family, and friends already listen to you enough, and you need a more objective form of support. Perhaps your family and friends live too far away or are too busy to provide the help you seek on a regular basis. Or, you may want a level of emotional support that they are not prepared to give. If any or all of the above apply, a support group might work for you.

> *We have stories to tell, stories that provide wisdom about the journey of life. What more have we to give one another than our "truth" about our human adventure as honestly and as openly as we know how?*
>
> RABBI SAUL RUBIN

You will not be alone. Approximately fifteen million Americans attend about 500,000 support group meetings a week, according to a 1990 cover story in *Newsweek*. Between 1980 and 1990 the number of such groups quadrupled and, by all indications, they are continuing to multiply. The actual numbers could well be higher than these estimates; many leaderless support groups spring up in living rooms and kitchens independent of any coordinating organization and remain invisible to those doing the counting.

While the most numerous types of support groups focus on recovery from addictive behavior and follow the twelve-step model developed by Alcoholics Anonymous, others serve different purposes and take a variety of forms. Cancer patients attend groups to help them deal with the emotions that come with the disease and, if possible, heal themselves; small-business owners gather to overcome isolation and to share tips and contacts; men and women join same-sex groups to deepen their understanding of themselves and their common issues; and minorities of all kinds band together to provide one another the encouragement and resources they need to survive in a culture that discriminates against them.

The process of really being with other people in a safe, supportive situation can actually change who we think we are. . . . And as we grow closer to the essence of who we are, we tend to take more responsibility for our neighbors and our planet.

BILL KAUTH

No matter how different these groups, they share one quality: every member is a peer. No expert tells the others how to fix their problems or achieve their goals, and no one person functions as leader. If members do lead or otherwise facilitate meetings, they usually rotate the task. Support groups also provide a safe place for members to talk, on a regular basis, about their lives—how they are feeling, what is going well or badly, their hopes, dreams, fears, and disappointments.

Some call these rapidly proliferating mutual-help groups the "new community," or, in the case of the spiritually oriented twelve-step groups, the "new church." Neighborhood churches have traditionally held communities together by the threads of shared religious faith. But today a growing number of people are yearning for emotional honesty and acceptance rather than dogmas and sermons. At some churches, more people reportedly attend the weeknight meetings of Alcoholics Anonymous, Overeaters Anonymous, and other twelve-step meetings than show up for worship services on Sunday.

WHY SUPPORT GROUPS ARE PROLIFERATING

Support groups of every stripe have begun flourishing in America because people are tired of going it alone in a fast-paced, competitive world. They are also tired of relating in superficial, fragmented, or status-conscious ways. Growing numbers of people yearn for regular doses of honest talk, healthy emotional connections, and practical support. And many are not finding enough of this in their families, among their friends, at their church or synagogue, or in their neighborhoods. This yearning has become evident in a problem many twelve-step groups now face: more and more of those flocking to meetings are not alcoholic or otherwise obviously addicted—they simply want or need regular peer support.

One young man in his twenties, a recovering substance abuser and an AA participant for four years, enjoys the new friends he has met through meetings a lot more than he did his former drinking buddies. His new relationships involve more intimacy and authenticity. "You can talk about feelings," explains Ray, "and not have to worry about your friends gossiping about you afterwards." (Participants at twelve-step meetings identify themselves by first names only and pledge not to reveal confidences outside the group.) It's not unusual, he adds, for a man to hug another man at a meeting and say "I love you." With his old friends, Ray says, "I thought I was having fun, but I really wasn't. He admits he was scared much of the time and realizes now how much these friends lied, talked behind one another's backs, and focused primarily on materialistic pleasures.

I regard my support group as a community because each member meets my definition of a friend. I could ask any of these people for a loan. They might not give one to me, but I would feel free to ask.

TONY BACZEWSKI

Besides being safe places to express feelings and admit problems, support groups fit well into America's busy, mobile culture. Anyone can join or form a support group, any time, anywhere, for any purpose. If the first one you try does not work for you, you can leave and join or create another. If you move to a different city, you can readily find or form a support group there to meet your particular needs. Support groups need not demand a lot of time or a commitment to a belief system, nor must they be formally structured. Some groups meet just once a month for two or three hours, with the only structure an agreement to give each member a chance to talk for a few minutes without interruption.

One group like this, the five-member Entrepreneurs Group, provides support for people in business for themselves and, in most cases, by themselves. "Self-employment can be a lonely business," remarks member Tony Baczewski, a gourmet chef and caterer. For him, meeting with a group of people whom he trusts and who understand from personal experience the challenges of being a sole proprietor provides a precious taste of community, even if they only meet monthly and rarely see one another outside the meetings. "This is a warm group," Tony continues, "I know these people, and we talk about very personal things, in confidence." The other members include a photographer, a writer, an editor, and a study-skills teacher. Tony has asked for and received editing help on a promotional letter and telephone support when he was on the verge of losing a client and feeling angry and unsure how to proceed.

How Support Groups Can Generate Community

While Tony's Entrepreneurs Group and Ray's AA meetings feel like community to them, according to our definitions such groups function more as proto-communities, at least within their scheduled structures. They meet only at prescribed times, within a set format, and for a specific purpose. Members tend to come and go, and sometimes the groups themselves disband after a few months or years. Participants in open-format twelve-step groups can move around from one location to another and attend as many groups and meetings as they wish. The very label "anonymous" reveals the limits of intimacy inherent in the twelve-step kind of structure.

Loneliness is one of the biggest problems for alcoholics. And the love that they get in recovery, I think, is very powerful. It's what helps them change.

DOT MOONEY

Support groups do, however, function as training grounds on which individuals can gain confidence and the communication skills necessary to move toward full, conscious community. Most people in America feel lucky if they have one or two friends in whom they can confide or with whom they can explore ideas or let off steam. Even in the old, traditional extended families, neighborhoods, churches, and towns, people often could not speak openly about their feelings and the most painful of their problems. While many members of these communities dedicated themselves to caring for one another at a practical level, even the most loving among them did not always provide support at the emotional level—especially if the needy person's problems fell outside the range of social acceptability. Family and friends whispered about such subjects as divorce, rape, and alcoholism and did not even mention incest and homosexuality. Today, support groups broach these and countless other subjects formerly considered shameful or taboo and model emotional honesty and peer encouragement.

They also serve as meeting places where people can connect with others whom they may wish to weave into their personal networks. Within these webs of personal community, support groups often shine as important nodes of connection. For some, such as Ray, they function as primary, indispensable nodes. Ray attends three to five AA meetings a week and has met virtually all his current friends through these gatherings. In contrast, Tony's Entrepreneurs Group serves as a secondary node, helpful but not essential. His socializing only occasionally includes group members. If this group of supportive friends fell apart, Tony's life would not change significantly, though he would certainly miss the others' support.

Although you may be disappointed if you expect a support group to provide you with a fully functioning community, the sustenance you receive and the skills and attitudes you develop there may be just what you need to prepare for such community. Support groups allow you to be yourself, to tell the truth about both your weaknesses and your strengths. You also learn how to listen to others without judging them and offer help without trying to fix them. With the positive yet realistic support of your group, you develop the confidence to set and accomplish your own goals and develop the kinds of relationships you desire.

Alice's Story

One woman, a committed churchgoer who grew up in the kind of large, loving, extended family that many people pine for these days, discovered that her forms of traditional community—church and family—could not provide the kind of emotional and educational support she needed when she finally admitted to herself that her husband was an alcoholic.

A journey of a thousand miles must begin with a single step.

Lao Tzu

As a youngster, Alice, the second of five children, felt anything but alone in a world peopled with grandparents, aunts, uncles, and cousins. Even after she and her immediate family moved hundreds of miles away to a ranch, she often found herself surrounded by relatives coming to the country for a visit. They played, worked, and went to Catholic services together. Alice married into another extended Catholic family and, over the course of fourteen years, produced seven children of her own. The children attended Catholic school during the week, Mass on Sunday, and rambunctious family gatherings every Christmas and Easter.

Despite this apparent wealth of connection and support, Alice experienced profound loneliness. When she became aware of the seriousness of her husband's drinking problem, she felt she could not turn to her parents, her brothers and sisters, her cousins, or even to her parish priest for help. She was afraid they would think less of her husband and regard her as a bad wife. She remembered her father harshly criticizing an aunt for leaving an alcoholic husband after years of serious abuse. The priest, Alice feared, would simply preach to her, counseling her to keep quiet about the problem to save face for the family.

When Alice finally did venture into counseling through Catholic Social Services and brought up the alcohol issue, her counselor dismissed it as a minimal problem. Her husband, who was neither physically abusive nor a falling-down drunk, did not fit the classic stereotype of an alcoholic. He would become quietly but embarrassingly soused whenever the couple went to a party or would drink himself into a stupor at home after work. Finally, a friend from high school days, whose ex-husband was an alcoholic, gently asked Alice whether alcohol was a problem in her home. When Alice admitted it was, the friend, a longtime participant in AA, suggested attending an Al-Anon meeting. Al-Anon, the initial offshoot of AA, provides peer support for relatives and friends of alcoholics. On the spur of the moment one day, Alice drove past the church where she had intended to attend a service, and continued on to her first Al-Anon meeting. "It was the first place," she says, "where I could talk about what was going wrong in my house and no one would judge me for it. Instead, the others talked about what was happening in their houses."

Today, ten years later, Alice feels blessed and supported by the circle of friends she has made through Al-Anon and by the meetings she attends three times a week. Over the years, she has built friendships with a core of women members whom Alice considers her primary community outside her family. They travel, shop, and go to movies and plays together, in addition to supporting each other emotionally. When one of Alice's sons experienced a drug-induced breakdown and had to be hospitalized, her Al-Anon groups helped pull her through.

When I speak of the healing of the community, I speak of a whole people, not just ourselves [those of us in recovery]. Because when we heal, the children heal, the family heals, the mother heals, the grandfather heals, the grandmother heals. Everyone heals when we heal.

KENNY HALL

Before joining Al-Anon, Alice did not have friends she could confide in, even though she interacted with many people through church and her children's schools. Through her support groups, she discovered what real friendship feels like and, most importantly, began to believe it was possible for her.

Alice also learned about her own role in the family addiction system. "At first, I thought nothing was wrong with me," she admits. "I figured that if my husband stopped drinking everything would be okay." Now she realizes how her own controlling behavior contributed to the problem. Alice has learned to acknowledge her feelings, ask for what she needs, and drop a lot of the control. "I now let my husband decide whether to stay home or join me and others on a family trip." As she has practiced healthier ways of relating, both in her groups and at home, other family members have begun to do likewise. After Alice made her fateful detour ten years ago and began attending Al-Anon meetings, she stopped trying to turn her husband into a non-drinker, choosing to change herself instead. She considers it a bonus that her husband has not touched alcohol for two years and has begun participating in couples therapy with her.

Her twelve-step support groups have enabled Alice to claim a life for herself and, in the process, to build a strong personal community. She no longer has to go it alone. Paradoxically, as Alice has acknowledged her limitations and increased her interdependence, she has become more empowered and independent.

THE TWELVE-STEP MOVEMENT: A PIONEERING MODEL OF EFFECTIVE PEER SUPPORT

The network of twelve-step groups, now worldwide, differs radically from most organizations in America. Its power lies not in financial or political clout nor in the status of its leaders. It owns virtually no assets, refuses to take a political stand on any issue, and raises no member above the others. The power the network does generate—and that has enabled it to transform millions of lives and spread throughout the world—arises from the compelling effectiveness of its program and the decentralized, organic nature of its organizational dynamics.

Anyone can start a twelve-step group by spreading the word and arranging for a meeting place. If members feel their current group does not meet their needs, they can break away and start a new one. Those founding the new group can revise the wording of the standard opening statements slightly to reflect their purpose.

What makes a space safe? To the extent people feel confident that what they say will not be used to attack them, that their confidences will not be broken, and that they will not be taken advantage of or abandoned in a difficult spot—then they will risk being open.

TOM ATLEE

And so the network, an excellent example of a living system, grows and changes in response to needs and pressures within and without while still retaining its identity. What gives its rapidly proliferating groups continuity and a recognizable dynamic is a meeting format, a manual (known as the "Big Book" and written by the founders of Alcoholics Anonymous), and a set of slogans such as "One day at a time" and "Keep it simple." No one at the top determines who can or cannot be a member or what kinds of groups can or cannot form, and no bureaucratic central office collects dues and polices chapters to make sure they are toeing the party line. Even three of AA's strongest critics—Stanton Peele, Archie Brodsky, and Mary Arnold, authors of *The Truth About Addiction and Recovery*—who blast the program for its rigidity, acknowledge that chapters vary so widely that some barely resemble the parent organization.

The groups have developed several formats. Some are public and open to anyone, while others are private and limited to membership by invitation only. Either of these can follow a speaker format in which one person tells his or her story or a circle-sharing format in which anyone who wishes can take a turn talking about her or his life. But regardless of a particular group's procedure, participants can be sure that no matter which meeting they attend in whatever city in the world, it will open and close with approximately the same prayers and statements. They also know that when they speak, no one will interrupt them or discuss or interpret what they have shared.

THE LIMITS OF TWELVE-STEP GROUPS

While, for millions of people such as Alice and Ray, twelve-step groups serve as a vital catalyst for personal recovery and the creation of healthy community, these groups do not provide an answer for everyone. If you do not have an addiction or an addicted loved one, a twelve-step group is not the ideal place to find mutual support and to meet people you might want to incorporate into your community. You would be better off finding or creating a peer group that serves your primary interests and needs.

As twelve-step groups have gained more adherents, their success has bred controversy. Many critics voice dismay about the religious overtones, even though twelve-step participants insist that the "higher power" to which they turn over their lives can be God, nature, their own inner strength, or a universal spirit—however each person chooses to define it. The movement, say twelve-steppers, provides not a religion defined by faith in specific beliefs but a practical spirituality through which participants can experience a power greater than themselves and allow this to help them recover from their addiction.

There may be advantages in not *turning one's support group into one's intimate community, for often what we need to be supported* about *are the conflicts and struggles we're involved in with our intimates.*

STARHAWK

Some women and members of minority groups have trouble with the program's heavy emphasis on admitting powerlessness and making amends for personal wrongdoing while ignoring the social and political factors that lead people into addiction. As one critic, Charlotte Davis Kasl, author of *Many Roads, One Journey: Moving Beyond the Twelve Steps,* points out: "Most women suffer from the lack of a healthy, aware ego, and need to strengthen their sense of self by affirming their own inner wisdom." The last thing they need, she believes, is a feeling of powerlessness. Another observer, however, views the organization as a feminist model. "There is no one person who speaks for any twelve-step group," explains Marguerite Judson, host of the public radio program "Community in Recovery." "Every group is self-supporting; there are no membership requirements and no officers. The power is at the periphery of the organization, and that's one of the ways I define feminism." Some believe the women's movement contributed significantly to the current explosion of AA offshoots. "It was the women's consciousness-raising movement," notes an article in *Newsweek,* "that first extended the self-help concept beyond alcoholism."

Despite the lack of any external, centralized authority, certain twelve-step members act as if there were one. Elizabeth Reed, a psychotherapist and Methodist minister who participated in groups for several years, comments that such members can become as rigid as fundamentalist Christians, insisting that the program is the only way to make change and using the fourth step, which requires "a searching and fearless moral inventory of ourselves," to berate others with judgments. "Reform movements that open closed systems inevitably become institutionalized and oppressive themselves," Reed points out. "We bring our individual dysfunctions into any system," she adds, noting that in twelve-step groups "one or two dysfunctional people can shut the system down."

Twelve-step groups possess fewer defenses against such behavior because they are leaderless and open to all comers. While this leaderlessness encourages people to take responsibility for their own life, Reed explains, on the down side, members who have not done sufficient work on their own addictive patterns can either flounder together or allow one person to take over and play therapist or become the "confronter." If the group is full of "pleaser types," she notes, "they can allow this one person to wreck the group." Wrecking one group, however, does not destroy the organization. When one group disbands, its members join other groups or start new ones.

Competitiveness breeds a you-against-me attitude that creates separateness and isolation, the food of addiction. Cooperation breeds a sense that we are all interdependent on one another, we all matter, and each of us has a role to play in the bigger picture. It teaches us that everyone can win.

CHARLOTTE DAVIS KASL

Some critics warn that the groups themselves can become addictive, providing another form of escape from the challenges of life. Jungian analyst James Hillman, coauthor of *A Hundred Years of Psychotherapy—and the World Is Getting Worse,* fears that the mushrooming of support groups focused on addiction represents an undermining of community rather than a strengthening of it. "Now our emotional loyalties are tied to other fat people, or other alcoholics. It's selfish. It's drawn a tremendous energy away from other causes, away from politics and ecology. They [addiction recovery groups] have drawn citizens into thinking of themselves as patients, rather than citizens."

While acknowledging the tremendous value of the twelve-step movement in helping millions stop addictive habits and build support structures, therapist Tina Tessina warns against the assumption, promulgated by many twelve-step groups, that addiction is a lifelong disease without cure. In *The Real Thirteenth Step,* she writes, "For many long-term recovery group members, it is no longer enough to remain 'clean and sober,' to learn the Steps, to be a part of the 'family.' Life beyond the group, beyond recovery, calls to them; human beings have an innate need to grow, to accomplish, to achieve." They can, according to Tessina, graduate from the group and move toward healthy, autonomous living.

Not everyone recovers from addiction, and many find twelve-step groups exactly the kind of supportive challenge they need. Despite its limitations, the program provides an experience of mutual support for millions of people that is often deeper and healthier than any they have experienced in their traditional families, churches, and civic organizations.

We believe that in proto-communities such as twelve-step groups, people can plant the seeds for conscious community. As they move beyond the recovery group, telling their truth and accepting one another without judgment at home, school, church, work, and in other settings, they will feel less need for banding together around specific addictions.

Beyond the Twelve Steps: Tailoring Support Groups to Meet Members' Needs

A little bit of me would pop out and no one went away. They just kept listening, understanding, and caring. It was so amazing. So I'd share a little more and a little more. Slowly I stopped feeling so rotten inside.

Sex and Love Addicts Anonymous member Gerri

A number of peer-based groups have begun to adapt or augment the twelve-step process to fit their own needs. For example, non-spiritual alternatives to AA have arisen, including Secular Organizations for Sobriety, Rational Recovery, and Methods of Moderation. In 1976, Jean Kirkpatrick founded Women for Sobriety, a program that attempts to identify the unique recovery needs of women.

More and more members of twelve-step groups are choosing to explore a wider variety of supportive group processes. Participants in one small, private Codependents Anonymous meeting wanted to receive a response when they spoke, and even to sing, dance, and drum together—interactions not possible in the strict twelve-step format. So they organized four all-day gatherings outside the regular weekly meetings for more wide-open sharing. Members taught each other everything from simple songs to bread sculpture. "It fed energy back into the group and opened up the process," reports one of the initiators, Alexander. "Some of us may take the group out of the safe twelve-step container and start a new kind of group."

Two African-American groups have also moved beyond the strict twelve-step format and risked greater intimacy. One of these, a group of recovering addicts, was featured in Bill Moyers' public television program, "Circle of Recovery." When Moyers asks Tony, the group's founder, what the six men get out of their meetings that they do not get in a traditional twelve-step group, Tony replies, "It's simple. There is no dialogue or debate—or what's the word? cross talk—in twelve-step meetings, and we cross talk here. We dig. We really get into it with one another." While some of these men also attend traditional twelve-step meetings, none would think of missing their small, Sunday-night gatherings in one member's apartment. One ex-convict in the group tells how the other men "showed me how to live, how to be a black man," and emphasizes how important it is for him to be able to see other black men staying sober.

Part of the challenge and the reward of this men's group is that it brings same-sex members of an oppressed minority together in a safe place where they can confront not only their addictions but also the pain of their oppression, including their internalized versions of it. "When you remove the drugs," says Kenny, a member who now works as a drug and alcohol counselor, "I'm still black, ugly, worthless. I'm still no good. That's recovery for me—to challenge those demons. To one day [be able to] look in the mirror and . . . say 'I am worthwhile, I am okay' on a daily basis." The group, for him, is a mirror he can look into.

The other group is all women. Gladys Fermon, a twelve-stepper for seven years who considers AA "home," realized that she needed to "go a step further" to get emotional support in the wake of her father's death. "My body was grieving," she says, "and I needed to be held by a black woman, not in a sexual way but like a mother. I needed to be shown that I was lovable even when I was crying." Her own mother, who had given Gladys the message that crying would make her sick, had rarely expressed physical affection toward her daughter. "As a child, when I kissed my mother, I'd look back and see her wiping the kiss off her face," recalls Gladys.

What amazes me and heals me over and over again . . . is the incredible power of the human spirit to build and rebuild loving communities, to break open our hearts again and again so that we might truly know each other and feel moved once more to trust, to give, to receive.

DUNCAN CAMPBELL

Through a friend, Gladys heard about the peer support groups fostered by the Bay Area Black Women's Health Project, an independent regional organization associated with a national network. At the meetings—small, informal gatherings in a member's home, not unlike Tony's men's group—Gladys learned that "I could cry, cry, cry, and get up and function. I didn't get sick, and no one tried to talk me out of my feelings." And sadness was not the only emotion expressed. "Sometimes women even get up and dance or sing," says Gladys. "We have a good time together."

Although Gladys comments that she has "never experienced anything so safe as these groups," she also acknowledges that they are "more intimate and more risky" than twelve-step meetings. "In twelve-step meetings," she points out, "you can sit there and not speak and no one will know what you are thinking or feeling." Some people need the option of sitting out a meeting without saying anything, or at least knowing that no one will comment on their sharing when they do speak. But for those ready for more, the above groups demonstrate three variations on how you can move beyond twelve-step groups in your own way.

FINDING A PEER SUPPORT GROUP THAT WORKS FOR YOU

You may not need a weekly meeting where you can share your pain. Perhaps you simply want a group that can give you tips and encouragement as you change careers or struggle to raise a teenager. To find the appropriate group, you first need to clarify the kind of support you desire.

Some groups focus on problems—recovering from addictive behavior, dealing with an illness or disability, negotiating a crisis, or relating to a friend or family member who has a problem. Other groups, such as The Entrepreneurs Group, single-parent groups, professional networks, and most men's and women's groups, are more growth-oriented than problem-oriented. A look at two networks of such groups can give you an idea of the possibilities.

I find this especially striking and essential to successful forms of community: that a person's intellectual and spiritual advancement was a community concern. It was the goal of all to uplift each and every member of the community in a real spirit of love and compassion.

RICK MARGOLIES

A growing number of peer support groups, inspired by Barbara Sher and Annie Gottlieb's books *Wishcraft* and *Teamworks!*, call themselves Success Teams and serve to help their members realize their dreams—professional or personal. "A Success Team," the coauthors explain, "is a small group of people whose only goal is to help every member of the team get what he or she wants." While these teams vary tremendously in their focus and composition, they all follow the same simple format: they meet weekly or every other week for no more than two hours; consist of no more than six members who divide the time equally among them; and focus on helping members identify their goals, develop specific steps and timelines to reach these goals, and offer each other support in following through on these steps. This support might involve brainstorming, sharing contacts and other resources, rehearsing a crucial sales pitch or interview, or venting frustrations in a safe setting. At every meeting, members report on their progress (or lack of it) since the last meeting and commit themselves to taking specific steps toward their goal for the next one. Sometimes, a team member will ask another to serve as a buddy between meetings by giving a supportive phone call or helping out in some other way. One woman kept postponing signing up for an acting class that both excited and intimidated her. Her teammates called her the day of the next class to give her encouragement. She attended the course and enjoyed herself thoroughly. Another woman got the raise she wanted after a teammate, a human resources consultant, coached her on how to ask for it. Like twelve-step programs, Success Teams have spread rapidly to form loosely organized but far-reaching networks.

The members of The Entrepreneurs Group met through a similar kind of network, the Briarpatch—a community of business people who believe in sharing information and resources, being honest and open, and putting the quality of their products and services above pure profit. Named after the briarpatch in the folk tales of Uncle Remus—a thorny place in which Br'er Rabbit lived a simple, happy life protected from predators—the organization started in the San Francisco Bay Area and has spread as far as Japan, Sweden, and New Zealand. Members in most locations pay voluntary dues, receive a member directory and a newsletter, and can phone the coordinator for emotional support and resource referrals. New and old members, affectionately known as Briars, also brainstorm at monthly brown-bag lunches and attend occasional workshops sponsored by other Briars. If a member wishes an on-site business consultation, she or he can call on a volunteer team of technical consultants.

Sometimes support groups develop spontaneously as a result of some shared, intimate activity. In Carol Cowen's fiction writing group, which started out as a seminar, the seven women participants have become close despite their different ages, backgrounds, and marital status. "We encourage each other to go deeper and deeper inside ourselves," Carol notes. Together, they now feel comfortable revealing sensitive personal truths in their writings. In supporting each other's creativity, they have learned how to give feedback in helpful ways and to trust the group wisdom. They also share publishing ideas and discuss editors and agents. Some have formed friendships that extend beyond the group.

Help thy brother's boat across, and lo! thine own has reached the shore.

HINDU PROVERB

Locating and Assessing Existing Groups

You can locate an existing group by asking friends, reading the classified ads in local or specialty publications, checking community bulletin boards, calling a self-help clearinghouse, or contacting your public library. For twelve-step groups, the telephone book is an excellent place to start. Many groups list numbers in both the white and yellow pages. If the specific recovery group you are looking for is not listed, call another one for a reference. In the yellow pages, look under headings such as Alcoholism Information, Support Groups, Crisis Intervention Services, and Human Services Organizations. Also, see this chapter's Resources section.

Finding a support group that works for you is a little like deciding which of your acquaintances you wish to cultivate as a good friend. You may not always feel comfortable in the group you choose, but you should feel safe, trusting that you will not be attacked or judged and that your sensitive revelations will not be disclosed outside the group. You might also sense whether the group is willing, over time, to help you grow and expand your world, even if this means you eventually leave the group. As in friendship, the giving goes both ways, so in assessing a group, notice how you feel about providing support as well as receiving it from this particular collection of people. You may need to shop around until you find a group that serves you well and that you can serve in return. While Alice, for example, felt immediately at home at the first Al-Anon meeting she attended, Ray went to a number of different AA meetings before he found some he wanted to stay with.

Mutual help groups are a powerful and constructive means for people to help themselves and each other. The basic dignity of each human being is expressed in his or her capacity to be involved in a reciprocal helping exchange. Out of this compassion comes cooperation. From this cooperation comes community.

PHYLLIS SILVERMAN

Because many peer support groups serve a specific type of need, their populations appear less diverse than those of other forms of community and proto-community. The sameness can be either comforting or disturbing. For Gladys, who joined the Bay Area Black Women's Health Project, it was important "to be in a community of my own kind—with other black women." On the other hand, a friend of ours who joined a cancer support group felt, at first, overwhelmed by the collective fears and pain associated with the main characteristic they had in common. Within the bounds of sameness, however, tremendous variety can exist. The cancer patient discovered that the individuals in the group were complex people and that collective hope can spring from one person's comment or the warmth of sharing. Gladys was surprised at how different the BWHP members were from other black women she had known—so at ease with one another, laughing, talking, and hugging. When you are evaluating a group, give it a chance to show its whole personality before making a final decision to leave or continue.

Some support groups, affiliated with larger service-oriented organizations such as the Black Women's Health Project, provide you with opportunities to grow and expand your world beyond the group. They offer, as Felicia Ward of the Bay Area BWHP puts it, a vehicle "for moving from personal sharing to collective action." When people come into a small peer group in pain or in the middle of a major life transition, Ward acknowledges, they often need months or years of pure support in a safe setting, but once they have regained confidence and self-esteem and improved their relational skills, these members can begin to reach out to others and become healthy change agents in the larger world. Gladys Fermon eventually felt confident enough to initiate and co-facilitate her own BWHP groups after taking trainings from the regional organization. In Atlanta, where the national BWHP was founded in 1984 by Byllye Avery, the organization is helping to establish an African-American women's wellness center, among other community projects.

You need not be in pain to feel a desire for giving and receiving support. Paul and Diana von Welanetz founded The Inside Edge, a southern California breakfast group, in 1985 after returning from a citizen diplomat trip to Moscow. Their purpose was to meet with other leaders and professionals, to help each other expand their personal potential and make significant contributions to the larger community. Today, two Inside Edge chapters, one in Orange County and one in Beverly Hills, serve more than a hundred active, dues-paying members and a host of drop-in guests. "It's a wonderful place where you can grow, be free, be nurtured, and have family," says member Art Messing. "It's different from a biological family, which supports you in doing what they think you should do. Inside Edge provides support for what *you* want to do. It's where we go to get charged up."

At the Tuesday meetings, which begin at 6:30 a.m., groups at each table take turns speaking for a few seconds on a topic the featured speaker will address. Once, when a healer was on the schedule, each person mentioned an area in his or her life that had experienced healing in the past year. Other speakers have included writers, philosophers, astronauts, psychologists—anyone who can provide inspiration. "Often I've heard just the right talk, exactly what I've needed to hear on a given day," says Art. The meetings, which include time for greetings and hugs, conclude about 8:30 with a song or a poem. Attendees often hang around afterward. The group also hosts social events and an annual Interdependence Picnic.

Several spinoffs—more specific support groups—have developed, including Women's Edge, Men's Edge, and Writers' Edge. The groups are self-selecting: anyone can initiate an Edge group and anyone can join.

Starting Your Own Peer Support Group

If you want to be sure a support group fits your needs, and you wish to have a say in who participates, start your own. This can be as simple as calling two or three friends and asking them to each bring another friend to an initial meeting. If your current friends do not have the same needs for support that you have or are not willing or able to participate in a regular group, you can place an ad in a local newspaper or post fliers on community bulletin boards to attract members. A middle way exists between these all-friends, all-strangers extremes. Often you only need to know one other person who, in turn, knows people or groups among which you can drum up members without advertising to the public. Teaming up with another person to initiate a group can make the process more fun and less intimidating.

If you are planning to start your own support group, consider several key issues—purpose, size, time considerations, format, task/process ratio, and diversity of membership—before calling the first meeting.

Purpose: Clarify your primary reason for initiating the group. Do you wish to focus on personal support? Professional? Or a combination of both? Consider how you would define success for the group. List the changes you would like to experience in your own life as a result of meeting regularly with peers.

Size: In determining the number of members for your group, consider how much time you want to provide each person to share and receive help at every meeting. Five to nine members is generally a good number, depending on how much time you allot for the meeting. Most veterans of support groups agree that you are wise to start with more members than you ideally wish to have, because some are bound to drop out.

We cannot find reality simply by remaining with ourselves or making ourselves the goal. Paradoxically, we only know ourselves when we know ourselves in responding to others.

MAURICE FRIEDMAN

Time considerations: Clarify whether you wish the group to continue indefinitely or for a specified length of time, and how often you are willing and able to meet. Consider how much time and intensity you will need to accomplish your key purpose. Bill Kauth, author of *Men's Friends: How to Organize and Run Your Own Men's Support Group*, recommends a minimum of six weeks for specific skill-learning or problem-solving groups and six months for open-ended growth-oriented groups, meeting either weekly or every other week. Some support groups continue for years.

Format: Determine the level of structure that will help you accomplish your purpose. If your group is primarily task-oriented, it may wish to adopt a fixed procedural format that includes regular times for the setting and monitoring of goals. If your group is more relationship-oriented, you may choose a less structured, more spontaneous format. For both goal-oriented and relationship-oriented groups, we have found that a personal check-in at the beginning of each meeting helps build the trust that makes groups work. In diverse groups, this check-in can serve to break down stereotypes and reduce the likelihood of polarization when conflict arises, as it inevitably does in any healthy, truthful group. (See Chapter Fourteen for more meeting suggestions.)

Task-process ratio: Consider to what extent are you willing to commit to building conscious community with one another. Are you prepared to work with conflict, develop intimacy, and share secret parts of yourselves? Some support groups are primarily task-oriented, while others are process-oriented, preferring to focus on group dynamics and individual behavior rather than accomplishing a goal. Most people are more comfortable with one type than with the other. Strong polarization between task-oriented and process-oriented people can undermine a group. To prevent this, set aside time regularly to examine and recommit to the ratio of task and process that works for the group.

Diversity of membership: Consider how much diversity your group's membership can embrace while remaining safe enough to accomplish your pur-

Teaming Up to Start a Group

Fred Olsen used a team approach successfully when he decided he wanted peer support in his new and unusual profession and a greater sense of community in his newly adopted hometown. After working for years as an engineer for NASA in Washington, D.C., Fred chose to turn one of his primary interests, dreamwork, into a new career. Dreamwork is an approach to self-understanding and personal growth that uses dreams as vehicles to tap inner resources. Because he knew that a large number of dreamworkers lived and worked in the San Francisco area, Fred moved there, after completing an extensive training, to set up his private practice. When he learned that no support group existed for his colleagues, he resolved to form one. "I needed such a group," he says. "Dreamwork isn't highly supported in our culture. If you're not mainstream, there's an acute need for validation of your vision and ideas."

The first thing he did was call a colleague, Linda. The two spent an evening zeroing in on what each was looking for. What they had in common, they discovered, was a desire for a space where anyone who is involved with, or has a deep interest in, dreams can share his or her own perspectives—with no one discipline considered right or wrong. Fred and Linda called two others, inviting them to get together for a potluck and "see what happens."

What happened was the formation of a solid core group of dreamworkers, who then invited more people involved with dreams—writers, therapists, artists, and so forth—to join. Now the group's informal membership list contains more than fifty names. At the monthly meetings, members share food as well as ideas and feelings. Outside the meetings, members help with each other's individual projects and go to each other's events. They think of one another as family.

pose. Should the group be limited to friends and acquaintances or open to strangers? Only men or only women? Members of a certain profession?

While gathering friends is certainly easiest, getting them to let go of their ingrained socializing patterns may not be so easy. You may find yourselves chatting more than giving one another thoughtful, honest feedback. Acquaintances can be ideal charter members: you know them well enough to trust that they will fit in and contribute, yet not so well that you view each other in fixed ways. While starting with strangers can be risky, it also can be surprising and refreshing. If you want a group in which you can deal with some of the hidden or shameful aspects of your life, you may find it easier to be open with strangers who share a common problem than with friends.

When we come from a group whose culture has been systematically denied or stolen, we need spaces of separation, safe places in which to nurture each other, to grow, to be ourselves without fear or pressure. . . . Without such places, we have no base from which to connect with others who are different.

STARHAWK

If you decide on a group of strangers, be prepared to screen candidates by phone to ascertain whether they will be compatible and not dominate the group. Ask them why they are interested in a group, what they expect to gain from it and what they feel every member should contribute. Listen carefully to their answers and notice how well they listen to you. If you hold your first meeting at a restaurant or other public place, you will probably feel safer, and you can observe who meshes with whom.

In determining the appropriate amount and type of diversity, bear in mind that while the group needs fresh perspectives and new information, it also needs enough commonality to minimize arguments and ensure full participation of all members. Some groups, such as open twelve-step meetings, share at a deeply personal level despite diversity in race, sex, class, religion, lifestyle, and politics. A commitment to confidentiality helps, along with an agreement to abide by a fixed procedural format.

For others, such agreements do not provide the level of safety they desire. To achieve this, they restrict the membership more narrowly—to gay men only, or to Asian women, for example. When deep gaps in understanding and centuries of oppression have separated certain population groups—such as men and women, blacks and whites, gays and straights—from one another, groups limited to members of only one side of the divide can generate greater safety and, with that, greater intimacy. The African-American men's and women's groups described earlier demonstrate the intimacy and healing such restricted membership can generate. Because of their common race and backgrounds, the women and men in these groups are able to reveal fears and other feelings they could never show in mixed-race and mixed-gender groups. The self-esteem each gains through this loving and respectful interaction enables them to function with greater honesty and effectiveness in the diverse world in which they live and work. When narrowly defined affinity groups such as these challenge their members to take what they have learned back out into the world, the groups contribute indirectly to the building of more diverse forms of community.

No matter how carefully you plan your support group, you can be sure of one thing: over time, it will change as it takes on a life of its own. Rejoice in this, for it signals the presence of a healthy, living system.

Resources

Recommended books

Teamworks! by Barbara Sher and Annie Gottlieb (Warner Books, 1989)

Men's Friends: How to Organize and Run Your Own Men's Support Group by Bill Kauth (E.Q.L.S. Publishing, 4913 North Newhall St., Milwaukee, Wisconsin, 53217; (414) 964-6656).

Beyond Therapy, Beyond Science: A New Model for Healing the Whole Person by Anne Wilson Schaef (HarperCollins, 1992)

Surplus Powerlessness: The Psychodynamics of Everyday Life and the Psychology of Individual and Social Transformation by Michael Lerner. Published in 1986 by the Institute for Labor and Mental Health, 5100 Leona, Oakland, California 94619; (510) 482-0804. Discusses the effectiveness of support groups.

Many Roads, One Journey: Moving Beyond the Twelve Steps by Charlotte Davis Kasl (HarperCollins, 1992)

The Real Thirteenth Step: Discovering Confidence, Self-Reliance, and Autonomy Beyond the 12-Step Programs by Tina Tessina (Jeremy P. Tarcher, 1991)

The Recovery Resource Book: The Best Available Information on Addictions and Codependence by Barbara Yoder (Fireside/Simon & Schuster, 1990)

Organizations

American Self-Help Clearinghouse, St. Clares-Riverside Medical Center, Denville, New Jersey, 07834; (201) 625-7101. Provides information on and referrals to national self-help groups and local self-help clearinghouses. Also consults with those interested in starting a new type of self-help group not yet available in the United States. Publishes *The Self-Help Sourcebook* ($9 ppd.).

National Self-Help Clearinghouse, 25 West 43rd Street, New York, New York, 10036. Send a self-addressed, stamped envelope to receive information. Publishes the *Self-Help Reporter* five times a year ($10/year) and many other educational materials, including *How to Organize a Self-Help Group* by Andrew Humm.

Alcoholics Anonymous (AA), AA World Services, Box 459, Grand Central Station, New York, New York, 10163; (212) 870-3400 and (212) 870-3199 (TTY)

Secular Organizations for Sobriety International Clearinghouse, P.O. Box 5, Buffalo, New York; (716) 834-2922

The Inside Edge, P.O. Box 692, Pacific Palisades, California, 90272; (213) 649-1442 (Beverly Hills); (714) 964-3833 (Orange County)

Ft. Negley
COMMUNITY
GARDEN
PARTICIPENTS:
FT. NEGLEY NEIGHBORHOOD ASSOCIATION
CHATTANOOGA VENTURE
CHATTANOOGA NEIGHBORHOOD ENTERPRISES

SIX

Turning Neighborhoods and Cities into Communities

ONLY A GENERATION AGO, many Americans were able to enjoy the intimacy of small-town life even in the heart of a big city. My (Carolyn's) older brother, John, discovered this a few years after we moved to the Sunset District, then an Irish-Italian working-class neighborhood in San Francisco. On his way home from school one day, John visited the local bakery. He treated himself to a chocolate eclair, headed across the street, and was just biting into the creamy confection when he heard a loud male voice from above bellow, "John Shaffer, what do you think you're doing?" John froze and looked skyward. Was it God checking on his every action as the nuns at school had warned him? Then, as John tells it, "I noticed our family dentist, Dr. Erigero, sticking his head out his second-floor window and yelling at me to think of my teeth." Although John was not delighted with such close community at that moment, he certainly could not complain about the loneliness and anonymity of big-city streets.

Neighborhood people kept a trained eye on passing life from behind the curtains and Venetian blinds of the front windows of their houses facing the street and both sidewalks. . . . It wasn't being nosy or busybody so much as the real need to turn one's back periodically on the household with all its demands, to see what was going on in the world.

NORBERT BLEI

Jane Jacobs, in her classic *The Death and Life of American Cities,* called the phenomenon John experienced "eyes on the street" and credited it with keeping many dense urban neighborhoods safe. Today, however, it is difficult to imagine neighbors choosing to become this involved in the activities of others. Even if dentists had office windows that opened and clients who lived within walking distance, it is improbable that these health professionals would, like Dr. Erigero, literally stick their necks out to protect clients from their own behavior or from street dangers.

Of course, wealthier Americans have been withdrawing into their own neighborhoods and clubs for generations. But the new secession is more dramatic because the highest earners now inhabit a different economy from other Americans. The new elite is linked by jet, modem, fax, satellite and fiber-optic cable to the great commercial and recreational centers of the world, but it is not particularly connected to the rest of the nation.

ROBERT B. REICH

No More Eyes on the Street

Grownups watching out for children other than their own is only one aspect of neighborhood life that has suffered over the course of a generation. Another is children playing with children spontaneously. As one mother in Berkeley, California, commented, "My kids can't cross the street when they feel like it. There are too many cars, going too fast. We have to make dates with the kids across the street—sometimes days in advance—for our kids to play with them."

Neighborhood community has deteriorated for adults as well. Women, especially those staying home to raise their families, have traditionally woven and maintained the social fabric of their neighborhoods. Today, with more women in the workforce, fewer have the time to organize potlucks and block parties, or to drop in on one another for coffee and conversation.

Urban neighborhoods used to be like villages, integrated systems in which people of all ages knew and interacted with one another and in which almost every essential product or service was available within walking distance. Shopkeepers watched out for the kids and performed other informal community services. Over the last few decades, corporate franchises have replaced many mom-and-pop operations, and the clerks who staff them feel little connection to the neighborhood.

Discouraged by urban decay and fearful of crime, people who can afford to have fled to homes in the suburbs which, in turn, are becoming sprawling metropolises with crime problems of their own. In these suburban residential enclaves, they find that neighborly personal contact is often rarer than it was before. Meanwhile, the abandoned urban centers deteriorate for lack of attention.

In both the suburbs and the cities, the main thing next-door neighbors have in common these days is socioeconomic class: they have similar incomes and pay about the same in taxes. The more successful and affluent have, U.S. Secretary of Labor Robert B. Reich warns in a *New York Times Magazine* article, seceded from the less fortunate four-fifths of society. "In many cities and towns," says Reich, "the wealthy have in effect withdrawn

Assessing Your Neighborhood

How does your neighborhood—or the neighborhood to which you are considering moving—rate in terms of community?

- Does the design of the houses, apartment buildings, and blocks encourage interaction?
- How pedestrian-friendly are the streets? Are there enough sidewalks?
- Can you travel where you need to go—work, school, shopping, etc.—on foot or by public transportation easily?
- How strong is the neighborhood identity? Does the neighborhood publish its own newspaper? Support a community center?
- Is there an active neighborhood association? Do its issues extend beyond keeping property values high? Does it reach out to other neighborhoods?
- How active are the local merchants in community affairs?
- Are most businesses locally owned, so that the owner-residents have a stake in the neighborhood? Do the people who work in the businesses live in the neighborhood?
- Are there plenty of trees? What about community gardens?
- Do you see a diversity of people—different ages, races, economic classes—and do these groups interact with each other?
- Is there plenty of street life, and is it safe?
- How, if at all, does the neighborhood welcome new residents and new businesses?

Let us all take responsibility not only for ourselves and our families, but for our communities and our country.

Bill Clinton

their dollars from the support of public spaces and institutions shared by all and dedicated the savings to their own private services."

In some areas, even the houses discourage interaction, like the neighborhood that columnist Barbara F. Newhall described in the *Oakland Tribune:* "Houses up here pretend they aren't here at all. They turn away all comers. They are built low and out of sight. They hide behind camelias and runaway ivy. Six-foot-high fences—and there are more and more of these every day—keep the children in and the deer out. They also firmly rebuff the human eye and ear. . . . You can live down the street from a family with kids your own children's age and never know it."

If you are starting to feel a little depressed by the above analysis, take heart. There are signs of hope. Certain cities have revitalized their downtowns or are turning decaying industrial areas into thriving commercial and residential neighborhoods. A few architects and planners, in league with visionary developers, are creating whole towns instead of additional bedroom communities segregated by economic class. Citizens are taking the initiative in reclaiming formerly blighted, crime-ridden urban neighborhoods. A few are revisioning their entire cities and creating multicultural community in the process.

People can experience their human potential for cooperative effort and interdependence through the staging of hands-on urban barnraising events. Witnessing the growth of community as people work together for a common goal has been a ray of hope to me, a glimpse of human potential in a world besieged by violence and wars.

KARL LINN

Individuals are reconnecting with their neighbors in simple ways that involve neither bureaucracies nor politics. Sometimes you can start rebuilding community with just a little consistent attention and a few small but firm steps in the right direction—or, as songwriter Betsy Rose puts it, "trust in the neighborhood, faith in each other and the common good."

Banana Kelly and Other Do-It-Yourself Neighborhood Revivals

It was not faith, exactly, that prompted Harold DeRienzo to begin organizing a burned-out, rubble-strewn neighborhood in the South Bronx. It was partly impatience and partly youthful idealism (he was twenty-three). Many of the young men coming to play basketball at the settlement house where Harold worked hailed from a banana-curved block of Kelly Street, where the city was preparing to tear down three vacant buildings. Everyone had given up on "Banana Kelly," as that section of the street was called. City government considered it hopeless, and the private sector was disinclined to invest in such a blighted area.

"It looked like Dresden," Harold recalls. "Anyone who had any choice was leaving." Those who had not yet been able to escape were putting up with entirely too much, he felt. "Sometimes there was no water, so people were filling buckets from a fire hydrant and hauling them up through sixth-floor windows."

It doesn't have to be that way, thought Harold. So he began talking to the basketball players after the games, gradually persuading them that they could, by working together, "frame their own solutions." Eventually, the Banana Kelly residents spent less and less time playing basketball as they began organizing street cleanups and block parties. The group stopped the bulldozers from tearing down the abandoned buildings and prepared to take renovation literally into their own hands. Harold put his own commitment on the line by moving into the neighborhood himself. He and the others were able to work around the city's bureaucratic system, partly by making special arrangements with individual city agencies and partly through "sweat equity"—a form of homesteading in which families renovate the dwellings they themselves will occupy. The effort was successful, Harold believes, because it enjoyed local support and did not challenge large developers (who were not interested anyway). There was also a bit of luck: in 1977 President Jimmy Carter visited the South Bronx "and suddenly sweat equity was 'the President's program,'" says Harold.

True belonging is born of relationships not only to one another but to a place of shared responsibilities and benefits. We love not so much what we have acquired as what we have made and whom we have made it with.

ROBERT FINCH

Once the project was under way, people began returning to Banana Kelly to participate. A sense of community began to emerge. Garbage disappeared from alleyways, a mixture of co-ops and single-family homes became livable, and flowers bloomed along the sidewalks. After saving their block, the Banana Kelly Neighborhood Improvement Association went on to save other blocks. The Association began to attract city, state, and private investment—when you are successful, everyone wants to give you money—and now administers a variety of social service programs and a multi-million-dollar budget. Harold worries, though, about the loss of the volunteer "we're helping ourselves" mentality. "Banana Kelly needs to be viewed as a vehicle for local empowerment rather than a channel for social services. To retain a sense of community, people have to have a sense that they're affecting their own lives."

Even when neighborhood endeavors require a smaller commitment, they can serve as models for others to adopt. Often these efforts are started by individuals who say, first to themselves and then to whoever will listen, "Enough—this has to change." Cynthia James, a volunteer minister in East Oakland who was fed up with drug-spawned shootings, moved her congregation into the street to hold prayer meetings and shine flashlights on drug deals. She and her husband even borrowed money to buy an apartment house known for its crack activity. Once the tenants were evicted, the church and neighbors rehabilitated the building and started a youth program in one of the apartments. The national Volunteers of America chose Cynthia's neighborhood as a pilot project for its anti-drug campaign.

These neighborhood activists were not content to wait for government to give them what they wanted and did not spend time blaming elected officials—or anyone else—for unsatisfactory conditions. Although they were not trained organizers, they simply did what needed to be done, and gained the benefits of group support in the process.

When joint efforts result in community solidarity, you can reap rewards that go far beyond monetary gains and safer, more pleasant surroundings. Needs for child care, street greenery, or simply mutual support often provide the impetus for projects that bring neighbors together on a deeply personal level.

Jeannie Hall describes how her neighborhood, the Brainerd area of Chattanooga, Tennessee, initially coalesced around a zoning battle and went on to become a model for caring and connectedness: "We had a lot of meetings over a long period of time, and eventually we started to talk about not only the zoning, but 'Wouldn't it be nice if we could get together for Christmas and have caroling and a bonfire and hot chocolate, and light candles?' The dreams started pouring out." Many of these dreams, she notes, had been "lying around dormant in the minds of individuals because it takes so much time to organize." But when a group starts exchanging ideas, suddenly people realize that, together, they have the resources and the energy to get things done.

The words community *and* commons *are from the same root. Traditionally, the commons in England were used to graze cows—common land, respected and maintained by all for the good of all. What happened to our concept of common spaces? They are all around us still—the streets, parks, air, beaches, ocean, rivers, streams, and forests—but for some reason we don't feel personally responsible for them.*

TREEPEOPLE

Today, her neighborhood association holds an annual Christmas celebration and a grand Fourth of July picnic that brings together young and old, singles and families for midsummer fun. Block captains have been appointed to monitor specific areas of the neighborhood and alert others to new residents, new babies, people who are ill, and older citizens who might need some kind of assistance. When one seventy-eight-year-old woman failed to attend the Fourth of July party, a neighbor brought her a plate of food. "I went to check on her later that evening and she said she had had several calls," says Jeannie. "She doesn't drive, and she could be really isolated, so people watch out for her."

The Neighborhood Commons

One visible sign that Jeannie's neighborhood had become a community was the city-owned circular park the neighbors turned into a pleasant gathering place. After obtaining an Adopt-a-Spot grant from the local Chamber of Commerce, they worked together installing picnic tables and benches and landscaping the area. Not only do they hold their annual holiday celebrations here, but they also meet and visit casually in this attractive, shady spot throughout the year.

The commons, once a given in every neighborhood, village, and town, is experiencing a revival as residents seek a sense of community. The ninety households along Enright Avenue near downtown Cincinnati created a commons in their formerly blue-collar, transitional neighborhood by turning backyards into organic gardens and holding an annual Harvest

Festival. They also raised $27,000 to purchase and preserve a wooded lot behind them that had been slated for development.

In Shutesbury, Massachusetts, several of the neighbors along one road purchased a house in common through a community land trust and turned it into a cooperative office center. Residents of what they call Hearthstone Village can use the computer, printer, copier, and fax machine there.

I challenge a new generation of young Americans to a season of service, reconnecting our torn communities.

BILL CLINTON

Members of Hearthstone Village, Enright Avenue, and Jeannie Hall's neighborhood also develop a sense of collective identity through a metaphorical commons. In their neighborhood newsletters, locals tell stories, share practical information, and express opinions, much as they would in front of the general store in days of yore.

Community gardens and tree-planting projects can serve as catalysts for community. Two nonprofit organizations, TreePeople in Los Angeles and Friends of the Urban Forest in San Francisco, organize sidewalk tree plantings in various city neighborhoods. As groups of citizens dig holes together, plant the saplings, learn how to care for them, and join in potlucks afterward, they get to know one another better. Besides beautifying their blocks and improving the air they all breathe, they develop feelings of kinship with each other, their neighborhoods, and the nature that surrounds them all. This sense of connection often forms the basis for future joint activities.

REVIVING CITYWIDE COMMUNITY: THE CHATTANOOGA STORY

Citizens of Chattanooga revitalized an entire city without waiting for government intervention. They did it by initiating highly participatory processes that roused the population from polarization and apathy, created a new sense of identity and pride, and stimulated community building in several different ways.

In the early 1980s, Chattanooga was a city in decline. Devastated by economic recession, traditional manufacturing industries were laying off employees and even closing down. The city's infrastructure—schools, transportation, housing—was rapidly deteriorating. The disaffected working class blamed the small, elite class who lived on "the mountains" (the hills surrounding the city on two sides) and, so the "non-mountain" folks thought, made all the decisions. In fact, no one was really taking responsibility and assuming the kind of leadership the city needed.

Two people found the situation intolerable, though they came from different backgrounds and neighborhoods: Marty Landis and Gerald Mason. Today, both Marty and Gerald are enthusiastic, committed citizens whose pride in their city is widely shared.

Our whole society has told people over and over that "we're going to give you this and give you that, do this for you and do that for you"—the whole welfare system is set up to teach people that. You tell them that often enough and it gets hard for them to buy out of it.

MARTY LANDIS

Marty Landis and the Visioning Process: Experiencing Citizen Empowerment

Although Marty had been born and raised on Lookout Mountain, one of the upper-income neighborhoods in Chattanooga, and worked at a social service agency, she felt powerless. "I used to get up on my soapbox and say that housing, transportation, day care, and education are the real keys to the poverty trap," she says. "But there wasn't any way to get anything done about it because the systems were so entrenched. I was frustrated, depressed, and angry at the system. I knew that as soon as my two kids were grown, I would leave Chattanooga. I'd go anywhere. I just didn't want to stay here. Then along came Vision 2000."

Vision 2000 was the first initiative of a project called Chattanooga Venture, which was launched in 1984 to get as many people as possible—newcomers, old guard, rich, poor, black, and white—involved in creating the city's future. The founders of Chattanooga Venture had done their homework: when they studied other cities that had experienced a turnaround, they discovered that every one had created a new coalition involving diverse segments of the population. The successful cities had invited more people to the table, rather than leaving the visioning process to a few movers and shakers making decisions behind closed doors. The Venture founders were determined to bring in new ideas and to make Chattanooga a model of citizen involvement. In Vision 2000, more than seventeen hundred people, including Marty Landis, participated in a total of thirty-nine meetings, over the course of four months, to develop specific goals for the following decade.

As soon as she entered the conference room for her first meeting, Marty recognized some of the city's "power people." "They were saying, 'We care about what you say and we want you to tell us what your vision is for the year 2000.' I stood up and said, 'I'm sick of sitting in meetings where people listen and don't do anything. If you don't do something, I'm going to be mad as hell.'" Marty was shortly to learn that the people who were supposed to do something included herself.

The Vision 2000 process was similar to that used in a number of business "visioning" meetings to elicit ideas and agreements. Each of the participants joined a smaller group, according to which one of six topics they wished to discuss: people, places, play, work, government, or future alternatives. Once in a group, each person in turn stated what he or she thought was a key issue or idea. A facilitator wrote each idea on the wall. The group then discussed and prioritized the ideas. "Not only did they get up there on that wall," exults Marty, "they got printed in a book!" Finally, she knew she had been heard.

Thou shalt love thy neighbor as thyself.

MATTHEW 22:39

But giving everyone a chance to speak his or her mind was not the end of the process. Vision 2000 also generated a Commitment Portfolio of thirty-four goals, which became Chattanooga Venture's—and soon the city's—agenda. It also generated excitement and community spirit, which had long been dormant. Eager volunteers formed task forces to carry out the goals, many of which were achieved within the first few years.

One was the formation of Neighborhood Network, which spurs the development of neighborhood associations, helps them share information and resources, and facilitates their working together on issues that cross neighborhood borders. Marty Landis, who had left her social work job to recover from burnout, found new fire as Neighborhood Network's coordinator. She invites representatives from the associations—who come from both rich and poor areas of the city—to come together and experience the same processes she found so valuable in Vision 2000. "My goal," she says, "is to rekindle the spirit of Vision 2000 through working with the neighborhoods."

Marty no longer has that powerless, others-in-control feeling. She feels connected to and supported by those in the former "power structure" because she has discovered that she and they are committed to the same goals. The new members of her professional community—whom she had previously considered unapproachable—include the founding chairman of Chattanooga Venture and executives of the Lyndhurst Foundation, which provides a great deal of funding for Venture. All treat each other as valuable sources of skills and knowledge, have learned to trust each other, and know they are part of the same system. "Now, when I need some help on an issue, I know who to call for the first meeting," says Marty.

Chattanooga Venture continues to pursue community goals through public-private partnerships and citizen involvement. Accomplishments include a riverside park that is the first phase of a master plan for developing twenty miles of riverfront land, the Tennessee Aquarium as the anchor for the riverfront parks, a performance hall that serves as a memorial to Chattanooga native Bessie Smith, a human relations commission, and the city's commitment to upgrade all substandard housing within a decade. With twenty other organizations in the area, Venture sponsored a conference on the environment to highlight what midsized cities can do to be both economically and environmentally prosperous.

A second communitywide goal-setting process—ReVision 2000—attracted twice as many participants as its predecessor. Public meetings in nine different locations reached people where they live.

Anyone who is "helpful and hopeful" can join Chattanooga Venture. As its first chairman, Mai Bell Hurley, says, "The fabric of civic commitment is a fragile piece of work which demands an open-minded tolerance, a sense of hope, and a desire to help. It asks—it calls out—for trust and confidence."

We have largely lost the sense that our capacity to live well in a place might depend upon our ability to relate to neighbors on the basis of shared habits of behavior.

DANIEL KEMMIS

Gerald Mason and Family Reunion: Bringing Blacks and Whites Together

Unlike Marty Landis, Gerald Mason was a relative newcomer to Chattanooga and a "non-mountain" resident. But like her, he felt angry and frustrated by the apathy and polarization he saw when he arrived from Knoxville in the early 1980s. Although, as an African-American, he was all too aware of the racially based tensions and divisions across the city, he also recognized that "just as many whites were negative about Chattanooga as blacks. They thought, 'We're not going anywhere, there aren't good jobs here, there aren't good schools.' The only positive thing everyone agreed on was the beauty of the geographic setting."

For Gerald, the experience that triggered enthusiasm about the city was his participation in Leadership Chattanooga, a course sponsored by the Chamber of Commerce. He had never known anything like it before. Suddenly he found himself in a series of intense, all-day discussions with about twenty-five other citizens—liberals and conservatives, whites and minorities, "mountains" and "non-mountains"—arguing about social, educational, political, and health care issues. "In our class," he recalls, "we were all very assertive. We polarized along racial lines the first month." After bringing in a consultant from Washington, D.C., however, the group was able to coalesce into a real team.

"We had all kinds of stereotypes about each other," says Gerald. But because they were able to express their feelings openly and own up to their mistakes and misperceptions, "we just clicked about the second month in our twelve-month period. We're still networking today." They also network with Chattanooga Venture members; Gerald became a member of Venture's board of directors.

Deciding to take personal responsibility for putting some of their ideas into action, a group from the Leadership Chattanooga class founded Partners for Academic Excellence (PACE), which gets parents involved in improving the educational system. Gerald became PACE's first executive director, then left to become a partner with his wife Diane in running a day care center she had started.

Once his community spirit had been ignited, however, Gerald could not stop thinking about new ways to bring people together, especially people from different races. One evening, as he was watching TV news on Martin Luther King's birthday, he suddenly sat upright. The program was about a large biracial group in Montgomery having dinner together. "That's it!" he thought. "What's keeping blacks and whites from coming together as a community is our inability to be together socially. You can work with other kinds of people, go to school with them, but until you break down the social barrier, you aren't going to be comfortable." A brainstorming session with an office colleague yielded the Chattanooga Family Reunion.

By this time, Gerald had a lot of contacts in the city, so he sent a letter to "two or three hundred" black and white citizens, inviting them each to bring a member of the opposite race to Sunday brunch at a restaurant. There would be no agenda; the purpose was purely social and everyone would pay for his or her own meal. More than a hundred people showed up for that initial meeting, and after that the brunch became a monthly event. The Family Reunion always met from 12:30 to 3 p.m. after church, since "Sunday is the most segregated time in this community," Gerald says.

At first the attendees were wary, tending to stick to their own groups, but gradually they began interacting with those of the opposite race whom they did not already know. Gerald arranged for different restaurants to "host" the brunches each month, and for invitations to be sent out. Locations varied from the toniest country club in "the mountains" to an eatery in the heart of the ghetto. Judges mingled with tenants of housing developments, and the mayor and city commissioners showed up, too. Gerald notes, "If you weren't involved, you'd be considered lacking in social graces."

Much business networking resulted, and the brunch bunch became involved in each other's projects. A core group of more than fifty became regulars, many of them deepening their friendships by visiting each other's houses.

"Before the Family Reunion, I had not been in any white homes for dinner," Gerald says. "Now we're constantly getting invitations—and we've had more whites in our home." A particularly close friendship has developed between the Masons and the Radpours, a white family. "We've gone on family picnics together. When I was in the hospital the whole [Radpour] family came out to see me. We're just part of each other's extended family now, and feel very comfortable." The Mason and Radpour children occasionally visit each other at college.

Because Gerald could not continue shouldering the monthly responsibility of organizing the brunches—and no one else volunteered to do it—the Family Reunion convenes only about twice a year now. But its substance continues in other forms. In addition to the interracial friendships that grow and extend into wider communities, there have been special events such as human relations forums and a citywide evening of twenty-five dinner parties, some hosted by blacks and some by whites, each inviting people of the opposite race.

Chattanooga now has, Gerald believes, both the chemistry and the hope needed to transform itself, and he is enthusiastic about the opportunity to make personal contributions. "I'd never seen a city where an outsider can come in and immediately become a player," he declares. "Chattanooga allows people to do that."

Three Keys to Creating Civic Community

The stories of Marty Landis, Gerald Mason, and others in this chapter illustrate how community can be created in neighborhoods and cities where it does not happen naturally. They reveal key principles that apply more than ever today. Neighborhoods no longer are, and may never have been, the cozy, one-dimensional, and monochromatic enclaves of Ozzie and Harriet's day. And old-style, paternalistic urban governance no longer works.

First, while sameness was the glue that held traditional communities together, today's neighborhoods and cities must not only tolerate but embrace diversity. Fundamental to the success of Chattanooga Venture and Leadership Chattanooga was the realization that broad-based citizen participation is essential to spark new ideas and sustain community spirit. Neighborhood cohesiveness can be counterproductive if it means that neighborhoods look out only for their own narrow needs and ignore or undermine those of other neighborhoods and the city as a whole. Chattanooga's Neighborhood Network and Family Reunion demonstrate that different types of communities can gain strength from each other. When one low-income neighborhood, Alton Park, faced a toxic waste problem that included a polluted creek, others in the Network joined in a well-publicized campaign to convince the city to do something about it. The neighborhood associations helped city government and their own members grasp that each is part of a dynamic larger system. Working together to improve the health of one part has contributed significantly to the health of nearby neighborhoods and the city as a whole.

Second, the process by which diverse strands are transformed into a closely woven tapestry is often as important as the resulting programs and projects. The communication and decision-making processes used by Chattanooga's Vision 2000 and Leadership Chattanooga provided safe places in which people could express their ideas, argue, and fight for their issues. Marty, Gerald, and others began to see each other as individuals rather than stereotypes and to develop the trust in each other that forms the basis of true community.

Finally, whether you live in the South Bronx or a city in Tennessee, community happens only when power is shared and individuals take responsibility. Presenting a plan for approval is vastly different from gathering people together and allowing ideas to emerge. When people realize that their ideas count and that they can personally make something happen, something does happen. When they wait to be given something, they might wait forever.

Citizen work initiatives ought to be the starting point of most, if not all, forms of publicly supported activities. Policy formation should begin with the question: "How much work can organized citizens perform for themselves?"

RAY SHONHOLTZ

DESIGNING CITIES AND NEIGHBORHOODS TO ENCOURAGE COMMUNITY

The ease with which you can turn urban and suburban residential areas into communities depends partly on the way these areas are designed. And for the last few decades, a large portion of them have been designed as though their residents—their taxpayers, their youth, their community pillars—were automobiles rather than people.

Developers and governments design cities and suburbs today so that automobiles can get around just fine; they can go wherever they want to go, really fast, and be with all kinds of other automobiles at any time of the day or night. People, on the other hand, are hemmed in by freeways—which are like sidewalks for autos—while enjoying no sidewalks themselves. If you live in a new development, you cannot go to the main library or City Hall or the theater without crossing dangerously busy streets or getting into a car and navigating freeway exits—even if you are only a few minutes, as the crow flies, from your destination. Trapped in your car, you have little interaction with others.

To accommodate driving and parking, suburban neighborhoods feature multi-laned streets and low-density housing, which discourage community as well as gobbling up unnecessary space and other resources.

Older people, children, and others who cannot drive become isolated and dependent.

Meanwhile, expanding freeway systems funnel more and more automobiles into the centers of clogged cities, resulting in desperate proposals to get people out of their cars and into public transportation. Traffic-weary citizens would be delighted to comply—if only they could get where they needed to go in a reasonable time. But the proposals usually involve penalizing drivers by higher tolls and parking fees, rather than providing sound alternatives.

"Leaving home" for the professional middle class is not something one does once and for all—it is an ever-present possibility. Thus the pressure to keep moving upward in a career often forces the middle-class individual, however reluctantly, to break the bonds of commitment forged with a community.

ROBERT N. BELLAH AND COAUTHORS

Finally, a few renegade architects are beginning to challenge these scenarios by designing entire new towns in ways that acknowledge human needs for community. And developers, tired of having their parameters dictated by traffic engineers, are starting to turn these visions into reality. The best-known projects are Laguna West, an 800-acre "antidote to urban sprawl" created near Sacramento by San Francisco architect Peter Calthorpe and estate developer Phil Angelides, and Seaside, Florida, a small resort town designed by neotraditionalists Andres Duany and Elizabeth Plater-Zyberk. Calthorpe, Duany, and other forward-thinking planners are savvy enough to realize that, today, they cannot make the car disappear (in fact, the two-car family is a proliferating species), nor can they do away with such automobile-spawned conveniences as the shopping mall. Viewing urban and suburban development from a whole-systems perspective, they call for mixed-use development that is convenient for pedestrians, mass transit, and autos and that takes environmental, housing, and employment concerns into account.

Imagine living in a town where you can do most of your errands on foot in five minutes, not counting the time you stop and talk to friends and shopkeepers. The tree-lined street you live on is narrow enough, and the buildings close enough to the street, that you can call across to your neighbor's porch or balcony. Dwellings, set companionably close together, complement one another in style but differ in size, cost, and density. They include apartments, townhouses, single-family homes, and dwellings with "in-law" units occupied by elderly parents or college-age kids. You can walk to nearby small office buildings as well as parks, playgrounds, health and entertainment complexes, and commercial and government centers. If you work at home, as people are increasingly doing these days, you need not fear isolation; people congregate daily at the main library and post office, which are also within walking distance, to read the bulletin boards and exchange information.

When you need to travel outside the main part of town, you take the trolley, or you go around to the back of your house to get the car. On the street in front, which looks quite friendly without rows of blank-faced garage doors, youngsters can play safely under the protective gaze of many "eyes on the street." Wide sidewalks and plentiful trees—which you and your neighbors planted—help keep the air fresh. Air pollution poses little problem anyway because residents rarely need to drive their cars within the town.

Elements of this scenario are already in place, though not all in the same place. Even Laguna West and Seaside have been criticized for placing too much emphasis on private lots and failing to achieve the mix of incomes they envisioned. Part of the problem is the need to revise old zoning restrictions and overcome people's natural resistance to change. To speed this process, designer/builders are giving public presentations, incorporating local architects with a sense of the area's history and personality into design teams, and inviting citizens and officials to comment on the developing project at each step of the way. Citizens who yearn for community-friendly neighborhoods help by making their voices heard in planning meetings and pressing for necessary zoning changes.

Besides implementing community-friendly design in the construction of new cities and suburbs, citizens can also introduce it into established towns. Garrett Park, Maryland, a suburb of Washington, D.C., proves the point. In 1877, Garrett Park was constructed around a building that housed a general store and a post office. When the building came up for sale in the 1970s, the town bought it and proceeded to turn it into a commercial center—not a typical shopping mall but what one real estate broker called the "soul of the community." The tenants—carefully selected by town officials, who also set management practices—include the Town Store and Café with a "yes shelf" of toys that kids can play with; a fish market whose proprietor also sells fresh fruit, breads, beer, and wine; and a beauty salon that also sells plants. Rather than resisting the small-scale commercial development in their neighborhoods, residents of Garrett Park have welcomed the Town Center because they can control the kind of business that operates there.

One key to making this town commons work as a community meeting place is a post office, still located in the original building, to which residents must come to pick up their mail. The town has fought continuously to keep the postal service from delivering mail door to door. As a former mayor put it, "A post office that requires people to come together is more important than retail businesses." Garrett Park, luckily, has both.

Incorporating small town centers in new neighborhoods is no longer as difficult as it was. Incorporating them in existing single-family neighborhoods is still very difficult. It is also important, because only 1–2% of the nation's housing is built new each year.

PATRICK HARE

Sustainable planning refers both to the process of planning and its focus. Good planning examines the overall, cumulative effects of proposed changes in land use, and judges them in the context of the region's natural features such as climate, watercourses, seismic history and animal and plant life cycles. In addition, it is developed at the grassroots level with active citizen participation in setting the agenda and proposing policies.

PETER BERG

A development on another front that promises to create more community-friendly cities is the budding "ecocity" movement. Its advocates—environmentalists, community organizers, architects, and city planners from all over the world—are focusing on how to make cities healthier and more people-oriented. In 1990, more than seven hundred people convened for the First International Ecocity Conference in Berkeley, California. The local ecocity group in Adelaide, Australia, hosted a second such conference in 1992.

Every institution in the city should have concern for the whole city, and not just concern for its segment of the city or, more commonly, concern solely for itself. Often the most high-minded organizations have little regard for the community around them. I described the situation facetiously at a national meeting of voluntary organizations recently by saying: "A voluntary group may be profoundly and high-mindedly committed to care of the terminally ill and never notice that the community of which it is a part is itself terminally ill."

John W. Gardner

Steps You Can Take

You can begin to forge community bonds in your neighborhood by simply striking up a conversation with your neighbor, or by joining forces with others to start a community newsletter. The possibilities can take a few minutes now and then or involve more time but reap greater rewards. Here are just a few.

Neighborhood Initiatives

- Take time to learn the names of your local merchants and their employees, not to mention the folks who live next door to you. Then decide whom you might like to know better and begin sharing ideas and feelings with them.
- Children and pets are good icebreakers. Approach another parent, or send out postcards, suggesting a babysitting co-op. One mother created a once-a-week neighborhood commons by talking the owners of a local gym facility into opening its doors to parents and children every Thursday afternoon when it was usually closed. The parents chatted and sipped tea while the children played. If you are a dog owner, arrange with others to convene in a park, with pets, at a specific time each week.
- If your neighborhood does not publish a newsletter or newspaper, start one. You can begin with a simple typed sheet. Not only do you get to know your neighbors better by interviewing them for articles and by visiting merchants to solicit ads, but you also help them become better acquainted with one another through the publication. A neighborhood newsletter can reinforce or create a neighborhood's sense of identity.

- Find a place to hold neighborhood meetings and events. Places of worship usually prove good bets because they tend to have large spaces that are not used every day of the week and because their congregations are built-in communities that can reach out to others. San Francisco's Noe Valley Ministry, for example, is much more than a place for Presbyterians to gather on Sundays. The building also houses the offices of the neighborhood newspaper and a co-op nursery and draws a diverse group of residents to such events as jazz concerts, monster movies for children, art exhibits, Scottish dancing classes, and theater games.
- Organize small events that will bring different age groups together—such as storytelling by elders in the neighborhood library.
- Contact the local police department and ask for help in sponsoring a block meeting to discuss safety. Plan for a social time, with refreshments, afterwards.
- Start a neighborhood salon (see Chapter Three).
- Invite your next-door neighbors for dinner and suggest a meal rotation, with one household at a time cooking for the whole group one day each month.
- Place an ad suggesting the formation of a theater group.
- The next time you get together with neighbors who are interested in strengthening community bonds, bring along a book or article as a discussion starter. *Community Dreams* by William R. Berkowitz (see Resources) is one of our favorites. It is chock-full of ideas on turning a neighborhood into a community.

I first knew my neighborhood was special when I rented my house. The historical society came by with the house's genealogy, the list of people who had lived there before me, done up like a family tree. As I became rooted in the past, I felt more responsible for the present.

BILL BERKOWITZ

City Initiatives

- Check the above list to see what might apply on a citywide basis.
- At a meeting of your neighborhood association, suggest collaborating with another association in the city on an issue the two have in common.
- Invite local architects and planners with vision to speak to your community group.
- Request that some city parkland be made available for citizen planting of trees and community gardens.
- If you work for a large corporation, find out how it can contribute to the neighborhood around it. Encourage the company to seek local input before taking action.

- At civic meetings, introduce processes that encourage new people to become involved, help participants feel safe and listened to, and encourage sharing of decision-making and responsibility.

"Participation in shaping the larger world beyond family and friends is a deep human need, as real as the need for a satisfying private life," says Frances Moore Lappé, coauthor of a forthcoming book on "living democracy" and co-founder of the Center for Living Democracy. In fact, private life and the "larger world" are parts of the same whole. Individuals, neighborhoods, cities, and the natural environment are linked so closely that personal issues cannot be isolated from civic issues. The power of ideas and shared vision can transform a neighborhood and the larger systems of which it is a part, and in the process transform the individuals who participate.

This deep-seated attachment to the virtue of neighborliness is an important but largely ignored civic asset. It is in being good neighbors that people very often engage in those simple, homely practices which are the last, best hope for a revival of genuine public life. In valuing neighborliness, people value that upon which citizenship most essentially depends. It is our good fortune that this value persists.

DANIEL KEMMIS

RESOURCES

Recommended books and periodicals

Community Dreams by William R. Berkowitz (Impact Publishers, P.O. Box 1094, San Luis Obispo, California 93406; 1984)

A Green City Program by Peter Berg (Planet Drum Foundation, P.O. Box 31251, San Francisco, California 94131)

Sustainable Cities: Concepts and Strategies for Ecocity Development edited by Bob Walter, Lois Arkin, and Richard Crenshaw (Eco-Home Media, Los Angeles, 1992)

A Colorful Quilt: The Community Leadership Story edited by Carl Moore (National Association of Community Leadership Organizations, 525 South Meridian Street, #102, Indianapolis, Indiana, 46225; 1988). Case studies of leadership programs.

The Simple Act of Planting a Tree: Healing Your Neighborhood, Your City, and Your World by TreePeople with Andy and Katie Lipkis (Jeremy P. Tarcher, 1990)

Reinventing Government by David Osborne and Ted Gaebler (Addison-Wesley, 1992)

Neighborhood Caretakers: Stories, Strategies and Tools for Healing Urban Community by Betty and Burt Dyson (Knowledge Systems, 1989)

Community and the Politics of Place by Daniel Kemmis (University of Oklahoma Press, 1990)

The Facilitator's Manual by Carl M. Moore with Eleanor Cooper and Karen McMahon, a step-by-step manual for developing community visions—or setting goals for an organization—and turning them into reality. Order for $10 from Chattanooga Venture, 506 Broad Street, Chattanooga, Tennessee, 37402; (615) 267-8687.

CommonWealth: A Return to Citizen Politics by Harry C. Boyte (Free Press, 1989)

Sustainable Communities: A New Design Synthesis for Cities, Suburbs, and Towns by Sim Van Der Ryn (Sierra Club, 1986)

How to Save Your Neighborhood, City, or Town: The Sierra Club Guide to Community Organizing by Maritza Pick (Sierra Club, 1993).

What Can We Do? Guidebook for the Citizen Empowerment Seminar by Tova Green, Francis Macy, and Bill Moyer (New Society, forthcoming)

In Context #14, Autumn 1986: Theme—"Sustainable Habitat: Buildings, Resources and Community." #29, Summer 1991: Theme—"Living Together: Sustainable Community Development." #33, Fall 1992: Theme—"We Can Do It!: Tools for Community Transformation." Order from *In Context,* P.O. Box 11470, Bainbridge Island, Washington, 98110; (206) 842-0216.

"Urban Barnraising: Building Community Through Environmental Restoration" by Karl Linn, *Earth Island Journal,* Spring 1990

Small Town (bimonthly newsletter, $30/year) Box 517, Ellensburg, Washington, 98926

The Urban Ecologist (quarterly newsletter) and reports on ecocity conferences, available from Urban Ecology, Inc., P.O. Box 10133, Berkeley, California, 94709; (510) 549-1724.

The Neighborhood Works (bimonthly magazine), 2125 W. North Ave., Chicago, Illinois, 60647; (312) 278-4800

The Responsive Community (quarterly journal), 714 Gelman Library, The George Washington University, Washington, D.C., 20052; (800) 245-7460. The communitarian movement seeks to balance individual rights with obligations to community.

Organizations

Center for Organizational and Community Development, 377 Hills South, University of Massachusetts, Amherst, Massachusetts, 01003; (413) 545-2038 or -2231. Provides training, consulting, and educational manuals to empower citizens, leaders, and communities in their work for social change.

Center for Living Democracy (CLD), Rural Route 1, Black Fox Road, Brattleboro, Vermont, 05301; (802) 254-1234. Also, Living Democracy Learning Center (LDLC), 2400 Olympic Boulevard, Suite 3300, Walnut Creek, California, 94595; (510) 945-1882. CLD provides workshops and lectures on "living democracy" and trains citizens in dialogue, active listening, creative conflict, negotiation, political imagination, and public judgment. To schedule these interactive presentations and workshops, or to receive a catalog of learning tools, contact Molly Hamaker, director of LDLC in Walnut Creek. Co-founders of CLD and LDLC Frances Moore Lappé and Paul Martin Du Bois have coauthored an excellent book reframing democracy not as something people have but something people do. *The Quickening of America: Rebuilding Our Nation, Remaking Our Lives* will be published by Jossey-Bass in April, 1994.

Community Service, Inc., P.O. Box 243, Yellow Springs, Ohio, 45387; (513) 767-2161. Has facilitated and followed the movement toward community in neighborhoods, towns, and intentional communities since 1942. Publishes *Community Service* newsletter.

Chattanooga Venture, 506 Broad Street, Chattanooga, Tennessee, 37402; (615) 267-8687. Provides resources and services for community building.

Association of Community Organizations for Reform Now (ACORN). National Office; 730 Eighth Street, SE, Washington, D.C., 20003; (202) 547-9292. Organizing and Support Center, 1024 Elysian Fields Ave., New Orleans, Louisiana, 70117; (504) 943-0044. Newsletter: *US of ACORN.*

National Center for Neighborhood Enterprise (NCNE), 1367 Connecticut Avenue, NW, Washington, D.C., 20036; (202) 331-1103. Promotes social and economic problem-solving by and for low-income Americans. Technical assistance and publications focus on new strategies and self-help approaches to seemingly intractable problems.

Neighborhood Reinvestment Corporation, 1325 G St., NW, Ste. 800, Washington, D.C., 20005; (202) 376-2642. Provides training to individuals in organizations committed to improving the affordability, economic vitality, and quality of community life.

Safe Streets Now! a division of the Drug Abatement Institute, 1221 Broadway, Plaza Level, Suite 13, Oakland, California, 94612; (510) 846-4622. Teaches neighbors how to organize at a grassroots level and provides them with empowerment tools to help them take back their streets from drug dealers by using small claims court. Publishes *Neighborhood News.*

Industrial Areas Foundation (IAF), 36 New Hyde Park, Franklin Square, New York, 11011; (516) 354-1076. Community organizing.

National People's Action, National Training and Information Center, 810 North Milwaukee Avenue, Chicago, Illinois, 60622; (312) 243-3035. Offers a wide range of technical assistance for community groups. Newsletter: *Disclosure.*

Center for Community Change, 1000 Wisconsin Ave. NW, Washington, D.C., 20007; (202) 342-0519. Committed to building the power and capacity of community residents, working through grassroots organizations to improve conditions in poor and minority communities. Publishes *Community Change* newsletter.

Community Design Exchange, 923 23rd Ave. E., Seattle, Washington 98112; (206) 329-2919. Facilitates partnerships among people, their government, and community support organizations to achieve mutual visions for a shared future. CDE brings to its work twenty-five years of experience building community through design, organizational development, and communication technology.

National Civic League, 1445 Market Street, Ste. 300, Denver, Colorado, 80202-1728; (303) 571-4343. Brings together business, nonprofit, and government sectors—and diverse interests and perspectives—to address community problems. Publishes *The Civic Review.*

Communitas, Inc., P.O. Box 374, Manchester, Connecticut, 06045; (203) 645-6976. This network facilitates the inclusion of all people, including those with disabilities, into community life. Publishes the *Whole Community Catalog,* the six-part *Community Inclusion Series,* and a newsletter, the *Communitas Communicator.*

Videos

Urban Barnraising Part I: Restoring Community Through Building Neighborhood Commons and *Urban Barnraising Part II: Education for Service and Transformation,* videos available from Urban Habitat Program, Earth Island Institute, 300 Broadway, Suite 28, San Francisco, California, 94133-3312; (415) 788-3666.

SEVEN

The Workplace as Community

Those few American corporations that manage to convey a genuine sense of community and belonging to their employees are thriving as a consequence.

THOMAS J. PETERS

AT THE QUAKER OATS pet food plant in Topeka, one production worker's performance deteriorated until he finally made a serious mistake that would have caused some companies to fire him. Instead, three fellow members of his work team began counseling and working with him on a weekly basis until his performance was up to par.

The founder of Harbor Sweets, a Massachusetts candy company, insists that his diverse work force operates on total trust, with no time clocks, no efficiency measures, and no secrets. Productivity is high because, he says, "love is good business."

"I know this is going to sound sort of hokey, but I work here because of the family feeling," says a manager at Levi Strauss & Company in San Francisco. After twenty-two years with the company, he cannot imagine leaving.

Community, family feeling, and love in the workplace? Isn't this the turf where workers ally themselves against bosses, managers build shark-infested moats around their fiefdoms to keep out other managers, and the favorite game around the water cooler is one-upmanship? While offices and factories may continue to display their unique brands of internal politics, a new wave has been sweeping through America's businesses that promises to make a sense of community—"We're all in this together, so let's support one another"—much more commonplace.

After decades of viewing business organizations as profit-driven machines and workers as expendable parts, a growing number of corporate leaders are beginning to perceive these organizations as living systems driven by people, their needs and their vision. They have come to this "new paradigm," as *Fortune* and others christened it, not out of altruism or a sudden spiritual conversion but from the strong, even desperate, desire to maintain a competitive edge in a rapidly changing global economy. They are discovering that paying attention to people, including them at all levels in the visioning and decision-making process, and providing a supportive work environment pays high dividends, monetary as well as psychological.

> *If we do not design our organization consciously to facilitate the attitudes and behaviors we want, some of our organizational arrangements will almost certainly channel energy and attention in ways which are contrary to our purposes.*
>
> ROGER HARRISON AND CELEST POWELL

Besides improving the bottom line, always a strong motivator for revising the corporate culture, community in the workplace has its own rewards. Both line employees and top managers are finding that they yearn for a sense of support and connectedness in the arena where they spend the bulk of their waking hours.

Even large organizations are starting to practice what many smaller businesses, nonprofits, and activist groups have been doing for years: treating workers as whole human beings with families, spiritual lives, and values that deserve attention along with their job descriptions, and viewing the organization itself as inseparable from the environment in which it operates. Peter Senge, author of the popular management tome *The Fifth Discipline: The Art and Practice of the Learning Organization,* warns that to survive, firms and their employees must learn to think systematically, seeing patterns, interrelationships, and interdependencies rather than chains of cause and effect. They must not, he declares, lose their sense of connection to the larger whole.

Systems thinking, with its awareness of global connectedness, creates a more inviting climate for conscious community than we have seen in previous decades. In some firms, in fact, community is a declared goal. James Autry, former president of Meredith Corporation's magazine group, goes so far as to suggest an executive bumper sticker: "If you're not creating community, you're not managing." Autry wrote a book with a title you would not have seen on the shelves a decade ago: *Love and Profit: The Art of Caring Leadership.* One chapter asserts, "The job is the new neighborhood."

This growing awareness in the business world does not automatically ensure the creation of conscious—or even functional—community. Awareness is one thing, actions another. But across the nation, innovative community-building ideas are taking hold—some spontaneously and joyfully, others with difficulty and a little pain. Implementing these ideas requires commitment of time and energy, as well as learning new skills

What Can Grassroots Activists Teach Businesses?

The Great Peace March for Global Nuclear Disarmament in 1986, in which more than 600 people walked from Los Angeles to Washington, D.C., led San Francisco psychologist/consultants Sam Kaner and Eileen Palmer to wonder whether organizations might be able to learn something from grassroots peace activists. Although these activists possess few economic resources, endure physical hardships and long hours, and receive no financial reward, they exert extraordinary efforts to achieve their goal and, in the process, develop strong, resilient communities. What accounts for this unusual bonding and commitment?

Kaner and Palmer concluded that in such "communities with a mission," the members' needs, values, and lifestyles are fully integrated with the organization's purposes and structures. Each task is dedicated to the vision, so that when people are performing the mission tasks they know they are expressing the vision. The organization sustains the whole person and allows members to stretch themselves. People's jobs are not separate from their personal lives, and boundaries with the outer world are unguarded yet handled with care and concern. Kaner and Palmer are now helping business organizations incorporate this activist model.

If Utopia is to emerge, it will do so primarily from the world of business.

M. Scott Peck

and throwing off old assumptions. If you are the head of an organization or department, you may have many opportunities to generate a climate of community. Even if you are not the boss, you can take steps to create a supportive work climate and encourage attention to group processes. And if you are choosing a new place of work, you can learn to spot indicators of functional or conscious community that can affect your decision.

Eight Qualities of Workplace Community

Knowing what community in the workplace looks like can help you increase it. In talking with chief executive officers, managers, employees, and consultants representing organizations both large and small, we have identified eight qualities that enable workplace community to develop and thrive.

1. Alignment of Values

When you hear a lot of "we" in employees' conversations about the company, that is one clue that individuals identify themselves with the organization. They see themselves as parts of the whole, reflecting the whole by pursuing a common mission that aligns with their personal values.

We all want a company that our people are proud of and committed to, where all employees have an opportunity to contribute, learn, grow, and advance based on merit, not politics or background. We want our people to feel respected, treated fairly, listened to, and involved. Above all, we want satisfaction from accomplishments and friendships, balanced personal and professional lives, and to have fun in our endeavors.

FROM LEVI STRAUSS'S ASPIRATION STATEMENT

One tactic companies are using to bring about this alignment is to gather people from all levels to create a vision statement indicating what the organization aims to be—different from a mission statement that says what it intends to do—and to brainstorm ways to realize the vision. This vision statement serves as the foundation for conscious community. A successful visioning process is not a one-shot exercise; to keep up with changing individual and corporate priorities, it should be repeated at least once a year. And if the company is to maintain integrity, an essential ingredient in community, the vision needs to be incorporated into daily business.

After employee teams developed Levi Strauss's first Aspiration Statement back in 1987, CEO Robert Haas looked his senior managers in the eye and told them, "I want you to live this." Discussions of the aspirations have been incorporated into performance appraisals, in-house courses on such topics as business ethics and diversity, and monthly management-employee forums. Today, people actually go around talking about whether certain actions are "aspirational."

2. Employee-Based Structure

Rigid, pyramid-style hierarchy, besides inhibiting communication and decision making, discourages community. A pyramid supports primarily those at the top. Friendlier structures emphasize interdependent networks and flattened or eliminated pyramids, while allowing for decision-making authority to reside with those who are most capable and knowledgeable. William L. Gore & Associates, the family-held company that makes Goretex fabric, has done away with the idea of supervisors. Each of the 5,300 employees is an "associate" and any employee may take an idea or complaint to any other.

To serve customers better, many companies are reorganizing to emphasize processes, such as flow of materials and order fulfillment, rather than functional departments, such as manufacturing and shipping. Their structure begins to resemble a set of intersecting circles and dotted lines, representing a cooperative, dynamic body in which each person or team shares information and responsibilities with others. Employees as well as customers benefit from the richness of this exchange.

The ultimate employee-based structure is the employee-owned company, in which people are literally invested in the firm. More than 11,000 American firms have some sort of employee stock ownership plan (ESOP), and many also involve employees in running the organization. When combined with other types of participation, employee ownership plans can contribute to improved sales and employment. In Philadelphia, an O&O (employee Owned and Operated) Supermarket opened in an old A&P market that had been closed in 1982 because of declining sales. In the first year, the O&O doubled the A&P's sales volume.

At Rainbow Builders in Massachusetts, each of the dozen or so employees is an owner, sharing in the profits according to skill level, marketability of skills, and need. Every day on the job site, the workers take a few minutes to stand in a circle quietly, with eyes closed, and attune with each other and as a group. Every week, they meet to discuss interpersonal as well as business issues. "It was one of the best work experiences I ever had," says Bruce Davidson, a co-founder of Rainbow who has since left to manage a major construction project at Sirius community, where he lives.

"The first winter," he recalls, "there wasn't enough business, but people kept coming to the meetings every week anyway. We talked about how we might start another business together if the construction one didn't go." Rainbow has gained a reputation for honesty, quality, and being easy to work with. "When you're having a good time, and you equate the success of the business with personal success, you do things a little beyond what's expected," says Bruce.

An organization should, by definition, function organically, which means that its purposes should determine its structure, rather than the other way around, and that it should function as a community rather than a hierarchy, and offer autonomy to its members, along with tests, opportunities, and rewards, because ultimately an organization is merely the means, not the end.

WARREN BENNIS

3. Teamwork

In a community-supporting organization, people work in teams rather than alone whenever possible. The organization clarifies roles but does not attach them to specific people. Instead, it expects employees to learn one another's skills and provides continual opportunities for them to do so. Each team rotates leadership so that everyone has a chance to demonstrate the skills and knowledge they have acquired.

In self-managing teams at the Quaker Oats pet food plant, employees hire, evaluate, train, and counsel each other as peers. All team members share responsibility for production, quality, safety, maintenance, and sanitation, rotating from job to job according to a schedule they develop together. When one man fell off a catwalk and injured his shoulder, he traded jobs temporarily with a fellow team member whose work required lifting smaller loads. "We do everything we can to help our fellow workers," an employee comments.

Union and white-collar workers who produce Saturn cars share all major decisions, whether they involve personnel, suppliers, advertising, or quality. If you want to work at Saturn, you have to demonstrate communication skills and an ability to work well in teams.

Task forces at Levi Strauss used to be created by management but now operate by self-selection. "The company newsletter informs us when a task force is being set up and we're invited to join if we're interested," explains Mary Ann Michaels, director of fulfillment services.

In most vital organizations, there is a common bond of interdependence, mutual interest, interlocking contributions, and simple joy.

MAX DEPREE

4. Open Communication

In workplace community, communication flows randomly—upward, downward, sideways, from outside in and from inside out. If you feel an item warrants the president's attention, you can stroll over to his or her office and bring it up directly. The organization actively seeks feedback from the outside and encourages internal questioning.

People do not avoid sensitive communications, such as criticism. They handle them face to face rather than relying on memos, and the criticism always focuses on "How can we do this better next time?" Some organizations institutionalize this process. For example, IBM, Procter & Gamble, National Semiconductor, and other firms have a formal procedure for upward feedback, in which employees rate their managers on the latters' people-management skills and then join them in open discussions about how to work together better.

Such honest upward and downward communication generates a high level of trust because no one feels that management is lying to them. You do not have to be "political" or act as if you always know what you are doing. Leaders do not isolate themselves behind closed doors or guard information in order to play power games. Since there is little secrecy, it is not necessary to remember whom not to tell.

Recognizing that openness and involvement are linked, managers share information that used to be for their eyes only. For example, at Manco, Inc., a packaging manufacturer in Ohio, CEO Jack Kahl posts charts in the cafeteria that list daily sales, shipments, and billings, as well as information on marketing, general expenses, and monthly profit and loss. Many members of the Briarpatch, a mutual support organization of small businesses, follow a policy of "open books," allowing customers as well as employees to peruse the financials.

In workplace community, even gossip takes on a friendly, caring tone. People make an effort to get to know their fellow workers and are willing to let themselves be known. They listen to each other's concerns, hopes, and fears, and do not say only what they feel others want to hear. They are not afraid to express emotion. Jim Autry of Meredith told us that when he had to fire a longtime friend for sexual misconduct, both sat in Jim's office and cried. He believes that all emotions should be expressed in the workplace—except anger, because "you can't think or act properly when angry."

5. *Mutual Support*

Once they have developed such a level of trust, workers become not only willing but eager to help each other complete projects. When one person is having personal problems, the others, rather than pretending not to notice, rally around to give aid and support.

Support bubbles over into play and fun. When *Industry Week* asked various types of employees why they felt their jobs were no fun any longer, the most typical response—given by 49 percent—was, "We're not a team." Good-humored teasing reflects acceptance of others' foibles. At Lightworks Construction in Bethesda, Maryland, for example, employees annually present each other with "dubious achievement awards" illustrated by anecdotes.

6. *Respect for Individuality*

You cannot separate building community from building individuals. And the health of all contemporary communities—businesses, neighborhoods, families, and shared residences—depends on diversity. Healthy communities value ethnic, racial, and gender differences and actively seek the perspectives of all groups, not because they are required to but because everyone senses the opportunity for better decisions and richer community experience.

Forcing people into predesigned molds, or expecting them to conform to rigid "standards" such as dress codes, beardless faces, or party-line behaviors, discourages community. A letter to newspaper etiquette columnist Miss Manners complained about "enforced retreats" that require employees to "spend weekends at some resort, presumably [on] their own time," where they must listen to pep talks, play silly games, and "endure what is in effect a 49-hour staff meeting." The letter writer was not simply refusing to be a team player. She might have felt less hostile toward company retreats if they were voluntary, did not require her to give up part of her personal life, and offered her a chance to express herself in her own way.

Companies have evolved various ways of demonstrating their respect for diversity and individual expression. Some companies let workers design their own jobs. Others offer courses in diversity. Some allow all employees to decorate their work space any way they want—which helps co-workers get to know them better. Behind these initiatives lies the concept that employees are whole persons, not just jobholders or interchangeable cogs in the corporate wheel.

We must stop "going to work" or "staying home" but must think of our lives as a continuum of endeavor, a collection of works *making up a larger work that is our lives.*

JIM AUTRY

Companies that acknowledge employees as whole persons assume they have families and other relationships that are as important to them as their jobs. Company policies—child and elder care, flextime, job sharing, time off for personal matters, on-site fitness programs, reimbursement for self-development courses—reflect this perspective.

Child care centers on company premises represent more than a practical acknowledgment that working parents are more productive when they are not juggling schedules. Such centers also demonstrate caring and offer an opportunity for community building. A mother who has been taking her daughter to an on-site day care center at Patagonia, Inc., declares that working anywhere else would be difficult: "She's grown up with all the kids here."

7. *Permeable Boundaries*

Community-friendly organizations acknowledge interdependence and avoid an "us and them" mentality. Barriers between unions and management dissolve into partnerships. Decision makers value the organization's contribution to its employees, suppliers, customers, surrounding community, natural environment, and the world at large just as much as its contribution to its stockholders, even in times of economic instability. All are recognized as part of the same system. Some firms invite vendors and customers to company functions and encourage employees to devote company time to community service.

Because "work" and "life" are not separate concepts, employees' personal lives spill over into the office or plant. For example, staffers at the Minneapolis offices of *Utne Reader* socialize both on and off the job and have met each other's friends. Says editor Lynette Lamb: "I miss my co-workers even when I go on vacation." Publisher Eric Utne keeps a drawer full of toys for his young sons to play with when they drop by the office. Even his dog has visited the editorial suite. Another editor, Helen Cordes, brought her daughter to the office twice a week until the infant was eight months old.

Companies used to recoil in alarm at the very prospect of married people working together. Now, they are realizing that couples who discuss office business at home often develop greater identification with, and commitment to, the company. "I've actually seen personals ads on company bulletin boards," says consultant Michael Doyle.

8. Group Renewal

When *Utne Reader* expanded its staff a few years ago, the group became less cohesive. Roles and reporting relationships were not clear, and personality conflicts were beginning to erupt. So Eric Utne closed the office for two days in the middle of the week and took the entire staff to a spa an hour away. There the entire group relaxed, hiked, biked, indulged in massages, and got to know each other. They shared stories about how and why they had come to work at the magazine. As they developed a sense of the group as a community, they more easily discussed roles, responsibilities, and action plans. After that, the magazine scheduled periodic half-day retreats to follow up on the action plans and maintain the cohesion that had emerged at the spa.

Companies that ignore the total person will receive a very painful lesson in terms of the costs of employing a person who has physical and/or mental ailments or whose family life is a source of stress.

ROBERT H. ROSEN

Once a month, the entire staff of Lightworks Construction meets outside the office environment with a professional team builder. Any employee can bring up any topic. "Often we discuss and resolve interpersonal conflicts in the group without the help of the facilitator," says company president David Johnston, adding that these monthly meetings make everyday work run much more smoothly.

Community-conscious organizations hold regular renewal sessions, involving as large a portion of the staff as possible, to improve teamwork, clarify values, and review and recommit to the organization's vision and mission. At these conclaves, retelling corporate history and celebrating corporate milestones aid in the bonding process.

The Perils of Workplace Community Building

Organizations committed to workplace community strive to embody most or all of these eight qualities and, in doing so, enjoy the intrinsic rewards that they bring. But, treading a road few have traveled before, these organizations also encounter hazards along the way, especially as the pull of old patterns and fears threatens to stall or reverse their forward progress. A workplace in which teams manage themselves, people rotate roles, and the organizational chart (if there is one) looks more like a pancake than a pyramid represents a new kind of beast. Not everyone is likely to trust it right off, especially given the centuries of labor-management strife that preceded its emergence. Also, many Americans, having grown up in a culture that reveres the fiercest competitors and the most ruthless fast-trackers, find the concept of interdependence difficult to embrace.

Many people consider their jobs as something they have to do, a burden imposed from the outside, an effort that takes life away from the ledger of their existence. So even though the momentary on-the-job experience may be positive, they tend to discount it, because it does not contribute to their own long-range goals.

MIHALY CSIKSZENTMIHALYI

A Question of Balance

"Hold on a minute," a senior-level veteran of a harsh business battleground might say. "If I focus on community and don't pay enough attention to the task of making money and beating the competition, I won't survive and neither will this business." A lower-level employee skilled in detecting phony motivational ploys might add, "And how do I know that, after I begin taking initiative and helping my co-workers more, the bosses won't suddenly change the rules once again to suit their interests while ignoring mine?" Both of these fictional adversaries make important points.

A highly successful construction company that exemplified all eight of the above qualities began losing its competitive edge when a recession struck. The employees had focused so much on their interpersonal relationships that they had neglected to take the steps needed to bring in new business. When the financial crunch came, they split into factions, thus damaging community as well as productivity.

The employees at a manufacturing firm began enthusiastically supporting one another and the company when a new owner took the reins. This incoming CEO, whom we shall call Trent, told the employees in total earnestness that he wanted them to participate fully in the business and its profits. Over the course of two years, a strong family feeling emerged in the organization. Work teams taught each other skills, and employees willingly helped out fellow workers. After a while, however, the employees noticed that this particular family operated under the thumb of a Big Daddy. Trent was not the hands-off type of manager he claimed to be, or possibly even wanted to be. "He did a lot of checking up," reports a consultant. "His secretary was his spy." And he was quick to intervene when he perceived that things were not going the way he wanted them to. As a result, community spirit ebbed away.

Balancing task and relationship, authority and freedom, and the needs of the individual with those of the group prove to be the primary challenges of workplace community. Businesses need to make a profit to stay alive. But survival can also depend on relationships. After investigating "Whatever Happened to the Class of '83?" Curtis Hartman in *Inc.* concluded that "the survivors have built systems of relationships inside and outside their companies that depend more on trust and mutual advantage than on authority and delegation."

Terry Mollner, director of the Trusteeship Institute, which helps companies become worker-owned, declares relationship the key to transcending the polarities between the individual and the group and freedom and authority. Mollner believes that capitalism—a system in which the freedom of the individual takes priority over the interest of the group—and socialism—one in which group interests take priority over individual freedom—both contain inherent flaws because they are based on materialism rather than love and caring. He advocates the "third way": focusing on relationship first. He likes to point out that if two people have an apple to share, both capitalism and socialism assume that what is most important is who gets the bigger piece. But what is really most important is the relationship between those who are doing the dividing. "If we're friends," he says, "I'll gladly give you the bigger piece, because what we're really concerned about is our relationship." If relationship comes first, he continues, hierarchy no longer functions as a control device and can be appreciated for its efficiency. By allowing a role for hierarchy and other task-oriented or efficient structures within a relationship model, the "third way" compensates for the potential weaknesses of the purely support culture.

Are the present changes in business and organizations a fad or a passing trend that may last a while and then be replaced by another new idea? Or are these changes part of a much broader pattern representing a fundamental shift in which the value priorities of the entire society are going through reassessment (as is the underlying image of reality) and even the purpose of the corporation is being redefined? There is much contemporary evidence to support the latter view.

WILLIS HARMAN

Stresses and Shadows

Incorporating community into the workplace poses additional challenges. Michele Hunt, Vice President for Quality and People Development at Herman Miller (until she was promoted, she held the title of Vice President for People), is delighted to work for an organization that is committed to individual growth and to building high-quality relationships among workers, managers, customers, and the larger community. "Everyone talks about love and joy," she says. "You're a whole person here. I've been offered quite a bit more money to go to another company, but I haven't been able to leave." One disadvantage, however, is that "you become so engaged. I have to send my people home and make them take vacations." Another is the necessity to be truthful, even when the truth is painful. "I have to walk into a colleague's office and say, 'This is how I'm feeling.' We're constantly confronting each other in ways people don't usually do at work." She adds, "I still fight against my urge to control and mistrust. Vulnerability isn't easy. But we are coached along the way."

Although community building reduces stress in the long term, the training required to break old patterns may feel stressful in the short term.

A worker at the Quaker Oats pet food plant comments that the self-managing work teams require people to develop management and communication skills that workers in traditional plants do not need. Although the company offers training programs to develop these skills, "it's hard to maintain this system. It takes constant work, constant maintenance, constant attention. It tends to stray—there are moments of everyone being very enthusiastic and then people get a little bit tired." Team leaders often find it difficult to deal with people who have their own ideas on how to do things and argue their point of view with heat and passion. Vendors and others outside the company sometimes become irritated when they cannot figure out who's in charge.

As Michele Hunt's comment suggests, a heightened feeling of commitment and identification carries with it the danger of workaholism—which even the Japanese are beginning to see as a disease. Several of the companies mentioned in this chapter as examples of community friendliness show symptoms of this disease, which is common in high-performance, achievement-oriented cultures. Again, a sense of balance is important, as it is in any living system.

Diversity in the work force presents its own challenges. For example, certain employees do not want to be empowered and self-managing, and their needs must be considered along with everyone else's. Also, not every manager is willing to implement an enlightened CEO's philosophy of openness, trust, teamwork, and respect for individuality. "From what I know of other companies, ours is better," comments a Levi Strauss employee. "But that doesn't mean it's perfect. There are pockets of wonderful, supportive people and pockets of dysfunctional, patronizing folks. That's diversity at its finest." Acknowledging and incorporating the shadow side of diversity—and any other challenging feature of the workplace—is as much a part of the ongoing adventure of building community as are words of reassurance and gestures of support.

If You Are the Boss

The impetus for creating community in the workplace usually starts at the top. If you are the head of your organization or department or the owner of a business, the following six steps will help you initiate the community-building process:

1. Set aside some time to be alone and to look into your own heart. Ask yourself why you want community in your organization and what, specifically, you expect to gain from it personally. (You might want to use the exercises in Chapter Three to increase your clarity on this issue.) What would your ideal community-friendly organization—the one where you want to work, the one with which you want to be identified—look like? In this vision, how does your day begin, and what goes on from hour to hour?
2. Think about what your typical day, and the typical day for others who work with you, looks like now. Do you notice a large gap between this picture and your vision of the ideal? Quickly now: What are some fast and easy ways to begin closing that gap?
3. Ask yourself how much control you are willing to relinquish. For entrepreneurs, letting go of one's brainchild can be a painful process. However, it is necessary not only for community but for growth.
4. Invite some—or all, if it is a small group—of your employees to join you in a visioning process that will include creating community. At this point you may want to hire a consultant with experience in running visioning workshops. To avoid unrealistic expectations and later disillusionment, communicate clearly, in advance, the limits of this exercise. Let your employees know how budget and other constraints affect decisions. Before launching this visioning process, you may need to prepare employees to take part effectively by arranging for courses in interpersonal skills, such as cross-cultural communication and conflict management.
5. Model the behavior you want to see. Bring your family to the office. Spend time talking to people who are several levels below you. Answer all questions honestly and do not be afraid to show feelings. Keep your door open. Send cards and notes. Invite everyone to celebrate milestones together. Demonstrate trust. Solicit (do not just be open to) criticism of the way the company does things and the way you do things. Contribute your time and energy to the surrounding community.
6. Think beyond your own workplace to the larger system in which it operates. For example, if you own a small business, you might consider joining Business Partnership for Peace, a 300-company consortium that shares ideas and resources, invests in third-world village banks, lobbies Congress, and conducts joint neighborhood improvement activities. A recent merger between BPP and Busi-

Modern organizations and the promise of the "good life" have separated us from traditional ties to the land, to our families, to the community, and perhaps most importantly, from the connection to our own spirit. In this process, millions of us have been cut off from our hearts' desire—to be a part of a larger community of endeavor that is worthy of our best effort.

JUANITA BROWN

nesses for Social Responsibility—a smaller group but one that includes companies of all sizes—has further strengthened the network and its member businesses, as well as rewarding the individuals who take an active role.

When you become a global citizen on the inside, your external identity begins to expand to accommodate this new belief. This is true for organizations as well as individuals.

CYNTHIA F. BARNUM

Although we do not fully realize it as yet, men and women are on an equal playing field in corporate America. Women may even hold a slight advantage since they need not "unlearn" old authoritarian behavior to run their departments or companies.

JOHN NAISBITT AND PATRICIA ABURDENE

A number of studies indicate that if you are a woman, community-fostering behavior may come more easily to you. One scientific study indicated that women are more likely than men to use input from various regions of their brains, including those that control feelings, in performing verbal tasks. Women also can more readily recall complex patterns of apparently unconnected items. Such cerebral differences may help account for differences in so-called feminine and masculine styles of management. Researcher Judy B. Rosener reported in *Harvard Business Review* that women tend to "encourage participation, share power and information, enhance other people's self-worth, and get others excited about their work."

Sally B. Helgesen, author of *The Female Advantage: Women's Ways of Leadership,* says that women talk with employees more frankly than men do and create "webs of inclusion." Dr. Deborah Tannen's studies of men and women in conversation reveal that women use conversation to create or deepen intimacy, while men use it to establish status. "If a man struggles to be strong, a woman struggles to keep the community strong," Tannen writes in *You Just Don't Understand: Women and Men in Conversation.*

None of this implies that men cannot create community. The process requires a set of skills that anyone can learn. Although consensus building and listening have long been considered feminine skills, the workplace offers proof that women have not cornered the market on such skills. In corporate settings, those initiating community-friendly changes at the top and writing books about the process tend to be men. Prime examples are Herman Miller's chairman Max DePree, author of *Leadership Is an Art* and *Leadership Jazz,* and the above-mentioned Jim Autry. Of course, this is hardly surprising since men still hold most of the top management positions. They are also most likely to land book contracts to express ideas that, coming from men, seem striking.

We believe that, as more women are either promoted into positions of power or start their own companies—and as they have less need to look and act like men to fit in—their natural community-encouraging style will begin to permeate organizations. We also remain hopeful that, as newer generations of men experience the rewards of healthy community, they will increasingly ally with women to build such community in the workplace.

If You Are Not the Boss

If the person at the top of the organization creates a climate that discourages community, community is not likely to happen, at least not on a large scale. Managers and even other workers will snuff out attempts to be open and inclusive before they have a chance to spread, since people tend to do what the boss wants. But if your environment is welcoming, or at least not inhibiting, you can take steps to create pockets of community that can serve as models for the rest of the work force. One or more of the three following suggestions may work for you:

1. If you are a member of a task force or work team (self-managing or not), or if you supervise a small group, initiate moves toward conscious community. Encourage the members to take time, say at the beginning of the work day or before group meetings, to "check in" with each other and reflect together on how well the group is meeting individual and collective needs. Make sure everyone on the team has a chance to speak briefly without interruption, if he or she so desires. Also, build in procedures that guarantee that any concerns requiring a response receive one. Introduce others to the communication, decision-making, and conflict resolution procedures described in Part Four of this book.
2. Reflect on your own needs and behavior. What do you want from your work life and home life, and how do these relate to each other? If you have any differences or conflicts with other members of your work group, how have you contributed to these? Do you risk self-disclosure? Do you support others' interests? How might you make some changes in the way you do things around the office or plant that would encourage community?
3. When you review the elements of community listed earlier in this chapter, you may conclude that your present organization has a long way to go in this direction. Talk with another person or persons, preferably change agents (they are easy to identify) about your community visions anyway. These co-workers may have been craving more community also but did not know how to get started or whether they would find any allies. Together, you may be able to make a difference.

The team exists to accomplish a result. The community exists to support its members while they fulfill their purpose. . . . When partnerships, management teams, and organizations build communities, they tap into a greater and deeper reservoir of courage, wisdom and productivity.

Peter Gibb

If your efforts at building workplace community repeatedly fail, and you receive no support from higher-ups, you may wish to look for work elsewhere or consider starting your own company. Both these options take courage, especially in tough economic times, and neither guarantees automatic workplace community. Nonetheless, the eight qualities of community and the examples of successful and not-so-successful experiments described above can help you develop criteria for the kind of workplace you want.

Excellence in management will be achieved through an organizational culture of civility routinely utilizing the mode of community. Such organizations will be so dramatically successful, that is, cost effective, that their sister institutions—no matter how initially threatened—will flock to discover their secret and imitate them.

M. SCOTT PECK

If you are not ready or able to leave your unsupportive work environment, consider forming a support group of others confronting similar issues. The collective wisdom and creativity of the group may help you cope with or change the situation in fresh ways, and the caring support of the others will certainly help you feel better.

As the business world continues to embrace whole-systems theories, and as organizations keep demonstrating the emotional and financial gains from such initiatives as self-managing work teams and labor-management partnerships, conscious community in the workplace appears likely to increase. Organizational development consultant Peter Gibb puts it this way: "In each of us, there is a tug of war between a desire for independence and autonomy on the one hand, and a need to belong on the other. Part of me (the rebellious child) wants to show you (the parent) that I don't need you, or your community; that I can make it on my own. But another part, I think the deeper part, knows full well that the greatest independence comes from interdependence, the greatest growth comes from committed partnering, the highest impact comes from acting in concert with others."

Greater community in the workplace will be good news for everyone, not just those commuting to offices and factories each day. People who learn interactive skills in the workplace can transfer them to non-work settings, ranging from families to governments. Governments, in fact, have traditionally looked toward business to develop models for decision making, problem solving, and conflict resolution. As business becomes increasingly global, successful models of interdependence can spread beyond institutional and geographic boundaries, planting seeds of international cooperation and peace.

RESOURCES

Recommended books and periodicals

New Traditions in Business: Spirit and Leadership in the 21st Century, edited by John Renesch (Sterling & Stone, 1991)

Love and Profit: The Art of Caring Leadership by James Autry (Morrow, 1991)

The Living Organization: Transforming Teams into Workplace Communities by John Nirenberg (Business One Irwin, 1993)

The Healthy Company by Robert Rosen (Jeremy P. Tarcher, 1991)

The New Paradigm in Business edited by Michael Ray and Alan Rinzler (Jeremy P. Tarcher, 1992)

Second to None by Charles Garfield (Business One Irwin, 1991). Teamwork-based businesses.

Leadership Jazz: Weaving Voice with Touch by Max DePree (Currency/Doubleday, 1992)

Leadership Is an Art by Max DePree (Doubleday, 1989)

The Female Advantage by Sally Helgesen (Currency/Doubleday, 1990)

On Becoming a Leader by Warren Bennis (Addison-Wesley, 1989)

A World Waiting to be Born: Civility Rediscovered by M. Scott Peck, M.D. (Bantam, 1993)—particularly the last section, on community in the workplace.

The Fifth Discipline: The Art and Practice of the Learning Organization by Peter Senge (Currency/Doubleday, 1990)

Understanding Employee Ownership by Corey Rosen and Karen M. Young (ILR Press, 1991)

Creative Work: The Constructive Role of Business in a Transforming Society by Willis Harman and John Hormann (Knowledge Systems, 1990)

At Work: Stories of Tomorrow's Workplace (bimonthly newsletter), Berrett-Koehler Publishers, Inc., 155 Montgomery Street, San Francisco, California, 94104-4109

Business Ethics (bimonthly magazine), 1107 Hazeltine Blvd., Suite 530, Chaska, Minnesota, 55318

Organizations

Co-Op America, 2100 M Street NW, Suite 403, Washington, D.C., 20037; (202) 872-5307. Networking, information, and support for democratic, socially responsible businesses and community-based economics.

TWG (The Washington Group), c/o John Adams, Resources for Human Systems Development, 2914 27th St. N., Arlington, Virginia, 22207; (703) 524-8126. Network interested in transforming large organizations. Produces a bimonthly newsletter and a member list.

Businesses for Social Responsibility (incorporates Business Partnership for Peace), 1850 M Street, NW, Suite 750, Washington, D.C., 20036; (202) 872-5206

Also see resources in Chapters Fourteen, Fifteen, Sixteen, and Seventeen.

EIGHT

Electronic Communities

There's a rich emotional soup a-boiling up there on the networks; more and more people are leading multiple lives simultaneously. It's an excellent adventure.

JON CARROLL

WHEN KATHLEEN WAKES SUDDENLY at 3 a.m., she feels the familiar sharp twinge of panic. Although it has been well over a year since her husband of three decades was killed by a drunk driver, she is still vulnerable to surges of anxiety and loneliness. Lying there in the dark, she longs for someone to talk to, someone who understands and cares. But where can she find such a sympathetic ear at this hour? Her friends would surely be willing to listen, but she does not want to wake them up. Nor does she want to call her grown children, who are having enough problems of their own.

Gently, Kathleen slips out of bed and pads into the next room, where she switches on her computer and logs onto SeniorNet, an electronic network for people fifty-five and over which spans the U.S. and Canada. Soon she is typing out her thoughts and feelings to friends she knows are really there for her—even though they may not be "there" on the network with her at exactly that moment. These people, most of whom she has never seen or even talked to on the phone, will respond with empathy and concern when they log onto SeniorNet and see her message.

As her words travel from her computer through her telephone line to her friends' computers, it feels good to let her emotions out. She does not have to be embarrassed if her eyes fill with tears, because no one can see her. She need not feel guilty about unburdening herself, because many of her fellow networkers have been through the same situation.

"When I first made contact with people online," Kathleen says, "I realized that SeniorNet is an unbelievably caring community. It's been my lifeline, and I've run across some really wonderful people. One of them has a sister-in-law whose husband died, so she knew how I was feeling and was very sympathetic. Later another lady joined whose husband had died, so I found I could give something back by listening and responding to her feelings. I can see she's improving by the way she's expressing herself."

We are exploring a frontier where cultural and technological change converge. . . . We believe that wise use of computer-mediated communications is an essential part of creative action in these times.

TRUDY AND PETER JOHNSON-LENZ

One night, Kathleen recalls, a phone-line glitch caused her to get bumped off the network. "I was new to networking and kept hitting keys to see if I could get back on. This meant my name just kept coming up on other people's screens. A couple in San Francisco became worried and tried to call me." They could not get through because Kathleen had only one phone line and that was tied up. So they phoned the police in her Oregon town, who came to check up on her. "These folks really cared," she says with wonder.

Even without seeing the other networkers, she knows their distinct personalities. When she sees that her friend Melmac (his network name, or "handle") is online at the same time she is, she pages him and the two move to a private conference to chat. "It's more immediate than mail and better than the phone—I'm not really a telephone person," she says. Although she uses SeniorNet only for conversation, some of her network buddies—including her sister—take advantage of the online Monday night bingo games and Wednesday night parties. Others share their hobbies and their interests in literature.

SeniorNet is just one of hundreds of electronic networks that have been springing up rapidly around the world. From different locations and time zones, people are getting together online to socialize, plan events and political movements, form support groups, engage in philosophical discussions, and share personal details of their lives.

But is this really community? Or is computer technology actually a subtle destroyer of community?

There is no denying that computers, with their awesome power, already have altered our lives and will continue to do so in ways we can scarcely predict. Whether or not we use a personal computer or know the difference between a modem and a hard drive, these electronic processors have changed forever the way we relate to one another, just as the telephone did more than a century ago. Computer technology has nearly eliminated, for example, many of the daily face-to-face transactions that used to seem essential, such as talking to a human teller when we want to withdraw money from our bank account. More and more of us even manage, by telecommuting, to avoid going to our offices.

Some technology watchers claim that the computer causes alienation, tension, paranoia, and anxiety. It engenders such striving for speed and perfection, they say, that hostility erupts when life fails to measure up. People who are glued to their terminals become less and less able to relate to others face to face. "Our computers can talk to each other but our people can't," one manager of a high-tech company laments.

In a virtual community we can go directly to the place where our particular interests are being discussed, then get acquainted with those who share our passions.

HOWARD RHEINGOLD

Jeremy Rifkin warns, in *Time Wars,* that the emerging computer culture operates at such speed and deals in such abstractions that it is threatening to separate us from human experience and the rhythms of nature. "We are entering a new temporal world," he predicts, "where time is segmented into nanoseconds, the future is programmed in advance, nature is reconceived as bits of coded information, and paradise is viewed as a fully simulated, artificial environment."

To be sure, our present-day high-speed, stressful lives reflect the advances of technology. Far from saving time, such devices as personal computers and fax machines have simply created more for people to do. Because you can now work and produce faster, you are expected to do so. When you send that fax message or electronic mail to someone who used to be perfectly happy to wait a week for a letter, you can expect an instant reply and thus more to do. Stress levels rise as you struggle to accomplish more within the same number of daily hours. And in a speeded-up life, it can be difficult to find time for community building.

Berkeley psychologist Craig Brod, who has traced many of his clients' problems to America's love affair with the computer, is among those who take the dim view. In his book *Technostress,* he declares that, as our computer use increases, "we are diminishing and altering our sense of self and of others, creating new barriers to what we long for: intimacy, continuity, and community."

Others, however, point to the computer's potential for enabling us to form relationships with people we would never otherwise have a chance to know. This device expands the notion of what community means by freeing it from certain traditional assumptions about place, time, sensory information, and physical ability. In many ways, electronic networks behave much like the other types of communities mentioned in this book. They are full of emotion, personality conflict, celebration, and challenge, and they go through life-cycle changes. They also raise new community-building issues that demand new approaches and solutions.

Not All Networkers Are Nerds

That personal comments can appear in such an impersonal setting, that anyone who subscribes can read a man's description of emotional breakdown or a woman's bald statement—"I'm back from the doctor and he tells me I have cancer"—does not depreciate that message's power. The very indifference, implacability, of a medium as public as The WELL only amplifies the human cry that appears on the screen in words and phrases. I feel sometimes as if I'm walking the streets of a big city, reading graffiti that's just been scrawled on a wall.

JUDITH MOORE

Craig Brod asserts that in electronic networks, "there's none of the guts of what it means to be in a community. In fact, the very people who want to connect to community by computer wouldn't have time to participate in the community that was in front of them. If I tried to get them to come and paint the local school, I doubt that I could get them away from their machines."

His comment indicates how personal computers have stretched the traditional concept of community from a physical place to a symbolic place. It also illustrates a pervasive belief about electronic networks—and their users—that has colored our reactions to them.

Many are concerned that people who use computers for personal networking are techno-nerds who have hung around the infernal machines so long that they've become machine-like themselves, with no warmth, sociability, or unpredictable foibles. This belief, however, collapses into misleading stereotype when we realize that personal computers are now ubiquitous features of homes, offices, and schools. It is becoming harder and harder to find anyone—housewife, student, business manager, retiree, or homeless person—who has never set finger to computer keyboard. All these categories of people are represented in electronic communities. It is true that such communities, which are more diverse than most other types, include nerds who are not very good at traditional forms of interaction. Some of these people cause problems. And many others blossom online.

Some network users are children, for whom computers are no more mystifying than touch-tone telephones. Children even participate in network communities designed especially for them—such as KIDS, a project that gets children in the ten-to-fifteen age group involved in global dialogue with their peers from Tasmania to Texas.

Using a variety of conferencing systems, networks, and electronic mailboxes, the KIDS kids introduce themselves (sometimes in their own languages, sometimes in English, most people's second language) by answering four questions: Who am I? What do I want to be when I grow up? How do I want the world to be better when I grow up? What can I do now to make this happen? Then they go on to chat about such topics as school, hobbies, the environment, and their hopes for the future. Subscriptions are free. All participants need is access to a computer with a modem—the device that connects the computer to a phone line or satellite. Often, participation in KIDS is a school project. These young pioneers, and others like them, are the community-builders of the future . . . starting now, in the present.

Computers can open the door into community for people who might otherwise have been shut out, such as Wanet Miller, who became paralyzed from the neck down as a result of an automobile accident in 1974. "Everything changed in that moment," he recalls. "My marriage fell apart, I fell apart." Lacking a family support system, he decided to move with a colleague from Phoenix to Berkeley, where people from the Mormon church became his first new friends.

Still, he felt isolated. Although Wanet is a naturally engaging and gregarious man, "it was hard on me to see all the things I couldn't do, so I didn't go out," he says. "I became a hermit except for visits from church people." Then, despite the fact that he'd hated computers for years, he was so bored he decided to purchase a Commodore. With the aid of a friend, he figured out how to rig it up so he could work it with a stick held in his mouth. From then on, his world began opening up.

First, he helped out his church community by preparing computerized mailing lists. Then he took on other information-organizing projects and eventually the church committees began holding their meetings at his house, bringing dinner along to add a social dimension. When he bought a modem so that he could communicate with a friend who had one, he was suddenly presented with new possibilities for connectedness.

One by one, he joined computer networks: CompuServe, Prodigy, America Online, and local computer bulletin-board systems. Not only did he meet a variety of new acquaintances—including other disabled people—he was able to enhance his own feelings of self-esteem by using the computer for activities that had formerly been problematic, such as shopping and banking. In fact, he now assists his growing circle of friends by helping them make airline reservations, do research, and shop online for electronic equipment.

Today, Wanet spends at least three hours a day online. For him, the computer is his link not only to electronic communities but also to the wider community. "The world," he says joyfully, "is interesting again."

A second eroding belief about electronic communities is that they replace personal, in-the-flesh contact. On the contrary, networking by computer usually supplements and even encourages what network users call meeting "f2f" (face to face). However, the process of developing closeness evolves differently. As several users have observed, in traditional place-based communities you meet people and then, if you choose, get to know

With the power of computer-mediated communications, it is possible to expand dialogue, to show people that individuals can be effective, and to organize groups of strangers into communities. There are few more important tasks at every level, from the neighborhood to the planet, in the days ahead.

HOWARD RHEINGOLD

them; with electronic communities, you usually get to know people first and then decide whether to meet them f2f.

Some network communities set up regular gatherings for their participants. The WELL (which stands for Whole Earth 'Lectronic Link) holds monthly get-togethers in the San Francisco area, although many WELLites hail from other parts of the country—the world, even. Members of ECHO (East Coast Hang Out), a smaller, cozier network composed mostly of New York City residents, arrange picnics, dances, bowling parties, members' art shows, and other events. If someone is having a birthday party, an open invitation is likely to appear on the ECHO network. Many members gather over beers on alternate Monday evenings at the White Horse Tavern in Greenwich Village, which happens to be located near the home/office of ECHO's founder, Stacy Horn.

When we sit down to write a letter, we make the most of that postage stamp. If we don't have time to write a whole page, we put it aside and wait until we have more to say. On a network, we constantly chitchat—we can send several messages back and forth in a day, regardless of where we live.

JOHN HELIE

What happens when online acquaintances meet f2f? That depends on the type of network. For ECHOids it is not a big deal, since most of them can arrange meetings spontaneously, on short notice. For others, it can be tremendously exciting. Neesa Sweet, a video scriptwriter in Chicago who belongs to several online groups, recalls the first time she attended a convention of the Electronic Networking Association. "We looked at each other's name tags and started hugging and kissing as we recognized each other. It was very touchy-feely." When she's traveling through a town where one of her network friends lives, she telephones. "I'm a very people-oriented person and this is a great way to meet more people," she says.

It is not uncommon for a couple to meet on the network, then get together in person, and finally marry. This is a bit like marrying your pen pal, except that the getting-to-know-you stage progresses more quickly and more multi-dimensionally. Courting couples can have private conversations by exchanging electronic mail, and they can also join each other in public conferences on issues as general as Culture, as intimate as Sexuality. The give and take can be instant or as soon as someone feels like replying.

The possibilities for using electronic networks as an avenue for exploring community issues are just starting to be discovered. John Helie, director of an electronic network called ConflictNet for professionals in the conflict resolution field, describes how the intricate dynamics of this network community surprised him. "When I created ConflictNet, I envisioned it as a way for people in the field to meet and support each other. After a while, though, I began to get the idea that some members thought ConflictNet was for online client mediations. But that wasn't what they meant either. After being flagged several times to go in and read conferences where problems were coming up, I realized that they wanted a way to work out conflicts with each other by using the network."

John successfully mediated a dispute between two members who were both officers of a nonprofit organization, but lived in different cities, by combining three-way electronic network discussions with voice conference calls by telephone. "Eventually, the two people met face to face, and that was when we brought the mediation to closure," he reports. "For us, the electronic network was an adjunct to our other means of communication, not a replacement."

More and more, human to human need not mean face to face.

THE NEW YORK TIMES

How Computer Communities and Physical Communities Mix

The line between network community and traditional, place-based community often becomes blurred. A few years ago, the City of Santa Monica launched the world's first teleconferencing network operated by a municipal government. Called PEN, an acronym for Public Electronic Network, its purpose was to link residents to City Hall, giving them a chance to ask questions and express their opinions. But according to Kevin McKeown, chairman of the PEN Users' Group, "PEN grew to be much more of a citizen-to-citizen phenomenon, with a culture of its own."

All residents of the city were offered free use of PEN, where they could read city information, send messages to their representatives in City Hall, and join teleconferences to debate issues with each other. All they had to do was register. To participate, they could either use a home computer or drop into a library or school and use one of PEN's nineteen public terminals. This meant that, for the first time, all kinds of formerly disinterested or disenfranchised people had a chance to influence city government. And they did.

Among the public issues that generated intense interest online was the perennial problem of homelessness. Online comments from homeless individuals spurred some PENners to form a PEN Action Group that met not only via computer, but also in person in a local library. When a few people with scraggly hair and shabby clothes showed up for one of these f2f meetings, they were recognized for the first time as the homeless whose cause the group had been championing. They had been so articulate online that most of the others had been unaware of, or had forgotten, their status. "That meeting broke a lot of our stereotypes," says one action group member.

The homeless people explained how lack of early-morning showers, access to clean clothing, and storage space for belongings was an obstacle to finding jobs. So the PEN Action Group developed a proposal called SHWASHLOCK—a system for providing SHowers, WASHers, and LOCKers for homeless people—that was later adopted by the Santa Monica City Council. "The otherwise 'hidden' homeless themselves were part of this process from start to finish," says Kevin McKeown, "because of the level playing field their ideas enjoyed on PEN."

In the world of online computer networking, there are some similarities between electronic mail, computer bulletin boards, and computer conferencing. In all three kinds of systems, for example, people can log on at different times and from different locations. What differentiates true computer conferencing is the emphasis on supporting a group of people as a group.

METASYSTEMS DESIGN GROUP

One of the PEN Action Group's founders was Michele Wittig, a psychology professor who had never before been interested in her home city's politics—or, for that matter, in electronic discourse. But when she joined PEN after reading a newspaper announcement, she became intrigued with Santa Monica issues. She also discovered online that Kevin lived only four blocks from her, and the two joined forces in other projects. When a city council—and PEN—member informed her that there was an opening on Santa Monica's Women's Commission, Michele applied and soon became one of the commission's most active members. Without her online community, Michele says, she would never have become a vital part of her neighborhood community.

Network habitués are fond of comparing their online conferences to gatherings in a neighborhood café hangout. You meet your pals regularly, hear about what's happening or pick up old conversations where you left off, and are introduced to new folks who share some of your interests. But unlike actual café conversations, you do not physically see your friends, rub elbows with them, or absorb the visual and tactile ambience of a favorite hangout.

In a few major cities, however, those who enjoy both online hangouts and the physical café variety can experience both at the same time. In certain coffee houses in and around San Francisco, for example, you can plunk down your cappuccino next to a tabletop terminal and log onto SFNet for a bull session or a foray into the Love Connection, a computerized personals column. It is easier and less risky to make a connection this way than to hail a stranger at the next table who is buried in a newspaper. Why violate social norms when you can find willing conversational partners online? In fact, SFNet has become such a conversation piece that people have met standing next to each other over the terminal. Wayne Gregori, the entrepreneur behind SFNet, plans to extend the network into other cities, such as Seattle, New York, maybe even Paris. Having an electronic discussion with someone sipping mocha on Montparnasse would certainly lend a whole new dimension to the term "café society."

Group support and group rituals are becoming as common in online communities as in families and neighborhood social circles. Life passages from birth to marriage to death are celebrated together. One poignant event was The WELL's reaction to the news that one of its members—a brilliant but controversial man whose comments had spiced up dozens of conferences—had committed suicide. Before he killed himself in the "real" world, he had committed "virtual" suicide by erasing almost all his old WELL postings. He had disappeared from the planet . . . or had he? After struggling with shock, denial, grief, and anger online, his fellow WELLites suddenly pulled together for a memorial service. Screenfuls of heartfelt comments and tributes poured in from all corners of the network. Networkers even managed to create a new file of his old postings, which had been saved on a backup disk.

In the real world, you'd have to go to multiple conventions—or a university—to find as many experts in one place. In these new villages, you can get fast feedback from peers or question specialists with equal ease. But it's no free ride. In the electronic community the price of admission is a willingness to share knowledge.

GLENN MAR

NEW PROBLEMS, NEW SOLUTIONS

Despite the many similarities between networks and traditional communities, it would be a dangerous mistake to assume that the two behave in exactly the same way. Computer communities, in fact, have given rise to so

THOUGH THEY ALWAYS TRIED TO PRACTICE SAFE LINKAGE, MONA STILL CONTRACTED LARRY'S COMPUTER VIRUS.

many new communication issues and problems that it is a constant challenge to come up with solutions.

Take, for example, the lack of visual and aural cues in electronic interactions. On a network, you can get to know each other's minds and spirits without considering age, education, ability, race, physical appearance, or other potential barriers. But by the same token, you are vulnerable to deception, intentional or unintentional, and misperception. It is possible to build up a complex picture of another person in your mind and then have to do a lot of mental rewiring after an f2f meeting. Liz is a bubbly young blonde who's probably a little chubby since she said she's addicted to chocolate, you might think, and then be surprised to meet a slim, shy, fiftyish Liz with short dark hair. A balding, rotund man can represent himself as a sex god—or even as a woman.

When intentional deception is discovered, the results can be emotionally shattering—as in the case of "Joan," a network regular who became immensely popular on CompuServe even though she was, she revealed, mute, disabled, and disfigured. An intense, dramatic person, Joan was also a generous and thoughtful friend, particularly to other women on the network. She nurtured these friends through physical and emotional distresses, even sending cards and gifts. But although she exchanged detailed secrets, life histories, and even flirtations with fellow networkers, she would not meet anyone face to face—for a reason that eventually became clear: "Joan" was in reality a male psychiatrist named Alex, who was attempting to see what it felt like to be female and to experience woman-to-woman intimacy.

When the others found out about the deception through a gradual series of suspicions and revelations, shock and anger reverberated throughout the network. People spoke in anguish about victimization, betrayal of trust, and "mind rape." Writing about the incident in *Ms.* magazine, Lindsy Van Gelder, one of the many people who had grown emotionally attached to "Joan," declared that "Many of us online like to believe that we're a utopian community of the future, and Alex's experiment proved to us all that technology is no shield against deceit. We lost our innocence, if not our faith."

What is noteworthy about this type of disillusionment, however, is the way the electronic community goes about healing itself. In the Joan/Alex incident, as in the case of the online suicide, both men and women expressed their emotions and responded to others' comments in a sort of group soul-searching. Three factors facilitated this community process: members could communicate their feelings when they felt them, at any time of day or night; they tended to speak more honestly and freely than if they were confronting one another face to face; and everyone involved could "hear" the others' comments exactly as they had been made, without the distorting effect that occurs when stories are passed serially from one to another.

A less dramatic but more pervasive issue than online deception is the typical communication glitch that can cause what network users refer to as "flaming": a rash of anger or general craziness that spreads through the conversation like wildfire. When participants cannot see facial expressions or body language and cannot hear tone of voice, it is easy to misinterpret someone's words. It is also easy to go off on a tangent and sweep other communicators along. Claude Whitmyer, a WELL participant, recalls an incident when "one guy made a crack that another person—not even the one he was addressing—took to be sexist. Someone else reacted and then more bystanders joined in and pretty soon it was way out of proportion."

Networkers have developed several ways to mitigate misunderstandings. Online hosts or moderators for a particular conference keep track of conversations and try to nip communication problems in the bud. And individuals take personal responsibility for making sure their communication is clear by using typed signals to amplify their words. For example, participants type "just kidding" or, abbreviated, "j/k." Network language includes a range of "emoticons," symbols composed of punctuation marks that indicate subtle emotions and body language and look like stylized faces turned on their sides. These include the smiley face :-), the wink ;-), and the frown):-(. Some users are careful to type "hmmm" to show that they have heard what another participant has just said and are considering their reply.

These are among the civilized approaches to communication problems. Sometimes, however, network communities do not appear very civilized. When they realize they can say whatever they want, without interruption or even an admonishing glance, they have been known to act like a bunch of unruly children after a meal of Halloween candy. Or, as Kevin McKeown says, "otherwise nice people can get downright nasty." He was surprised when this happened in the PEN Action Group.

"When PEN was set up," he explains, "we consciously decided to require the use of individuals' real names, which are automatically appended to every response and message. Given that most PEN participants live within two miles of each other, we hoped that flamers would be dissuaded by the very real possibility of a knock on the door in the dead of night. Great theory, but it didn't work."

A few males on PEN ("mostly adolescents," says Kevin) began writing scenarios in which various PEN women were subjected to sexual domination and other degrading behavior. On some networks, a moderator would have summarily thrown them off and not allowed them to sign on again. But PEN was operated by the City of Santa Monica, which as a government entity had to be very careful not to infringe on free speech.

If I had to pick a single word to characterize the impact of PEN [Public Electronic Network] on Santa Monica, it would be . . . "empowerment." When traditional social cues are lacking, individuals become equals, judged on the strength of their ideas.

KEVIN MCKEOWN

Enter the PENfemmes, who took matters into their own hands. Online, they organized a women's support group that met face to face, decided to ignore their attackers, and sent calming messages to each other by personal electronic mail.

Like many other types of communities, however, PEN began to evolve through new stages. According to Michele Wittig, rudeness on the network continued and complaints began to outnumber helpful suggestions. Politicians, who formerly were interactive participants, began to read only. When fewer and fewer citizens posted comments and questions, the network became dominated by a few strong-minded participants, and broad-based, meaningful dialogue degenerated. As a result, PEN changed its focus, becoming more useful—and used—as an information database. The decline of online community, however, did not affect the rewarding personal relationships that had been formed as a result of introductions on PEN.

ORGANISM OR ULTRA-MACHINE?

Computer networking gives rise to fundamental questions concerning functional and conscious community: Is computer technology turning human users into machines? Or is it enabling machines to become more human? And what does this mean for humans who use the technology to develop community?

While technology critics like Sherry Turkle, author of *The Second Self: Computers and the Human Spirit,* and Jeremy Rifkin warn that humans are beginning to think of themselves as computers rather than the other way around, a case can be made for computer systems, and the electronic network communities they spawn, mirroring living organisms and ecosystems.

Like living organisms—and unlike our old notion of machines—these network communities emerge spontaneously in response to diverse, intrinsic needs for connection—political, social, emotional, intellectual. Self-creating and self-regulating, they tend to spurn hierarchy, resist control, and expand amoeba-like in all directions, crossing physical borders and psychological boundaries. A computer network "has a life of its own, just as an economic or biological ecosystem does," writes Bernardo Huberman, author of *The Ecology of Computation.* These networks exemplify the shift in worldviews that many ecologists, new physicists, and systems thinkers believe humanity is now experiencing: a transformation from a mechanical model of reality to an organic one.

Each [ECHO] board I have been on is unique, has its own personality, which comes from the sum of the personalities of its users and which grows and changes with them.

OWL X WHITNEY

Members of a network community often show concern not only about their own and each other's well-being, but about the network itself and its relationship to other communities. They treat each network like a living being, talking affectionately about its personality: "ECHO is a salon for hip New Yorkers." "The WELL is huge, quirky, and intellectual." The Meta Network, whose 300 or so members include futurists, humanistic psychologists, and political activists, declare themselves committed to making the world better.

A lengthy discussion on The WELL was titled, "The WELL as Superorganism—and Possible Prototype for . . . ?" In this conference, some participants pictured the network as a three-dimensional entity, organized on different levels with connections between levels. But is it a tool or more like a dream? Each node on the network, member Howard Rheingold theorized, is a jewel reflecting the rest of the net. Might the network evolve its own consciousness? others wondered. What would constitute reproductive success? What are the spiritual dimensions?

The analogy to a living organism tends to stretch thin when it comes to self-regulation. At times, the dynamics of these network communities appear as out of control as a body without an immune system. It is difficult, in some cases impossible, to screen participants. As a network gains members, content can balloon into unwieldy proportions: a single topic can generate hundreds of responses, some of them paragraphs long, and can give birth to numerous branches or subtopics. Also, as with PEN, a small group of "toxic" members can poison the network for everyone.

Another disconcerting aspect of such network communities is that people can leave at any time, simply by no longer signing on, and others may not realize that they have left until weeks or months later. Computer communities tend to be characterized more by fluidity than by cohesiveness and stability.

WELLites argue periodically about what happens to their words once these words penetrate the ethers and become part of the group consciousness. How can they make sure no one "steals" their ideas? Networks are also plagued by larger issues: How can you keep sensitive information confidential? Who is liable for remarks made on a network? If the federal government starts up a network carrying information that affects all our lives, will it be able to "lock out" certain participants?

Acknowledging the need for self-regulation within electronic networks as well as for mutual support and protection against unfair government intervention, Mitch Kapor, founder of Lotus Corp. and a network enthusiast, has formed an organization with the express purpose of helping to "civilize the electronic frontier." His Electronic Frontier Foundation intends to help make electronic communication "truly useful and beneficial to everyone, not just an elite; and to do this in a way that is in keeping with our society's highest traditions of the free and open flow of information and communication."

Instead of asking, "What is the information that matters and how do we most effectively manage it?" companies must start asking, "What are the relationships that matter and how can the technology most effectively support them?"

MICHAEL SCHRAGE

Whether you believe electronic communities exemplify the ultimate in democracy, or are elite enclaves of the well-off, generally depends on whether you are viewing them from inside or outside. Within a given milieu, networks can be supremely egalitarian, barrier-dissolving communities in which everyone has an equal chance to be "heard." In companies that have installed electronic mail networks, for example, anyone can send a message to anyone else. If you want to ask the president a question or express your opinion, you do not need to wait outside his or her office under the bland gaze of the secretary.

William Gates, founder and president of Microsoft, Inc., runs his software company primarily via a computer network through which most of the 5,000+ employees can participate in decision- and even policy-making. When the consulting firm Interaction Associates was going through a painful reorganization and self-examination, the company set up forums on electronic mail so that people at all levels could exchange feelings that they might not have felt free to express face to face.

Sometimes, to be sure, reliance on electronic communication can go too far, actually inhibiting community. Craig Brod tells the story about a newspaper journalist who called to interview him and ended up complaining about her own workplace. "They're making us use electronic mail," she said, "and now I can't even talk to Sally in person." "And where is Sally?" Brod wondered aloud. "Five desks from me," was the reply.

More encouraging is a 1991 RAND Corporation study of two groups of employees at the Los Angeles Department of Water and Power. Both groups were able to meet in person and talk on the phone, but one group also exchanged messages on an electronic network. That group, the study found, worked together more closely and became better friends than the other. Moreover, says the study's coauthor, Tora Bikson, "A year after the

How to Create a Healthy Online Community

- Do not be too intimidated by the technology. Although there are a lot of new commands and procedures to learn at first, there are also people who are willing to help you. For many users, learning to network is easier than learning to program a VCR.
- Be open and honest with other members of your community. Type in your phone number, a brief biography, and your full name even if these are not required.
- Be courteous and sensitive, and express yourself clearly so you will not be misinterpreted.
- Log on and participate regularly.
- For each conference you join, identify your host, moderator, and/or process observer. If there is none, suggest someone experienced in facilitation and conflict resolution.
- Remember that, although network communities make participation convenient, they can also consume inordinate amounts of time. It is easy to get hooked into spending hours a day online that might be better spent in face-to-face bonding with your nearest and dearest. Do not read everything on the network—learn how to select what interests you most—and do not waste time in frivolous wandering or online banter.
- Celebrate online and f2f. Connect by phone also.
- Move toward conscious community by initiating and participating in discussions about your community's goals, ethics, liabilities, and communication style. Keep asking, "What should we all be doing together?" "How can we link up with other communities (electronic and non-) to produce positive change?"

The electronic environment is a rich context in which doing work and sharing work become virtually indistinguishable, and the frequency and spontaneity of interactions equally facilitate task and social exchange. . . . The use of even relatively low technology systems of the sort we employed seems promising not only for work group support but also for the communication of affect and the establishment and maintenance of durable social ties.

Tora K. Bikson and J. D. Eveland

experiment ended, the 'electronic' group was still in communication, and a social support network for retirees had grown out of the original network."

But many do not have access to a computer and a modem. And even if they did, some of them could not join in the online conversations because they cannot read, write, or spell well enough. To such outsiders, electronic network communities look like another kind of private club from which they are excluded. Only strong political will to lessen the gap between the haves and have-nots will enable the full democratic possibilities of computer networking to unfold.

An Electronically Connected and Empowered World

The giants of American communications are locked in a struggle to build and control a vast web of electronic networks. These so-called information highways will be of glass fiber and will deliver an abundance of services to offices and houses—video images, phone calls, helpful data in many guises. They promise to change the way people work and play. In the view of some technologists, they could affect American life as profoundly as railroads, interstate highways, telephones, and TV.

ANDREW KUPFER

Despite the thick floor of poverty and illiteracy that keeps the underclasses from benefiting from electronic communities, the phenomenon of computer networking is exerting a tremendous leveling force—and its global implications are profound. Because of electronic communications, it is no longer possible for governments or hierarchies to put a lock on information. When violence erupted in Tiananmen Square and in the Persian Gulf, when disaster was first suspected at Chernobyl, when tanks headed toward Leningrad for the attempted coup, news flashed instantly around the world from computer to computer. Phone lines were not always necessary; some inter-country connections could be made by satellite and hand-held phones. If the official news media were muzzled, citizen-to-citizen communications were not. And along with firsthand news reports, the networks carried messages of support and understanding. Many consider the Soviet people's use of electronic networking a major factor in stopping the 1991 coup.

Global community building happens through such organizations as the San Francisco–based Institute for Global Communications, the umbrella for PeaceNet, EcoNet, and ConflictNet. These networks have sister organizations in a growing number of cities around the world, including Moscow. Subscribers, from students to national policymakers, share information on everything from political action to how to dispose of radioactive waste. They use the network to produce, edit, and distribute newsletters, plan demonstrations, coordinate food drives, and lobby the United Nations. "The forces for peace," says PeaceNet's director, Howard Frederick, "have the same information as governments." And their views, on the network, have the same weight.

Because local community issues today are interrelated and extend outward into global issues, they must be dealt with at many levels simultaneously. Computer networking has become invaluable—even essential—for disseminating information and coordinating action. It empowers local organizations by linking them with others that share their values and visions. And in a mobile society, where few people stay in one family, job, or physical location long enough to put down roots, computer networks can be the tendrils that maintain connection among far-flung individuals and groups. For example, Chinook, a non-residential learning community near Seattle, established its own network (ChinookNet), which enables members, associates, and former members to stay in touch, continue to offer each other personal support, and share ideas on topics of mutual interest.

The future of electronic community is a moving picture. Certainly, as technology becomes cheaper and public access more widespread, the phenomenon will grow and become more powerful. Each new technological advance will raise new issues. A form of "virtual reality," which makes use of specially designed gloves and miniature video screens mounted in goggles, will let people move images, appear in each other's worlds, and even "touch" each other. How real is virtual? This is a question that will continue to be debated earnestly in online discussions.

It's as easy to program a dictatorship as a democracy in the electronic medium.

MURRAY TUROFF

Jeremy Rifkin and Craig Brod fear that people will be seduced by computers into substituting virtual community for the flesh-and-blood variety, while Mitch Kapor touts electronic forms of communication as "a healthy antidote to the corrosive effects of the power of large, centralized institutions, private and public, and to the numbness induced by one-way, least-common-denominator mass media." All make important points. Electronic technology can turn people into machines and suck the lifeblood out of human interaction, but only if we forget that it is a tool rather than an end in itself. One Oregon-based organization, the Institute for Awakening Technology (IAT), dedicates itself to reminding us that electronic technology is, or can be, a tool that we shape rather than one that merely shapes us. "Technology serves best," say IAT founders Peter and Trudy Johnson-Lenz, "when tailored in support of human values, meaning, and purpose." When the Johnson-Lenzes coined the term "groupware" in 1978 to identify a type of electronic networking, they defined it as "intentional group processes plus the software to support them." They chose to include the software "in the minds and hearts" of those using the technology as well as that in the computer.

One of the social organizations IAT convened between 1988 and 1992 is what it calls a Virtual Learning Community™ for self-development education. The community, whose members around the country communicated electronically through a host computer in Oregon, used a variety of groupware formats for various purposes, including online workshops and mutual support circles.

IAT is currently developing programs for group work by computer that help people solve problems, resolve conflicts, and explore political issues. The Institute believes that electronic democracy can be a lively, deliberative process provided that participants retain the power to frame the issues in their own words rather than responding to frameworks created by others; that they engage in dialogue rather than just voting thumbs up or down; and that they have an opportunity to reflect, consider, and deliberate rather than simply give quick opinions.

Used with wisdom and compassion, computer networks help people adapt to the sometimes frightening new world that technology itself has helped to create. Ignoring electronic technology can be as much a hazard as misusing it; those who cannot adapt to the computer's pervasive presence will eventually isolate themselves. It is essential to stay alert to both the dangers and the incredible opportunities that networks present—to use technology to build real solidarity.

RESOURCES

Recommended books and periodicals

Technostress by Craig Brod (Addison-Wesley, 1984)

Virtual Reality by Howard Rheingold (Summit, 1991)

Leading Business Teams: How Teams Can Use Technology and Group Process Tools to Enhance Performance by Robert Johansen and colleagues (Addison-Wesley, 1991)

Time Wars: The Primary Conflict in Human History by Jeremy Rifkin (Simon & Schuster, 1987)

Computer Mediated Communications by Matthew Rapaport (John Wiley, 1991)

Computer-Mediated Communication Systems by Elaine Kerr and Starr Roxanne Hiltz (Academic Press, 1982)

Whole Earth Review, Summer 1991, section devoted to "electronic democracy"

Organizations

Center for Information Age Technology, New Jersey Institute of Technology, Newark, New Jersey, 07102; (201) 596-3437. Offers support to organizations, individuals, and government and operates a computerized conferencing system called EIES (Electronic Information Exchange System).

Institute for Awakening Technology, 695 Fifth St., Lake Oswego, Oregon, 97034 (503) 635-2615. Groupware (computer-augmented group process), action research, facilitation, and design services. Publications include "Groupware for a Small Planet," and the bulletin *Using Our Differences Creatively*.

Networks

America Online, Quantum Computer Services, 8619 Westwood Center Dr., Vienna, Virginia, 22182; (800) 227-6364

SeniorNet, 399 Arguello Boulevard, San Francisco, California, 94118; (415) 750-5030

The Meta Network, Metasystems Design Group, Inc., 2000 North 15th Street, Suite 103, Arlington, Virginia, 22201; (703) 243-6622

The WELL: The Whole Earth 'Lectronic Link, 27 Gate Five Road, Sausalito, California, 94965; (415) 332-4335

ECHO, 97 Perry Street, Suite 13, New York, New York, 10014; (212) 255-3839

PeaceNet, EcoNet, and ConflictNet, Institute for Global Communications, 18 DeBoom Street, San Francisco, California, 94107; (415) 442-0220

CompuServe Information Service, Box L-477, Columbus, Ohio, 43260; (800) 848-8199

Part Three

New Ways of Living Together

NINE

New Options in Residence Sharing

Many condominiums and cooperative developments are built with privacy, not community, in mind.

DORIT FROMM

FOR MARIE, DIVORCED AND living on a restricted income, the primary impetus for moving in with others was financial. "My rent," she says, "got to where I couldn't manage it." She considered herself lucky to have found an organization that arranged for her to share a rambling suburban house with four other adults and a child. But after living alone and enjoying her privacy for twenty years, Marie found it difficult to adjust to her new roommate situation, which included adults of different ages, genders, and cultural backgrounds, plus three-year-old Zoe.

Only after she fell and broke both wrists did she realize how much of a community her household was. Lois cooked for her, Stephanie bathed her, Mike took her out on drives, and others did errands and laundry. "I was totally astounded," Marie exclaims.

Stephanie, Zoe's mother, cheerfully acknowledges that none of the adult roommates had anything in common before they moved in together, and they still mostly lead separate lives. But she loves her huge, U-shaped house (she could not have afforded more than a studio on her own) and her living situation in general. "It started out as economic necessity, but now we stay together because we're a family."

Judy Timmel and Gary Fields, by contrast, were financially secure enough to consider buying a home of their own. Yet they had no intention of making that kind of investment—until they went to a meeting of a group considering an urban venture billed as "cohousing." Judy had read about cohousing, an approach to residential living that combines private and shared living spaces, and was curious, but "hadn't really expected to be so taken with the idea. It struck a chord with me—it reminded me of the neighborhood I had growing up in the Midwest, that I had been missing but not really consciously." They committed themselves to the venture right away. Says her husband Gary, "I wasn't too keen about buying anything, but I thought this would at least be socially responsible."

Look at all those private houses which are locked up all day. What a waste! You may not realize these houses get lonely just sitting there, hour after hour. Let's encourage daytime occupancy, like bringing in musicians looking for a place to practice, for example, or people working the night shift, or people needing a quiet place to study or work at home. Let's have them use some of this bedroom-community space, fight crime, make money, and keep the block pumped up during the day.

BILL BERKOWITZ

Their new dwelling contains their own complete two-bedroom apartment plus extensive common areas shared with several other households. The group spent nearly two years meeting once a week to plan their custom-built community. By this time there is little they do not know about one another. Although Judy and Gary committed not only time but more than $200,000 to their new home, they feel that what they receive in return is worth the investment.

Between these two extremes is Wes Nisker, a writer who could not afford the cohousing option but liked the idea of shared living. Divorced, with a four-year-old daughter who lived with him half the time, he dreamed of a family-like situation "without the pressure and exclusiveness of the nuclear family." Although he was not actually searching for a group house, when friends told him about one near his ex-wife's neighborhood, he decided it would be convenient for both him and his daughter. After meeting the residents and ascertaining that they shared his values, he rented two rooms in the group's stately, eight-bedroom home. He was pleased that his daughter enjoyed the companionship of seven other adults, one toddler, and assorted dogs and cats.

When Wes decided, years later, to send his daughter to a high-quality public school in another town, the two of them moved. But when they—Wes in particular—found they missed their intentional family and the twice-a-week communal meals, they returned.

More and more Americans yearn for the sense of extended family that comes with shared living. They do not want to grow old or raise their children in a neighborhood or an apartment complex where they hardly know the other residents—where if one of them died or had to be hospitalized, the neighbors would barely take notice. Many of these Americans do not regard themselves as social pioneers or avid communards. Some who have acted on the impulse toward shared living, like Wes and Marie, did not even intentionally search for community in making their arrangements, yet have come to appreciate this social connectedness as much as, if not more than, the practical aspects of living with others.

Some who long for a more communal form of living put off acting on this desire for fear that they will have to give up too much. They view the choice as a rigid either-or dilemma: either they enjoy privacy and control over their living space, but feel lonely and isolated, or they find the social connectedness and mutual support they seek, but lose their privacy and control. The stories and models that follow reveal a more flexible set of choices. Today, options for residence sharing vary as widely as the motives of the residents.

American housing stock is largely designed for the mythical "typical American family," a two-parent household with children and with only one parent employed outside the home. Reality, however, is more complex: only about 20% of American households fit this "typical" description. Can you imagine the shoe industry designing all our shoes in only one single "typical" size? America is a diverse nation and we need alternative housing options.

KEN NORWOOD

THE REWARDS OF SHARING

By now it is no secret that the classic "American Dream" of the single-family home has become, for a growing number of people, just that: a dream, well out of financial reach. In 1991, the Census Bureau reported that 57 percent of all households in the United States could not afford a median-priced house with a conventional mortgage.

The dreamers are changing, as well as the dream. Fewer and fewer families fit the old nuclear model. Even if you do buy a house of your own, you may be too busy to enjoy it, you may have to struggle to keep up the payments while you support your children or parents, or you may find yourself alone in it after a divorce or the death of your spouse. In addition to feeling isolated behind your own four walls, you may be uncomfortable about the environmental effects of single-family neighborhoods.

"Single-family living is more costly—socially, environmentally, emotionally, and in dollars—than shared living community," says Ken Norwood, planner-architect and founder of the Shared Living Resource Center in Berkeley. "For example, a small family living by itself in a suburban house requires a disproportionate amount of water and sewer lines, paved streets, and land. Solar energy usually isn't cost-effective for one family. With no opportunity for buying in bulk, the family uses an excessive amount of packaging, which generates a lot of waste, creating an increased demand for landfill and depletion of the ozone layer. And the family is overdependent on the automobile, which is the prime source of excessive energy and fuel consumption as well as a key contributor to poor air quality."

Growing numbers of Americans are countering the housing trends of recent decades. They have decided that living in an isolated unit, whether it be a single-family dwelling or an apartment, is not for them. *Lifetrends,* an analysis of social trends for the near future, reported that programs to foster shared housing increased by 800 percent from 1981 to 1988. Such programs have continued to proliferate, and many of their clients are solidly middle class. More and more people, including those married and well-off financially, have discovered that they can enjoy a better home with fewer resources if they share, and they are willing to exchange a certain amount of control over their territory for the enriched connections and ethical satisfactions offered by shared living.

Urban communes may be the forerunners of "postbiological" families, where biology no longer determines status, role, who lives with whom, and how decisions are made within a family grouping.

ROSABETH MOSS KANTER

TRENDS IN SHARED LIVING: FROM COMMUNES TO COHOUSING

Back in the late 1960s, the term "shared living" conjured up images of hippie crash pads inhabited by the young and impecunious. Since the inhabitants of such dwellings were rebelling against authority and the "straight" society, they tolerated few rules. Believing that "all we need is love," those at the most casual end of the communal living spectrum developed no systems for sharing tasks or building community together. As a result, their communes—most of which were barely functional and not at all conscious—did not last long. Neither did the more conventional arrangements put together by students and post-students negotiating their passage from dependence on family and educational institution to independence.

Although the latter phenomenon continued (and does to this day), the early hippie communes began to be replaced in the 1970s by more stable, structured cooperative households involving people of varying ages. These groups started setting up systems for managing their living arrangements: formal or informal house meetings, written agreements, work schedules tacked to the wall. They became more purposeful and often more selective. In the wake of the human potential movement, these groups began to take more interest in developing relationship skills.

From the 1980s on, as group living processes became further refined, a systems orientation to shared housing began gradually to emerge. Many households started paying attention not only to their own group dynamics but also to the way they related to the environment and the surrounding community. For example, a group house in Palo Alto issued a standing invitation for outsiders to participate in its "eating club" every Friday night. Other households made it a point to participate in, or even spearhead, neighborhood activities. Recycling became standard practice.

We have found that a major issue in many cooperative households today concerns how to achieve the best balance between individual expression and commitment to changing group needs. Another issue, not so commonly discussed but growing in importance, is how the physical design of housing affects relationships within and without. These two issues form the core of the high-commitment type of shared living called cohousing—a phenomenon that has captured the imagination of thousands and is spreading across the country like grassfire.

Some people think they are in community, but they are only in proximity. True community requires commitment and openness. It is a willingness to extend yourself to encounter and know the other.

DAVID SPANGLER

COHOUSING: HIGH COMMITMENT, HIGH APPEAL

Imagine a living situation in which you enjoy your own private, self-sufficient unit (including kitchen), know your neighbors well and see them often, and share with them extensive common areas such as dining room, large kitchen, garden, workshop, office space, children's playroom—whatever you have all agreed on. This integration of private and shared living spaces defines the essence of cohousing.

A wife/husband team of architects named Kathryn McCamant and Charles Durrett imported the concept into the United States after investigating successful experiments in Denmark. On their return to California, they formed The CoHousing Company to promote the realization of their dream type of community. Variations of cohousing, sometimes going by other names such as "village clusters," were simultaneously being introduced by architects, developers, and potential residents. But Chuck and Katie—as they are known to dozens of U.S. cohousing groups—managed to secure the CoHousing-with-a-capital-H trademark and associate it with a process that is as important as the product. Their book, *CoHousing: A Contemporary Approach to Housing Ourselves*, became the cohousers' bible. They subsequently moved into a cohousing community themselves.

Cohousing is organized, designed, planned, and managed by its residents, with the aid of development professionals. The residents determine how the project looks, how they own and finance it, and how they make decisions. Cohousers also design the housing to encourage community: they conveniently locate common areas so that encounters are natural and built-in, and they plan roads and parking lots so that cars stay on the periphery. A large common kitchen and dining room allow residents to cook and eat some meals together. Most cohousing groups try to create multigenerational communities of singles and families.

The satisfying mix of independence and interdependence, privacy and intimacy holds great appeal. You can experience a kind of extended family while still enjoying the company of other friends in your own private space. On nights that you work late, you can come home to a dinner that someone else has cooked. You take your turn at cooking another time. Your children can feel secure in their own home yet can also readily talk and play with other children and with the adults in their cohousing neighborhood—who can take turns watching over the children. You can engage in common projects with your neighbors without having to share the same ideology. You can also enjoy support and companionship without always needing to make a plan to get together.

With our common meals, common chores and intentional plan to interact, cohousing gives us the framework to break down the barriers. It is an ingeniously gentle way to prod people of different backgrounds and ages to get to know and trust each other.

JON GREER

Forms of Cohousing: Tailored to Members and Site

Cohousing is a concept, not a blueprint. You can readily adapt it to urban, rural, and suburban settings and vary the form depending on the needs and desires of the members.

The first U.S. cohousing community moved in together in 1991. The Muir Commons group settled in Davis, California, a medium-sized town in an agricultural valley. A fifteen-minute drive from Sacramento, Muir Commons houses forty-four adults and twenty-two children on a three-acre site that is part of a larger planned community. Because the developers used the cohousing segment to satisfy the city's affordable-housing requirement, the cost to residents was low for that area: $96,000 to $110,000. The houses consist of duplexes, triplexes, and fourplexes grouped near informal meeting areas along the main pedestrian path. On summer evenings, residents congregate on the long front porch of the large common house.

Landscaping, particularly the edible type, sets Muir Commons apart from other cohousing developments. Residents—some of whom are affiliated with the University of California at Davis, a major center for horticultural research—grow their own fruit trees: peaches, cherries, apricots, pears, plums. They also plant both summer and winter vegetables in an impressive 3,700-square-foot plot. To balance this high level of cultivation, they have left some of the grounds naturally wooded. Both adults and children work in the community's orchards and gardens, and many contributed "sweat equity" to complete paths and landscaping.

The Doyle Street cohousing community in Emeryville, California—where Judy and Gary live—looks and feels quite different. The first U.S. cohousing settlement to be located in a central urban neighborhood, it began with an abandoned factory. The architects, CoHousing founders Chuck and Katie, designed a second-story addition to the original 8,000-square-foot building that allowed for twelve condominium units with lofts.

The high ceilings and illusion of two stories make the units seem larger than they are: 700 to 1,525 square feet. The group devoted more than 2,000 square feet to common facilities, which include a central sitting area with a fireplace.

Although the Doyle Street development boasts no gardens, and the neighborhood looks somewhat bleak, the residents tend five plots in a community garden two blocks away. The Doyle Street community also enjoys the amenities of nearby Oakland, Berkeley, and San Francisco. The Doyle Street residents ponied up $135,000 to $250,000 to be cohousing pioneers.

I was continually amazed at the [Muir Commons] group's determination to honor their processes, to respect one another's opinions, to listen, to concede, to wait and to attend countless hours of meetings. With that kind of energy and history, I'm confident that the community will be a wonderful success.

DON LINDEMANN

These and other cohousing settlements, as far afield as Washington State, Colorado, and Massachusetts, vary in size, landscaping, legal structure, cost, and design. One feature shared by all, however, is the communal kitchen and dining area. This is, according to more than one cohousing dweller, the soul of the community. Muir Commons holds communal dinners four or five evenings a week, plus brunches on weekends. Adults sign up in two-person teams to cook one or two meals the following month. One resident commented, after a Saturday of cooking and eating a particularly delicious meal with his cohousemates, that his living experience was like "a summer camp that goes on forever."

The process of developing and managing cohousing, however, hardly resembles a laid-back summer camp idyll. It can take up to three years of intensive planning, learning, decision making, and community building from idea to move-in, and new issues continue to emerge afterward. Except for the visionary communities described in Chapter Eleven, cohousing requires the highest level of group skills of any of the shared housing types we have found. It also provides the greatest amount of self-determination.

The Process: Not for the Faint of Heart

The journey begins when initiators—usually potential residents, but sometimes developers or architects—post a notice or ad that attracts other interested parties to an initial meeting. Those who show up at this and successive meetings begin to exchange ideas, desires, and personal dreams.

Participants who share a serious intention to embark on a cohousing venture become the *core group* and begin to form committees: membership and recruitment, financial and legal, philosophy, site search, and steering (to coordinate efforts and produce agendas). The *umbrella group,* which includes the core group plus those who have no immediate plans to live in cohousing, continues to meet as a whole. New people join while others depart. Sometimes a trained facilitator conducts a workshop on meeting skills or on consensus decision making, a process adopted by most cohousing groups.

The core group chooses its legal structure—partnership or corporation—and the form of community ownership, for instance, condominium or cooperative. It also finds a site, which for many groups becomes the toughest task of all.

The core group then begins working with architects and developers. Some groups insist on hiring Chuck and Katie, even bringing them in at earlier stages, since they have experience not only in designing cohousing but also in facilitating interactions with developers, securing financing, and teaching group skills. Others prefer to select their own designers and builders.

A natural shakeout period occurs when members must make their first significant financial investment. At this point, those unwilling or unable to make a commitment drop out. Even for those who stay, money often continues to loom as a sensitive issue. Some potential cohousers become diffident about revealing the extent of their resources, even when they must in order to obtain construction financing. "I think it's harder for cohousing groups to talk about money than it is to talk about sex," commented a member of a Seattle group. One solution, some cohousers have found, is to work through a mortgage broker, who can determine the financial capabilities of both individuals and the group. In Emeryville, the developer assumed financial responsiblity and established prices for the units.

Financial issues continue to arise throughout the design phase and test the efficacy of the group process. The greater the sameness of the individual units, and the simpler the common areas, the lower the cost. To meet an acceptable price, members have to agree, not only with each other but also with the developer on common specifications, from use of common areas right down to the color of the paint. The potential for conflict is enormous, as is the need for self-knowledge, knowledge of the rudiments of construction and financing, communication and decision-making skills, stamina, and dedication to the well-being of the community.

Relationships with the wider community can also require attention and work. After being turned down by the Planning Commission twice, the Doyle Street group had to appeal to the Emeryville City Council. "Every member got to know everyone on the commission and the council," says Gary. Commission members had complained that not enough parking space had been included, but Gary thinks they were really suspicious about what the group was up to. Neighbors were concerned that the new residents would change the character of the low-income, racially mixed neighborhood. Although the cohousers had sought diversity, their group ended up white and middle class, partly because of the cost involved. The group invited neighbors to several open houses while construction was proceeding, and gradually everyone's suspicions began to fade.

Not surprisingly in a process this demanding, some potential cohousers drop out early. Others join after some of the decisions already have been made, ensuring themselves fewer months of hassle but also less influence. As new people come in, the core group must bring them up to date. Sometimes the whole collaborative process becomes messy, as members try to balance individual and group needs throughout all the changes.

However, cohousing groups that have persevered, meeting week after week for years and building consensus along the way, say they have formed deep and lasting bonds. By the time they move in, they know each other's needs and opinions and have learned to work together on issues close to their hearts. They may not like everyone else equally, but they feel like family. They have become a conscious community.

Cohousing pioneers caution the growing numbers who contact them for information that it takes a certain type of person to enjoy building this kind of community. Chris Hanson, founder of the Winslow (near Seattle) cohousing group, says that "cohousers are people who believe they can create their own future." They also have to relish group process.

Even after members have settled into their new digs, they continue the collaborative decision-making process. The Muir Commons group, for example, kept struggling over the issue of openness versus privacy. Should they reconsider their policy of no fences separating the backyards? They finally compromised on a range of acceptable fences and lattices that would not completely divide neighbor from neighbor.

An Evolving Model

Jennifer Madden, a cohouser who has written a master's thesis on this form of shared living, notes that a major difference between the European model and the American one is that the latter is "overbuilt" to maintain privacy. The pioneer U.S. cohousers designed large kitchens for individual units, for example, even though they also had common kitchens and knew that they could live more affordably if they pooled more of their square footage. She believes that future developments will venture further from the ruggedly individual American tradition.

As cohousers, architects, and developers increasingly share information, they not only make the road smoother for one another and future groups but also continue to innovate. Enthusiasts have established cohousing networks, including a conference on the computer community called The WELL, and are promoting discussions with cohousers from Europe, where this type of housing has been thriving for more than twenty years. Some of the European ideas—such as designing some units specifically for the elderly and handicapped, and including neighborhood facilities within the plan—are being discussed in a few cohousing groups here. With government funding and sweat-equity programs, even cohousing for the poor is a possibility.

Already, cohousing has become an integral part of budding ecovillage developments in Los Angeles and Ithaca. Since these developments fall into the category of visionary residential communities, you will read more about them in Chapter Eleven.

In previous centuries, households were made up of at least six people. In addition to having many children, families often shared their homes with boarders, relatives, or servants. Relatives usually lived nearby. These large households provided both children and adults with a diverse intergenerational network of relationships in the home. The idea that the nuclear family should live on its own without the support and assistance of the extended family or surrounding community is relatively new, even in the United States.

KATHRYN MCCAMANT AND CHARLES DURRETT

OTHER PATHS TO SHARED LIVING

Despite its appealing blend of private and common space, cohousing may not be your cup of brew. It requires a significant chunk of capital in addition to considerable time and energy. If you are looking for a simpler, less costly type of shared living arrangement, other options abound, as Wes and Marie discovered. Neither had to come up with more than first and last month's rent and a cleaning deposit. Both knew that if the situation did not work to their satisfaction they could move out fairly easily and find another.

Although renting space in existing residences requires a smaller investment of both time and money than cohousing, it does not free you completely from meetings and group decision making. Even households like Marie's and Wes's require agreements among members. Innovative Housing, the organization that put Marie's group together, leased the house, screened the potential cohabitants, counseled them on shared living, and remains available to mediate disputes. In Wes's house, after several members left and long-simmering conflicts rose to the surface, the residents revised their rules and meeting procedures and mandated one member to serve as resident manager and facilitator.

You may have special needs or preferences regarding whom you live with and the amount of space you need. If you are a single parent, you may want to share a house with other single parents who understand your situation and are willing to take turns with child care. Or, if you are an artist or craftsperson and wish to alleviate the isolation that comes from solitary creativity, you may choose to band together with other creative types in a renovated warehouse or other large facility in which each living unit includes a spacious studio. Whether you are an upscale professional or someone just managing to scrape by, you can find or create a situation that possesses at least the potential for community.

Perhaps enduring commitment to those we love and civic friendship toward our fellow citizens are preferable to restless competition and anxious self-defense.

ROBERT N. BELLAH AND COAUTHORS

How One Diverse Household Became a Community

Several years ago, when a group of friends who shared a passion for nonviolent political action decided to look for a house to buy in San Francisco, they faced several challenges common to shared living arrangements. The story of how they met these can help you in your journey toward residential community, even if your situation differs in many details from theirs.

A power inequality existed from the start in this group devoted to the ideal of equality. Only a few of them had accumulated enough money to pool for the down payment. Legally, these few would become the owners and the others would rent from them. Also, the group included singles, couples, and families whose varying needs were not always likely to mesh. In this diverse group, gender and cultural differences were also sure to stir up conflict.

To deal with these differences up front and make their process as conscious and effective as possible, the group met with Ken Norwood, the director of the Shared Living Resource Center. First, Ken took them through a series of exercises zeroing in on individual values, needs, concerns, financial resources, priorities, and visions. Next, the group held brainstorming meetings, some facilitated by Ken, to develop criteria for location and size of the desired house. They used these criteria to produce a wish-list flier to take around to realtors. Before long, the group found a two-flat Victorian, with a view and a garden, that showed possibilities.

By that time, however, the original core group had discovered, through the exercises and brainstorming, that they were not as compatible as they had thought they were. "There were some personality conflicts and differences in child-raising philosophies," one member, Starhawk, recalls. "Then, once we had chosen the house, one family decided they didn't like the neighborhood, so they backed out before escrow closed."

Starhawk, author of the feminist spirituality classic *The Spiral Dance* and several other books, bought the house with her mother (who did not intend to live there) and her friend Rose (who did) as minority investors. The core group, whose membership was shifting, turned its attention to the structure of the house itself. They wanted the physical architecture as well as the social architecture (interpersonal agreements and procedures) to support community.

The physical structure presented challenges. Long and narrow, the house had too few bedrooms and no areas large enough for group members to congregate. With Ken's help, the core group worked out a new design, which includes a large combined kitchen/dining room/living room, where everyone loves to hang out, and a room for celebrations and other kinds of group gatherings. What had been two flats and an attic stacked on top of each other became an integrated three-story house with connecting stairways. The different-sized offices and bedrooms reflect the individual personalities of the members, while the common areas signal their shared desire to interact as a group. The value of an individual's private space, plus a fixed amount per person, determines the amount of rent the nonowners pay Starhawk.

As this household learned early on, families do not always blend readily with singles and couples. But the group did not give up on its ideal of such a diverse household. The current residents, most of whom have been together more than three years, include eight adults, four children, and—on weekends—two teenage daughters of one member.

The two-parent family in this group consists of Laura, Charlie, and their little daughters Florence and Aminatou. For Laura, the homesharing situation proved ideal because it enabled her to stay home with the children without isolating herself from the outside world of adult ideas. Dinner discussions tend to be lively and politically sophisticated. "I don't feel I'm missing out on much," says Laura. Although some of the other adults occasionally help take care of the young children, most of the time they are too busy or away at their jobs, so Laura joined a babysitting co-op.

"I come from a culture where it's normal to live with many other people," says Charlie, who was born in Senegal, West Africa, and feels quite at home in his current situation. An artist, he has contributed vividly to the house in the form of colorfully painted and textured walls, sometimes in exchange for rent. "I'm living with people I can count on," he declares. "Three years ago I didn't sense this, but now we're beginning to say we're creating a family. Sometimes there are frictions, but in our house meetings we tell the truth from the heart." The household has easily absorbed this family because, as Starhawk says, "they're relaxed about their relationship and have strong connections with others in the house. Earlier we had another family here, with one child, and they coalesced into a tight nuclear family. The rest of us felt we were skulking around the edges."

There has been some turnover among the housemates: two adults left amicably because their life situations had changed, and a single mother of the two older children moved in. All involved discussed these changes openly and thoroughly.

House meetings, held every three weeks after dinner, provide a forum for everyone to bring up practical or interpersonal issues. After check-in, during which residents catch up on each other's lives, the meeting proceeds according to an agenda posted several days earlier. Members take turns facilitating meetings and taking notes. They make decisions usually by consensus (including the decision to incorporate the single-parent family), occasionally by default. Since Starhawk pays for most of the renovations, she usually makes the final choices in this one area, but not before presenting her plans to her housemates for approval. The group divides household tasks according to an agreed-upon schedule. Everyone signs up to prepare two to three dinners a month.

As in most shared housing situations, from cohousing to co-renting, a certain amount of miscommunication and conflict is inevitable. If issues cannot be resolved one to one or in house meetings—as was the case when Starhawk's group wrangled over what room should be assigned to a new resident—the members call in a mediator.

Without careful consideration of physical, psychological, and procedural structure, this house could easily have failed to become a community. In this case, early attention to the design of the house as well as to compatibilities and differences among the potential residents forestalled many problems. The group that finally jelled has committed itself to both harmonious relationships and personal growth, and members are willing to consider themselves a family—a unit greater than the sum of its parts. They have established procedures to handle the daily workings of the household as well as to deal with disagreements, and they have learned group skills. They also make it a point to have fun together—to throw parties, take trips to the country, or go bowling as a group.

Finding Your Shared Housing Situation

Not all shared living requires as much intention as the participants in Starhawk's household opted for or as cohousing demands. The kind you choose will depend partly on how consciously you wish to build community and the amount of time you are willing to devote to this process. If you are considering living with others, first clarify the type of situation that will work for you; then, assess your own needs and qualities. Armed with this knowledge, you can begin seeking a compatible set of housemates.

Locating a Group Household

There are three ways that couples maintain the intimacy of their relationship while living communally: They stay in touch with their need to be alone together, they understand that total openness can endanger intimacy, and they are careful not to run away from fights with each other.

ERIC RAIMY

If you prefer to join an existing group household, you might begin your search by asking friends for recommendations. Other avenues are shared housing agencies, roommate referral services, newspaper ads, and community bulletin boards.

When you find a potential household, prepare to be interviewed by those already living there. Use your self-analysis to help answer their questions. Be sure to ask them about house policies: How much togetherness do they expect? What are their procedures for sharing tasks, holding meetings, making decisions, and resolving conflicts? How do they handle household finances? What rules or expectations do they have regarding guests, smoking, sex, drugs, pets, sound levels, and relationships of non-parents to children in the household?

If you feel uncomfortable with a group even though their answers satisfy you, take your emotional response seriously. If possible, check with people who have lived in the household before or who have had other contacts with the group. Spend time with the group or individual members outside the formal interview process.

Starting Your Own Household

Your own shared household can also begin with those you already know and like—friends, colleagues, and acquaintances—as well as people referred by shared housing agencies. Cohousing meetings are good sources of compatible housemates who are interested in conscious community; even if you do not become a cohouser, you may meet others who gravitate toward the same kind of homesharing that you want.

Once you have identified some potential housemates, call a meeting. If the group is large, notice which subgroups develop within it and which you feel most compatible with. Schedule follow-up meetings that require the kind of participation you desire in a household. These will usually shake out the curious from the committed. When you have assembled a compatible group, meet several times for planning and socializing. Find out how well you work and play together.

Shared Housing Self-Assessment

- What do I most want to change about my present living situation? For example, would I like a larger house, lower monthly expenses, or a more sustainable lifestyle? Do I want to learn more about relationships, enjoy more companionship, or include children or elders in my life? Do I desire more support for myself or help with child rearing? Do I long for a family?
- What balance of privacy and closeness do I want? Which of my possessions am I willing to share? With how much conflict and group process am I comfortable?
- How great a time commitment—hours or days per week—am I willing to make? How large a financial commitment? Do I want to buy or rent?
- What are my assets as a housemate or cohouser? What qualities might make me difficult to live with? Am I willing to work on these? What group skills do I possess?
- What type of housemates would I like? Do I prefer non-smokers, non-drinkers, vegetarians? How similar to me do I want them to be in age, race, gender, political persuasion, sexual preference, spiritual orientation, marital status? How do I feel about pets and children? How important is neatness?

Long-term communities must invariably struggle over the degree to which they are going to be inclusive. Even short-term communities must sometimes make that difficult decision. But for most groups it is easier to exclude than include. . . . Communities do not ask "How can we justify taking this person in?" Instead the question is, "Is it at all justifiable to keep this person out?"

M. Scott Peck

Be sure to draw up an agreement specifying how you will handle finances and run the practical aspects of the household, what modifications to the physical structure you wish to make, how the group intends to relate to one another and the surrounding community, and how you can change this agreement. (Some cohousing groups and homesharing agencies can provide model agreements.) You may want to employ a facilitator at this point, or even earlier.

Resources

Recommended books

CoHousing: A Contemporary Approach to Housing Ourselves (Second Edition) by Kathryn McCamant, Charles Durrett, and Ellen Hertzman (Ten Speed Press, 1993)

Shared Houses, Shared Lives: The New Extended Families and How They Work by Eric Raimy (Jeremy P. Tarcher, 1979)

Collaborative Communities: Cohousing, Central Living, and Other Forms of New Housing by Dorit Fromm (Van Nostrand Reinhold, 1991)

The Group House Handbook, by Nancy Branwein, Jill MacNeice, and Peter Spiers (Acropolis Books, 1982)

Living Together: A Year in the Life of a City Commune by Michael Weiss (McGraw-Hill, 1984)

Family, community, education, ecology, peace, civil rights, careers, hobbies—they all need attention, but it's so much ground to cover. We need a cooperative system that's decentralized enough to focus on the individual issues within each category, yet integrated enough that the individual efforts complement each other. Then we as a society can accomplish what we as individuals keep trying to do by ourselves.

GEOPH KOZENY

Organizations

The CoHousing Company, 1250 Addison, Suite 113, Berkeley, California 94702; (510) 549-9980

Innovative Housing, 2169 E. Francisco Blvd., Suite E, San Rafael, California, 94901; (415) 457-4593. Currently focuses on finding shared living situations for the needy, but also publishes a cohousing newsletter.

Shared Living Resource Center, 2375 Shattuck Ave., Berkeley, California, 94704; (510) 548-6608. Provides consultations, slide talks, and workshops about group houses and village clusters. Also offers design and planning services. Publishes a newsletter and other resource materials. Does not provide housemate referrals but does offer counseling on shared living and community building skills.

Co-Op Resource Center, 1442A Walnut St., Berkeley, California, 94709; (510) 538-0454. Nonprofit educational resource center. Publishes information on forming co-ops, including housing co-ops. Also conducts periodic seminars, trainings, and conferences.

Co-Op Camp Sierra, 1442A Walnut St., Berkeley, California, 94709; (510) 538-0454. Runs an annual family camp in California's Sierra Nevada Mountains. Includes a week-long institute on cooperative housing.

National Association of Housing Cooperatives, 1614 King St., Alexandria, Virginia, 22314; (703) 549-5201. Provides publications and trainings, including a yearly training conference.

California Mutual Housing Association, 1678 Shattuck Ave., Suite 72, Berkeley, California, 94709; (510) 548-4087. A "co-op of co-ops" that works to maintain and expand the supply of permanently affordable, resident-controlled housing in California. Provides training, management, development, and advocacy services for housing co-ops, resident-controlled buildings and associations, tenant associations organizing for ownership, nonprofits, and community groups.

Cooperative Resources and Services Project, 3551 White House Place, Los Angeles, California, 90004; (213) 738-1254. Coordinates the LA Ecovillage demo and sponsors a shared housing network. Has a lending library which includes an audio/video collection.

Center for Cooperatives, University of California at Davis, California, 95616; (916) 752-2408. Research, education, and outreach for cooperatives of all kinds in California. Publications include *Cooperative Housing Compendium,* edited by Katie Cohen and Lois Arkin, 1993.

Also see resources for Chapters Ten and Eleven.

TEN

Alternatives to the Retirement Home

SOCIAL SCIENTISTS LOVE TO track the baby boomers, those Americans born between 1946 and 1965 who, if only because of their sheer numbers, are shaping American society. Between 2011 and 2030, this large group of people will be turning sixty-five, at which point they might more fittingly be known as elderboomers. You can be sure that even before they reach their sixties, these boomers will dramatically change the way Americans approach retirement and grow old. The generation before them already has begun to do so, developing options their parents never imagined. In reporting on one set of such options, new forms of shared living for elders, we will give you a taste of the kind of mutual support and connectedness—as well as autonomy—that is possible for singles and couples heading into the autumn of life.

A renewed sense of group cohesiveness, freedom from full-time work pressures so they can follow where their instincts might lead, and discontentment over not quite living the adult life they thought they would, will produce an elderculture reflecting some of the spirit of the 1960s youth culture.

JERRY GERBER AND CO-AUTHORS

Such shared living may not only provide an attractive option but a necessary one as the United States confronts the enormous challenge of housing and caring for its senior citizens in the decades ahead. By 2030, the U.S. Census Bureau estimates, more Americans will have reached the age-sixty-five-and-over bracket than will be under the age of eighteen. This elderboomer bulge of about 66 million Americans will exceed by two and a half times the sixty-five-and-over population segment in 1980. Already, the surge in the number of elders has accompanied a decrease in the amount of affordable housing available. Even those elders fortunate enough to own their own homes may find these increasingly difficult to maintain as they (both the homes and the owners) grow older. And, because families today are so often separated by physical and emotional distance, moving in with relatives may prove impossible or undesirable.

Where everybody is going to live, and with whom, loom as challenging questions, whether you identify yourself as an elder, a potential elderboomer, or somewhere in between. If your parents have reached retirement age, you already may be helping them to determine how they want to live. Even if you are on the low side of midlife yourself, you may have glimpsed the future and decided to begin early to plan not only how to keep a roof over your head but also how to nourish community in your life as you grow old.

It is estimated that half of the residents of nursing homes are mentally and physically fit enough to be leading active, productive lives.

JOHN LOBELL

The housing needs of the healthy and reasonably active seventy- to ninety-year-old include not only economical shelter, but also safety and companionship.

CHESTER A. WIDOM

THE PROBLEM WITH CONVENTIONAL APPROACHES

Each of the three most common current models for living out your later years—nursing homes, continuing-care retirement communities (CCRCs), and living in your own home—present serious drawbacks, especially for middle- or low-income people desiring conscious, diverse community. Most nursing homes provide for basic physical and medical needs but offer little in the way of privacy, autonomy, personal attention, and cultural stimulation. Unfortunately, many elders end up in such institutions even when able-bodied because their families or the state can find no other place for them. With the over-eighty-five segment of the population now the most rapidly growing age group, this trend will continue unless new approaches grow and spread.

Continuing-care retirement communities—which make up the fastest-growing segment of the senior-citizens' housing market, according to *Consumer Reports*—appeal to those in high-income brackets. CCRCs are part residence, part insurance policy: in return for a hefty entrance charge plus a monthly fee, they promise you meals, a place to live for the rest of your life, and nursing care if you should need it. About a third of them are large facilities operated by hotel corporations. While many friendships undoubtedly flourish in these settings, residents tend to interact with a narrow range of people through highly programmed activities. Although many older people enjoy life in their CCRCs, these developments remain too expensive for fifty percent of the elderly. A few CCRCs are on such shaky financial ground that they fail to deliver what they promise.

No wonder eighty-six percent of the elders recently surveyed by the American Association of Retired Persons declared that they wanted to stay in their present homes forever. It does seem more reassuring to remain in a familiar place. But, besides being increasingly difficult to maintain, that place may be very lonely if your mate has died, your children live far away, and your friends do not stay put.

In adolescence, when so many interests are shared with others and one has great stretches of free time to invest in a relationship, making friends might seem like a spontaneous process. But later in life friendships rarely happen by chance: one must cultivate them as assiduously as one must cultivate a job or a family.

MIHALY CZIKSZENTMIHALYI

THE POSSIBILITIES OF SHARED SOLUTIONS

Fortunately, you need not be limited by the above three choices as you plan your later years, nor need you become paralyzed by fear at the prognostications of social scientists. Their projections assume that the culture will continue to operate as it does now, with the well-off paying top dollar for private solutions and those not so well off competing for slices of a smaller pie of public support. These projections do not take into account the effect of attitudes and approaches that go "outside the lines" of the current culture. A trend toward small-scale, voluntary communities of mutual support already has begun to generate creative solutions for elder-friendly shared living, including multi-generational arrangements. Some groups have developed these privately, while others have forged innovative bonds between the private and the public sectors.

Sharing housing with others—your own house or another dwelling—offers a way to preserve emotional stability, heal feelings of loss, renew a sense of family, provide physical security, and keep your mind alive through learning from others. It can ease financial stress and make continued independence possible through interdependence.

If you are a boomer approaching elder status, you are likely to be more receptive than your forebears to sharing schemes that encourage community. As Jerry Gerber and his coauthors point out in *Lifetrends*, "Given their experiences with communal living while young, [boomers] should have fewer inhibitions about sharing housing than has any previous generation of elders. Many will either live together in arrangements they improvise for themselves or find created by government, or be friendly with people who do and will be considering doing so themselves. Their needs for social support and intimate friendship will engender familylike networks within these communities, even if the stated goal of the undertaking is merely to provide a place for them to live."

As elders learn about new kinds of housing options and create others, they and those who follow them will realize that packaged, institutional living and living alone no longer remain their only alternatives. A range of shared-living options is emerging that provides varying degrees of self-determination, intimacy, and financial investment.

When small groups of unrelated [older] individuals join forces and share a common space, it benefits them and the community at large. More housing is available for younger families, homes are kept in better repair, there is a reduced need for support services, and the cost to the community of nursing-home care is cut in half.

JANE PORCINO

COOPERATIVE HOMES FOR SENIORS: INDEPENDENCE PLUS COMMUNITY

When Jim Slavin was widowed at the age of eighty, he continued to live in the home he had shared with his wife until he found it too difficult to maintain the house and yard. He then moved into a 160-room complex for seniors, but it did not take him long to realize that "this hotel living wasn't for me." At a friend's suggestion, he applied to live at Harvest House, and when his application was accepted, Jim found a real home again.

Harvest House, a two-story estate just outside the town of Syosset, Long Island, is administered by a warm, feisty nun in her sixties named Sister Jeanne Brendel. Sister Jeanne, who had been working with the elderly for more than two decades, had determined that what many of them needed was a place where they could feel independent but also part of a family. While she gathered funds through her network of fellow religious, she set up a nonprofit foundation and searched for a house. Harvest House turned out to be just what she was looking for, except for one thing: the neighbors would not permit a colony of older people living in their backyard. Undeterred, Sister Jeanne and her lawyer took the case as far as the New York Supreme Court, which ruled in her favor.

Today, she says, "our residents are our goodwill ambassadors." In fact, many friends, relatives, and neighbors who visit end up volunteering to help out. And Harvest House can use all the volunteers it can attract. There is no staff, and although all the residents—the house has room for eight plus Sister Jeanne—pitch in to cook and clean, their advanced ages prevent them from doing heavy chores. Harvest House is not for people who need nursing care. It is for seniors who like what Sister Jeanne calls "relational" living. It has generated such a positive response that she has started a similar residence in nearby Suffolk County.

"When a man's wife dies," Jim Slavin muses, "he loses three-quarters of his life, not just half. The wife was the one who created the comforts of home, the one who was the binder and nourisher. Here, I have the same kind of domestic situation I had before, except that my wife isn't here." Jim, whose energy belies his years, enjoys helping prepare dinner and serving the drinks and appetizers before everyone sits down at the table. Some of the food comes from the vegetable garden tended by one of the other house members.

While Harvest House holds no regular house meetings and posts no sets of rules and regulations, its members expect that all will treat each other with respect. Everyone contributes to the best of his or her ability and pays attention to the others' needs. While only Sister Jeanne and one other house member own cars, both happily give the others rides to town with them.

The rent at Harvest House is minimal for that area, and the living gracious. Its facilities even include a swimming pool. But to Jim, it is the spirit of the house, facilitated by Sister Jeanne, that makes it an attractive home. This spirit is infectious. "One couple, who are friends of mine, are so delighted with the house that they come over and prepare dinner for us once a month," says Jim.

Many seniors find cooperative living with peers a satisfying solution to two age-aggravated problems: financial constraints and loneliness. Today, these seniors can choose among a variety of forms, each with different degrees of independence and privacy. An organization in West Hollywood, California, called Alternative Living for the Aging, offers several of these choices.

Like Sister Jeanne Brendel, ALA founder Janet Witkin identified a strong need for non-institutional housing that would enable seniors to take charge of their own lives while enhancing each other's. And like Sister Jeanne, she formed a nonprofit organization to turn her dream into reality. ALA now manages five co-op houses for people sixty-two and older, and also matches up older people to share housing in their own homes or apartments.

In two of the co-ops, residents enjoy private bedrooms and baths, which they stock with their own furnishings, and share the rest of the house. Five evenings a week, a cook prepares their dinner; residents set the table and clean up on a rotating basis. A cleaning service cleans the common areas twice a month. The other co-ops resemble independent "apartment communities" in which each person or couple resides in a complete private unit but shares responsibility for the running of the overall facility. In all the co-ops, members meet together regularly with ALA staff to iron out any issues and to solidify their identity as a group.

"You could live in a big apartment complex and never know your neighbors," comments Edie Margolis, a resident of El Greco, an ALA apartment community. "But here, everybody's family. We help each other.

Many successful [homesharing] matches involve persons who share commonalities such as age, education, cultural background, interests, and health histories. Certainly there are exceptions. In one case a person with severe vision problems was matched with a person who enjoyed good vision but had trouble hearing. The two were able to help each other live fuller, richer lives by assisting each other in filling in what each had previously had to miss.

JO HORNE

One of us commented that this is an oasis in a social desert, and I really agree with that."

Edie's fellow residents in the gracious, Spanish-style building consist of a dozen other people ranging in age from sixty-four to eighty-two ("But don't let that eighty-two-year-old's age fool you. He's the most active of all of us"). Fausto and Conchita are a couple and the rest are singles. Although the co-op schedules no formal communal dinners, residents regularly gather for conversation at the umbrella table in the central courtyard, and a spontaneous potluck sometimes results.

Americans 60 and older have changed little in their strong preference (78% in 1986 and 75% in 1989) to live in a neighborhood with people of all ages. If they had to move into an apartment, however, respondents in 1989 (40%) are more likely than those in 1986 (32%) to prefer a "senior citizen" building to one for all age groups.

AMERICAN ASSOCIATION OF RETIRED PERSONS (AARP)

The El Greco association, composed of all the residents, makes decisions about such topics as community gardening. As in the other ALA co-ops, the El Greco residents look out for one another by way of a buddy system. "My buddy Muriel and I use night lights and mini-blinds," Edie explains. "If the blinds in the other's apartment are closed in the morning or the lights are on, we go see if everything is okay." On the pantry door in each apartment, ALA has provided residents with a list of all the other El Greco members, along with emergency phone numbers, names and addresses of closest kin, types of ailments and medications, and names of doctors.

Even large institutions can nourish the growth of community if they are managed with the right structure and attitude. In Minneapolis, you could drive right by a massive white brick building, which looks something like a hospital, and never guess that dozens of community-building activities are going on inside—or that the participants enjoy a median age of eighty-four. Seventy-Five Hundred York, the building's address and its name as well, is the oldest senior cooperative in the country. Opened in 1978 by the Ebenezer Society of the Norwegian Lutheran Church, it has retained the spirit of fellowship that was a way of life for its founders.

As a cooperative, 7500 York is run by its 440 resident owners, who select the board of directors and, as members of various committees—Finance, Property, Food Service, and so forth—guide the board in policymaking. Subcommittees such as Life Enrichment, Music, Gardening, and Neighbor Awareness work in partnership with the staff, which is still managed by the Ebenezer Society. The original director, Ray Johnson, spelled out the assumptions that continue to characterize the co-op's spirit: older people want to live independently, but also desire to be part of an independent community which decides its own destiny; they want to cooperate in the development of a community which cares about each other; they are creative and talented; there is some wellness in every older person that enables that person to contribute to the life of the community.

Thus you can find a ninety-two-year-old expert repairing equipment ranging from coffeepots to VCRs, as well as an eightyish woman who has had a knee replaced serving on two committees, playing the saxophone, and coordinating projects for the Children's Home Society. Residents routinely trounce the staff in croquet tournaments.

The members of 7500 York reach out not only to the neighborhood and city community but also to future residents of their own building. They send newsletters to those on the waiting list and host events for them. By the time these hopefuls actually move in, they feel like part of the family.

I think of age as a great universalizing force. It's the one thing that we all have in common. . . . Aging begins with the moment of birth, and it ends only when life itself has ended. Life is a continuum; only, we—in our stupidity and blindness—have chopped it up into little pieces and kept all those little pieces separate.

MAGGIE KUHN

Multi-generational Homes: Helping Seniors Stay Young at Heart

While residents of senior co-ops feel comfortable sharing living arrangements with their peers, others simply do not want "to live with a bunch of old folks," as one crusty senior put it. If you would rather share with people of different age groups, you are likely to find an increasing number of multi-generational options within your reach, including cohousing and the other shared-living arrangements described in the previous chapter. Those developing such options often actively seek a mix of older and younger people. The mix works well at Santa Rosa Creek Commons, a private cooperative in Santa Rosa, California, and at The Avenue in Madison, Wisconsin, a cooperative venture developed by private and public organizations.

Eighty-plus Helen Perkins, one of the founders and oldest residents of Santa Rosa Creek Commons, recalls that a larger group, mostly Quakers, of which she was a part talked about living together for years. Some members, Helen reports, bought country property near Santa Rosa in 1970 and developed it into a neighborhood that they call Monan's Rill. "But some of us decided we weren't rural, so we bought this place."

The Commons, a twenty-seven-unit low-rise complex, which looks from the outside like other apartment complexes in the neighborhood, has functioned as a multi-generational, mixed-income cooperative since 1982. Its midtown location qualifies it as urban today. Santa Rosa has grown exponentially over the past decades from a small farming town to a bedroom community for San Francisco commuters to a city in its own right.

Elders outnumber the younger members of this cooperative in part because the lender required that half the owners be over sixty-five. The Commons designated some units, by arrangement with another funder, as low-income rental housing. The thirty-five adults and twelve children who live here deepen their friendships by gathering for regular meetings and celebrations in the common building, sharing their stories, and working together on the property. Residence agreements require that everyone commit at least eight hours a month to the cooperative, including serving on any two committees. Helen says most people put in a lot more time than that. She herself devotes around thirty hours, some of them to yard work. Somehow she still finds time to produce a newsletter for her local Quaker meeting and to volunteer her services to such organizations as the Guatemalan School Fund and the Peace Network.

One of the casualties of the decline of community has been the bond between the youngest and the oldest citizens. This is no small loss to community: The bond between young and old is unique in its capacity to build in the young their attachment to history and renew in the old their attachment to the future.

RICHARD KORDESH

In the Quaker tradition, cooperative members make all decisions at the Commons' monthly business meetings by consensus. Although the children do not participate directly in the decisions, they provide input and are listened to with respect—but they occasionally get their grammar corrected. The Parents and Children's Committee actually includes children. "Oh, I get irritated at the children sometimes, or rather at parents who expect the rest of us to look out for them, but I guess they keep me young," says Helen.

A minuscule turnover rate and a waiting list of several years testify to the desirability of The Commons. Any prospective resident must survive an extensive application procedure—months of attending meetings, writing letters, being interviewed, and filling out forms. The procedure itself intentionally weeds out those with commitment problems. The Commons takes commitment seriously. It also pays attention to process and to the community's progress along the spectrum from functional to conscious. Once a year, the members hold an evaluation meeting to determine how they can improve their sense of community.

Helen hopes she will never have to leave the Commons. But if she becomes unable to handle the physical responsibilities, she plans to move to a Quaker retirement home in Santa Rosa. She wants the Commons to remain a vital residence for the able-bodied.

If you prefer a less stringent commitment but still seek cooperative living, new alternatives are opening up. "Across the country," reports *Lifetrends,* "old hotels, hospitals, churches, schools, and factories have been transformed into elder housing through federal grants from the Administration on Aging along with efforts by local government agencies and private nonprofit organizations. Many of these projects provide a community as well as a home." The Madison Mutual Housing Association and Cooperative exemplifies such efforts and serves other generations as well. In partnership with Wisconsin Power and Light Holdings Inc., as well as various government agencies and organizations that serve the elderly, the nonprofit

MMHA sponsors two housing cooperatives designed, as an MMHA brochure declares, "to provide quality living for a mix of people reflective of the current neighborhood—young professionals, families, older adults, and people in need of physically accessible housing—and is affordable to a mix of incomes."

One of these developments, The Avenue, illustrates what a concerted effort by individuals, government, and private business can accomplish. Remodeling of an old hospital and medical school created a four-building, forty-unit residence with one-, two-, and three-bedroom apartments, among them six that are fully accessible to people in wheelchairs. Picnic tables in the central courtyard feature extended tabletops to accommodate the wheelchairs. The Avenue adjoins central Madison's Graaskamp Park—the state's first park designed to accommodate disabled people—which was also developed by MMHA.

Home-matching services are forming in various places around the country. However, they still aren't keeping pace with the potential demand. Communities can help close this gap by organizing services to bring people together to satisfy their housing needs. The results can be better communities, with more available and affordable housing, and better lives for many people.

LEAH DOBKIN

Designed by a respected nonprofit architectural firm, Design Coalition, and co-sponsored by Access to Independence, Independent Living, and Options in Community Living, The Avenue includes a spacious community room that provides a pleasant meeting place not only for residents but for members of the surrounding neighborhood as well. As with Sister Jeanne's Harvest House, however, neighbors were suspicious or even hostile when MMHA announced development plans. But after the organization invited them to take part in planning meetings, foes turned into fans. The neighbors ended up helping to decide everything from the location of parking entrances to the type of applicants who would be accepted. Kids even contributed their ideas—climbing structures and a sledding hill—to the design of Graaskamp Park. The Avenue's residents participate in selecting and interviewing newcomers and in making management decisions along with MMHA. The cooperative expects all members to join committees to maintain the property.

MMHA took advantage of a federal tax credit for low-income housing, and WPL Holdings provided nearly half the funding as an equity investment, from which it expects a healthy return. More than a hundred other individuals and companies invested as well, receiving not only financial benefits but also the satisfaction of helping to build neighborhood community. If you belong to a housing cooperative or a nonprofit organization that would like to emulate The Avenue, MMHA offers information as well as training in such topics as board management, meeting and decision-making skills, conflict resolution, starting housing cooperatives, and racial sensitivity.

As the idea of shared housing gains respectability and government regulations ease, Americans can look forward to more innovations in home-sharing that will welcome the elderly. Elders today can make lively, desirable companions for younger housemates. Rather than simply retiring from their jobs and from the world, many are taking on new part-time work, starting their own businesses, volunteering, and consulting. More and more are enrolling in courses and often combining education with travel. As the boomers become elderboomers, they will continue to challenge themselves and society through personal growth endeavors and social activism. And, as they free themselves from the dual burden of child-raising and earning a family-sized income, they will have more time to devote to such passions. Housemates should not assume, however, that elders will be willing to provide free child care or act as mom and dad to the group. These vital seniors are more likely to feel that, at last, they can pursue their own interests.

I work more now because at this time of my life I am not disturbed from my aim by outside pressures such as family, passionate relationships, dealing with "who am I?"—those complications when one is searching for one's self. I have no doubt who I am.

JEANNE MOREAU

SHARING A HOUSE—YOUR OWN OR SOMEONE ELSE'S

Some seniors have discovered the benefits, and challenges, of sharing on a smaller scale by moving in with someone else who appreciates the companionship and the lower living costs. But if you have grown attached to your own home, you may dislike the idea of leaving it when you grow old, even for a fancier house. In that case, you might consider taking in a housemate—someone either your own age or of a different generation. You can avoid the dangers and the hassle of screening potential home-sharers by arranging for an agency to conduct the initial evaluations.

Eighty-eight-year-old Estelle Gannon could not imagine leaving the community that had been her home for twenty years, or giving up her rosebushes and fruit trees. But her legs got so bad she had to use a motorized cart to get around. She had too much room in her house and not enough energy to keep it in good shape. So Project Match in San Jose, California, found her a series of temporary housemates who were happy to look after Estelle and to help with the house and garden in exchange for a room for only $200 a month. One of them, Toni Mefford, a forty-five-year-old secretary, faced a two-hour daily commute between her job and her own home in another town. Toni freed herself from this grind by staying with Estelle during the week and traveling to her own house only on weekends. This practical solution brought rewards Toni had not expected. The women became such fast friends that, Toni reports, "I hate leaving her."

Innovative Housing, as well as Project Match and ALA, matches seniors with peers or with younger adults who, like many people recently, find themselves facing a tight and expensive housing market. These agencies require both homeowners and tenants to complete questionnaires, provide references, and participate in face-to-face interviews. College and university offices often provide more informal matching services to seniors who live near the campus and want to rent a room to a student.

The person we are today is the person we will be when we are old. If there are special preparations to be made for old age they will have to be changes we make in ourselves today.

MICHAEL PHILLIPS

If you do not relish the idea of sharing your personal space with a housemate, you may prefer a more elaborate option, offering more privacy: a new rental unit built right within your house. Patrick Hare, a Washington-based consultant, estimates that about one of every three single-family homes contains enough surplus space to accommodate one of these "accessory apartments." He warns, however, that constructing one of these units may involve expensive permit fees and annoying regulatory mazes.

You might consider renting an apartment adjacent to that of a family member. Another option, ECHO housing (Elder Cottage Housing Opportunity), involves installing a prefab stand-alone unit on a relative's, usually an adult child's, property. Patterned after an Australian program that calls the units "granny flats," ECHO housing provides closeness without intrusion, a happy solution for many families.

Laying the Foundation Now

The best time to plan for post-retirement living is pre-retirement. If you think you might want to share living space with others as you grow older, begin now to figure out what kind of sharing you would prefer.

Jane Porcino, gerontology expert and author of *Living Longer, Living Better: Adventures in Community Housing for Those in the Second Half of Life*, firmly believes that you need to put conscious effort into creating community that will sustain you as you grow older. After raising seven children in a suburban house, she and her husband, Chet, by then in their sixties, moved into a large apartment building near New York City's East River. There they discovered that not all New Yorkers, despite their reputation, prefer to keep their doors shut and their business to themselves. Chet sent letters to sixteen people in their building, inviting them to help start a monthly potluck dinner and discussion group. "Every one of them responded," Jane reports, "and at our first meeting we could see how hungry for community they were." The dinner group, which ranges in age from

Before Plunging into Elder-Friendly Shared Living, Ask Yourself These Questions

- Will I be the type to share housing when I am older? Am I flexible, or am I becoming fussy, picky, and attached to a fixed routine? Am I relatively free from emotional problems?
- Where do I want to live as I move toward the end of life? Do I want to be in an urban or a rural area? What kind of climate would I like best? Do I want to live near friends, family, a college or university, medical facilities, or a religious center?
- What size group appeals to me most? Should I look for an extended family or a more separate, private situation? Do I prefer an intergenerational group or would I rather live with peers? Am I willing to open my home to others?
- What kind of financial resources will I have?
- If I do not stay in my present home, shall I move into an established residence, use the services of an agency, join a cooperative to plan a community, or start my own shared housing?

To further help you decide whether such shared living is for you, review the questions at the end of the previous chapter.

Why can't we build orphanages next to homes for the elderly? If someone's sitting in a rocker, it won't be long before a kid will be in his lap.

Cloris Leachman

fifty-five to seventy-five, discusses books or a topic such as parenting your adult children.

Over time, group members have begun to share cars, attend the theater together, and help each other in emergencies. Once, when heart problems sent Chet to the hospital, others in the group joined Jane there to keep her company. "We haven't pushed for community. Developing trust takes time, and we want to just let it evolve," says Jane, who also belongs to a women's support group.

Two of her children have become involved in the Pioneer Valley cohousing group in Massachusetts and would love to have their parents join their community. Although the intergenerational aspect of Pioneer Valley attracts Chet and Jane, they also love the excitement and convenience of New York—as well as their dinner group—and prefer to remain in the city. Since they may not be able to afford to stay indefinitely in their non-rent-controlled apartment, Chet and Jane have joined a New York City cohousing group that is exploring options for metropolitan shared living. Because the two of them are willing to make the effort to create community, they will undoubtedly enjoy a wide circle of support and companionship until the end of their lives.

Sophie Otis, a San Francisco psychotherapist, started planning her post-retirement community long before she knew she would need it. She and six other members of her women's group, after observing their parents become isolated as they aged, decided that they did not want to follow suit. "We wanted to continue having stimulation, support, and the emotional challenge of relating," Sophie recalls.

Where we live and how we live is such an intrinsic part of our daily existence that even thinking about making a change can be unsettling. But once you get started, simply by reaching out for information you begin to make connections with others engaged in the same search.

MICKEY TROUB FRIEDMAN

Although the women had known each other since their children attended the same cooperative nursing school in Manhattan Beach, California, many changes had occurred in their lives since then: marriages, divorces, remarriages, moving to new locations. Still, the women had stayed in touch and kept up with each other's shifting family lives. By the time they were well into midlife, according to Sophie, "we were determined to put our rocking chairs on the same porch."

With their spouses and partners, they began researching types of communities and looking for property both in northern California and in southern California. The northerners found a site first: twenty acres on the Navarro River in the Anderson Valley, three hours from San Francisco. By this time, another couple had joined the group, and the full complement of eleven people—singles and couples ranging in age from forty-five to sixty-three—put together a legal general partnership and bought the property. They then hired an architect to help them design two buildings with plenty of community rooms, including a library and that porch for the rocking chairs. Ramps and wide doors make everything wheelchair accessible. They are turning two small existing buildings on the property into bunkhouses where visiting children can stay, thus encouraging multi-generational community.

Despite forbidding commute distances, the partners have met faithfully once a month, in either the north or the south of the state, to plan their community. Although similar to cohousing groups in several ways—for example, they make consensus decisions on everything, including building design—this group enjoys more common history and homogeneity than most. The majority have known each other for many years—their children grew up as extensions of each other's families—and share values, such as a commitment to reduce demands on the earth. And, because they were all financially secure homeowners to start with, they have found making money decisions relatively easy. Still, the members discovered much to learn about themselves and each other. "We're becoming more like a family as we see how we fight," reports Sophie, who finds the learning process invigorating. "We know our friendship can endure conflict now. We can tell each other what we want." She adds, "This is the most exciting thing that's happening in my life right now."

What though youth gave love
and roses,
Age still leaves us friends and
wine.

THOMAS MOORE

Given their age differences and various retirement plans, the group members will not move en masse to the Anderson Valley. Some will settle there earlier than others. Those who are still years away from retirement will visit the place periodically while they sort out how they want to wind down their careers. Their shared housing arrangement resembles a semi-retirement community, with future security built in.

As the stories in this chapter illustrate, with a little research and planning you can achieve the kind of life you want as you grow older. The process will be easier if you begin now to learn the communication, decision making, and conflict resolution skills that will make you a compatible community member. By remaining open to new ideas and pursuing your own individual development, you will become both an interesting and a congenial housemate. And whether you opt for shared residence or not, you will find that the best old-age insurance consists of lively, even challenging, interactions with other people.

RESOURCES

Recommended books and articles

Lifetrends: The Future of Baby Boomers and Other Aging Americans by Jerry Gerber, Janet Wolff, Walter Klores and Gene Brown (Macmillan, 1989)

Living Longer, Living Better: Adventures in Community Housing for Those in the Second Half of Life by Jane Porcino (Continuum, 1991)

Age Wave: The Challenges and Opportunities of an Aging America by Ken Dychtwald and Joe Flower (Jeremy P. Tarcher, 1989)

Caring Strangers: The Sociology of Intergenerational Homesharing by Dale Jaffe (JAI Press, 1989)

"Perfect Match" by Sue Briante in *San Jose Mercury News,* January 22, 1992

Shared housing facilitators

Note: There are dozens of shared housing resource centers around the country. Seek out one near you through the ones listed here or through your state and local social service agencies for housing or the aged.

National Shared Housing Resource Center, 136½ Main Street, Montpelier, Vermont, 05602; (802) 223-2667

Project Match, Inc., 1671 Park Avenue, Room 21, San Jose, California, 95126; (408) 287-7121

Alternative Living for the Aging, 937 N. Fairfax Ave., West Hollywood, California, 90046; (213) 650-7988

ECHO/Project Share, 3102 Telegraph Avenue, Berkeley, California, 94705; (510) 845-9030

Innovative Housing, 2169 East Francisco Blvd., Suite E, San Rafael, California, 94901; (415) 457-4593. Publication: *Prolonging the Good Years: Guidelines for Planning and Implementing Nonprofit-Sponsored Shared Housing for Seniors*

Madison Mutual Housing Association & Cooperative, The Livery, 200 North Blount Street, Madison, Wisconsin, 53703; (608) 255-6642. Provides information on developing and running a housing cooperative.

Other organizations

The Gray Panthers, 311 S. Juniper St., Philadelphia, Pennsylvania, 19107; (215) 545-6555. Fifteen dollars gets you their newsletter, but no one is excluded for inability to pay.

American Association of Retired Persons (AARP), 1909 K Street, NW, Washington, D.C., 20049; (202) 434-2277. Publishes *Housing Options for Older Americans, Understanding Senior Housing for the 1990s,* and *A Consumer's Guide to Homesharing.*

Patrick H. Hare Planning & Design, 1246 Monroe Street, NE, Washington, D.C., 20017; (202) 269-9334. Provides information on accessory apartments, and zoning requirements.

Also see resources for Chapters Nine and Eleven.

ELEVEN

Visionary Residential Communities:

R & D Centers for Society

In the communal vision of the ideal life, relationships are loving; work is meaningful; behavior is self-fulfilling. The closeness to other people is mirrored in a closeness to nature and the supernatural. Machines serve people and nature, not the reverse.

ROSABETH MOSS KANTER

SALLY SNYDER'S HEART WAS pounding so hard that she almost had to pull off the Interstate. The magnitude of her decision had suddenly struck her. After more than a year of serious consideration, she and her two children were about to join an intentional residential community in rural Oregon, an hour and a half from the nearest city.

For years Sally had longed for an opportunity like this, and both she and the residents of this family-style community, Alpha Farm, sensed a good fit. Yet her mind pummeled her with questions: What will it really be like to live at Alpha? Can I do the work the community will expect of me? Will my kids fit in?

A few years later, Sally laughs about her panic attack on Interstate Five. Even though the going has not always been easy, she knows she has made the right decision for herself and her children. "I've always wanted to work for positive change in the world," she comments. This full-time immersion in new ways of living has given her a chance to do that. Alpha residents make decisions by consensus, share their income, and, as their literature professes, seek "to nurture harmony within ourselves, among people, and with the earth."

Previously, Sally had lived in Eugene, working at a job she liked but considered "neutral" when it came to social transformation. Besides, working full time outside her home prevented her from spending enough time with her then nine-year-old daughter and eight-year-old son. At Alpha, the work-family-recreation aspects of Sally's life blend into each other. Her forty-five-hour-per-week work commitment can include, for example, gardening—which had always been a passion of hers—volunteering in her children's classrooms in a nearby town, and putting her small-business expertise to use by keeping the books at Alpha-owned stores.

Before World War II intentional community seemed to be a prophetic gesture outside the mainstream of society. But now the intentional communities movement is one of society's crucial growing points.

GEORGE INESON

Sally most appreciates the parenting support she receives. "I like not having to be the 'heavy' all the time," she comments. "Here other adults can be special friends to each of my kids, and there's a parenting team that meets every week." One of these special adult friends to her kids has turned out to be special to her as well. As Rick became closer to the children, his relationship with Sally deepened. Eventually they began living as a family, and Rick and Sally chose to have a child together.

If you, like Sally, dream of living in a residential community where you and others integrate your work, play, family life, and social and spiritual ideals, you will be happy to know that Alpha is one of hundreds of such communities scattered across North America, each with its own vision and approach to shared living. If you find these endeavors intriguing but not for you, you may still wish to read on. You may discover that you can adapt the life skills and community-building arts these visionary groups have been honing for years to your own family, workplace, or neighborhood. Most of today's intentional residential communities view themselves and the systems they employ as models for the wider culture. "We're the research and development centers for society," quips Corinne McLaughlin, co-founder of Sirius Community in Massachusetts. Visionary residential communities, which are among the few places you can find deep community, continuously develop—and in some cases have pioneered—many of the methodologies we describe in the last part of this book.

VISIONARY COMMUNITIES COME OF AGE

Although Sally's living situation turned out even better than she had expected, her jitters on the verge of joining her visionary residential community were only natural. She was about to make a long-term commitment to values and a lifestyle significantly different, in many ways, from those of the dominant culture. If you choose to make such a commitment to a communal way of life, you may find the experience somewhat like marrying outside your race or social class. Your family and friends may not understand or may feel threatened by your choice, and the larger society will hardly encourage it. You had better be convinced that your new life will be innately satisfying, because you may not find much external support for the union.

The local group is only a small fragment of the total world; when isolated the community may develop personal tensions and internal preoccupations to the point that wider perspectives tend to fade. The result can be a self-centered community that is as pathological as a self-centered individual.

GRISCOM MORGAN

But while your commitment to your community's vision and way of life may separate you from much of mainstream culture, it will link you with a long tradition of communards typically labeled "Utopian." The word itself comes from the title of Sir Thomas More's sixteenth-century book, *Utopia*, describing a perfect political and social system on an imaginary island. However, the practice of attempting to establish such idealistic systems and communities dates much farther back. In 200 B.C., for instance, the Essenes banded together in what is now Israel to escape from corrupting materialism and embrace purifying spiritualism.

In the 1800s, the Utopian movement in the United States spawned the Shaker, Oneida, and Amana communities, among others. The Shakers still exist, although their tradition of celibacy has thinned their ranks. A wave of idealistic back-to-the-land commune-ism, paralleling the rise of urban hippie communes, swept the country in the late 1960s. And from the 1970s on, intentional residential communities, mostly land-based like those of the previous century, have been springing up and taking hold. Today an estimated five hundred thrive in North America alone, many of them linked in a loose network that spans the globe.

These days, most such communities prefer not being labeled Utopian. Not only has this term acquired a pejorative meaning, suggesting pie-in-the-sky, unrealistic goals, but it also describes a tradition of communities that purposely chose to isolate themselves so that, like the Essenes, they could retain their purity in an impure society. Unlike these Utopias of the past, most of today's visionary residential communities ground themselves in contemporary reality and encourage interaction with, even participation in, the surrounding culture. Many operate guest programs that welcome outsiders onto their campuses, or run businesses that serve the larger community. They encourage their members to balance individual needs with those of the group even if, at times, this means spending time off-campus. These contemporary visionary communities tend to operate as integrated, open systems with permeable boundaries between the individual, the group, and the outside world. Some emerging forms structure themselves as hybrid, or variegated, communities—part residential, part non-residential—to incorporate a wider range of members and affiliations.

Certain characteristics of visionary residential communities distinguish them from other forms of cohabitation:

- The inhabitants make a conscious commitment to live in close, highly participatory association with like-minded people.
- A common vision of a better way of life provides the glue that holds them together. Their common purpose includes modeling this better way for the larger society.
- They adopt a social and economic contract that matches their vision and involves ownership of property.

Community means different things to different people. To some, it is a safe haven where survival is assured through mutual cooperation. To others, it is a place of emotional support, with deep sharing and bonding with close friends. Some see community as an intense crucible for personal growth. For others it is primarily a place to pioneer their dreams.

CORINNE MCLAUGHLIN AND GORDON DAVIDSON

Most of these settlements are fully conscious communities; some of them could be described as "deep" communities. Their inhabitants demonstrate a strong commitment to their own and each other's personal growth as well as the group's growth. Trusting themselves and one another, they acknowledge their interdependence and willingly dedicate themselves to working through conflicts. The communities thus become family-like, but emotionally closer and more honest than many conventional families.

How Visions Take Form: A Sampler of Communities

These commonalities notwithstanding, visionary communities come in an amazing variety of forms: agrarian and urban, large and small, restrictive and laissez-faire, religious and secular, located in all parts of the country. If you are seeking such a community, you can choose one that matches your particular interest—psychological development, education, or ecologically sustainable living, for example—or your spiritual orientation. You can pick a community that pools all money and most possessions or one where each person or family unit supports itself financially. Each community manifests its own personality, as you will see from the examples below.

Alpha Farm, a Country Family

Alpha Farm's 280 bucolic acres in Oregon's coastal range are sprinkled with gardens, orchards, and a hayfield. An eclectic assemblage of buildings includes a barn, a chicken coop, and assorted dwellings ranging from large houses with common spaces to cabins, trailers, and yurts. Days begin at dawn, when members milk the cows and feed the chickens, and end late, after mostly vegetarian communal dinners and evening farm chores.

As a way of reaching out to the wider community, Alpha operates several businesses: Alpha-Bit, a bookstore and café in a nearby small town; a rural mail delivery route which the U.S. Postal Service pays the community to operate; Alpha Enterprises, which includes construction and architectural services; and Alpha Institute, which provides consulting and training in group living processes. Members also barter with their neighbors, trading farm products for such necessities as tools, machinery, and auto parts.

Equality comes in realizing that we are all doing different jobs for a common purpose. That is the aim behind any community. The very name community means let's come together to recognize the unity. Come . . . unity.

SWAMI SATCHIDANANDA

Alpha's two dozen members, couples and singles ranging from infants to golden-agers, consider themselves a family and pool all their resources. As new members join, they turn over all their money and property, as well as their debts, to the community. (If they leave, they take back whatever they came with.) The community considers children important and incorporates members' other relatives into its extended family. When Lief McCurrach's sixty-eight-year-old father developed emphysema and could no longer take care of himself, the community took in both the father and Lief's seventy-two-year-old stepmother.

"We are all committed to learning how to live together in a genuine way, finding a balance between the I and the we," Sally Snyder comments. "We have an agreement that if you have difficulty communicating with anyone, you are encouraged to find others to sit down with you and help work things out." Caroline Estes, who, with her husband Jim, co-founded Alpha Farm in 1972, serves as a teacher and professional consultant in the areas of group facilitation and consensus decision making.

Should you be interested in the possibility of joining Alpha Farm, you will probably begin with a three-day visit, participating in the group's work schedule. If you ask to be considered for membership, all members will interview you in turn. If you and the others mutually say "Yes," you become a resident for a year and then make a formal vow to commit "for the foreseeable future."

Ganas—for Those Who Love City Living

While most visionary communities tend to be rural, some thrive in urban environments. One of these, Ganas, has put down roots on Staten Island, New York, just a half-hour ferry ride from downtown Manhattan. Sixty-some residents dwell here in five large, adjacent houses and two down the

Your vision should be bigger than what you think you can create.

FRED OLSEN

SEX, LOVE, AND DEEP COMMUNITY

If your community stresses intimate connections with others in the group, you may find that getting to know someone's heart, mind, and soul at a deep level leads to sexual involvement. Certain questions immediately surface: How do you preserve any privacy? What if your partner has previously been—or is currently—involved with someone else in the community? What happens if you break up but both want to remain in the community?

Sally Snyder of Alpha Farm recalls that when her involvement with Rick began, "the limited privacy was disconcerting at first." On the other hand, romance in a fishbowl "does keep you really honest in your relationship. You can't idealize it, and you can't focus just on that one person and leave your other relationships sitting for a while. The community has helped us resolve issues between us."

Before he and Sally grew close, Rick had broken up with another woman at Alpha. "The group gave her a lot of support, but she eventually left," Sally reports. "People do stay in communities after breakups, though. The friendships that have been able to evolve out of that process are really remarkable."

Susan Fisher of Stelle would undoubtedly agree. Her first husband and current husband both live in the community. "I see my first husband nearly every day," she says, adding, "My new husband's ex-wife is my best friend. We've blended our families." This sort of thing, she admits, is "unusual even for Stelle. But the community has supported everyone."

street. Although Ganas is not primarily a child-oriented community—currently only two of its residents are children—two adult members are planning a separate house for single parents where child care will be part of the situation.

The diversity of Ganas's population mirrors that of its multi-cultural neighborhood and the city itself: Chinese, Japanese, South Americans, Swiss, Russians, and Australians mingle with North Americans, some of whom instruct their housemates in English as a second language. While you can look out the window and see trees, squirrels, birds, and raccoons in the common back yard, inside you find video, audiotape, and book libraries as well as TVs, VCRs, computers, and copiers.

Activities at Ganas move at a faster pace than at Alpha, as befits the urban setting. After a one- to two-hour planning meeting beginning at 7:30 every morning, residents rush off to work at city jobs, household tasks, or one of Ganas' three urban recycling businesses within walking distance of the community: Every Thing Goes, Every Thing Goes Furniture, and Every Thing Goes Clothing. Like Alpha, Ganas strives to support the wider community. For example, its residents spearheaded a weekly neighborhood cultural festival along the Staten Island waterfront.

Living together is an art.

WILLIAM PINCKENS

An arm of the Foundation for Feedback Learning, which was founded in 1976, Ganas is fiercely committed to interpersonal communication. Its residents aim to grow as close to each other as possible through total disclosure of deep feelings and of responses to others' behavior. "I've had problems in my life expressing feelings and opening up to people, and I've felt misunderstood," says member Thompson Reichert, a computer systems troubleshooter. "That's not possible here." The feedback initially included use of biofeedback machines, but these have long since broken down. The group now emphasizes one to one or group interaction, and often videotapes the latter. Members who miss planning meetings take responsibility for bringing themselves up to date by viewing the video.

The social-economic structure consists of three layers, or concentric circles. Members of a nine-person core group, who plan to spend the rest of their lives together, own the property, pool their income, make economic decisions with input from other members, and share their lives so intensely that one member describes it as "like being married to eight other people." If one of them wants to take a trip spending pooled money, the others have to approve. A larger group of members live in the community houses, some of them working in the community businesses and participating in end-of-the-year profit sharing. People who visit for open-ended periods of time, contributing work, energy, and money to varying degrees, form the outermost circle of membership. All can attend meetings.

Ganas stresses a combination of autonomy, self-governance, and willingness to care about others. The community has no formal joining-up process and insists on only a few rules: no violence to people, things, or privacy; no exploitation (everyone carries his or her own weight economically); and no illegal activity. Members eat everything from vegetarian meals to meat to junk food, and drink wine with dinner if they care to. While the community serves evening meals in two dining rooms, people can prepare their own food whenever they like.

Although Ganas claims to encourage differences of opinion in its decision-making process, a visitor immediately notices that the opinions of Mildred Gordon, a senior member of the core group, tend to dominate. Mildred, whose professional experience in group process spans many years, acknowledges that "we practice consensus decision making but it doesn't look like it. I find out what other people want and present it." No one seems to mind. Other core group members join her in an effort to see that everyone in the community gets what he or she wants.

Stelle, a Prairie Town

One large Midwestern community—more than 150 people on 240 acres—offers even more autonomy than Ganas, although it did not start out that way in the early 1970s. Stelle, Illinois, ninety miles southwest of Chicago, resembles a small, modern town, or suburban development, in the middle of a prairie. Stelle boasts its own water, sewer, and telephone systems and even its own Chamber of Commerce. Residents live in individual houses, work at their own jobs—most of them in small businesses run by Stelle people, others outside the community—and manage their money independently. If you want to join Stelle, you need only buy, build, or rent a home there. Besides homes, Stelle's community consists of a combination office building–community center, a private school, a factory building, an orchard, and undeveloped, green land.

Stelle embodies the friendly, cooperative qualities of idealized small-town life along with the attitudes and skills of an ecologically aware community. "It has elements of both a neighborhood and a family," says longtime resident Susan Fisher, "and the longer you're here the more it feels like family. There's lots of intimacy and support, and we read each other very well." The profile of a person who would be attracted to Stelle, she believes, is someone "interested in community but self-reliant, maybe even a rugged individualist. Our binding values are education, personal responsibility, and communication." The communication includes a commitment to working through problems together. "It's easier to walk away," Susan points out, "but that would be a shallower way of living." The Stelle community also demonstrates a commitment to low-cost, earth-friendly technologies. Many of its homes serve as prototypes for energy-efficient design, and researchers in the community have been developing alternative energy sources and other ecologically sound technologies for years.

Residents share meals in the community center several times a week, as well as participating in potlucks and seasonal celebrations. Groups organize spontaneously to put on workshops or form study groups on various philosophies, psychological techniques, and healing. The Stelle Community Association, a homeowners' and renters' group which maintains the common facilities, serves as the only "government."

Young people find Stelle hospitable. About a quarter of the community's population is under the age of eighteen. Some of those who grew up in Stelle and have gone away to college pay return visits to talk about how much the community has meant to them. Their parents are proud that they are carrying Stelle's peaceful, community-oriented principles into the larger world.

Ecovillages—Modeling Planet-Friendly Living

With its small-town self-sufficiency and ecologically sound technologies, Stelle could be considered a prototype of an emerging form of visionary residential community called an ecovillage. Ecovillages take a whole-systems approach, integrating housing, food production, energy, business, the natural environment, and group processes such as consensus decision making and creative conflict resolution. They aim to promote sustainable human development, model ideas for the preservation of the planet, and support themselves as self-sufficiently as possible into the indefinite future. Some ecovillages are integrating cohousing into their plans.

Ecovillages in the United States have sprung up in widely divergent locales, including lakefront land in Oregon; the environs of Ithaca, New York; and an abandoned dump site in Los Angeles. Says Lois Arkin, the chief steward of Los Angeles Ecovillage's vision, "I feel strongly that we have to make deep and radical shifts in our thinking, from linear to cyclical, from 'competitive edge' to 'cooperative edge.' We have to know *why* we're not using pesticides, and *how* to recycle right. We have to work for transformation wherever we are and with whatever we have."

To give their visions form, ecovillagers need to educate and win the cooperation of their neighbors and the public at large. L.A. Ecovillagers and others work hard to involve the surrounding community in planning and development. Ecovillage at Ithaca is affiliated with Cornell University, which helps with research, ideas, and education.

Members of Cerro Gordo, located on about 1,200 acres on Dorena Lake near Eugene, Oregon, spent more than twenty years developing agreements with neighbors and local government agencies. Envisioning their ecovillage as a self-supporting "symbiosis of village, farm, and forest," they commissioned an extensive ecological study in 1973–74 to determine how many people the land could support without harming the environment. Before the end of the decade, the county had approved zoning for the first phase of development and families began moving onto the property. Then, however, disputes between county and state planning agencies stalled the building process. "Oregon has the most rigorous statewide environmental protection in the country," says founder Chris Canfield. By the time Cerro Gordo cleared the final hurdles in 1989, some families had had to leave.

But Cerro Gordo is attracting new members and has formed a nonprofit organization linking residents, future residents, and supporters with a network of people and organizations interested in sustainable living. Key members periodically go on tour to spread the ecovillage concept.

Beyond the sharing of commodities and services with one another, the true luxury of the communal system is the experience of mutual support and caring—a luxury that is often difficult for even the richest people in the private property system to provide for themselves.

ALLEN BUTCHER

Shenoa, a Variegated Community

Another emerging form of visionary community incorporates both residential and non-residential members and defines itself as much by its vision and mission as by its geographical location. Such a community may develop several nodes of activity—some rural, some urban or suburban.

One such variegated community, Shenoa Retreat and Learning Center in northern California's Mendocino County, includes residential, occasionally residential, and non-residential participants. The staff lives on campus and comprises the residential community; the Land Stewards, members of the nonprofit organization that purchased the land in 1990, mostly live and meet in nearby cities but spend some time on campus in collectively owned retreat cabins that they designed and financed; and a wider, non-residential circle of participants initiate and take part in Shenoa-related activities both on and off campus and provide various kinds of support, from spiritual to financial.

Members of all these overlapping circles implement the vision and mission of Shenoa—which include living in harmony with nature and fostering community—by linking it with the greater San Francisco Bay Area through community gatherings, food programs, and other projects. Through the Daily Bread Project, for instance, Shenoans distribute organically grown produce from the Shenoa garden to free food kitchens in the Bay Area. Several public events also have helped strengthen Shenoa's urban node. Two of these, called Growing Community gatherings—held in Oakland and organized by Bay Area residents—enabled city dwellers interested in creating more community in their lives to meet one another and learn about community-building skills and resources.

Shenoa, like the community that inspired it, Findhorn in northern Scotland, dedicates itself to "the positive transformation of our world." Multi-nodal and multi-form communities such as Shenoa exemplify a way of interacting with the larger society without becoming absorbed in it. The interaction inspires the larger society to change by demonstrating the positive effects of new ways of living and also assures that new ideas and fresh perspectives continue to flow into the visionary communities. This mutual exchange grounds members in real life, stretches and refines their vision, and prevents them from becoming stagnant and ingrown.

Life in common among people who love each other is the ideal of happiness.

GEORGE SAND

Some visionary communities that began primarily as residential settlements have begun to evolve into hybrid, multi-nodal forms. Sirius, for instance, which always fostered interaction with the larger society, now includes, besides its core group of residents, a network of two hundred associate members who contribute financially and in other ways. Some associates live at Sirius but choose not to be core group members, others live nearby, and still others reside in distant parts of the country. The network of associate members includes Hearthstone Village, a group of some fifty people living on the same road as Sirius, in a closely knit neighborhood-type community of their own. The Villagers often participate in preparing and sharing community meals at Sirius, and belong to the Sirius food-buying co-ops and garden.

The Spirit within the Forms

At Ganas and Stelle, you can engage in any spiritual pursuit or none at all and feel right at home. In other communities, varying degrees and types of spirituality form part of the glue that binds residents together. Residents of Alpha Farm, who (like those in Sirius and Shenoa) honor the oneness of all life, used to hold a spiritual meeting once a month but now simply express their beliefs through their actions. Sirius considers itself a spiritual community, encouraging regular group and individual meditation as a way of focusing community efforts. "We . . . emphasize contacting our own inner source of Divinity for guidance, rather than relying on outer teachers," write cofounders Gordon Davidson and Corinne McLaughlin in *Builders of the Dawn: Community Lifestyles in a Changing World.* "Members are free to follow whatever spiritual disciplines are most inspirational and helpful to them."

In contrast, the members of Ananda World Brotherhood Village dedicate themselves to the teachings of Paramahansa Yogananda, as interpreted by his disciple and Ananda founder, Swami Kriyananda (J. Donald Walters). The community's members, who reside at its headquarters in the Sierra foothills of northern California and at several branches including one in Italy, attend religious services regularly, meditate, and trust in the wisdom of those closer to the Master. They make decisions through "dharmacracy," that is, tuning into the "dharma" (a Sanskrit word meaning cosmic order or law) of each situation. One member defines dharma as "that which will bring us closer to the light."

To truly educate and serve, we must embody our philosophy and "walk our talk." This is not easy. How do we stay in tune to nature and Spirit while operating a business? How do we allow for our own healing and nurturing and still get everything done? How do we handle our emotional upsets responsibly, without suppressing legitimate dissent? How can we hold ourselves in a positive light while dealing with our shadows and woundedness in the process of healing the planet? These are questions we grapple with daily, questions familiar to other groups and centers pioneering new models, trying new systems.

MARIE SPENGLER

Alpha, Sirius, Shenoa, and many other visionary communities perceive a deep connection between spirituality and nature. The newly emerging ecovillages, while not necessarily spiritual in an overt sense, dedicate themselves to ecological principles with as much fervor as Ananda members devote themselves to the dharma.

Revolution, Evolution, and Flexibility

If your motivation for joining a visionary residential community is to escape the rapid changes of postmodern life, your search may prove frustrating. As these communities move through the natural stages of development and interact with the surrounding environment, they learn to stay flexible. At times they undergo profound change.

Sirius, for instance, transformed its economic system from a totally communal one, in which all members pooled their income and paid expenses out of the common pot, to a blend of private enterprise and communal sharing. Today, members collectively own the land and the community houses and operate the garden and the food cooperative, but individually take responsibility for generating and spending their personal income. The original system simply did not work financially, even after community members meditated together and tried to clear up any personal and interpersonal blocks to the flow of income. Finally, they decided the problem might be the system, and they agreed, by consensus, to change it. "Within a few months," reports Corinne, "this unleashed tremendous creativity, and our income rose."

Over time, Sirius also attracted so many families with children that it began to orient itself more to the needs of the younger set, even though that required a stretch for some of the unmarried and childless members.

Occasionally the departure of the founding visionary results in serious and often painful reevaluation of the community's vision and goals.

Such was the case with Stelle, founded in 1973 by Richard Keininger, author of a survivalist text called *The Ultimate Frontier.* As part of its original mission, Stelle focused on preparing for upcoming world upheavals. As it turned out, the major upheaval occurred within the community itself when Keininger left, with some of his followers, under a cloud. Accused of sexual misdeeds and other forms of manipulation, he had aroused the hostility of many members and had polarized the community. When he departed, however, Stelle felt cut adrift and floundered for more than three years, with everyone asking himself or herself, "What do I really believe?" Eventually, Stelle was reborn in a new and very different form. Originally, it had operated under strict rules: mothers did not work outside the home, men had to be clean shaven, women had to wear skirts, and so forth. Now Stelle imposes virtually no rules at all, and individualism has replaced the guru mentality.

We started off trying to set up an anarchist community, but people wouldn't obey the rules.

ALAN BENNETT

The community did not, however, completely abandon its original philosophical underpinnings. The Stelle Group, composed of those who remain interested in Keininger's ideas, has moved back to Stelle, where it operates as one organization among several within the community. The Group, which focuses on education and philosophy, publishes a quarterly journal, *The Philosopher's Stone,* and runs an accredited, award-winning private school. It has also developed, under grants from the Illinois Department of Energy, prototypes for an energy-efficient greenhouse and an ethanol plant.

LEARNING FROM VISIONARY COMMUNITIES

If you want to acquire information and skills from these visionary R & D centers that you can apply in your workplace, neighborhood, or friendship-based community, you can find plenty of opportunities to do so. Most offer classes and workshops for the general public and publish books, journals, and newsletters. Some of the experienced leaders of visionary communities serve as consultants on organizational issues. Gordon Davidson and Corinne McLaughlin of Sirius now spend eight months of the year in Washington, D.C., teaching "New Paradigm Politics" at American University and helping organizations develop new forms of leadership and governance. Alpha Farm's Caroline Estes consults for industry and for Evergreen State College. She also facilitates meetings of the Green Party and bioregional congresses.

To find out more about these and other kinds of community-building services, you can contact either the communities themselves or organizations that link visionary residential communities with one another. (See Resources at the end of this chapter.)

If you are particularly interested in sustainable living, the international ecovillage and ecocity movement sponsors conferences, publishes newsletters, and hosts public presentations and slide shows. Sister-city ecovillage developments have sprung up in, among other places, St. Petersburg in Russia and Senegal in West Africa.

The greatest challenge of community life is to create synthesis, embracing diversity in a unified whole, resolving differences with the healing spirit of love and dedication to the good of the whole.

CORINNE MCLAUGHLIN AND GORDON DAVIDSON

FINDING A COMMUNITY THAT MATCHES YOUR VISION

If you are seriously considering joining a visionary residential community, you have probably already begun to ask yourself many questions about your readiness and the challenges involved. Such communities can be as demanding as they are rewarding. You gain priceless companionship and support and a sense of larger purpose, but you must be willing to devote much time and energy to communication and collective decision making. In a visionary residential community, you can expect any unresolved relationship issues from your family of origin—authority, abandonment, and codependence issues, for instance—to be replicated in magnified form.

To help you decide whether a visionary residential community is for you at this point in your life, we suggest that you follow these seven steps:

1. Take some time to sit quietly (meditation is helpful here) and tune into your own heart and mind. Ask yourself: Am I a truly social person with minimal need for privacy? Am I willing to delve beneath the surface in my feelings and relationships on a daily basis? Do I want to integrate all or most aspects of my life? Am I willing to put many of my outside interests on the back burner to have time to pursue a vision of a better world? Am I mature and confident enough to think and act in terms of the good of the whole community without losing my individuality? Am I willing to work on my communication skills, confront my personal issues, and engage in conflict resolution?
2. If, after this exercise, you feel that you are a good candidate for visionary community, begin to zero in on your core vision and values. Imagine what an ideal world, and your ideal community, would be like. What is most important to you—children? ecol-

ogy? gender equality? planetary transformation? Do you yearn to reconnect with the rhythms of nature, or do you envision yourself in an urban setting? How important do you consider spirituality, and how would you like your chosen community to manifest it? What degree of intimacy would you prefer?

3. While you are mulling over these questions, research the options available. A good place to begin is the *Directory of Intentional Communities,* which contains descriptions of more than 350 communities in North America and abroad—from The Abode of the Message to Zendik Farm. The directory also includes useful articles on cooperative living in general. Read other books on intentional community (see Resources). By this time you will have begun to clarify and refine your vision.
4. When you have identified a few communities that appear to mesh with your personal vision and values, write for their literature. Tell a little about yourself and ask how to arrange for a visit.
5. Plan a visit to your chosen community, or communities, in accordance with the procedures each settlement suggests. Do not just drop in. Members of visionary communities generally operate on busy schedules, which they may need to adjust to give you attention and answer your questions. Be prepared to pitch in with the cooking, gardening, cleanup, or other work projects, and follow the group norms. Not only is this courteous, but it is also the best way to get a real feeling for the community and the manner in which its members work together. Plan to spend several days to a week or more in the community, if that is convenient for the members.
6. During your visit, observe closely how the members act and interact. What holds them together? Do they appear to be "walking their talk?" Are they working for something larger than their individual needs and the needs of the immediate community? (If so, they are on firmer ground and will stabilize more readily when power or control issues arise than will those focused on narrow self-interest.) Does the form of leadership and governance feel comfortable to you? If the community stresses family-like relationships, would you like these people to be your family? Be open about your needs and feelings but do not criticize individuals or group procedures. Remember that you are a guest.
7. Follow the joining-up procedure the particular community has established. But do not rush your decision. Few people find instant,

Work is appreciated, and good work is appreciated a lot! This is true on the smallest commune or the biggest kibbutz. Work opens doors to friendship and mutual confidence that no amount of conversation will accomplish.

KAT KINKADE

deep rapport with the first community they visit. You may need to spend time in several communities, and make repeat visits to one or more, before you feel comfortable making such a major shift in your life.

If you are considering starting your own visionary residential community, you will need to do all this research and more. Most such communities have developed innovative forms of land ownership as well as economic structures and group processes. They have dealt with financial, interpersonal, and developmental problems. Take advantage of what they have learned—remember that these are the R & D centers for community seekers.

RESOURCES

Recommended books and periodicals

The Search for Community: From Utopia to a Co-operative Society edited by George Melnyk (Black Rose Books, Montreal, 1985)

Builders of the Dawn: Community Lifestyles in a Changing World by Corinne McLaughlin and Gordon Davidson (Sirius Publishing, Shutesbury, Massachusetts, 1986). Profiles several visionary residential communities and explores issues such as leadership and governance, spirituality, and balance.

Seeds of Tomorrow: New Age Communities That Work by Oliver and Chris Popenoe (Harper & Row, 1984)

Earth Community: Living Experiments in Cultural Transformation by Susan Campbell (Evolutionary Press, 1983)

Directory of Intentional Communities: A Guide to Cooperative Living, published and regularly updated by the Fellowship for Intentional Community, c/o Sandhill Farm, Route 1, Box 155, Rutledge, Missouri, 63563; (816) 883-5543. Describes some of the communities below, plus hundreds more.

Cooperative Housing Compendium, edited by Lottie Cohen and Lois Arkin, 1993.

Communities: Journal of Cooperation, headquarters is at Stelle (see below).

Communities: Journal of Cooperative Living (published quarterly by the Fellowship of Intentional Communities, $18/year), 1118 Round Butte Dr., Fort Collins, Colorado, 80524; (303) 224-9080.

Growing Community: A Quarterly Newsletter on Creating Healthy Community From the Ground Up ($21/year), 1118 Round Butte Dr., Fort Collins, Colorado, 80524; (303) 490-1550. Addresses group process issues and provides excellent practical information on everything from zoning laws to energy independence to child-rearing in community. Includes a survey of communities currently forming and a list of resources for community. (The name "Growing Community" is used under license from Growing Community Associates, of Berkeley, California. The newsletter is not otherwise formally connected with GCA.)

Communities mentioned in this chapter

Note: Many communities publish their own newsletters and journals.

Alpha Farm, Deadwood, Oregon, 97430; (503) 964-5102

Ganas, 135 Corson Avenue, Staten Island, New York, 10301; (718) 720-5378 and 981-7365

Stelle Area Chamber of Commerce, 127 Sun Street, Stelle, Illinois, 60919; (815) 256-2212

Los Angeles Ecovillage, Cooperative Resources and Services Project, 3551 White House Place, Los Angeles, California, 90004; (213) 738-1254

Ecovillage at Ithaca, Anabel Taylor Hall, Cornell University, Ithaca, New York, 14853; (607) 255-8276

Cerro Gordo, Dorena Lake, Box 569, Cottage Grove, Oregon, 97424; (503) 942-7720

Shenoa Retreat and Learning Center, P.O. Box 43, Philo, California, 95466; (707) 895-3156. Provides a site for workshops by outside individuals and organizations as well as by people affiliated with the community. Founding visionary Stephan Brown offers a weekend course for people who are interested in starting their own residential community or retreat center.

Sirius Community, Baker Road, Shutesbury, Massachusetts, 01072; (413) 259-1251. Offers weekend on-site workshops on such topics as "Creating Community Where You Are" and "Living Lightly on the Earth"; nine-month training programs for New Age leaders, and credit courses through the University of Massachusetts. Sirius is building a new community/conference center with seating for 130 people, as well as a commercial kitchen and living space.

Ananda World Brotherhood Village, 14618 Tyler Foote Crossing Road, Nevada City, California, 95959; (916) 292-3065 and -3464

Networks

The Fellowship for Intentional Community, P.O. Box 814, Langley, Washington, 98260; (206) 221-3064

The Federation of Egalitarian Communities, c/o East Wind Community, Box DC-9, Tecumseh, Missouri, 65760; (417) 679-4682

Also see resources for Chapters Nine and Ten.

PART FOUR

Starter Kit:

A Map, Some Basic Tools, and a Few Warnings

TWELVE

Coming Together, Growing, and Parting:

Natural Phases in Community Life

Every breath we take encompasses the circle of birth, death, and rebirth. The forces that push the blood cells through our veins are the same forces that spun the universe out of the primal ball of fire.

STARHAWK

WHEN ALISON TOLD HER women's group why she was leaving, they responded with shock. In this group of women who had been meeting monthly in one another's homes, Alison was a charter member and a mainstay. For more than three years, she and the others had shared hopes, fears, and dreams about their lives as well as the state of society. They had cried and laughed together and celebrated regularly. Over the years, as new members joined and old ones left, a core group of original members had remained, providing stability and continuity.

It was even harder for the group to hear the reasons Alison gave for her departure. She felt deeply disappointed by the lack of real intimacy in the group, including its refusal to grapple with conflict and competitiveness within its ranks. Whenever she had tried to raise such issues, she had felt cut off and shut out. She wanted more honesty, more risk-taking, a group willing to delve more deeply into its own interpersonal dynamics.

As Alison explained her decision to stop attending meetings, the group's shock turned to anger, guilt, and, for some, a sense of failure. Whatever intensity Alison had been missing in previous meetings quickly flared up this evening as members argued, demanded explanations, and revealed secrets. Did Alison know that she had been the cause of Anne's and Lena's leaving some months ago, even though both had publicly given other reasons? Neither had liked the way Alison tried to direct the group. By the end of the evening, nearly all the women had become aware of their problems with the group's dynamics. Two months later, only three members were continuing to meet.

Hanging in results in a positive outcome. Confrontation turns to love and respect; chaos gives way inevitably to deeper levels of community.

RABBI SAUL RUBIN

This splitting apart and the sense of failure that accompanied it could have been avoided. If this women's group had been aware of the natural phases of community life and trained in the skills needed to make the transitions, they could have saved themselves much grief, deepened their intimacy, and possibly continued to support one another for many more years. Alison, by uncovering hidden agendas and power struggles, could have helped the group face the end of its childhood innocence and begin another phase in its growth. Instead of viewing the arguing and departures as a sign of failure, the women could have perceived these as healthy, if painful, steps toward maturity as a community.

To help you avoid such unnecessary group tragedies, this chapter provides you with a guide through the various phases of community life, illustrated with stories of how groups have both failed and succeeded at making the transitions from one phase to another. While such a map will not remove the risk and effort involved in creating community, it will give you a chance to prepare for what lies ahead. With a larger perspective on group development, you will not view every difficult transition as a setback or a failure. A sense of the terrain and its challenges can help you and others in your community accept one another with empathy and good humor and avoid the most dangerous pitfall of all, the kind of despair that led Alison, Anne, and Lena to give up on their women's group before challenging it to change.

Remember, however, that a map cannot fully capture something as alive, complex, and multi-dimensional as the unfolding life of a community. While community life develops over time, it does not do so in strictly linear fashion. We chose the term "phase" rather than "stage" in describing this development to convey its cyclical as well as linear movement. Think of the phases of the moon. While the moon moves through its relationships to the sun and the earth in a linear progression, it also repeats the whole cycle every twenty-eight days. Similarly, a community's developmental phases tend to repeat themselves as a series of sub-cycles within a larger cycle.

Have you ever thought you were long finished with the insecurities, jealousies, and chaotic emotions of adolescence, only to find them arising in new forms after the breakup of a love relationship or the loss of a job? Do not be discouraged if your group or community goes through a similar repetition of earlier phases even after it has seemed to settle into a stable, mature phase. This may happen when you welcome new members or say goodbye to old ones, when you start a new project, or when you engage in group revisioning and renewal processes.

The good news is that you do not have to endure endless repetitions of these phases at the same level of awareness. The more conscious your community becomes, the more you learn from each turn of the cycle. When you combine linear and circular motion, you get a spiral. Each set of phases represents one turn of the spiral. The fifth phase, transformation, releases you from that level of the spiral and allows you, if you choose, to move up to the next. Of course, community, like life, is complicated and unpredictable. Be prepared to repeat cycles at the same level now and then and to experience mini-cycles within larger ones.

These stages of the community building process are not linear; they do not necessarily happen in order with one stage immediately following the other. A group may touch emptiness and then quickly return to chaos. Or a group in chaos may go back to a more subtle form of pseudo-community. Community building is a dynamic process.

FOUNDATION FOR COMMUNITY ENCOURAGEMENT

FIVE PHASES AS RECURRING CYCLES

We are not the first authors to observe that community moves through identifiable phases on its road to maturity. Susan Campbell, author of *The Couple's Journey: Intimacy as a Path to Wholeness* and *Earth Community,* has noted that community phases resemble those a couple passes through on their journey toward intimacy and conscious loving. In *The Different Drum,* M. Scott Peck describes four phases that occur in his community-building workshops and elsewhere. Consultants Kay and Floyd Tift point out in their workshops that community life cycles parallel the seasons of the year and also the developmental phases an individual moves through over the course of a lifetime.

The phases of community life we delineate here most closely resemble Campbell's, although we take the model a little further to include a last but not necessarily final phase: transformation, which includes rebirth. In releasing old forms and assuming new ones, your community might expand, change its focus, or disband.

The five phases of our model are:

One—Excitement: Getting high on possibilities

Two—Autonomy: Jockeying for power

Three—Stability: Settling into roles and structures

Four—Synergy: Allowing self and group to mutually unfold

Five—Transformation: Expanding, segmenting, or disbanding

Most traditional families, communities, and organizations suppress Phase Two by not acknowledging their power struggles and become stuck at Phase Three, preferring the safety of familiar roles to the risk of moving into undefined terrain. Long-term conscious communities that allow themselves to experience fully each of the five phases learn, in each one, that which helps them move on to later phases. While these communities may repeat phases, they tend to move to a higher turn of the spiral each time they do so.

PHASES OF COMMUNITY DEVELOPMENT

A rough comparison of other systems with Shaffer and Anundsen's

Peck	Pseudocommunity	Chaos		Emptiness / Community	
Tifts	Spring/ Childhood	Summer/ Adolescence	Autumn/ Adulthood	Winter/ Golden Age	
Campbell	Romance	Power Struggle	Stability	Commitment / Co-Creation	
Shaffer/ Anundsen	Excitement: Getting High on Possibilities	Autonomy: Jockeying for Power	Stability: Settling into Roles and Structures	Synergy: Allowing Self and Group to Mutually Unfold	Transformation: Expanding, Segmenting, or Disbanding

Phase One: Excitement—Getting High on Possibilities

Starting a community, or a group with the potential of becoming a community, is a lot like falling in love. The world looks new and the possibilities endless. You focus on the positive outcomes, not the problems bound to crop up along the way. Like lovers, you perceive one another in all your fresh beauty and potential. You and others in the group may feel seen and heard for the first time, and sense an immediate intimacy with one another. You imagine how these other people will fill the gaps in your life, rescue you from the mundane, help you fulfill your dreams, and make up for the disappointments you have experienced in previous groups and relationships.

In describing the couple's journey, Susan Campbell labels this phase "romance." Ah, you may say to yourself as you take in the others' smiles, at last I can find real connection and support. You forget that those smiling back at you come to this group with their own disappointments from the past and emotional holes that they hope the group will fill, and that they are probably projecting onto you a set of expectations as unrealistic as the ones you are projecting onto them.

Enjoy this romantic phase thoroughly, but do not expect it to last forever. Remember that mutual projection is generating much of the excitement you experience; that, in this early phase, you and the other group members are connecting with hopes, dreams, and fantasies more than with real people. The bonds created may be genuine but do not yet go deep. Remind yourself also that, as delicious as the thrill of this first phase may be, it represents only a foretaste of the deeper satisfaction that comes from persevering through the inevitable disillusionment to forge the deeper, more substantial bonds of Phases Three and Four.

The developmental task for your group at this phase consists of exploring possibilities and creating a shared vision or purpose. Your alignment with this common purpose will help you persevere through the rough spots ahead. Do not be seduced by the fantasy of instant community.

The women in Alison's group assumed that they had achieved intimacy, but the bonds that the members had woven were not strong enough to survive Alison's challenge. They were still at the phase that Scott Peck calls pseudo-community, "an unconscious, gentle process whereby people who want to be loving attempt to be so by telling little white lies, by withholding some of the truth about themselves and their feelings in order to avoid conflict." It is a pretense, he says, that precludes true community.

In pseudocommunity a group attempts to purchase community cheaply by pretense. . . . It is an unconscious, gentle process whereby people who want to be loving attempt to be so by telling little white lies, by withholding some of the truth about themselves and their feelings in order to avoid conflict. . . . Pseudocommunity is conflict-avoiding; true community is conflict-resolving.

M. Scott Peck

In an individual life passage, Phase One corresponds to birth and childhood—or the spring season of awakening. Just as children need strong adult guidance and dependable structures to develop a clear sense of who they are and what they can do, groups often survive Phase One by invoking strong leadership or a firm set of rules and procedures. The "Big Book" of AA, the manual followed religiously by twelve-step groups worldwide, serves this function for a network in which new leaderless groups continually form and move through the infancy phase.

A genuine leader makes himself superfluous by drawing forth the leadership potentials of others, and speaking directly, but lovingly, to people's passivity and dependency on others' strengths.

RICK MARGOLIES

Often idealistic communities refuse to recognize the need for leadership and strong guidance in the early phases of growth. Fearful of replicating the domineering or manipulative power roles they have experienced in their families and the larger society, they commit themselves to total equality.

At the visionary residential community Sirius, the founding couple, Corinne McLaughlin and Gordon Davidson, initially believed themselves equal in power with every other member and established an economy and a governance structure in which members shared assets equally and made all decisions by consensus. Looking back, they realize that this equality was more an ideal than an actuality. "We expected everyone to be as committed, as hard-working, as high energy as we were," says Corinne, "and that did not happen." At one point, she and Gordon realized that they had to accept their own leadership position. "The main shift," notes Corinne, "was in us. We took more responsibility, inside of us. We said okay, we are the founders, we created this, we need to honor everyone's potential and help them develop their potential over the years." If Corinne and Gordon had not done so, becoming, in effect, the temporary mom and dad of the community, Sirius might never have survived childhood and developed into the stable, thriving community it is today.

Phase Two: Autonomy—Jockeying for Power

Campbell observes that in couples, the power struggle phase begins when the partners wake up to the awareness that the other person is not what they had thought he or she was. When the illusion of unity shatters, and the partners become disillusioned, disappointed, and angry, they tend to respond in one of two ways. Either they begin to fight for what they want, attempting to change the other to be the way he or she was supposed to be, or they unconsciously try to hurt the other in retaliation for the disappointment. The illusion of power, "the belief that threat, force, manipulation, or domination, no matter how subtle, can get us what we want," according to Campbell, becomes the main obstacle to achieving intimacy and wholeness. The power struggle phase comes to an end, she writes, "when we recognize who we are and what we do have, and give up our attachment to fantasies of harmony without struggle."

Autonomy, or the jockeying-for-power phase—which Peck calls "chaos" and the Tifts liken to summer and adolescence—serves an important developmental purpose. Through this phase, people in couples, families, and communities learn to assert themselves as individuals and to differentiate their needs from the needs of the others, or, as Campbell puts it, "to say who we are and ask for what we want." What those in authority tend to view as resistance also can be perceived, according to therapist Richard Olney, as the "thrust toward autonomy." However disruptive this rebel energy can become, at its root it represents a healthy yearning to survive and remain whole. Parents may not look forward to the power struggles of their children's teenage years, but most understand how crucial such struggles are for their offsprings' evolution from dependent children to independent young adults. All kinds of groups need to pass through a similar adolescent phase before they can enter a stable maturity. If their members feel free, within the safe container of the group, to develop and assert their independence and individuality, they will then be able to move to the next phases of interdependence.

At times, this experience of unity bursts upon us spontaneously, revealing the wonder and mystery of life—a taste of the Divine. And yet we also can create a sense of unity consciously, building it patiently, step by step, as we get to know each other, revealing more of our deeper selves, trading vulnerabilities, developing trust, keeping our hearts open as we work out conflicts and differences. As this process extends beyond the human world, we develop a sense of community with all other life forms who share the earth with us.

CORINNE MCLAUGHLIN AND GORDON DAVIDSON

A number of residential communities have experienced conflict and upheaval when, for whatever reason, they changed their leadership, modes of governance, or economic agreements. But by encouraging open communication and paying attention to both individual and group needs, some of these communities, such as Sirius and Stelle, have been able to stay afloat over the stormy seas and eventually achieve stability.

PHASE THREE: STABILITY—SETTLING INTO ROLES AND STRUCTURES

Just as the awkwardness and rebellion of adolescence do not last forever, neither does the chaotic autonomy, or jockeying-for-power phase of community life. If your group or community is willing to face its power issues and engage in healthy conflict, it will quite naturally grow beyond this phase to enjoy the stability that comes with confident adulthood. Once you and the other members have learned that you can express yourselves as individuals, even if this means criticizing the group, and be heard and accepted, you will begin to relax the rigid positions you may have developed. You will accept your own, others', and the group's limitations and set about focusing on the task the group has set for itself.

By staying together through the rough jockeying-for-power phase, members of your group or community can reaffirm your caring for one another and your dedication to the group's larger vision. Confident that you are respected as individuals and secure in knowing the rules of the game, you are better able to cooperate on common tasks. You enter the stability phase of community life, one that frees your community to pursue, in a more focused and aligned way, what it came together to do. This parallels that phase in a couple's life when the two partners have weathered the first big storms of their relationship and are more realistic in what they expect of each other and the relationship.

The role of beneficial authority is to return the function and responsibility to life and to people; if successful, no further authority is needed. . . . It is only by returning self-regulating function and responsibility to living things that a stable life system can evolve.

BILL MOLLISON

This settled phase is not without its pitfalls, however. The warning Campbell gives couples can serve communities as well: beware of becoming so attached to stability that you avoid novelty and change. "When the feelings of peace are so hard-won," she notes, "we do not like to let go easily. And so we make a god of our new-found comfort, forgetting that growth involves risk, pain and uncertainty, all of which may be felt as we continue the journey."

Whether your community consists of a network of friends and family, a support group, or a workplace team, or whether you live in an intentional residential community like Sirius, you will at some point notice that you have fallen, quite unconsciously, into ruts. You may begin to resemble an "old married couple." Some of you may naturally gravitate toward the supportive roles of attending to details and paying attention to relationships. You are the ones who coordinate food preparation and clean-up, organize telephone trees and other communication tools, and make sure birthdays get celebrated and disagreements settled. Others of you focus more comfortably on theory, business, and leadership tasks: articulating the mission of the community, setting the agenda, chairing the meetings, and handling financial matters. One of your group might serve as the resident critic who points out how the community is falling short. Another might be the peacekeeper, continually trying to smooth over disagreements and return the group to harmony. Often one person takes on the job of skeptic, questioning the feasibility of proposals and reminding the group of its limits, while another serves as visionary, keeping the dream alive and recalling for the group its possibilities.

While each of these functions is necessary to keep the community's wheels turning smoothly, allowing a member or small group to carry one role alone can lead to burnout, stagnation, and polarization. The long-suffering detail-tender can begin resenting the charismatic leader who never cleans up after him- or herself, just as the natural leaders can tire of holding so much responsibility and receiving flak from the increasingly resentful detail-tenders. The community as a whole suffers by a polarization that squelches the intelligence and leadership potential of the detail-tenders and keeps the leaders out of touch with the common wisdom that comes from hands-on practice and interaction with a diversity of people.

New members should be in joyous agreement with our style of life and our purpose. This is of paramount importance, for it means they fully understand and articulate with their own lives what we are about.

RICK MARGOLIES

Like the parents of any growing family, Corinne and Gordon at Sirius had to know when to relinquish authority and encourage other community members to take a larger role in defining themselves and the group. By the time we spoke with Corinne and Gordon, they had freed themselves of their mom and dad roles enough to spend eight months a year away from the community pursuing their own projects.

Many founders of communities do not make this shift. They expect the others in the group to be instantly mature and, when these members fall short, the group either disbands or the founders install themselves as permanent parents, believing they have no other choice. At this point, the community begins to resemble a cult. The founders do not grasp that their community, like an individual, is an organism that develops through predictable and necessary phases.

While power issues obviously dominate Phase Two, power also plays a role in every other phase. In Phase One, founders' power shapes and guides the community. In Phase Two, the non-founders challenge this person-based power. The more impersonal and bureaucratic, role-defined power that results characterizes Phase Three. In the synergy phase that follows, members and the group learn to respond more to an intuitive inner power than behave according to externally defined roles and rules. This prepares them for transformation, Phase Five, in which they discover the enormous power that becomes available to them when they release their attachment to a specific form.

PHASE FOUR: SYNERGY—ALLOWING SELF AND GROUP TO MUTUALLY UNFOLD

Just as many conscious couples today are challenging old role-bound models, so are many conscious communities. Individuals are no longer satisfied to fulfill just a part of themselves. They yearn to become whole, yet they also want connection with others within a larger whole. In Phase Four of community life, you learn to be and do both through the paradox of synergy.

In a synergistic relationship, what is good for the individual is also good for the whole, and vice versa. This does not mean that individuals can do what they please. The "good" in this definition refers to the essence, not the ego, of the individual. When you know that everything is connected to everything else, acting from your essence implies acting with both your own good and the good of the group in mind. The healthier each member of a community becomes, the more he or she contributes to the health and wholeness of the group.

So a major activity of a democratic community is developing the skills, procedures and attitudes needed for people to jointly create with their diversity.

TOM ATLEE

You know your community has entered the synergy phase when the visionaries begin paying attention to the numbers and the get-the-job-done types start tuning into the emotional climate and taking time to clear resentments and clarify communication. You also know you have reached it when the founders or the natural leaders among you can leave or take a back seat and your group continues to flourish as new leadership emerges from within the group. When Corinne, the co-founder of Sirius, began spending time away from the community, women members confided to her that they started speaking up more and taking leadership in situations in which they had previously deferred to her.

The members of Alexander's twelve-step group also experienced synergy when they chose, on occasion, to chuck the safe but limiting roles and rules of twelve-step meeting procedures and to spend a day freely talking with one another as well as singing, dancing, and otherwise expressing themselves artistically.

While you cannot make synergy happen, you can prepare for it by practicing willingness, listening to others and to your own inner wisdom, and continuing to open to a larger perspective that includes both sides of a polarity. In synergy, you move beyond narrow self-interest and the security of roles to take responsibility for the needs of the group, not out of self-sacrifice but as a way of expanding yourself as you serve the whole.

Foretastes of synergy can come early in the community development process as groups move through micro-cycles within their larger life cycle. A fledgling intentional community called Greenvillage enjoyed such moments when, as member Suzanne Arms put it, "we developed such comfort and trust with each other that our individual needs to 'have it our own way' just dropped away." Later, though, Greenvillage fell back into a sort of power struggle, a polarization between task-oriented people and people who liked to focus on interactive processes, from which it never recovered.

Synergy, in the sense described here, represents the epitome of conscious community. Yet it contains within itself two possible traps. The first is one that Campbell points out with regard to couples: the illusion that your relationship (or community) has done all it needs to do, and you can ignore the rest of the world. Systems do not work like that. A healthy small community within an unhealthy larger social system still has work to do. The second trap is the illusion that once you have achieved synergy you can count on the community staying the same. The truth is, community by its very nature is continually in flux.

As communities pass through their phases, they generally move along the spectrum from functional to conscious community. However, when cycles repeat, within phases or after a series of phases, the group does not become less conscious. Every turn of the spiral holds the potential for deepening a community's consciousness.

The lesson of the crossroads is that we cannot get off the old road and on to the new without going through this intermediate place. In cultural terms, this means that dis-integration always precedes re-integration.

ROBERT GILMAN

PHASE FIVE: TRANSFORMATION—EXPANDING, SEGMENTING, OR DISBANDING

In the last phase of its cycle, a community undergoes a death and rebirth of sorts, either expanding the boundaries of its group identity, segmenting into a number of smaller communities, or disbanding entirely and freeing its members to develop further in connection with other people and groups.

Often at this phase a group responds to an impulse to serve a larger community or, if it has already been doing so, it focuses its attention more fully on its service mission and perhaps expands into new projects. Sirius, for example, has been connecting with other visionary communities, contributing to the local community, and hosting other groups at its facilities since its inception. Members expect its educational and outreach functions to move into an expanded cycle with the increasing use of the community's new conference center.

The timing of such an expansion can be crucial to the health of a community. If a group has not developed a strong internal system that enables its members to feel supported and empowered, too fast an expansion outward, even for the highest ideals of service, can fatally weaken or splinter the membership.

Felicia Ward of the Bay Area Black Women's Health Project understands this well. Although the Project is committed to social change as well as interpersonal support, Felicia does not prod the support groups she coordinates to take on activist projects. Effective collective empowerment, she says, can only come when members feel empowered as individuals. When a woman is emerging from patterns of abuse that go back generations, notes Felicia, she may need sufficient time to heal before turning her attention back out to the world. Nonetheless, groups within BWHP's self-help network have been reaching out in various parts of the country. In Atlanta, Georgia, the National BWHP (NBWHP) established the Center for Black Women's Wellness (CBWW) in 1988. This nationally recognized program serves the women in three local housing projects by providing basic education, self-help group development, social service information and referrals, and preventive health services. Every year NBWHP also holds conferences in various cities across the United States. The 1993 conference, "Body and Soul: The Black Women's Health Agenda," which convened in Detroit, focused on refining a health care plan that meets the needs of African-American women and on developing strategies to inform and educate policymakers at the federal, state, and local levels about these needs.

A healthy organization—whether a marriage, a family, or a business corporation—is not one with an absence of problems, but one that is actively and effectively addressing or healing its problems.

M. Scott Peck

Sometimes even the most intimate communities and proto-communities reach a natural ending point, a time at which members' lives seem destined to move in new directions. Many groups formed to explore the possibilities of cohousing build close and supportive relationships, yet, because finding and developing property can take so long, some of the most dedicated potential residents drop out. A few of these people buy their own houses, in partnership with others or not, and some move on to other cohousing situations. If the original group continues, new members come in to fill the gap. This does not curtail the flow of interest and creativity, however; this flow simply moves back and forth across the boundaries of individual groups. A number of cohousing groups that never made it past the phase of dreaming and planning continue to meet occasionally, to keep the cohousing dream alive and to deepen their relationships with each other. In the San Francisco Bay Area, cohousing groups from different areas have come together to share experiences and insights.

A fledgling community group that I (Carolyn) belonged to met religiously at eight o'clock every Sunday morning for more than two years. We explored ancient and new forms of spirituality; we played volleyball together, ate potluck meals, and told our life stories. We even traveled to a small town in Oregon one long weekend, scouting for a community in which we could settle and be neighbors. But, one by one, members of our Sunday Circle moved to other towns and farms and cities, and we stopped meeting.

Navigating the Five Phases

Your awareness of your community's phase, and of what is in store down the road, can help you travel that road less haphazardly and with less stress. Here are some suggestions:

- Take some time, as a community, to determine where your group is in its life cycle. If you conclude that you are in one of the later phases, notice whether you have suppressed any of the earlier ones. If you have, do not be surprised if you need to deal with them later. But do not try to push the group into any phase for which it is not ready.
- If you feel you are stuck in Phase Two—preserving individual autonomy by jockeying for power—familiarize yourselves with the meeting and communicating, decision making, and conflict resolution processes discussed in Chapters Fourteen through Sixteen, and determine how these might help you become unstuck. Do not be surprised if some members leave during this phase.
- If you conclude that you have been too comfortable for too long in Phase Three—developing stability by settling into roles and structures—consider exchanging roles and trying out new skills. Or, take time out for a retreat to renew and reenvision your community.
- If you believe you have achieved synergy as a group, discuss the possibilities for a new, broader vision and set of goals.
- If you fear that your group is falling apart, talk about whether a frank and open discussion of differences might bring members closer, or whether the group's natural end is at hand. If disbanding seems to be appropriate, take a look at Chapter Seventeen to see how you might conclude as consciously as possible, on a note of hope and friendship.

Dreaming that love will save us, solve all our problems or provide a steady state of bliss or security only keeps us stuck in wishful fantasy, undermining the real power of love—which is to transform us. For our relationships to flourish, we need to see them in a new way—as a series of opportunities for developing greater awareness, discovering deeper truth, and becoming more fully human.

John Welwood

Now, at our occasional reunions, we marvel at the directions our lives have taken and the extended families and communities we have formed since experiencing that prototype in the mid-1970s. I do not regret that the circle scattered. In fact, today I have to laugh at the thought of the dozen or so of us living together, even as neighbors. We have taken such different paths. Instead, I bless the Sunday Circle for revealing the depth of connection that is possible, through utterly simple forms of gathering and sharing, in this seemingly splintered world.

RESOURCES

Recommended books

Transitions: Making Sense of Life's Changes by William Bridges (Addison-Wesley, 1980)

The Truth Option: A Practical Technology for Human Affairs by Will Schutz (Ten Speed Press, 1984). Describes three phases in the development of relationships.

The Couple's Journey: Intimacy as a Path to Wholeness by Susan Campbell (Impact Publishers, 1980)

The Creative Imperative by Charles Johnston (Celestial Arts, 1986). Offers a developmental model appropriate for communities.

Necessary Wisdom by Charles Johnston (Institute for Creative Development, 1992)

Power Equity and Groups by Carol Pierce (Equity Associates [see below], 1988)

The Partnership Way: New Tools for Living and Learning, Healing Our Families, Our Communities, and Our World by Riane Eisler and David Loye (HarperSanFrancisco, 1990)

Organizations

Growing Community Associates, P.O. Box 5415, Berkeley, California, 94705; (510) 869-4878. Co-founders Carolyn Shaffer and Sandra Lewis and associates offer workshops, trainings, and consulting services to the general public and to groups and organizations. Using the processes described in *Creating Community Anywhere,* they teach the strategies and skills of cooperation and help organizations navigate the phases of community life.

Foundation for Community Encouragement, 109 Danbury Road, Suite 8, Ridgefield, Connecticut, 06877; (203) 431-9484. Helps individuals and organizations learn how to build and sustain community according to the principles and processes described by M. Scott Peck in his books *The Different Drum* and *A World Waiting to Be Born.* Offers to the general public community-building experiences, workshops, skills seminars, and conferences. Specially designs such programs for organizations upon request. FCE also provides management consultation and is developing an in-depth community-building leadership training for large corporations and the general public.

Center for Organizational and Community Development, 377 Hills South, University of Massachusetts, Amherst, Massachusetts, 01003; (413) 545-2038 and -2231. Provides training, consulting, and educational manuals to empower citizens, leaders, and communities in their work for social change.

Equity Associates, 21 Shore Drive, Laconia, New Hampshire, 03246; (603) 524-1441. Workshops and literature on the dynamics of power equity groups.

University Associates, Inc., 8517 Production Ave., San Diego, California, 92121, (619) 578-5900. Publishes guidebooks on group process, conflict resolution, communication, etc.

Also see resources for Chapters Fourteen, Fifteen, and Sixteen.

THIRTEEN

Becoming Whole:

Embracing the Shadow Side of Community

I would rather be whole than good.

C. J. JUNG

A right relationship with the shadow offers us a great gift: to lead us back to our buried potentials.

CONNIE ZWEIG AND JEREMIAH ABRAMS

WHEN CELEST POWELL AND Roger Harrison first began spending time at Shenoa Retreat and Learning Center, they relished the camaraderie they found among staff and guests almost as much as the beauty and solitude of the redwood groves. They had been looking for a community with a vision and a spirit that matched their own and thought this might be the place. After they invested in a limited partnership at Shenoa, they threw themselves into organizing potlucks and other community-building activities. When visiting Shenoa, Celest sometimes rose at dawn to bake breakfast muffins for staff and guests.

All that changed several months after Celest and Roger were invited to attend a series of meetings of Shenoa's board of directors as candidates for the board. Soon they stopped traveling to Shenoa except when compelled to do so for a meeting. Even then they found themselves arriving at the latest possible moment and leaving as soon as the meeting adjourned. Both had begun to feel unwelcome in what they had earlier experienced as their community.

What happened to bring on this change? The genesis of the problem was a fiscal crisis at Shenoa. Celest and Roger had insisted that the group confront the painful numbers head-on and publicize the deficit to all those concerned. Celest proposed that, if all debts could not be paid, the center should develop a plan for closure. Roger went so far as to suggest that the limited partners be allowed to vote on whether the center should continue to operate past the point of being able to repay their investments. The latter suggestion appalled some board members and angered most of the staff when they received word of it. Shenoa was the staff's home as well as their workplace, and they resented the idea that a group of off-site lenders might have the power to close the place. "The board and staff considered the fiscal crisis as one of life and death for the center," Celest explains, "and many viewed Roger and me as being on the side of death."

In group situations most of us can always point to one person and say, "If only that person were not here, things would go more smoothly." . . . [That person] represents and reflects back to us some aspect of ourself we are not comfortable with. . . .

MICHAEL LINDFIELD

The next time Roger and Celest came to Shenoa, the two received a frosty reception from many staff and board members. At one critical board meeting, a member questioned whether Roger and Celest held any hope for the center. As Celest remembers it, this person told her that if she could not acknowledge the role of faith as well as finances in determining its future, Shenoa was not the place for her.

Celest and Roger admit that their alarmist ways of saying things contributed to a polarized atmosphere. At that critical board meeting, for example, they arrived late, missing the initial round of personal sharing and an especially upbeat discussion of a potential new investment plan. Roger did not help matters by describing the center, in the first words out of his mouth, as a sinking ship.

Celest believes she and Roger, for a time, were treated as scapegoats: identified as the ones responsible for worsening a difficult situation and shunned. The pain of being treated with animosity and excluded from conversations led her and Roger to avoid the center, thus deepening their alienation from the community.

Identifying one person or group as responsible for a community problem and shunning them, or even forcing them to leave, is a strategy that communities have resorted to for eons. Ironically, scapegoating actually represents a community's misguided attempt to heal itself by excising those parts it considers diseased. The process is not unlike surgically removing a cancerous tumor from a human body. This strategy might work for a time, but if the patient never deals with the conditions that gave rise to the tumor, chances are other tumors will appear or the person's disease will express itself through different symptoms. If the Shenoa board and staff, for instance, had gone so far as to ban Celest and Roger and their bad news from meetings, the center conceivably could have faced much more serious problems—limited partners upset that their investments would never be paid back, charges of mismanagement, and a bankrupt retreat center.

Instead, after unconsciously falling into the ancient scapegoating pattern, Shenoa woke up and chose an alternate route to community health, one that resembles holistic models of bodily healing. Such models acknowledge pain and difficulties—the symptoms—as signs of imbalance within the system as a whole. Rather than treating, or surgically removing, a certain part of the body, the holistic healer treats the whole person, taking into account emotional, mental, and spiritual stresses as well as physical imbalances. Similarly, a community operating from a systems, or holistic, view of reality regards members who cause problems or raise unpleasant issues as messengers or symptoms of a disease for which the community as a whole shares responsibility. Instead of rejecting the messengers, the community welcomes their disturbance as a sign that the system may need rebalancing.

Families, churches, businesses, and governments become sick by refusing to face painful realities. If they allow themselves to become conscious of their painful issues, however, then they can work on organizational healing and grow into painful but joyful maturity.

M. SCOTT PECK

Although the Shenoa board initially resisted focusing on the bad financial news, most members soon acknowledged that facing this pain provided the key to recovery and long-term health. The board chose not only to listen to Roger and Celest but also to include them in decision making by voting both in as members. In doing so, they practiced what M. Scott Peck calls "genuine civility." He describes this in *A World Waiting to Be Born* as "a form of healing behavior that demands often painful honesty and the scalpel of candor." What the Shenoa board cut away with this scalpel were not the messengers bearing the bad news, but the illusions that hid the seriousness of the situation.

Shenoa not only survived its financial crisis but developed an innovative investment plan, grounded in sound fiscal practice, that promises to sustain the organization for years to come. Several board members credit Roger's and Celest's sounding the alarm as the impetus for generating the new plan in time to avert disaster.

Although this confrontation with the shadow turned out well for the center, the process was hardly an easy one. Board members struggled with fear, anger, and confusion as they tried to put personal feelings aside and make decisions for the good of the whole. On key votes, some abstained or expressed minority positions but chose not to block consensus. Members continue to hold a range of opinions about what happened and why. Even Roger and Celest vary in their perceptions of the experience and in the feelings with which it has left them. Because Celest continued as a member of the board almost two years longer than Roger did, she has had a greater chance to heal her relationships with specific board members, yet she remains reluctant to return to the Shenoa campus for workshops or community gatherings.

"Neither of us ever felt really comfortable on the board," explains Roger. "It was extremely difficult, once having taken the role of 'shadow exposer,' to shed it, even though the group eventually came to be much more balanced. For certain of our relationships on the board, the wounds we gave, as well as those we received, never quite healed." He adds that he stayed on the board through and beyond the crisis "for reasons other than good fellowship." Celest concurs that her dedication to the larger vision of Shenoa, not the warm sense of community that she first experienced, kept her involved in board work.

There is no them; there is only us.

BILL CLINTON

Those familiar with family therapy models will recognize the systems approach that Shenoa chose as an extension of family systems theory. This model regards the entire family, not just the identified patient, as the one who needs help. The family, the larger whole, provides the context in which individuals members live, learn, and relate to one another. When the family system goes out of balance, the most sensitive member usually begins developing symptoms, becoming ill or acting out in some disruptive manner. This is not unlike what happens in a body. Under stress, the most vulnerable part—be it the throat, the heart, or the back—develops problems first. A family that perceives itself as a whole system acknowledges a chronically sick or rebellious child as a messenger whose pain signals a deeper, system-wide problem. While the family does not necessarily condone the behavior of the child, it honors the person and the message beneath the pain. Often, when listened to with respect and embraced in love, this child-messenger returns to internal balance and becomes a contributing part of the solution rather than a chronically nagging part of the problem. The family, in turn, gains an ally in its own healing process.

For a community, a crisis often signals the need to enter a new phase of development. Shenoa, for instance, used its financial crisis to move from the initial idealistic excitement phase to the more conflict-ridden autonomy, or jockeying-for-power, phase. The center could not simply patch up its wounds and pretend to look the same as before; it had to expose these wounds to the cleansing light. The board discussed its fiscal woes within the board meetings and with all of its stakeholders, engaging openly in conflict as it sought a proper course of healing action.

If your community is struggling through such a critical transition, you can take heart from the Shenoa story. After two painful years of financial scares and—essential for the teenage or autonomy phase—internal struggles around issues of identity and authority, the center successfully entered the next stage, stability. Members of staff, management, and board began to accept their individual and group limitations, develop and agree to goals and procedures, and settle into more defined roles and structures. The board, formerly a "parent" who made decisions at many levels, restricted itself to setting policy. Management took on a stronger role and, with the participation of a more empowered staff, developed a full set of personnel procedures. While the board and the staff continue to deal with challenging issues, neither automatically turns the other into the "bad guy."

We have talked of our personal bag, but each town or community also seems to have a bag. I lived for years near a small Minnesota farm town. Everyone in the town was expected to have the same objects in the bag; a small Greek town clearly would have different objects in the bag.

ROBERT BLY

FACE THE FACTS *AND* EXPECT A MIRACLE

The Shenoa story illustrates what has come to be known as "the rubber band theory of manifestation." Business management guru Robert Fritz, who gave the name to this theory, claims that taking a hard look at current reality is as essential to making a dream a reality as holding the vision of what one wants. According to Fritz, author of *The Path of Least Resistance,* the tension between vision and reality propels the creative process. It is as though there were a rubber band connecting the two. If you only focus on the vision, you never figure out the steps necessary to move from where you are to your goal. Likewise, if you spend all your time immersed in current problems, you become discouraged and give up on the vision.

Many who are drawn to creating community tend to be idealists, unafraid to dream big and trust in the strength of the vision. Some even believe in miracles. Many realistic, bottom-line business types, on the other hand, mistrust dreams and dismiss every non-traditional proposal when the numbers fail to compute. Yet, according to Fritz, the realists and the idealists have crucial perspectives and information to offer one another. Each helps uncover the undeveloped parts, or shadows, of the other.

Our personal shadow, says Jungian analyst Edward C. Whitmont, is "that part of the personality which has been repressed for the sake of the ego ideal." Or, as poet Robert Bly more graphically puts it, our shadow is the long, invisible bag we drag behind us filled with the parts of us that our parents, teachers, and peers do not like. "Since the . . . bag is closed and its images remain in the dark," explains Bly in *A Little Book on the Human Shadow,* "we can only see the contents of our own bag by throwing them innocently, as we say, out into the world." Bly is talking about psychological projection, the unconscious act of ascribing to others one's own anxiety-producing ideas or emotions. People unconsciously turn others into villains when they are afraid to acknowledge their own power and sexuality. They also can create positive shadow figures, such as superstars and superheroes, by projecting onto others the qualities they desire but believe they are lacking in themselves.

Honesty is the great defense against genuine evil. When we stop lying to ourselves about ourselves, that's the greatest protection we can have against evil.

JOHN A. SANFORD

DETECTING YOUR SHADOW

An Eight-Point Community Health Check

To identify the shadow issues of your community—your dwelling place, workplace, religious or social group—ask yourself and the group the following questions:

1. What are your group's values around harmony, diversity, and conflict? How do you treat members or non-members who disagree?
2. Can you detect symptoms of transplanted family dysfunctions? For example, do some members play Father/Hero or Mother/Caretaker roles, assuming inappropriate amounts of responsibility? Do others play the Helpless Child role, avoiding responsibility? Or the Teenage Rebel role, continually defying authority?
3. How does your community deal with bad news about itself? When something goes wrong, do people point fingers at one another or avoid the issue?
4. Do political factions or social cliques exist? Do people talk behind one another's backs, hoard information, or let others in on information too late to influence decisions?
5. How aware is the group of its power balances—for example, who controls information or money, makes decisions, and serves as spokesperson? Does the group examine imbalances regularly and agree to accept or modify them?
6. Do any members neglect families, personal lives, and their health to serve the community? Do some feel guilty if they aren't working long and hard for little compensation? Does your group seem to operate in a perpetual state of emergency?
7. How well do you balance task and process? Do you address both individual and group needs? Do you discuss relationship issues (including sexual politics) as well as business ones?
8. What kind of emotional climate generally exists? When you enter a group gathering, does your body tighten and do your defenses go on alert? Or do you relax and feel welcome and accepted? Do hugs and expressions of caring seem genuine or false? When tension arises, is the group willing to talk about it? How do non-members feel when they interact with your group?

Projecting a disowned part, whether of the individual or of the group, is not always a destructive thing to do. In fact, it can be the first step in attaining balance. For example, if you find yourself adoring a successful person or idealizing a creative group, you may be projecting onto them your own unacknowledged capacities for success and creative self-expression. Likewise, if you tend to turn authority figures into monsters, you may be ascribing to them unconscious yearnings for personal power that your parents and teachers taught you to view as evil. When you become aware of these motivations, you can choose to move toward wholeness.

One does not become enlightened by imagining figures of light, but by making the darkness conscious. The latter procedure, however, is disagreeable and therefore not popular.

C. J. Jung

The realistic number-crunchers and idealistic visionaries that every community needs often find one another hard to live with because they reflect each other's shadow. The number-crunchers, for example, may put down the visionaries for having their heads in the clouds but may secretly envy and even idealize those with the courage to dream. The visionaries may disdain the number-crunchers for being so materialistic, even while harboring hidden doubts about the strength of the foundations upon which their own dreams rest. Ideally, individuals in a community learn to wear both hats as they develop previously hidden aspects of themselves and reduce the size of their shadows. Members integrate the number-crunching and visioning skills within themselves so that no single person or subgroup has to bear the entire responsibility of either holding the vision or pointing out the limits of current reality.

Sometimes the dreams of community are small in scale; however, a gap between the real and the ideal can create pain nonetheless. A group of neighbors in a mid-sized city decided to tear their backyard fences down and create a communal space for their families to use. For years, while their kids were growing up, the concept worked beautifully. Parents chatted over coffee while they watched their youngsters play, families celebrated birthdays together, and those with green thumbs raised vegetables in the common garden. But they hadn't prepared for those kinds of events that no one wishes to imagine happening: divorces and despair. In the wake of one divorce, the ex-wife suffered a serious breakdown, turning from friendly and agreeable to nasty and unreasonable. The neighbors tried their best to respond with warmth and friendship, but she continued spewing venom until no one wanted to relax in the communal backyard anymore, much less take responsibility for maintaining it. As the situation deteriorated, tools began to disappear from the group toolshed or were returned dirty and broken, and one of the stable couples, Marta and Kurt, found themselves picking up after everyone else. Finally, they gave up on the common garden and, with it, the dream.

"If, in the beginning, we'd had a procedure for working through potential difficulties," comments Marta, "we might have been able to avoid this disintegration. We should have dreamed up every worst-case scenario we could think of, and written down how we planned to deal with these, and signed agreements." The neighbors' challenge lay not so much in acknowledging current reality but in honestly assessing future possibilities. The likelihood of breakdown—of individuals, families, and the community itself—remained in the shadow, or in denial. When communities deny the difficult side of group life, they can destroy the cohesiveness they are trying so hard to protect.

Sharing brokenness as well as heroism is an essential part of maintaining community. Both the darkness and light can be expressed.

FOUNDATION FOR COMMUNITY ENCOURAGEMENT

DENIAL AND CONTROL: FACING THE TWIN COMMUNITY-KILLERS

"The first time I entered Emerson House I sensed so much tension that I felt nauseous." Melanie, current resident manager of this shared household, is telling the story of how one community recovered from a serious bout of denial and control that almost destroyed it.

Emerson House in Philadelphia had been a shared household since the 1960s and, for more than five years, had served as a meditation center as well. One of its longtime residents, Ken, had developed a steady following as a meditation teacher. He lived at Emerson with his wife, Barbara, their young daughter and son, Abigail and David, and six other residents.

"I used to come here for meditation classes," Melanie recalls, "and imagine how together this house must be. I assumed that because its members meditated regularly, they must be exceptionally open-hearted and accepting of one another. I had come expecting to find a generosity of spirit and instead experienced the opposite. I sensed a contraction and a stinginess. House meetings were edgy and controlled. People were trying to keep things together but without giving one another any freedom."

The problem is a common one for groups of all sizes—from families to nations—that identify themselves with high aims. They strive so hard to be ideal that they deny, and throw into that invisible shadow bag, anything in themselves or their group that does not fit. At Emerson, this meant "bagging" conflicts, power issues, and sexual tensions. House members feared that to admit discord would be to acknowledge that they were not good meditators, living in harmony and responding to every challenge with calmness and compassion.

But what happens when the wife becomes jealous of her husband's friendships with other women in the household? When the daughter throws three tantrums a day, the son barges into rooms without notice, and the parents refuse to let other residents reprimand the children? When housemates get into arguments over who is not doing the dishes? At Emerson House, the response was typical of most family and community systems intent on maintaining a facade: massive denial and strenuous attempts to control one's own and others' behavior.

When Emerson resident Rachel asked others whether they were bothered by the children overpowering the household, they shrugged. No one wanted to admit that anything might be wrong, and they conveyed, not too subtly, the message that the dissonance existed in Rachel's imagination. After several weeks at Emerson, Melanie, a therapist for many years, grasped that, in this dysfunctional "family," Ken and Barbara acted the roles of mother and father. In this household of supposed peers, this couple managed to get their way on most decisions. Ken sat at the head of the dinner table—the power position—with his wife and children beside him. Swallowing feelings and going along with Mom and Dad's decisions were strategies that the others (except, to some extent, Rachel) had developed as children to survive in their families of origin.

I used to think I was considerate and cooperative. I usually blamed others for whatever went wrong. Slowly and reluctantly I realized how self-centered and self-righteous I was and how easily I could be careless, irresponsible, and destructive.

ARTHUR GLADSTONE

The only one spontaneously expressing her emotions seemed to be two-year-old Abigail. She screamed and cried out all of the repressed anger and fear in the household, serving as an emotional alarm bell. Most residents, however, wrote off her outbursts as false alarms, ascribing them to a childhood phase.

The household's unspoken problems came to a head about a year after Rachel and her partner Larry's son, Jonah, was born. In psychodynamic terms, this family system had difficulty stretching to incorporate two family subsystems within it. The already chilly relationship between "Mother" Rachel and "Mother" Barbara went into the deep freeze. Frozen feelings became the norm for the house, affecting even the members' relationships with the children. Rachel remembers a house meeting at which she begged the others to respond to Jonah when they entered or left a room he was in. "The poor little guy," she recalls, "would be waving his hand to say hello or goodbye and the adults would completely ignore him."

House members began to ignore one another as well. They ate together less frequently and rarely invited guests over for dinner or threw the house parties for which Emerson had been known.

By the time Melanie signed on as a housemate, about half the residents—including Ken, Barbara, and their children—had given notice and were preparing to move. The owner seriously considered putting the house on the market, but decided to appoint Melanie as manager instead.

Today, Emerson flourishes as a shared household and has regained its reputation for lively celebrations. Its members shout at one another on occasion, but more frequently they laugh together. Every Christmas, household members outdo one another dressing up as Santa Claus, Mrs. Claus, and the elves for the benefit of Jonah. New residents remark on the atmosphere of love that welcomes them at Emerson and remains even after the "honeymoon" phase.

The shadow acts like a psychic immune system, defining what is self and what is not-self.

CONNIE ZWEIG AND JEREMIAH ABRAMS

The shift in membership, of course, helped bring about this transformation. But equally important was a change in attitude about communication and conflict. Openness and honesty became primary values, even when this meant arguing in front of others and occasionally losing the calmness so prized by meditators. With Melanie facilitating, the household reviewed its traditional structures, policies, and procedures and decided which to keep and which to change. In effect, members brought unspoken rules and assumptions into the open and took a conscious look at them.

Ironically, as permission grows to complain and disagree, less of this seems to be happening. When disagreements arise and members begin arguing openly, the tension dissipates quickly. Such outbursts are now more like brief squalls that blacken the sky for a moment, fill the air with rain and thunder, and then disappear, leaving a fresh, clean feeling in their wake.

The Many Guises of the Shadow

Every group shadow wears at least two sets of masks that deflect attention from the deeper issues. One set usually appears shiny and bright: uplifted faces seeking light, hearts yearning to beat as one. The other is often sharp and menacing: scowling faces, fingers pointing in blame. Usually, as shadow issues emerge in a group, warring camps form. Each believes its own members are wearing the bright masks, and the others the menacing ones, although perhaps under a veneer of brightness.

As soon as a group splits into factions, each blaming the others, it has fallen out of truth. In an interdependent system, there are no sides. The masks are like the dark and bright faces of the moon, illusions created by the play of shadow and light. There is only one moon and it is round. That portion of the surface labeled the dark side this month may be in the light another month. Celest and Roger, Shenoa's messengers of gloom and doom in July, became, in some members' minds, wielders of the searchlight of salvation in November. Rachel, the troublemaker among one constellation of residents at Emerson House, transformed into a builder of community when a new constellation formed.

The shadow, by its nature, is elusive and hidden. It lives beneath conscious awareness in the dark alleys and underground tunnels of the personal and the collective psyche. Yet, you can begin to sense its outlines by studying your own and your group's psychological projections, just as you can gather sketchy information about the people sitting in a firelit cave by observing the shadows they cast on the cave walls.

To compose such a symposium of the whole, such a totality, all the old excluded orders must be included. The female, the proletariat, the foreign, the animal and vegetative; the unconscious and the unknown; the criminal and failure— all that has been outcast and vagabond must return to be admitted in the creation of what we consider we are.

ROBERT DUNCAN

Here are five common guises of the shadow in groups and communities, along with suggestions on how you can detect and deal with them.

1. The Harmony Trap

Both Shenoa Retreat and Learning Center and Emerson House fell into the attractive harmony snare. Holding harmony as an ideal is not the problem. The danger lies in ignoring the process that leads to harmony and that maintains it after it is attained.

Although people tend to view harmony as a fixed state or an end product, it is neither. Rather, it is continually in flux, not unlike your body's metabolism. Every time you eat a meal, your body's metabolism temporarily goes out of balance, processes the food, eliminates what cannot be used, and returns to balance. Not eating would also produce a lack of balance and the need for readjustment. If your body acted like many egos do and refused to admit that it was out of balance, it would be unable to make the needed adjustments. Holding on to the illusory ideal of being in perfect balance, it would ignore messages to the contrary, build up and retain toxins, and become sick or even die. Similarly, a community that pretends it is always in harmony and balance builds up emotional toxins under the surface that throw it more deeply out of balance. It becomes vulnerable to depression, fear, or rage among its members and death by slow attrition or sudden breakdown.

In Emerson House, members had repressed their anger and resentment for years. When it began to leak out through Rachel and little Abigail, it appeared ugly and chaotic. In this case, the commitment to emotional honesty that followed a shift in membership allowed the system to find balance again. At Shenoa, the shift occurred within the people on the board. Although board members did not at first encourage Celest and

Roger to ask hard questions, several made sure the two were not cut off when they did. Eventually, other members began to take on this critical function, raising tough issues even when Celest and Roger were not present.

Shenoa's "Declaration of Intentions," the equivalent of a vision statement, is dotted with the words harmony, oneness, and cooperation. Recently, board members have begun considering adding phrases that reflect the values of diversity and conflict—a sure sign that the organization is climbing out of the harmony trap.

What happens if I do not welcome some aspects of myself and banish them to a life outside . . . ? How can I find wholeness if some of the pieces are missing? . . .

Our anguished cry for wholeness is like a homing signal for all the hitherto ignored and repressed parts of ourself. . . .

MICHAEL LINDFIELD

If you sense that your community is in danger of falling into this trap, invite the group to discuss the issue in a non-threatening manner. You might suggest giving each member a chance to talk for a few minutes, without interruption, about his or her fears about confronting conflict and anger in a group setting. You also might talk about how the families you grew up in handled these behaviors and emotions. Find out what would make dealing with differences in the group safe for each of you. Acknowledge any disagreements about the value of airing conflicts as a means of achieving harmony and look for common ground. Those who have managed conflict successfully in couple relationships, and reached deeper harmony as a result, might share their experiences.

2. The Equality Trap

Another ideal that, if misinterpreted, can waylay a community is equality. Communities of friends and proto-communities, such as peer support groups, tend to operate on the unspoken assumption that all members wield equal amounts of power. Members of some communities that include management-staff hierarchies feel uncomfortable about the power differences, so they downplay these differences and create the impression that, beneath the titles, everyone is equal. Problems arise, as with the harmony trap, when the gap between the ideal and the real widens to the point of creating resentment or disillusionment among community members.

Emerson House fell more and more deeply into the equality trap as its members allowed inequalities to arise without acknowledging and agreeing to them. As Ken and Barbara's presence in the house grew to include family and meditation center, they took up more space, literally, than any other member. Outsiders often referred to the house as Ken's meditation center. He facilitated most of the house meetings and Barbara made most of the decisions about house maintenance and interior decoration. Yet, if anyone had asked the members of Emerson House at that time if they were a peer group, sharing power equally, they undoubtedly would have answered yes. Tension grew, nonetheless, as they sensed unconsciously that this was no longer the case.

Like harmony, equality is a fluid state. No group, no matter how committed to equality, ever shares power equally for more than a few serendipitous minutes at a time. Even in an informal peer group, a person with computer expertise, for instance, can play a more powerful role than those without it simply by maintaining the mailing list, sending out memos, and keeping the books. If the group holds meetings more often at one person's home than at the others', that person accumulates a subtle power. Members who happen to be more vocal and articulate than others also draw more power to themselves. Sharing power becomes a series of course corrections as members of a group, over time, attempt to balance perceived inequalities.

Gender continues to complicate inequality in groups. Because of differences in cultural conditioning, men may tend to dominate task-oriented discussions, while women may hold sway in those that deal with emotions and relationships. Even in the most enlightened communities, women often gravitate toward supportive functions and men to leadership ones. In Emerson House, Ken was not the only member with a reserved position at the dinner table. Another tall, powerful male, Alex, always sat opposite Ken at the foot of the table. And in house meetings during the dark days, when Ken did not facilitate, Alex usually did. Neither man was overtly sexist, nor were female members of the household consciously looking for father figures. Still, the male and female members of Emerson House allowed classic, gender-related power imbalances to emerge, possibly because these imbalances reflected those they grew up with in their own families.

To help your community steer clear of the equality trap, begin by initiating a candid discussion about power and responsibility. Your group might reduce the emotional charge by acknowledging up front that differences in power are inevitable and not necessarily bad. Then consider in which areas of your community life equality is important. Your group may be happy to let the same computer whiz update the mailing lists and keep the books for years on end, even if this does mean granting him or her more power. But you may not be willing to let the same few people lead the meetings or supply the refreshments month after month, especially if, in the past, the men have tended to do the leading and the women the serving.

To keep the gap between the ideal and real from growing too wide, consider committing yourselves to conducting an annual power audit. You could even turn it into a game. After figuring out who took on the most jobs in the most number of areas, and who sat in the power position at meetings and meals most frequently, award these people prizes. By the time you flush out all the hidden tasks and subtle status indicators, you might discover that the most self-effacing among you are actually the biggest power-mongers.

3. Unresolved Family Projections

Management and staff at a Maryland construction company felt like family. "I not only knew my employees' children by name," remarks president and owner David Johnston, "but I knew the names of their dogs as well, and I could tell you the last time their truck broke down on the highway." At the beginning of each weekly staff meeting, employees took time for individual "climate" checks, with each giving an emotional "weather report" and talking about events currently affecting their lives. "We considered ourselves a community within the business," says David.

He was understandably shocked when, in the face of a recession, this sense of trust and connectedness disappeared. As soon as employees realized that layoffs could no longer be avoided, they formed factions and began pointing fingers.

As in the case of Emerson House, members of this community had tended to project their unresolved family issues onto the group. David realized later that he had unconsciously taken on the role of caretaker in the company, much as he had in his family of origin. Likewise, many of the staff looked to him as the Daddy who was supposed to take care of them, especially in a pinch. So long as work went smoothly, no one noticed these unhealthy dependencies. Each was playing a familiar role and getting the rewards he or she wanted from it. Only when Daddy failed to take good enough care of them, and one or more of the employees faced the frightening prospect of having to leave this secure home, did the system reveal its weaknesses.

Looking back, David now recognizes the danger signs that he had missed. As the economy declined and construction contracts became more difficult to land, his staff tended to hunker down and commiserate with one another rather than take the offensive and market the company's services even harder. "It was a cold world out there," comments David, "and my people preferred the warmth of their internal community." As a result, the burden of bringing in the business and making the hard financial decisions fell increasingly on David's shoulders.

Today, David is determined this will never happen again. He has reorganized the company into separate intrapreneurial units, each of which must carry responsibility for its own bottom line. He now owns only a small fraction of the business and has learned to let go of his caretaker role. Employees who are running the reorganized company are discovering fast what it means to take initiative and bear responsibility. While rebuilding community is a slow process, David and the others know that, when their restructured venture matures, it will be the kind they can trust: an interdependent community of peers rather than a one-way dependent community of father and children.

Unresolved family projections and dependencies are nothing to be ashamed of. They are simply part of life. Becoming aware of these dynamics is a major first step toward resolving and detaching from them. Sometimes that is all you need to trigger changes in behavior.

Usually, the next steps take place at two levels: psychological work by individual group members to resolve their personal projections and group restructuring to encourage interdependence. The personal work might be as simple as reminding yourself that so-and-so is not your father or as complicated as embarking on a course of therapy to resolve ingrained childhood complexes. At a group level, a community might change a few procedures, as Emerson House did in rotating the leadership of its meetings, or it might completely restructure itself like David Johnston's construction company.

4. Hidden Agendas and Power Plays

If dysfunctional group dynamics go unchecked, trust can deteriorate and ugly power games emerge like monsters from the deep. When the recession hit David's company, the vice president, who had been David's best friend for years, refused to take any responsibility for the crisis even though he headed the company's financial department. Instead, according to David, this second-in-command began rallying disgruntled employees around himself and painting David as the bad guy. Finally, David had to fire his friend and partner of many years.

Secret power plays and hidden agendas can arise in even the most aware and best-intentioned communities. M. Scott Peck notes that organizations specializing in group dynamics often have the hardest time noticing when they themselves have slipped into pseudo-community. This proved true for a West Coast organizational development firm that prided itself on building community among its own associates and staff, while helping other companies create healthier, more productive work environments.

Several years ago, the forty-plus members of Interaction Associates began to realize that what they called workplace community was only a veneer. Beneath this surface of openness and mutuality, people were following their own personal agendas, trying to establish control of the company or their part of it, and not admitting what they were doing. The change was gradual and insidious. Eventually, "it didn't feel right or natural anymore," recalls one longtime associate, Peter Gibb. "There wasn't as much joy." Under the guise of being respectful in a consensus-oriented company, people would mask their truth. "They'd say things like, 'I think we ought to reexamine our compensation system' when what they meant was 'I don't think I'm getting paid fairly,'" reports Peter. Then they would go off in groups of two and three and complain to each other.

[The shadow] retains contact with the lost depths of the soul, with life and vitality—the superior, the universally human, yes, even the creative can be sensed there.

LILIANE FREY-ROHN

After a series of ineffective planning meetings, tensions came to a head in one confrontational meeting that amounted to filing for divorce. Members divided into two opposing camps, each of which wanted to win control of the organization. The camps formed around the two partners who had founded the company. One partner left, followed soon by others from the same faction.

Today the company is strong again, both as a business and a community, although the process of rebuilding has been long and painful. "Those of us who remained took the rebuilding process very seriously," comments Peter. "We started by examining why we were here, and then how to align corporate and individual interests with our commitments to each other and to our larger mission." Two of the commitments the organization has made to avoid falling into pseudo-community again could easily work for other groups, whether these are informal circles of friends or established organizations. At internal meetings, Interaction Associates sets time aside for individuals to speak from the heart about what they are learning (even from their own mistakes) as members of the organization. And, once a year, the company reaffirms its vision statement and makes sure its efforts lead in that direction.

Such preventive measures help groups avoid hidden agendas and power plays and the factions they tend to generate. Others include welcoming diverse points of view, developing communication guidelines, and training the group members in conflict resolution skills. If, despite these precautions, factions still form in your community, call an emergency meeting. You might bring in a skilled mediator to help bring the hidden issues into the open and encourage the community to work through them in as honest and respectful a manner as possible. Remember that the identified troublemakers are actually messengers revealing imbalances in the system as a whole. Look into the mirror that they hold up to discover the shadow of your community, then bring it into the light.

5. The Split between Task Orientation and Process Orientation

Only by making friends with the shadow do we gain the friendship of the self.

ERICH NEUMANN

One group of people intent on creating a neighborhood-style residential community seemed to have everything going for it. The members of the Greenvillage project were skilled and capable, had sufficient financial resources, shared key values, and were so dedicated to working together that they met faithfully every other week, for almost a year, to plan their community. But just as certain members believed the group was ready to purchase land together, the project collapsed.

At least two members think one of the key reasons Greenvillage fell apart was the group's inability to resolve the tension between the doers and the processors. While all members appreciated the need for process, some wanted to get on as quickly as possible with the tangible task of creating a physical village, while others were convinced the project would not fly unless they slowed down and spent more time getting to know one another, developing interpersonal skills, and building trust. Finally, the group decided to hold separate meetings for task and for process, but no one was required to come to any of these meetings. Greenvillagers never met again as a whole group, and when one couple announced that they had given up on the shared living dream and bought a house for themselves, the collective project fizzled.

The task-process split that helped undo Greenvillage is common in communities that seek deeper consciousness. Every such group will eventually need to decide how to balance its task and its process needs, and it will probably have to negotiate this balance more than once during its lifetime. Different members—depending on their ages, their life situations, and their natures—typically have different needs and paces. At certain points in their lives, such as a career transition or the imminent arrival of a child, some feel they have to complete a task soon. They do not have the luxury of "hanging out" in process. Others consider process the essence of community, whatever the tangible result.

Shenoa Retreat and Learning Center overcame a potentially fatal split between doers and processors when, during an emergency meeting, both camps reached the common clarifying insight that they needed one another to survive. This group "Aha!" came when one participant, board member

Celest Powell, sketched on the flip chart an organizational development model that proved pertinent. Celest drew a picture of a bicycle and labeled one wheel "task" and the other "process," explaining that "we need both for the bicycle to function, and it works best if front and back wheels are the same size."

With the gradual acceptance of the darker impulses within me, I feel a more genuine compassion growing in my soul.

CONNIE ZWEIG

Prior to this "Aha!", the task-process debate had taken place along staff-management lines. Staff feared that management was so concerned about keeping the business in the black that it was willing to sacrifice the carefully built community feeling among the staff to this bottom line. Management was afraid that staff's strong focus on maintaining community among themselves blinded them to the needs of the business and would lead to poor business decisions. After Celest drew her bicycle on the chart, one staff member spoke for the others, saying, "We care about task too. We know how important it is to run this place as a business and we're willing to do that. We just thought that we were the only ones who cared about process, so we always supported that side of the issue."

The way out of the dichotomy once again involved embracing the shadow, both as a group and individually, and taking steps to change behavior. At Shenoa, those in management began acknowledging and supporting the role of community in the operation, while the staff began educating themselves about budgets and cash flow and taking greater responsibility for the business part of the center.

If your community is experiencing tension between task and process, you have discovered one of your growing edges, an avenue to greater health. You might be more concerned if your group is feeling no such tension, either because you have collapsed into exclusive preoccupation with internal dynamics, or you are focusing so totally on task that you are no longer paying attention to how members feel or how healthy your group process is.

When a group becomes too absorbed in process, members neglect the business or shared purpose. Those members who yearn for a feeling of accomplishment feel frustrated or bored and eventually stop participating. The ones who stay can become addicted to the group and its process, using this perceived womb as an escape from the demands of outside life. Ironically, support groups, such as twelve-step groups designed to help members recover from addiction, can become an addictive process themselves if they do not provide a healthy dose of challenge along with support.

Conversely, groups or communities can become addicted to task. They can be so intent on getting the job done that they ignore the well-being of their members. Workaholism, as Anne Wilson Schaef and Diane Fassel point out in *The Addictive Organization,* is not strictly an individual disease. The group itself can serve not only as the fix, or the addictive substance, but also as the addict. Communities and organizations dedicated to noble causes and lofty ideals are especially prone to becoming fixes for their members. They can easily hook those who find their value and self-esteem primarily through externals—in this case, through doing good for others. Individual workaholics, in turn, can use the compelling mission of their group as an excuse for ignoring their own health, family, and friends. Both individuals and groups addicted to work undermine community by resisting the kinds of activities that create group bonding: teamwork, sharing feelings, and playing and celebrating together.

The workaholic's mask is one of the hardest to detect because those putting in long hours for a cause or a company look so virtuous and seem to be getting so much done for their organization. In addition, the culture rewards such behavior and tends to ignore its downside. Yet compulsive work habits hide deep-seated anxieties that can surface in disruptive ways. And, while those addicted to work look productive, they often waste time on less important tasks because, in their self-absorption, they have difficulty setting priorities that best serve the larger whole.

Healing and transformation come not only through individual members recovering from their personal addictions but also through the organization admitting that it, too, is an addict, so hooked on its own mission that it ignores internal problems and processes. To recover from its addiction, the group or community first needs to admit that it has a problem. Then it must be willing to ask for help and to reorder its priorities to allow time for interpersonal processing and group renewal. The group also may need to scale down its goals to match its human and financial resources.

If your community has become excessively focused on task, consider suggesting small steps toward bringing about a balance. You might begin each meeting with brief personal check-ins, the kind of emotional "weather reports" that the employees at David Johnston's construction company provided one another. Besides helping people connect on a relationship rather than a task level, these reports could indicate whether stress and overwork are becoming problems. If members are dropping out or becoming ill for reasons you believe are related to the stress level in the community, do not let them go silently. Invite them back to tell their stories in a safe setting where they will not be discounted or attacked. Often addicts remain in denial until their loved ones confront them with the consequences of their addiction. The same approach can work for communities. Skilled family therapists and organizational development professionals from outside an organization can often spot signs of work addiction. Invite one to work with you or to offer a workshop for the community that focuses on the balance between task and process. With or without the help of an outsider, explore this balance at a community retreat.

There is in God, some say, a deep but dazzling darkness.

HENRY VAUGHAN

A retreat or a skilled facilitator can also help if your community suffers from an excessive absorption in process. Both can assist you in defining your task and challenging yourselves to accomplish specific goals. If the employees at David Johnston's construction company had participated in a retreat designed to help them confront, in a supportive setting, the seriousness of the company's financial straits and together plan strategies for recovery, they might have spent less time in commiserating and more in drumming up new business.

6. The Sexual Coverup

Communities may be willing to talk about their internal power and money dynamics, but they usually do not even consider putting sex on the agenda unless a scandal forces them to. Yet, when a group is coalescing into community, the resulting intimacy often leads to sexual attraction. If inappropriately expressed, this powerful dynamic can ruin the community.

When sexual tensions or misbehaviors become too obvious to ignore, communities typically identify the offenders as soon as possible, get rid of them (the scapegoat syndrome), and shut the lid on the issue. They act as if the problem concerns only one or two individuals in the group and assume that, when these people are removed, the community will return to its original health. Rarely does a group or community examine a sexual flare-up as a symptom of imbalances in the system as a whole.

One community, a church in northern California, chose a different approach after members filed complaints about its pastor of twenty-three years with the National Conference of the United Church of Christ. Some complaints alleged sexual or romantic overtures to female members of the congregation.

Usually, once formal charges are brought against a pastor, either he packs his bags and leaves or the congregation kicks him out. In this case, for the first time in the history of the United Church of Christ, pastor and congregation agreed to work together in grappling with the issues, following the course of action recommended by the national conference. For the pastor, this included a six-month suspension from active ministry and a year-long prescribed course of psychotherapeutic work and clerical education. During this time the congregation engaged in its own healing process. For several months it held forums every Saturday morning at which members could speak their truth about the situation in a safe setting, with no third-party discussions, no crosstalk, and an agreement to keep whatever was said confidential. "It was a way of beginning to air the collective wound," notes one parishioner.

There is strong shadow where there is much light.

GOETHE

By facing the shadow as a community, members became aware of the underlying dysfunctional patterns of their pastor and of themselves as individuals and as a group. Some of those who had brought complaints acknowledged that their own codependent patterns played a part. They took the process as an opportunity to declare, "No, I'm not going to allow this to continue in my life." Small groups of parishioners began gathering privately in their homes and at Codependents Anonymous meetings to talk about their lives and to begin their personal healing.

"Sexual issues are difficult to share," notes psychotherapist Jonathan Tenney, "because we have such an enormous edge there—tremendous anxiety, fear, and unconsciousness. The power of the sexual experience is so overwhelming that we do one of two things: distance from it or blast through it. We never hang out at the edge." Tenney believes we need to create safe settings where we can explore our strong feelings about sexuality and use these as a source of transformation for ourselves and our communities. The Saturday forums developed by the California church provide one example of an attempt to create such a setting.

Some of the masks that groups wear to deny the potency and complexity of sexual energies range from "sex is an animal urge that we have transcended" to "sex is a holy, private matter" and "sex is no big deal." Removing these simplifying masks to reveal the complex mystery of sexual dynamics is not an easy operation. If your community feels ready to take up this challenge, we suggest you start slowly. As a preliminary step, you might create safe settings in which your members can speak honestly and with feeling about less explosive issues. As trust builds and your group develops clear communication guidelines, you may begin to explore sexual issues.

The rewards are usually worth the discomfort. When rumors of abuse ripped off the sunny, sex-is-a-lovely-and-private-part-of-our-lives mask that the pastor and parishioners had been wearing, the disclosure revealed not so much grotesque monsters and sacrificial victims as human beings with wounds—individual and collective—that had a chance to heal.

When a Community Becomes a Cult

Whole relationships, groups and even societies are big enough to use the disagreements of their members in creative ways. Disagreement is the stuff of which social intelligence is made.

PETER AND TRUDY JOHNSON-LENZ

When carried to extremes, projection, denial, and control can result in bizarre cultic abuse that makes headlines. The explosion of sex-tinted shadow material that triggered the California parish's painful soul-searching was a small firecracker compared to the bomb blasts of scandal that have rocked other groups. Top administrators of Rajneeshpuram, a guru-inspired religious settlement in rural Oregon, went to prison after being convicted of the assault and attempted murder of another highly placed member of the community. Jim Jones, the founder of San Francisco's People's Temple, led his followers into mass suicide at Jonestown, the group's Guyana compound, three days after gunmen from Jonestown had murdered a U.S. congressman and four others.

While vast differences exist between these extreme examples of cult behavior and the more commonplace shadow-related disruptions discussed above, the organizations in which both types occurred can trace their problems to a common pattern that arises from fear. "Behavior qualitatively similar to that which takes place in extreme cults takes place in all of us, despite our living in an open society, uncoerced, free to select our sources of information and our companions," contends psychiatrist Arthur J. Deikman in *The Wrong Way Home: Uncovering the Patterns of Cult Behavior in American Society.* He has found a pattern of four basic, interrelated behaviors that exist in extreme form in cults and in milder forms in virtually every social organization from the family to the school, the church, the corporation, and the media. Deikman labels these behaviors *compliance with the group, dependence on a leader, devaluing the outsider,* and *avoiding dissent.*

The first two behaviors, we have found, are common even in conscious communities, at least in early stages. Compliance with the group and dependence on a leader may well be bred into the human psyche as survival strategies and are appropriate, indeed crucial, for children. The second two, devaluing the outsider and avoiding dissent, are behaviors that conscious communities generally try to discourage. Yet being discriminating about outsiders and overriding dissent may sometimes be necessary. Certain outsiders may be sociopathic and may cause harm to the group or its members. And in an emergency or in a startup business that needs to move quickly, project or group leaders may not have time to resolve all disagreements before taking action. Sometimes a fine line exists between discriminating and devaluing, avoiding and overriding.

Integrating the Shadow

Nine Ways to Maintain Community Health

Here are some practical steps your community can take to integrate its shadow, avoid cult behavior, and maintain balance:

1. In business meetings, set aside time for personal sharing and discussion of interpersonal issues as well as for task-oriented goal setting and progress reports. In process and support-group meetings, spend some time taking care of business and occasionally reviewing your purpose and goals.
2. Clearly establish the acceptability of negative feelings. If necessary, develop processes to elicit fears, resentments, and sexual tensions—and to make such discussions safe.
3. If someone in the group is disruptive, make sure that person is heard and responded to with understanding. Listen for the underlying message, which may be the key to the community's health.
4. Look at your own family system to see whether you are carrying any dysfunctional patterns forward into your community.
5. Try wearing another hat: If you customarily focus on task and the bottom line, switch to process and vision—and vice versa.
6. If you are taking too much responsibility yourself, pass some on to others. If you're not taking enough, ask for more.
7. Don't be ashamed to ask for help. When your group needs to, call in an outside mediator or facilitator to help reestablish the balance of vision/reality, power, task/process, and group needs/individual needs.
8. While holding the vision and trusting in miracles, plan for worst-case scenarios.
9. Set aside regular times to review the group's vision, accomplishments, and internal dynamics and to play and celebrate together.

What distinguishes a cult from a healthy community is the degree and rigidity of behavior and the length of time the behavior continues. For example, if your community views all outsiders as potential enemies and operates in perpetual crisis mode, or the founders refuse to share power after the community has become stable and committed members have expressed interest in assuming greater responsibility, you may have cause for concern. Fear, the emotion that fuels survival strategies, operates as a safeguard in small doses. But when fear overwhelms the human impulses of love and trust—also essential for survival—and spreads unchecked like a cancer, it begins to threaten the health of the community.

The best way to prevent yourself or your group from falling into cult behaviors is to learn what they are. It's like knowing when you're getting drunk.

FATHER OF A CULT SURVIVOR

At the root of cult behavior lie excessive fear of the shadow and projection of it onto others. One man we interviewed, Joe, a psychologist who began studying cults after his daughter became enmeshed in one, calls this the "righteousness trap." It is akin to the harmony trap. Cult members are often people searching for a home-like community. They believe that, in the group and its leaders, they have finally found the perfect family and the ideal parents. To admit imperfection would shatter this safe haven. So they continually hold an unquestioned assumption, says Joe, that they "are never unkind or victimizers or politically incorrect or psychologically out of balance." Instead, they ascribe any such impurities to outsiders.

The best way to keep your community from becoming a cult is to continually expose its processes and dynamics to the light. Cults cannot withstand scrutiny. That is why many of them demand that members cut ties with family and friends, make the group their family, and treat questions about the community like arrows from the enemy. When government officials flew into Jonestown to investigate reported abuses, Jim Jones and his ruling clique ordered them killed. When the small, cult-like organization that Joe's daughter joined faced financial difficulties and had to allow its members to take outside jobs to support themselves, it began to lose its hold on these members. Unfiltered exposure to a broad range of people and belief systems undermined the narrow, fear-based beliefs promulgated by the cult. Most members, including Joe's daughter, eventually left and the group dissolved.

If you attempt to root out all cult behavior from your own community, however, or label any other group exhibiting such behavior a cult, you risk falling into the righteousness trap yourself. Every person and group has a shadow. This is as natural as the moon possessing a dark side and a tree providing shade. The path to health for individuals and groups lies in acknowledging the shadow and integrating it into conscious awareness. In this lies the secret of becoming whole.

When you assess your community for cultishness, take into account the phase the group is passing through and the circumstances in which the behaviors arise. If you note any of Deikman's four warning signs, ask yourself whether these represent temporary responses to a real emergency or an ongoing pattern that is no longer appropriate. Check with yourself also to make sure you are not simply projecting your own shadow onto the group. If you still believe the behaviors are not appropriate, bring the issue up in a meeting or suggest a group retreat to review the community's vision and process.

Clear communication can often resolve power plays, hidden agendas, lack of balance between task and process, and other shadow issues. The next chapter introduces you to the ingredients of healthy communication. It also offers suggestions for conducting meetings that take care of business while building stronger relationships.

In a dark time, the eye begins to see.

THEODORE ROETHKE

RESOURCES

Recommended books and articles

Meeting the Shadow: The Hidden Power of the Dark Side of Human Nature edited by Connie Zweig and Jeremiah Abrams (Jeremy P. Tarcher, 1991)

The Shadow Side of Community and the Growth of the Self, M. K. Woff-Salin (Crossroads, 1988)

Your Many Faces: The First Step to Being Loved by Virginia Satir (Celestial Arts, 1978)

A Little Book on the Human Shadow by Robert Bly (Harper & Row, 1988)

Avalanche: Heretical Reflections on the Dark and the Light by W. Brugh Joy, M.D. (Ballantine, 1990)

The Path of Least Resistance: Learning to Become the Creative Force in Your Own Life (Second Edition) by Robert Fritz (Fawcett-Columbine, 1989). Includes discussion of the tension-resolution, or "rubber-band," theory of creative manifestation.

The Paradox of Success: When Winning at Work Means Losing at Life by John R. O'Neil (Tarcher/Putnam, 1993). Explores the shadow side of success in the workplace and the hidden assets that individuals and organizations can unearth by acknowledging their shadows.

Shadow Dancing in the USA by Michael Ventura (Jeremy P. Tarcher, 1985)

People of the Lie by M. Scott Peck, M.D. (Simon & Schuster, 1983)

Faces of the Enemy by Sam Keen (Harper & Row, 1986)

The Disowned Self by Nathaniel Branden (Bantam, 1978)

Embracing Our Selves: The Voice Dialogue Manual by Hal Stone, Ph.D., and Sidra Winkelman, Ph.D. (New World Library, 1989)

Healing the Shame that Binds You by John Bradshaw (Health Communications, 1988)

The Dark Side of Love: The Positive Role of Our Negative Feelings—Anger, Jealousy, and Hate by Jane Goldberg (Jeremy P. Tarcher, 1991)

The Wrong Way Home: Uncovering Patterns of Cult Behavior in American Society by Arthur J. Deikman, M.D. (Beacon Press, 1990)

The Addictive Organization by Anne W. Schaef and Diane Fassel (Harper & Row, 1987)

"The Shadow: Embracing Our Totality" in *As Above, So Below: Paths to Spiritual Renewal in Daily Life* by Ronald S. Miller and the editors of *New Age Journal* (Jeremy P. Tarcher, 1992)

Other resources

"The Human Shadow," two ninety-minute audiotapes by Robert Bly available for $23.95 ppd. from Sounds True Catalog, 1825 Pearl St., Boulder, Colorado, 80302; (800) 333-9185.

"The Dark Side: Death, Demons and Difficult Dreams," a periodic twelve-day residential conference led by W. Brugh Joy at Moonfire Lodge, P.O. Box 730, Paulden, Arizona, 86334-0730; (800) 525-7718.

FOURTEEN

Communicating—in Meetings, in Groups, and One to One

Barriers [to authentic communication] include preconceived expectations, prejudices, cherished beliefs, the need to control, and the need to solve one anothers' problems.

FOUNDATION FOR COMMUNITY ENCOURAGEMENT

"I'M HURT AND ANGRY," Ed Margason exclaimed to the people gathered in his living room. They were all members of the Shenoa Land Stewards group, which collectively owns and maintains the Shenoa Retreat and Learning Center campus. "The three of us on the committee have been working so hard to get this garden project off the ground," Ed explained. "Now I feel like we're being accused of not doing our job well." Carolyn North, another member of the garden committee, agreed, adding that she had been awake most of the last two nights agonizing over whether she should even remain in the community.

As others in the circle took turns expressing their feelings and adding whatever factual information they thought might help, the group realized that the problem had been primarily one of miscommunication. It had started with an innocent question from the Land Stewards' group coordinator to its treasurer: Had the garden committee submitted a budget? The treasurer had mentioned the question to his wife, also a Land Steward, at the dinner table, and from there the story had turned into a version of the children's game of "telephone," in which a message becomes increasingly mangled as it is whispered from one kid to the next. No one had really thought the garden committee was not doing its job well, but as each party passed information along, he or she had added a negative spin to the comments of the previous person in the chain. By the time the message reached members of the garden committee, it sounded like a loaded, hostile accusation rather than a simple query.

One of the definitions of community is "an aggregate of people who have made a commitment to learn how to communicate with each other at an ever more deep and authentic level."

M. SCOTT PECK

Fortunately, the Land Stewards had built a solid foundation of mutual trust and respect and had developed an effective meeting format. Its members weathered what they called "the garden brouhaha" but realized that they needed to establish clear guidelines for communicating outside meetings as well as within them. They considered their dream of building a community together too important to endanger by faulty interaction patterns.

Why Communities Need Communication Agreements

Community cannot exist without communication, and the way people communicate determines the quality of individual and group relationships. As family therapist Virginia Satir puts it, "Communication is to relationship what breathing is to maintaining life." Healthy communication reconciles differences, deepens intimacy, fosters a sense of wholeness, and opens individuals to a broader view of themselves and of others. It is the primary avenue by which a group moves from functional to conscious community. By the same token, poor communication creates unnecessary barriers and allows the group's shadow to spread like a dark stain.

In traditional, homogeneous communities, members based their communication on shared backgrounds, learnings, and values. Although misunderstandings did crop up, people handled them by employing a shared "language" and by staying within communication boundaries prescribed by the traditional roles: authoritarian father figure; accommodating, nurturing, but influential mother figure; powerless child figure. With the increasing diversity of today's communities, however, these frameworks no longer fit the picture.

What you think of as common understandings may be shared by only a few members of the community. Individuals of different ages, family backgrounds, genders, professions, races, neighborhoods, and nations may share your community vision but employ vastly different modes of sending

Communication Agreement

This sample communication agreement represents a composite of actual agreements that various communities have adopted, plus a few ideas of our own. Use it as a template or discussion starter for developing your agreement. Be sure to put this agreement in writing, distribute a copy to everyone in the group, and post the agreement where new members and visitors can see it.

- *Take responsibility for your own feelings.* Do not expect others to read your mind. Use "I" statements and refrain from blaming.
- *Communicate directly with the person or persons involved in an issue.* Do not work through go-betweens or serve as a go-between for others. If someone asks you for information about an issue in which you are not directly involved, direct him or her to the proper source.
- *Do not speak critically about others behind their backs* unless you voice the same criticisms to their faces. To avoid unhelpful speculation, give specific names when you make a critical comment in a meeting.
- *State your position or concern before asking how others feel about it.* Do not set someone up to give a "wrong" answer. Be courageous and put yourself on the spot first.
- *Practice active listening.* Listen silently and with your whole self until the speaker has finished speaking. Then restate what the speaker has said and wait for a confirmation.
- *Provide continual feedback.* Do not allow resentments to build up, and do not forget to give positive strokes.
- *Respect and validate others' feelings.* If you do not agree or do not support another's statement, acknowledge what has been said, then make your point.
- *Use humor softly,* not sharply.

The solution is not a model, it's a path—and the key to that path is dialogue. . . . I believe the only way answers will emerge is through real talk among people. When everything is reduced to polarized issues, shrill name calling and sound-bite simplification, we've lost public talk about our values—the basis of all real problem-solving.

Frances Moore Lappé

and receiving messages. Also, instead of settling for partial personal development, many contemporary community and family members are seeking to express all aspects of themselves. Individuals are learning how to be both tough and tender, assertive and receptive, innovative and supportive. And they are discovering that helping each other in these efforts allows them to free themselves from the bonds of traditional roles.

Taking these new priorities into consideration, conscious communities are developing communication styles and meeting procedures that increase trust and support both individual and group development. If your community wishes to take a positive and time-saving first step toward these goals, you will want to begin communicating about communication. You might start by discussing and committing to explicit agreements. Kay and Floyd Tift, in their community-building workshops, point out, "You wouldn't think of driving a car in crowded city traffic without acknowledging the presence of and in most cases cooperating with legal traffic signals. Group life requires communication agreements for the same reason: to avoid wasteful collisions." To develop agreements, your group will need to understand the basics of effective, community-friendly communication.

Telling the truth brings about a state of lightness and energy in your body that few other things can engender. Hiding the truth blocks energy at a very fundamental, cellular level.

GAY AND KATHLYN HENDRICKS

INGREDIENTS OF HEALTHY COMMUNICATION

Healthy interactions within a community require that members communicate honestly, frequently, directly, and respectfully; that their words convey the same message as their emotions, body posture, and actions; that they are willing and able to listen as well as to speak; and that diverse members feel included, empowered to function in both leadership and support roles, and able to pursue the group vision while honoring individual needs.

Risking Honesty and Taking Responsibility

To communicate with honesty, you need to pay attention to your own personal truth and the truth that emerges through the wisdom of the group. Whether the group consists of two people or two hundred, no one person possesses the entire truth of a situation. Each person, therefore, can speak only his or her own truth. The larger truth develops in synergy with these individual expressions.

In practical terms, this means you become a more honest and more effective communicator if you speak from your heart and body than if you try to interpret someone else's behavior or motives. Talk about what actually happened and take responsibility for your own feelings. "I felt angry when you said such-and-such" is direct and difficult to argue with. (How can the other person deny that you felt what you felt?) "You made me angry" is interpretive, blaming, and likely to produce an argumentative response rather than a sincere expression of the other person's feelings.

Sometimes statements that begin with "I feel" can generate a similar response. "I feel that your actions are the cause of this mess" is an example. The statement does not describe a feeling; it makes an accusation. If you are not sure how to express what you are feeling, observe and comment on your body sensations: "I'm getting a pain in my chest as we're discussing this."

It's important to understand that every time you talk, all of you talks. Whenever you say words, your face, voice, body, breathing, and muscles are talking, too.

VIRGINIA SATIR

Using these "I" messages takes practice. If you are like most people, you are uncomfortable putting the emphasis on yourself. It almost seems egotistical. But it is really a matter of taking responsibility and allowing your real self to interact with others' real selves. This includes speaking directly to the person with whom you have an issue, rather than gossiping, using a go-between, or speaking in terms that are so abstract or general that your listener is not sure what you mean. For example, saying "Some people in this room aren't doing their part" is likely to generate confusion and defensiveness rather than inspire particular group members to participate more.

Since your real self is your whole self, you need to remember that words, however apt, represent only part of your communication. Your facial expression, tone of voice, and body carry your messages also, whether you intend them to or not. Studies reveal that such non-verbal cues constitute more than ninety percent of human communication. If these messages are not congruent with your words—for example, if you smile when you are conveying bad news—your listener becomes confused. The alert and caring listener, rather than responding only to the body language or only to the words, will do you a favor if he or she says, "I've noticed that you're smiling but what you've told me is very disturbing." This is an invitation to talk about your real feelings. Although few listeners are so candid, they will still—consciously or unconsciously—register all the messages you send and react to you accordingly.

You need not expect to feel comfortable in conveying bad news. It feels—and often is—risky to tell your neighbor that you are upset because he returned your tools in poor condition, or to inform your support group that you do not consider its process supportive. Someone might, in fact, respond to you with annoyance, rage, or real challenge. But suppressing feelings undermines intimacy and blocks conscious community.

The major communication problem in any type of community, says organizational consultant and trainer Betty Didcoct, is failure to clear up interpersonal disturbances early. "Little annoying things can be like little bricks," she points out, "stacking up until pretty soon you've got a wall. If something comes up that bothers me, I ask myself, 'Am I willing to let this go?' If not, it could be a brick." She adds that bricks can also be used to create pathways. Ed and Carolyn at Shenoa would agree. Although it was not easy for them to confess to the group that they felt so hurt and angry, they took the risk and did so with non-blaming "I" statements. Although the others reacted with a flurry of confused emotions at first, they quickly took the opportunity to practice their interactive skills and begin the healing process. Later the group developed a set of communication agreements that have helped members stay aware and forestall further disconnections.

In silence, we often say, we can hear ourselves think; but what is truer to say is that in silence we can hear ourselves not think, and so sink below our selves into a place far deeper than mere thought allows. In silence, we might better say, we can hear someone else think.

PICO IYER

Business organizations know the importance of continual performance feedback. It is unfair and counterproductive for a supervisor to surprise an employee with an unfavorable performance review when the employee has been unaware of any deficiencies. Good supervisors comment on performance and help employees improve, right from the beginning. Similarly, good community members—in work organizations and anywhere else—provide caring and constructive feedback to fellow members, on a day-to-day basis, as a way of creating a mutually growth-supportive climate.

To honor silence means to filter out the negative and allow the gold to emerge as a gift.

RABBI SAUL RUBIN

The Power of Silence

Both words and body language possess their own power, and so does another form of communication: silence. Most people, while they may know how to give someone "the silent treatment" as a form of punishment, are not nearly so familiar with the positive uses of silence. Yet people can use silence as an effective tool for community building.

In one of their business meetings, members of the Shenoa Retreat and Learning Center board were arguing over a budget item. One person strongly objected to spending funds for what she considered another's pet project, which caused the second person to become upset and defensive. When other members jumped in to try to settle the matter, emotions ran even higher. Finally, one member said, "Wait a moment, we are opening some old wounds here. Treating this like a factual business item is not going to work." She called for five minutes of silence. Everyone stopped talking. By the end of the five minutes, the board members felt calmer, and, in quiet voices, took turns reporting what they had experienced during the silent period. Suddenly the budget item seemed much less important than the relationships that needed healing. The board deferred the matter until the next meeting, when the members resolved it amicably.

Native Americans and Quakers represent two cultures that use the power of silence in a positive way. You can see an example of this positive use in the movie *Dances with Wolves,* when a Native American tribe meets to decide what to do about the white man who has come into its midst. One member talks, then another, then another, until everyone who wanted to say something has done so, and then they all sit in silence. Finally they get up and leave, and although at first it seems as though they have not resolved anything, they later reveal that they have all experienced the same truth.

In their silence, they were attuning with one another, as were the members of the Shenoa board after their emotional upheaval over a funding issue. Quakers often begin business meetings with periods of silent attunement. The attunement is not only with others and with the group as a whole but also with the self. Silence enables you to center yourself and listen to your inner voice. The Quakers would call this "opening to spirit," but you do not need to believe in spirit for it to work. You only need to listen.

Unless you listen, you can't know anybody. Oh, you will know facts and what is in the newspapers and all of history, perhaps, but you will not know one single person. You know, I have come to think listening is love, that's what it really is.

BRENDA UELAND

The Value of Listening

Listening is as central to communication as speaking. Until the recipient "gets the message," communication is not complete. If you have never *just listened* to another person, without reacting or responding, try it; you may be surprised at the power of your silent communication. Most people feel a desperate need to be heard. Yet attentive listening does not come naturally unless you practice it. You can easily allow your own biases, experiences, preoccupations, and your own desire to be heard intrude on your listening. You may also need to overcome a cultural bias that gives the assertive act of speaking higher status than the receptive act of listening. Listening is a learned skill, just as much as public speaking is.

If you typically begin forming your response before the speaker has finished, your listening skills need work. Because you are tuning out the speaker here and there, you are not likely to take in or process everything that is being said, so you are setting the stage for miscommunication. For example, you may hear that the person is leaving the group, but fail to hear the reason accurately because you are getting ready to express your dismay. As a result, your response may be inappropriate, you may alienate the speaker, and you may miss an important revelation about your group dynamics. Conscious communities practice active listening: silently empathizing with the person who is speaking and then summarizing, aloud, what that person has said so that he or she will have an opportunity to clear up any misperceptions. "As I understand it, what you just said was . . . Did I get that right?"

Effective Written Communications

Not all forms of communication occur in what computer scientists call "real time," that is, when the sender is delivering a communication at the same time the receiver is receiving it. Types of communication that occur outside real time include written notes or newsletters delivered to a mailbox and notices posted on a bulletin board, either physical or electronic. Like personal interaction, each of these modes contains its own risks. Yet communities need the flexibility of using whatever medium serves a particular purpose best.

Silence, then, could be said to be the ultimate province of trust: it is the place where we trust ourselves to be alone; where we trust others to understand the things we do not say; where we trust a higher harmony to assert itself.

PICO IYER

Become aware of when you are moved to speak and when you are not moved to speak.

FOUNDATION FOR COMMUNITY ENCOURAGEMENT

Stelle community uses a five-by-eight-foot Open Forum bulletin board in the community center's mailroom, which everyone visits daily to pick up mail. Residents post ideas, insights, articles, marriage and birth announcements, ads to sell bicycles—whatever you might find in a community newspaper. As its name suggests, the Open Forum board is also an arena for ongoing public discussions and expressions of feelings.

When Stelle's founder departed, leaving roiled emotions in his wake, voluminous Open Forum postings—not unlike computer network postings about sensitive issues—served as an outlet for frustration and pain and helped prepare residents for an in-person meeting. On another occasion, however, misuse of this medium almost caused frustration and pain. Stelle resident Susan Fisher tells the story:

"Someone who was upset with me wrote an open letter about me and put it on the board. Another person, who saw how critical it was, took the letter down and put it in my mailbox. The letter writer was furious and called me, thinking I had taken it down. Fortunately, this gave me an opportunity to say, 'If you have a problem with me, please see me directly.'"

Some group process experts advise against writing letters or notes when you have anything negative to communicate. The most well-intended notes may come across as hostile without the backup of tone, facial expression, or gestures. For expressions of love and appreciation, however, the written message, which can be referred to again and again, is hard to beat. Author Garrison Keillor sees letters as a way for people, particularly shy people, to "express the music of our souls," to "say a few things that might not get said in casual conversation." In an essay in *We Are Still Married,* he suggests a process that you may find useful if the members of your community or family are geographically scattered:

"Sit for a few minutes with the blank sheet in front of you, and meditate on the person you will write to, let your friend come to mind until you can almost see her or him in the room with you. Remember the last time you saw each other and how your friend looked and what you said and what perhaps was unsaid between you, and when your friend becomes real to you, start to write."

You can also write to people who are not distant; even a fellow community member you see every day will feel closer to you after receiving your appreciative, caring missive. A retired postman suggested to us that one way to expand community would be to send lots of "love postcards" to your friends and neighbors, so that mail carriers can read them too and share in the warmth.

Be patient toward all that is unresolved in your heart and . . . try to love the questions *themselves like locked rooms and like books that are written in a very foreign tongue. Do not now seek the answers, which cannot be given you because you would not be able to live them. And the point is, to live everything.* Live *the questions now.*

RAINER MARIA RILKE

How Personal Styles Complicate Communication

As communication has become more global and communities increasingly diverse, well-meaning people run a much greater risk of miscommunicating simply because their style of expressing themselves sends unintended messages. Cross-cultural studies reveal that your area of origin may determine both what you say and how you say it. In certain Arabic cultures, for example, people like to stand close together in conversation, while Americans are more comfortable at a distance of eighteen to twenty-four inches. Many Asians consider it impolite to pass on bad news or to come directly to the point. Even within the United States, people from disparate areas differ in the amount of time they allow as pauses between sentences. Family backgrounds, even within the same culture, condition people to communicate in different patterns.

J. Keith Miller, author of *Compelled to Control,* maintains that two types of communicators exist as far as openness is concerned: skunks and turtles. Skunks express feelings by spewing them out as a skunk spews out odor. Turtles do not share inner feelings at all. At first, these two types may attract one another—since they appear to balance or complete each other—and even marry. But then the turtles become frightened and the skunks frustrated by the other's style. Sometimes they give up trying to communicate with each other.

Pervasive cultural differences also exist between men and women. (Yes, male and female are in many ways different cultures.) Several sociologists and linguists, including Dr. Deborah Tannen, author of *You Just Don't Understand: Women and Men in Conversation,* have discovered that women tend to use language to create intimacy and consensus, while men use it to establish and maintain status. Men are more likely than women to express disagreement, to talk more often and longer in meetings, and to listen for problems and solutions rather than emotional context. According to Tannen, women's style is to tell the men everything that is on their minds, sometimes engaging in "troubles talk," as a way to become closer. Men, whose conversations with each other usually focus on doing something, have trouble figuring out what the women want from them. Trying to be helpful, they may jump in immediately with a solution, which women view as a conversation-stopper. Or, deciding that women just go on and on about nothing, men begin to tune them out. Men who dominate meetings and social gatherings clam up when at home with their wives, because they see no need to claim status there.

Cartoon character Cathy, after getting a terrible hairdo: "Oh, Irving, I just feel so ugly . . . I feel so stupid . . ." Irving: "Wear a hat." Cathy: "Wear a hat??" Irving: "Wear a hat. Call the salon. Make them fix your hair. Crisis over! What's the big deal?" Cathy, after slamming door in his face: "Men: all solution, no sympathy."

CATHY GUISEWITE

Men and women express emotion differently. Men sometimes perceive women as being *too* emotional, while women perceive certain men as overly rational. Such appearances can be misleading. *Fire in the Belly* author Sam Keen, who runs workshops on communication between genders, says, "When a man is being angry, look for the pain underneath. When a woman is in tears, look for the anger underneath."

When skunks and turtles, males and females, and people from different cultural backgrounds understand the other's mode of communication, they can often avoid hurt feelings and misunderstandings. As Tannen comments, "Not seeing style differences for what they are, people draw conclusions about personality ('you're illogical,' 'you're insecure,' 'you're self-centered') or intentions ('you don't listen,' 'you put me down'). Understanding style differences for what they are takes the sting out of them. . . . You can ask for or make adjustments without casting or taking blame." When you notice a miscommunication about to happen because of a style difference, point it out so that those involved can clear it up right away. Also, if your community is a safe place for you to develop new forms of self-expression, try out other styles yourself. You will grow as a communicator and begin to develop previously unused aspects of your whole personality.

MEETINGS: MINI-COMMUNITIES

In meetings, your community reveals its collective conversational style. You can let this evolve unconsciously or pay attention to it, noticing what works and what does not and refining your interactions accordingly. You can turn your meetings into regular opportunities for becoming more conscious and effective as a community—and more deeply bonded. Every meeting serves as a microcosm of community. Each is an organic whole within the whole that takes on a life of its own but also reflects the spirit of the larger community as well as that of the individuals who comprise it.

Responding to Different Needs

Most people associate meetings with doing business, although twelve-steppers may also link the notion of going to a meeting with receiving and giving support. Yet meetings can and do serve other purposes including networking, spiritual regeneration, and emotional clearing. Each of these types of meeting can build community. Problems arise, however, when the participants become confused about what kind of meeting they intend, or attempt to handle all these objectives in a single meeting. If John has not resolved his anger toward Maria, he may disrupt a business meeting when the group is discussing her suggestion. If Joan is expecting a spiritual deepening experience, she may feel impatient when the meeting focuses on supporting one member's emotional needs.

One of the most terrible responsibilities in the world is that of really being present, of being a presence for the other. We cannot achieve dialogue by an act of will, for dialogue is a genuinely two-sided affair.

MAURICE FRIEDMAN

For this reason, some communities hold separate meetings for separate purposes. Alpha Farm, a visionary residential community, devotes an entire day each month to working out emotional issues, which makes the monthly business meeting, held on another day, go much more smoothly. Workplace teams take time out for retreats to revitalize, socialize, and network. The Fellowship for Intentional Community, comprised of representatives from some 130 residential communities, divides its semiannual board meeting into three sections: a two-day "pre-meeting" in which the five-member Administrative Council refines the agenda, develops proposals, and clears interpersonal issues; a three-day meeting in which the council and Board of Directors make business decisions; and a three- or four-day "later committee" to clean up the minutes and discuss any decisions that the group deferred to the Administrative Council. FIC opens all meetings to anyone interested; people can choose to participate or merely observe. Between board meetings, members of the board and council, who are scattered all over the country, communicate almost daily by way of electronic mail.

Betty Didcoct, who serves on the Administrative Council, recalls a "major blow-up" when another council member became angry during the pre-meeting because he felt that others had failed to consider his position. The council took a full day to work through the issues raised by his frustration and others' reactions to his explosive style, but Betty emphasizes that the time was well spent. "He was going to leave the council in bitterness, which would have divided the whole group. Our meeting healed the split. I've seen a lot of groups bite the dust because they failed to heal emotions."

All real living is meeting.

MARTIN BUBER

Guidelines for Communicating in Meetings

- Share speaking time. Give every member a chance to make her or his unique contribution.
- Make your needs known to the group. If you are preoccupied in a way that takes you away from the group task, or if you have a particular personal agenda, bring it to the attention of the group.
- Speak to the point. Talk about the current agenda topic or acknowledge that you are changing to a new one. State your main point first, then offer background information, rather than building up to your main point.
- Avoid side conversations and interruptions.
- Respect time and format guidelines. If special circumstances require that you arrive late, tune in quietly to where the group is. If you are the facilitator, start and end the meeting on time.

Communities such as Alpha and the FIC understand the importance of taking care of feelings as well as business. Shenoa's communication agreement contains the statement, "Individual disturbances come first." Although Shenoans are committed to working out conflicts and providing emotional support to each other as part of day-to-day life, they recognize that someone might come to a business meeting angry or in pain. Others would then begin feeling unsettled and might find it difficult to attend to the task at hand. Shenoa asks each person to take responsibility for making his or her needs known to the group if they might disrupt the process. The community does not limit individual disturbances to emotional ones; a member might ask about opening a window to increase ventilation or excuse him- or herself to make a phone call to the babysitter. Although such concerns may seem trivial, ignoring them can increase significantly a member's discomfort and reduce his or her ability to focus on the discussion.

Building Inclusiveness

To embrace the diversity that gives a meeting its richness and the community its strength, the meeting process needs to be inclusive. When women or minorities feel intimidated or newcomers left out, the bonds of community begin to weaken. Communities have evolved a number of ways to ensure that meetings benefit from everyone's contribution.

Role rotation. This approach helps participants develop and broaden their communication skills and distributes responsibility for such tedious tasks as notetaking. It involves rotating the following four key roles:

We are not trying to win in a dialogue. We all win if we are doing it right.

David Bohm

1. The *facilitator* (sometimes called focalizer or discussion guide) starts the meeting; obtains agreement on the purpose, agenda, and closing time; introduces items for discussion; and closes with a summary of the meeting's content. This person does *not* take a "leadership" or partisan position and sometimes does not even participate in decisions. If you are acting as facilitator and an issue comes up about which you feel strongly, you may want to turn over your facilitator role to another member, at least temporarily. Some communities hire outside facilitators when particularly important and sensitive matters are on the agenda.
2. The *notetaker* records suggestions, decisions, and reasons behind the decisions—in the speaker's words, without putting a personal slant on anything. Writing on a flip chart enables participants to see a living record of the meeting as it progresses. The notetaker takes responsibility for recording the exact wording of agreements and for preserving the notes for future reference. Some residential communities and shared houses keep the notes in a specific place so that residents can refer to them whenever they like.
3. The *process observer* or *witness* monitors the quality of the meeting process and alerts participants to energy blocks. If, as process observer, you notice someone sitting with arms folded and frowning, you can say, "I want to make sure Lee's concerns have been heard." At the end of the meeting, the process observer summarizes his or her observations: Did the meeting start and end on time? Did it achieve its purpose? What can the group learn from the way participants performed their roles? How well did the group handle disagreements? This post-meeting review is essential for improving meeting and communicating skills.
4. The *timekeeper* keeps track of the time allotted for each agenda item, and for the meeting as a whole, and informs the group if it is about to run overtime. Timekeeping helps keep the meeting on schedule and ensures that no one issue dominates. However, the participants may agree, after the timekeeper informs them of the time, to extend a particular discussion.

Your group may choose to share roles within a meeting. For example, the facilitator can serve as timekeeper as well (although this demands extra alertness), and a guest can be invited to comment on process. In The WELL, a computer network community, a host moderates each conference, removes old material, encourages some discussions to move to other conferences, and endeavors to keep the flow of communication lively and interesting. This facilitative role used to be called "fair witness"—which illustrates how the two concepts blend into each other.

A woman who runs a counseling center noted that when she meets with women on her staff, it is not unusual for them to spend 75 percent of the time in personal talk and then efficiently take care of business in the remaining 25 percent. To men on the staff, this seems like wasting time.

DEBORAH TANNEN

Circle check. This technique provides each meeting participant an opportunity to speak for an uninterrupted period. (Sitting in a circle helps people direct comments toward each other.) Members can speak in the order in which they are sitting or in any order—also called "popcorn style"—as they are moved to speak. Many communities begin each meeting with a circle check to focus everyone's attention on the group. In this check-in, new members introduce themselves. Old and new members share their current states of mind, explore their successes and failures, and mention whether there is anything going on in their lives that might inhibit their full participation in the meeting.

Some communities use the check-in as a time for clearing—bringing up and dealing with interpersonal problems. In such cases, the group needs to avoid getting bogged down in negativity. In one shared household, each person first says something positive about what is going on in the house and then mentions something that is causing her or him concern. In another, meetings begin with two circle checks: the first go-around for confessing personal failings, such as "I didn't do the dishes when it was my turn," as well as irritations or complaints; the second for making positive statements about self and others. In one work team that consciously seeks to build community, each member checks in with a rueful "I blew it" statement, which relaxes everyone and ignites a spirit of cooperative problem solving.

Many communities consider the circle check before meetings essential to building trust and reducing the likelihood of polarization. When you hear someone very different from you speak from the heart about his or her feelings, you cannot readily write this person off as a mere type. Also, when you know that at every meeting you will have the chance to speak without interruption for at least a few minutes, you begin to feel more supported and empowered. At Shenoa, meeting participants never omit the circle check no matter how packed the agenda may be with pressing business items. Several board members and Land Stewards credit the bonding that has occurred during this simple check-in with enabling their groups to survive serious disagreements.

Circle checks also help keep the meeting flexible. If you come to a meeting upset about the death of a friend, for example, the group may decide to postpone the next agenda item to tend to your needs. Even in the middle of a meeting, the facilitator or another member may call for a circle check to take the temperature of the group if it appears that emotions are heating up.

A few simple silent reflections can be useful: Will my speaking serve me? Will the circle or community be served? Will the "bigger picture," life, God . . . be served? When doubts remain, it is usually best to take the leap. Boldness is rarely inappropriate.

JACK ZIMMERMAN AND VIRGINIA COYLE

Open-ended circle checks in large, diverse, or inexperienced groups might stretch out for hours and still result in uneven participation. Even in such a situation, however, you can make sure that everyone is heard. The civic organization Chattanooga Venture uses and teaches the nominal group technique, a planning process developed by Dr. Andre L. Delbecq at California's University of Santa Clara Graduate School of Business. The process has enabled hundreds of people attending citywide meetings to feel included and heard. Participants split into smaller groups, each with a trained facilitator. The facilitator gives each small-group participant a sheet of paper with a triggering question at the top—for example, "How can neighborhoods more effectively communicate with one another?" Everyone works silently and independently for a few minutes. Then each person in turn reads one idea, which a notetaker writes on a flip chart. After the group clarifies the meaning of each idea, each person writes on an index card what he or she considers the five most important items. The participants, who feel empowered and included by this time, then prioritize and discuss the items in a spirit of shared endeavor. Later, the meeting organizers publish a summary of each small group's suggestions.

The talking stick. To keep members from interrupting each other, many communities employ a "talking stick." If you hold the stick—or whatever object your community chooses to use—you may speak as long as you need to without interruption. When you finish, you pass the stick to the person next to you or to someone who has raised his or her hand. If no one wishes to speak right then, you place the stick in the center of the room, where someone else may retrieve it. The talking stick device works particularly well in giving shy people, newcomers, and children a chance to be heard.

An interesting variation helps groups limit and time each person's statement in a gentle, unobtrusive manner. The person to the left of each speaker holds a watch and times the speech. After the designated time—

two minutes, for example—the timer passes the watch to the speaker as a signal to finish. The person who just spoke then times the next person, and so on until everyone has had a turn.

In many of its computer network activities, the Institute for Awakening Technology uses an electronic talking stick–style circle that it calls a Virtual Circle. Each week the group, or its facilitator, poses a question or outlines an issue. Participants respond only once during the weekly round. They "listen" to one another by reading and reflecting upon the various responses that they call up on their computer screens.

Mutual understanding is a form of inclusive convergence in which everyone comes to understand all points of view, even though s/he does not necessarily agree with all of them.

TRUDY AND PETER JOHNSON-LENZ

For some groups, including certain Native American tribes, talking sticks represent far more than a discussion device. According to *Thinkpeace* editor Tom Atlee, who learned about talking sticks from a Native American on the Great American Peace March in 1986, the sticks embody what he calls the "wisdom-heart" of these groups, and are often artifacts of great beauty, simplicity, or significance. "Whoever holds the talking stick," explains Atlee, "is bound to speak their heart-truth as an offering to the group. They are mindful that they are speaking their unique facet of the group's voice, and that the group's whole voice must be heard."

Participants listen from their hearts, not their heads, and a member of the circle simply may hold the stick during his or her turn, letting a pregnant silence deepen. Some believe the listening, not the speaking, generates the power of such circles. In these groups, the stick does not make just one circle but goes around the group many times, "spiraling," as Atlee puts it, "deeper into the mystery, drawing up the group's evolving wisdom." This repeated going around impedes both domination of the group by one or two members and the kind of back-and-forth discussion that characterizes most communication. "Each statement," says Atlee, "arises newly from the present, deepening moment." Such circle councils become not only a potent method of community exploration but also a discipline for attuning to one another and to spirit.

Everyone's Responsibility

Even when a group uses circle checks and talking sticks, disruptions, domination, and distractions sometimes occur. A skilled facilitator can steer a meeting through such rough waters with comments such as, "We need to move on—could the two of you discuss this outside the meeting?" or "Let's take all the proposals first, as we agreed, and discuss them after we've heard them all." If men seem to be dominating the meeting, the facilitator

Three A's for an Effective Meeting

To be productive, satisfying, and supportive of community, meetings require certain physical and psychological elements that we call The Three A's: Agenda, Attitude, and Awareness. How well do your meetings reflect these three criteria?

1. *Agenda.* This is determined, if possible, at the previous meeting, and a working form posted or circulated well in advance of the meeting. Anyone who wishes can provide input to it. Everyone respects the agenda as a framework for accomplishing the task of community building.

2. *Attitude.* Participants come to the meeting with the intention of serving the group. They arrive on time so as not to distract or disrupt the flow. They welcome diversity and the opportunity to hear others' ideas, and are prepared to be flexible. They take responsibility for their own ideas, feelings, and proposals.

3. *Awareness.* Remembering that the meeting reflects the wholeness of the group, participants pay attention to both individual needs and group needs. They are sensitive to others' feelings in both areas. They keep the communication agreements and remind others of them when necessary.

might suggest that, for the next ten minutes or so, men and women speak alternately. The timekeeper can remind the group that time is running out and important agenda items remain to be handled. But in a meeting where creating community is a prime concern, balance between task and process, individual and group needs becomes everyone's responsibility.

Although at a particular moment you may not hold one of the four key roles, you may need to comment, in a spirit of love and support (and using "I" statements), on behavior that is destructive to the group. Do not let things slide to avoid criticism or conflict. A group of men who wrote an article called "Overcoming Masculine Oppression in Mixed Groups" point out, "It is no act of friendship to allow friends to continue dominating those around them." Besides being aware of their own tendencies—such as hogging the show, condescending, avoiding feelings through intellectualizing or joking, and treating women seductively—men need to alert each other when they observe such behavior, these authors believe. For individuals, whether men or women, to learn of their inappropriate or dysfunctional behavior in time to take corrective action serves not only them but the group.

In addition to serving as mini-communities where communication skills can be honed, meetings provide the setting for group decision making and conflict resolution. You will find these two related topics treated at length in the following two chapters.

Resources

Recommended books and articles

You Just Don't Understand: Women and Men in Conversation by Deborah Tannen (Ballantine, 1990)

Compelled to Control by J. Keith Miller (Health Communications, 1992)

The New People Making by Virginia Satir (Science & Behavior Books, 1988)

The Great Turning: Personal Peace, Global Victory by Craig Schindler and Gary Lapid (Bear and Company, 1989). About real dialogue—civic and personal.

Council by Jack Zimmerman and Virginia Coyle, a booklet about talking stick circles available from The Ojai Foundation, Box 1620, Ojai, California, 93023. Zimmerman and Coyle also do workshops on Council.

Salon-Keeper's Companion—a booklet describing various group processes, including Council. Comes as part of membership in Neighborhood Salon Association, c/o *Utne Reader,* 1624 Harmon Place, Minneapolis, Minnesota, 55403.

Listening: The Forgotten Skill by Madeleine Burley-Allen (Wiley, 1982)

How to Make Meetings Work by Michael Doyle and David Straus (Berkley Publishing Group, 1976). A classic.

People Skills: How to Assert Yourself, Listen to Others, and Resolve Conflicts by Robert Bolton, Ph.D. (Touchstone, 1986)

"How to Write a Letter" In *We Are Still Married* by Garrison Keillor (Penguin, 1990)

"Overcoming Masculine Oppression in Mixed Groups" by Bill Moyer, Bruce Kokopeli, Alan Tuttle, and George Lakey, *Win,* Nov. 10, 1977 (reprints available for $2 from Social Movement Empowerment Project, 721 Shrader St., San Francisco, California, 94117; (415) 387-3361).

"Dialogue at the Heart of Change" by Tom Atlee in *Thinkpeace,* January 1992. 6622 Tremont, Oakland, California, 94609; (510) 654-0349.

"Comparison of Dialogue and Debate," by Shelley Berman, in *Focus on Study Circles,* Winter 1993, available from Study Circles Resource Center, P.O. Box 203, Rt. 169, Pomfret, Connecticut, 06258.

Video

Speaking from the Heart, thirty-eight-minute video, available for $25 from The Ojai Foundation, Box 1620, Ojai, California, 93023.

Organizations

Chattanooga Venture, 506 Broad Street, Chattanooga, Tennessee, 37402; (615) 267-8687. Teaches other civic and nonprofit organizations the nominal group process to facilitate communication and goal-setting in large-group meetings. Publishes *The Facilitator's Manual* ($10).

Corporate Scenes, Inc., 2842 Prince St., Berkeley, California, 94705; (510) 547-5169. Offers business organizations seminars in interpersonal and team-building skills. CSI's "Active Communicating" seminars, based in the actor's discipline of creating effective communication, teach participants how to engage in the kind of real dialogue that forms the basis of true community in the workplace and elsewhere.

American Working Theater, 2842 Prince St., Berkeley, California, 94705; (510) 547-5678. Founded and staffed by the same people who run Corporate Scenes, Inc. (above). Provides similar communication and team-building trainings for inner-city groups and other nonprofit organizations.

Organizational Consultants, Inc., P.O. Box 330145, San Francisco, California, 94133; (415) 956-7690. Links consultants in the United States and overseas with groups and organizations—large and small—that wish to increase their effectiveness in communication, problem-solving, collaboration, and decision-making. Offers seminars on consulting for organizational effectiveness.

American Society for Training and Development (ASTD), 1640 King Street, P.O. Box 1443, Alexandria, Virginia, 22313-2043; (703) 683-8129 (customer support). A professional association whose members provide trainings and consulting services in communication, decision-making, and other community-building skills. Publishes the *ASTD Buyers Guide and Consultant Directory* (free to members, $55 for non-members).

FIFTEEN

Making Decisions and Governing

Rather than asking "What can I get from this land, or person?" we can ask "What does this person, or land, have to give if I cooperate with them?"

BILL MOLLISON

IN COMMUNITIES OF ALL kinds—from circles of friends to workplace teams—the way you make decisions and share power can either build or undermine relationships, strengthen or sabotage success, and renew or deaden vitality. No matter how small or informal your community may be, you are a governing body, and the choices you make, whether overtly or implicitly, constitute your system of governance.

Over the last few decades, corporations have learned that participatory forms of governance, more than authoritarian ones, not only boost productivity but also create a sense of community in the workplace. The brave ones have turned their neat, pyramid-shaped organizational charts into circular jumbles with leaders becoming servants and line employees experts. Many of these supposedly new forms of governance turn out to be not so new at all. They have been honed by visionary residential communities and social change groups for decades and the Quakers and native peoples for centuries. The lessons that corporations and communities have been learning about how to generate commitment and unleash creativity can serve your community well.

New Concepts of Power and Leadership

Especially in the West, leaders are heroes—great men (and occasionally women) who rise to the fore in times of crisis. So long as such myths prevail, they reinforce a focus on short-term events and charismatic heroes rather than on systemic forces and collective learning. Leadership in learning organizations centers on subtler and ultimately more important work. In a learning organization, leaders' roles differ dramatically from that of the charismatic decision maker. Leaders are designers, teachers, and stewards.

PETER M. SENGE

Any system of governance operates according to a particular set of power dynamics. For example, think about the many friendships among supposed equals in which one person does most of the initiating and the other most of the supporting. In your community, you can choose to make your power dynamics conscious and continually refine them to match your agreed-upon values and vision. If you instead choose to let power dynamics develop below the level of group awareness, you take the chance that they will mirror the values that each of you learned in your family of origin rather than those you now hold. You also risk falling into either the harmony trap, the equality trap, or both.

Members of the women's group that you met in Chapter Twelve made a silent choice not to question their internal power dynamics. No one wished to appear critical of other members and disturb the surface sheen of sisterhood. When a member became too uncomfortable with the resulting tensions, she left the group, giving some other excuse. Finally, this harmony trap, and the unresolved power issues that it masked, split the group apart.

The very term "power dynamics" suggests fluid relationships within an interactive system. More and more corporations are discovering that this interactive systems model works best in a rapidly changing, information-based culture. With easy access to information through technology, power (which depends on information) diffuses in non-linear fashion throughout organizations and neighborhoods and across national borders. People and institutions are beginning to perceive that power is not like a pie to be divided up, with some people receiving larger pieces than others. Rather, it is a dynamic that strengthens everyone as it is shared. In this information era, top-down controlling forms of governance—whether the father-knows-best approach in families or the boss-knows-best attitude in corporations—no longer work.

Businesses are finding out that sometimes the mailroom clerk or the customer knows best when it comes to redesigning a system for maximum effectiveness. Interdepartmental teams that include managers, clerks, and technicians, together with customers and vendors, are creating successful new initiatives. Because this approach works only in an atmosphere of trust and respect, effective leaders strive to create such a climate, inspiring others to commit to a common purpose, take personal responsibility for the greater whole, and care for their individual needs in the process. The more commitment that leaders can generate, the less control they need to exercise, and, as studies have shown, the greater productivity and creativity they can unleash.

While voluntary communities seem, by their very nature, to operate on trust and commitment, fear and the tendency to control can infect these affiliations as severely as they can hierarchical workplaces. In fact, fear-based dynamics, because they operate underground, can be more insidious in voluntary communities. In a hierarchical organization, everyone knows who holds the power to hire and fire, set the agenda, and control the purse strings. In "peer" communities, members might not be aware of undermining power issues until a crisis arises or the group begins to dissolve through attrition.

So long as several men together consider themselves to be a single body, they have but a single will, which is concerned with their common preservation and the general well-being. Then . . . the common good is clearly apparent everywhere, demanding only common sense to be perceived.

ROUSSEAU

No matter how committed you and other members of your community may be to shared leadership and participative decision making, you also may be vulnerable to the fear and control patterns that have shaped the social institutions of your culture, from family and school to church and government. Recognizing this and working as a group to change these dynamics can strengthen and deepen your community bonds. This requires developing, as part of your group governance, a clearly defined purpose or shared direction and finding ways to align new and old members with it.

A community is a group of all leaders who share equal responsibility for and commitment to maintaining its spirit.

FOUNDATION FOR COMMUNITY ENCOURAGEMENT

Without conscious attention to your values and system of governance, you may slowly lose members. In a culture in which people experience multiple, conflicting demands on their time from work, family, and friends, they tend to let slide any affiliation that does not contain an obvious built-in reward or a well-defined, compelling purpose.

If you wish to make your community's governance more conscious:

- Agree on why you are together and what vision and set of values you hold in common.
- Examine how you make decisions and whether this matches your purpose, values, and vision.
- Conduct an informal power audit, noting which members tend to take initiative, bear responsibility, and accumulate information, then consciously choose to agree to accept or change these current power dynamics.
- At least once a year, review, as a group, each of these areas, make any changes you desire, and recommit yourselves to your purpose and process of governance.

You may be happy to let others accumulate power in the form of information and skills if this means they take care of the administrative details that you abhor. But be aware of the tradeoff. If one of these volunteer administrators becomes sick or moves away, your community could lose time, money, and momentum trying to learn the accounting, membership, or other systems that this person maintained. In a worst-case scenario, volunteers who take on crucial organizational tasks may turn out to be more interested in accumulating power than in building community. Yours would not be the first organization to be taken over by people with hidden agendas who got their way by making themselves indispensable.

Full, free self-expression is the essence of leadership.

WARREN BENNIS

The civil group leader must not only be alert to the possibility that any member of the group may come up with the best solution to a given problem, but also then be prepared to follow that person's lead.

M. SCOTT PECK

One crucial governance issue that peer groups tend to sidestep is that of leadership. Although you may consider yourselves a leaderless group, no group remains leaderless for long. Below we explore new concepts of leadership and ways of developing flexible systems of governance.

Sharing Leadership

Conscious community, with its assumption that developing the potential of each individual benefits the full flowering of the group, stretches the concept of leadership beyond its traditional meaning. Max DePree, in his community-inspiring book *Leadership Is an Art,* defines a leader as a steward and as a servant of his followers. And who exactly is "the leader" and who are "the followers"? As DePree suggests, the leader is not necessarily, or not always, the head of the organization—the father or mother, as it were, of the family. Leadership is or should be a flexible concept. DePree advocates "roving leadership," in which people step forward and take charge, as needed, in their areas of competence, regardless of their place in the organization chart. "Roving leadership," he comments, "demands a great deal of trust and a clear sense of our interdependence."

It also demands that those who are not the anointed "heads" of anything take responsibility and demonstrate commitment to the group's purpose and vision. If you do not like the way decisions are being made in your group, it is up to you to speak up, tell your truth, stand up for what you believe in, make suggestions, and, if necessary, assume responsibility for carrying out your suggestions. Complaining does not constitute leadership or even good followership. Keeping quiet perpetuates discontent by driving it underground. If you happen to be the head of a group or organization, you need to create a climate in which those below you feel safe to speak up.

Many communities, particularly visionary residential ones, tacitly assume that the founder or "holder of the dream" is the leader. While this person can often serve as an articulate spokesperson and help other members stay conscious of the vision as they all grow together, he or she is not necessarily also the best person to take charge of everything from architectural design to the protein content of meals, now and forever. Trying to maintain tight control over all decisions, as Stelle community's autocratic founder belatedly realized, becomes self-defeating—and community-defeating. Founders who have been able, at the appropriate time, to let go of control have discovered that they and the community gain something more valuable than predictability. Shared and rotated leadership allows a whole range of insights and talents to emerge from the membership. In removing some of the burden from the shoulders of the dream-holder, group members deepen their own involvement and commitment. Roving leadership—on-the-spot decision making and action—keeps the community flexible enough to respond to the new ideas and challenges that inevitably arise as the community interacts with the world around it.

A community is like a ship; everyone ought to be prepared to take the helm.

HENRIK IBSEN

A form of government that is not the result of a long sequence of shared experiences, efforts, and endeavors can never take root.

NAPOLEON BONAPARTE

To distinguish the new kind of leadership from the authoritarian variety, David Spangler, co-leader of Scotland's Findhorn community for three years, coined the term "focalizer." This new-style leader, "like a lens, gathers together the elements and enables synthesis to take place through the focusing of these elements into a unity," writes David in *The Faces of Findhorn*. Stephen, a Findhorn resident, adds, "Leadership at Findhorn is based on a hierarchical pattern not of power, but of responsibility. If my responsibility, as focalizer of the publications department, is to ensure that deadlines are met, the way that's carried out is not to insist that someone meet a deadline but to share, in the most open and clear way possible, the reasons for it to happen. Being a focalizer, holding a broader awareness of the way a whole system operates, I try to share that awareness and allow each person to contribute his or her part." In a meeting, the focalizer serves as the facilitator and shares responsibility with the timekeeper, the process observer, the notetaker, and the other participants.

Massachusetts's Hearthstone Village, an informal community of neighbors, has evolved a simple shared leadership process called "eldering," which residents note has been used by Native Americans, Quakers, and others. It allows leadership to arise naturally. Whoever wants to initiate a project is free to do so. If others join, residents say that the person successfully eldered. Eldered projects have included the *Hearthstone Cricket* newsletter, a community land trust that purchased a house on the same road, and a self-service food store. No one in the eldering system has any authority over anyone else, nor is anyone coerced to participate.

Keeping Governance Flexible

We can release and actually use the enormous wisdom and power of our diversity instead of crushing it, isolating it, or smoothing it into a world of grey tolerance.

TOM ATLEE

As your community proceeds through its natural life cycle, you may observe that different people assume different types of leadership roles. The vision holder may step out of the spotlight while the designer of buildings takes center stage. A business entrepreneur who has launched a successful company may wisely hand the administrative reins to another member of the team with stronger day-to-day managerial skills. Learning to trust the group, to let go of one role and move on to another, becomes part of the growth process. Sharing and rotating the various roles—focalizer, relationship minder, event organizer, peacekeeper, gadfly, dream holder—will help keep your group from falling into stagnation or polarization and will strengthen the individual members.

In any system of governance, structure and hierarchy have their place. Across-the-board equality is a myth, as Sirius discovered when it attempted to hold onto a system in which everyone shared everything and made decisions as equals, despite varying levels of commitment and capability and varying needs among the membership. Sirius now operates with a governance system that blends consensus with hierarchy. A core group of longtime members assumes responsibility for major decisions, while eliciting input from—and, whenever possible, arriving at agreement with—the rest of the community. New York's Ganas, which is quite unlike Sirius in tone and focus, also finds the core-group system an effective way to balance individual and group needs, as do many other kinds of communities, from cohousing groups to neighborhood organizations.

Sirius, Ganas, and other well-established community R&D centers have moved from centralized to decentralized authority. Members assume responsibility for decisions in their own areas of interest and expertise. Each of Ganas's businesses, for example, is run by a separate team of people who do not need the acquiescence of the core group. At Alpha Farm, whose membership is so small that a core group would have to consist of all the adults, individuals make business and farming decisions within their own spheres of authority. Decentralization minimizes decision-making time and allows members to develop specific skills.

Since each community manifests its own evolving personality, yours will need to develop the form of decision making and governance that fits it best—and be prepared to change that form if it no longer seems to be working. In its formative stage, centralized authority may help solidify the group. But once the individuals have flexed their individuality, put their egos on the back burner, and embarked on the settling-into-roles stage, decentralization will probably provide a more natural form of governance. Later, as synergy develops, your group may want to experiment with rotating roles, giving each member and the group a chance to move further toward wholeness.

Making Wise Decisions: Tools and Suggestions

When we think about the people with whom we work, people on whom we depend, we can see that without each individual, we are not going to go very far as a group. By ourselves we suffer serious limitations. Together we can be something wonderful.

MAX DEPREE

Several years ago when a small philanthropic organization, Turtle Island Fund, began discussions on which proposals to support, most members felt certain they would fund one particular proposal and reject another. By meeting's end, they instead had funded the proposal they assumed they would reject and rejected the one that looked like a sure bet. They based their turnaround not simply on a rational discussion of pros and cons but on their collective interpretation of the pictures, body sensations, and verbal messages they received during the short meditation they engage in before making a decision, a process they call attunement.

Because the foundation members had learned to trust this intuitive approach to decision making, they were not surprised when both the yes and the no decisions produced positive results in unexpected ways. The project that received funding brought people together who would otherwise not have met and led to several fruitful collaborations, both personal and professional. The rejected proposal prompted the organization that had submitted it to reevaluate the way it worked with money. It renewed and strengthened itself as a result. The information Turtle Island gleaned from its attunement, and passed on to the organization, furthered this process.

Turtle Island Fund does not rely entirely on intuition. Its members spend hours studying each proposal and applying rational intelligence. But then, having done their homework, they allow the synergy of individual and group intuition to reveal an answer.

Sometimes emotions can cloud the intuitive process. Encouraging group members to express any fear, anger, or sadness they may be feeling about an issue before practicing attunement can yield clearer results. In this three-part procedure, the group first gathers facts, then clears emotions, and, finally, listens to intuition.

Turtle Island's recipe for wise decisions may sound unusual, perhaps on the new age fringe, but it is based on a key concept around which successful enterprises have been operating for years: Not all information comes to a group through direct and obvious channels. It seeps in from

How to Use Group Attunement in Making Decisions

Any time your group feels stuck or simply wants to tap its collective wisdom more effectively, you can take a few minutes of silence for group attunement. You can follow AMT's brain-cell method (see page 279) or the following process, modifying either to suit your group.

- When the facilitator asks you to go into silence, become aware of your own center. Focusing on your breathing can help you do this.
- Become aware of the center of the group and its connection with your center.
- Hold the issue the group is considering in your awareness and silently ask yourself what course of action is best for the whole.
- Notice any images, emotions, words, or physical sensations that arise without judging or analyzing them. If you become distracted, simply return to your awareness of your center, the group's center, and the question.
- When the facilitator calls an end to the silence and asks for your reports, describe what you felt, thought, heard, or saw, and what light that appears to cast on the issue in question.
- If a clear decision does not arise from this first round of group reports, you may wish to discuss the issue further and attune again, or postpone the decision while you gather more information and clear any emotional charges that remain.

Group intelligence is greatest when all points of view are integrated into a creative whole.

TRUDY AND PETER JOHNSON-LENZ

outside, wells up from inside the individual members, and emerges from a synthesis of members' thoughts, feelings, and reasonings. Even business executives who pride themselves on their rationality admit that hunches play an important role in successful management. "Logic and analysis can lead a person only partway down the path to a profitable decision," notes Roy Rowan in *The Intuitive Manager.* "The last step to success frequently requires a daring intuitive leap, as many chief executives who control the destinies of America's biggest corporations will reluctantly concede."

The individualistic ethos in American culture has led many executives to believe that these leaps must be made by one person, the one in charge, acting alone. But certain corporations—labeled Type Z by William Ouchi in *Theory Z: How American Business Can Meet the Japanese Challenge*, and including some of the largest and most successful companies in the United States—have been putting the lie to this. In these organizations, the decision-making process is typically consensual and participative and based on such implicit factors as "wisdom, experience, and subtlety" rather than dominated by such explicit control mechanisms as quantitative analysis and computer modeling.

Wisdom is often less a matter of choosing a particular view as the truth than of combining different truths in a balanced way.

ANDREW SCHMOOKLER

The types of collaboration that organizations use to reach agreement vary widely. Turtle Island Fund's attunement process hardly sounds far out compared to some of the approaches management consulting firms have been developing. Such a firm in Maine, called Advanced Management Technologies, came up with a problem-solving method for its own staff that demonstrates intuitive decision making at a group level along with the mysterious synergy that can develop between individuals and the group when the individuals include both themselves and the whole in their awareness.

Individual staffers imagined that each was a single brain cell, "feeding information to consciousness." Consciousness was represented by the table around which they all sat. Rather than trying to come up with a solution, they simply observed what took shape in that space. As one participant described the result, "For a long time there would be just this accumulating mass of information, impressions, judgments, feelings, jokes—more than you could ever hold in your head at one time—then suddenly the solution would be there for you and you'd look up and see it in everyone else's eyes as well. It was just obvious, and it felt like we were part of it . . . there was a sense of communal authorship." This "brain-cell" approach differed from typical brainstorming in that each participant stayed conscious of the whole. The firm's CEO, Michael Kelly, has since developed a computer program, used successfully by clients, that makes this seemingly free-form technique even more systematic.

In addition to turning within for information, organizations are learning the value of gleaning information from those outside who hold a stake in the decisions the organization makes. For businesses, this means including input from vendors, neighbors, and customers as well as management and staff in the making of major decisions. For cities and governmental agencies, it means inviting rather than discouraging grassroots participation. The city of Chattanooga was deteriorating and polarizing until, through a visioning process initiated by a citizen-based nonprofit organization, it secured the ideas and participation of more than seventeen hundred citizens, most of whom had previously felt excluded by the so-called power structure. Today the revitalized city has become a source of personal pride for these participants as they turn their ideas into reality. Going outside traditional organizational structures for information not only contributes to wiser, more effective decisions but also invigorates a community. The city has since held a second visioning process, inviting even more people to become involved in goal setting.

In our present society the governing idea is that we can trust no one, and therefore we must protect ourselves if we are to have any security in our decisions. The most we will be willing to do is compromise, and this leads to a very interesting way of viewing the outcome of working together. It means we are willing to settle for less than the very best—and that we will often have a sense of dissatisfaction with our decisions unless we can somehow outmaneuver others involved in the process.

CAROLINE ESTES

Even when a core group within a community assumes responsibility for major decisions, these decisions need to be based on the collective wisdom of the entire community. Otherwise the community runs two risks: making an unwise decision based on an incomplete picture, and generating misunderstanding and resentment by creating distance between the decision makers and the others. Core groups within communities can gather this information in many ways. They can, for instance, poll members, formally or informally; invite members outside the core group to participate with core group members in committees and project teams; hold small meetings with subgroups that include non-core-group members; or call open meetings with the whole community on specific issues about which the core group is making decisions.

As information must pass inward to the core decision makers, it also needs to pass outward to the rest of the group. Decision-making processes perceived as secret can create distrust and undermine community. The board of directors of Shenoa Retreat and Learning Center allays this problem by inviting staff and anyone else interested to attend the monthly board meetings and observe how the group makes decisions and reaches its conclusions. Non–board members can provide input, if they wish, through a process known as "fishbowling." The decision makers sit in a circle in the center of the room, while the others sit outside this circle (or fishbowl) and watch and listen, for the most part without participating. The center circle contains one empty chair, so that, if a person from the outer circle wishes to provide information or offer a comment to the decision makers, he or she simply takes this seat. The meeting facilitator invites the person to speak briefly before he or she returns to the outer circle. Primarily, those in the outer circle come to hear, to learn, and to surround the decision makers with their support.

CONSENSUS DECISION MAKING: AN AGE-OLD PROCESS GAINING POPULARITY

Unless you grew up in an intact native tribe or among Quakers—two kinds of community that historically have practiced consensus—you probably have experienced group decision making as a voting activity in which the majority wins and everyone else loses. Consensus decision making, which has become well developed in social change groups and is being adopted by all kinds of groups and organizations that seek community, is quite different. In its purest form, it requires that every member consent to the decision before the group can adopt it.

The notion of a group of diverse, strong-minded people coalescing behind decision after decision, and all feeling like winners as a result, may seem like a pipe dream. Perhaps it only works, you may think, when some people are willing simply to go along with a decision they dislike to avoid the pain of conflict.

There are a lot of organizations that operate by what they think *is consensus, but it really is not consensus at all. I've run into three top executives, for example, who have told me that they* "rule *by consensus"!*

M. SCOTT PECK

Actually, the opposite holds true. Consensus works only when people who feel uncomfortable about a proposed solution are willing to speak up and take the risk of engaging in conflict until a solution emerges that they and everyone else can support. Suppressing feelings and reservations deprives the group of the information it needs to make the wisest decision. If you go along with the majority for the sake of harmony or time efficiency while harboring doubts or resentments, you reduce the process of consensus to the equivalent of majority rule. This not only weakens the power of the process but also the long-term vitality of the community.

Consensus, like group attunement and AMT's brain-cell approach to problem solving, rests on the belief that every member of the group—however naive, experienced, confused, or articulate—holds a portion of the truth and that no one person holds all of the truth. It assumes that the best decision arises when everyone involved hears each other out about every aspect of the issue while keeping an open mind and heart. As participants let go of their positions and simply report information—including gut feelings, practical considerations, and sudden inspirations—the best course of action becomes evident. Everyone in the group then feels comfortable enough with the decision to participate in the action. Consultant Michael Doyle, who teaches organizations the art of consensus building, says that a lasting agreement contains three components: content satisfaction ("I liked the decision"), procedural satisfaction ("I liked the process"), and psychological satisfaction ("I liked how I was treated during the process").

How Practicing Consensus Can Build Community

While consensus requires a certain level of community to function and thus does not work for every group, it also deepens community as it is practiced. If you believe your family, circle of friends, neighborhood associa-

Gentlemen, I take it we are all in complete agreement on the decision here . . . Then I propose we postpone further discussion of this matter until our next meeting to give ourselves time to develop disagreement and perhaps gain some understanding of what the decision is all about.

ALFRED P. SLOAN

What You Need for Consensus to Work

- Trust that a wise decision or solution exists and that the group can find it.
- Commitment on everyone's part to the integrity and value of the group.
- Opportunity for everyone to provide input.
- Openness on each person's part to new information; willingness to listen and to pay attention to nuances.
- Willingness to engage in group processes—for example, acknowledging feelings and resolving conflict between members.
- Honest effort, at every step, to maintain perspective and discover what is best for the group, even when issues stir strong emotional responses.
- Patience; reaching consensus takes longer than majority vote, especially when conflicts become evident.
- Honesty and courage to communicate even an unpopular position.
- A facilitator with experience in the consensus process, who can discriminate between false consensus (people giving in to stronger members, resulting in weaker commitment) and true consensus.

tion, or workplace team is on the verge of becoming a conscious community, try practicing consensus as a means of making this shift. If you and the others are indeed ready for conscious community, you will increase your understanding of and your respect for one another as well as your awareness of yourselves as a group.

While you may spend more time reaching decisions based on consensus than on majority rule, once you have developed full agreement your group will move forward with great power and speed. No disgruntled minority will drag its feet or otherwise sabotage your success. All of you will own the decision as one that works for both the individuals and the group, and you will support it with your full energy. As an added benefit, you will know that you have tapped the wisdom and creativity of every member of your group and developed a solution more effective than any one of you, or any subgroup within your community, could have developed alone. With this information-rich process, you will not only perform your group tasks better but also deepen your relationships and grow personally.

A major difference between consensus and voting-based procedures is that, in consensus, discussion usually centers around the problem and related issues and not around proposals or motions. Consensus is a way of thoroughly exploring a problem, not an attempt to finalize a particular solution. The group should view any solution offered as just another territory to explore, until every member becomes clear that a particular solution is the best one.

Consensus is not group unanimity. Consensus is an integrated group will.

Randy Schutt and Lori Girshick

In consensus, if agreement comes too easily, you need to be suspicious. Conformist "groupthink" could be at work. Check to make sure that all participants have had a chance to contribute their best thinking and that the group is not ignoring important issues.

"The hallmark of a consensus decision is that it feels right," says consensus trainer Randy Schutt. "It feels like the true emergence of an integrated group will." Otherwise, you need to continue the process.

Overcoming Barriers to Consensus

You may fear that if your community chooses to operate by consensus, your meetings will bog down in endless discussions, with one or two people repeatedly blocking decisions. While blocking can become a problem in groups that have not built sufficient trust or developed a clear common purpose, it rarely occurs in groups that have done their relationship and visioning work. "In my personal experience of living with the consensus process for seventeen years," reports Alpha Farm's Caroline Estes, "I have seen meetings held from going forward on only a handful of occasions, and usually the dissenter(s) was justified—the group would have made a mistake by going forward."

Estes, a consultant on group process, views blocking as only one of several outcomes that can occur when everyone except one or two are in agreement. For example, the facilitator can ask those not in agreement whether they are willing, in Quaker terms, to "step aside." "This means," says Estes, "that they do not agree with the decision but do not feel that it is wrong. They are willing to have the decision go forward, but do not want to take part in carrying it out." Estes warns that, when two or three start to step aside, the group may not have yet reached the best decision.

In business groups, Michael Doyle declares, consensus works only when a clear fallback procedure exists. For example, he says, in hierarchical groups the leader can make the decision when the group seems unable to do so. In most horizontal groups, the fallback process is the majority vote.

SOME EXAMPLES OF COOPERATIVE DECISION MAKING

Eight people want to go out to dinner together and are trying to decide on a restaurant.

Decision Process	Description	Comments
Unanimity	Everyone's first choice happens to be a Mexican restaurant.	Nice if it works out that way and quick to decide, but doesn't happen very often.
Convincing Argument	One person likes a French restaurant—after presenting the advantages, everyone is convinced that this option is better than their original preference.	Sometimes works but frequently doesn't.
Follow a Popular Leader	One person wants to go to a German restaurant—everyone else wants to do whatever that person wants more than they want their own food preference; or they believe that that person knows better what is best for the group than they do.	Easy to make decisions this way, but often based on people's low self-esteem.
Compromise	Some want to go to a Thai restaurant, some want to go to the seafood restaurant, and some want to go to McDonald's so they decide to go to the seafood restaurant this time, the Thai restaurant next time, and to McDonald's after that; or they decide to go to another Thai restaurant that serves Thai dishes, seafood, and hamburgers, but none of the food is very good.	Nobody gets exactly what they want, but everyone gets part of what they want and everyone is treated fairly.
Implicit Majority	If 5 people want to go to the Thai restaurant, 2 want to go to the seafood restaurant, and 1 wants to go to McDonald's, they could decide to go to the Thai restaurant since that is what most people want—the others agree that they do	Usually satisfies most people, but the minority may feel ripped off, especially

The Winslow Cohousing group in Seattle, which operates by consensus without fallback, uses a clever visual tool to speed the decision-making process while empowering every member of the group. Each person brings to the meeting five 3″ by 5″ cards of different colors. At decision time, each member votes by raising one of these cards:

Green means "I agree—let's go ahead."

Blue means "I'm neutral or have only a slight reservation."

Yellow means "I have a question, or need clarification."

Orange means "I have a serious reservation, but not enough to block consensus."

Red means "I am against this and will block the decision."

Decision Process	***Description***	***Comments***
	not want to get in the way of what most people want. Without a formal vote, the group goes with the majority.	if they lose too many times.
Intensity of Preferences	Maybe the 5 who want Thai food are mostly interested in eating ethnic food, the 2 who want seafood don't like spicy food, and the person who wants to go to McDonald's cannot afford to spend more than $3. Here the people who don't like spicy food have a stronger reason not to go to a Thai restaurant than the people who like ethnic food have a reason to go so it takes precedence; but the person who wants to go to McDonald's absolutely cannot go to the other more expensive places, whereas everyone else can go to McDonald's, so they decide to go to McDonald's.	A type of least-common-denominator process that is satisfying.
Meeting Everyone's Needs ("True Consensus")	They decide to go to a Japanese restaurant (ethnic, but not spicy) and everyone chips in to cover the cost above $3 for the poor person.	• Everyone's true needs are met and a solution is found that everyone feels excited about. • Not a compromise or amalgam of people's original preferences, but a "third way"

Reprinted with permission from Randy Schutt's "Notes on Consensus Decision-Making" handout, dated August 8, 1992. Schutt thanks Susan Sandler for the example.

Everyone can see at a glance whether the group is in full agreement, or if not, what might be in the way.

An earlier and simpler version of this system, developed by organization development consultant Kay Tift, involves just three colors.

Green means go, or "Yes, I support your proposal."

Orange means caution, or "Before I choose, I have a question or comment."

Red means stop, or "I do not support your proposal."

As an alternative, Kay suggests using thumbs, with thumbs-up meaning yes, thumbs-sideways maybe, and thumbs-down no.

One adaptation that some groups employ is "consensus-minus-one"—

The problem is the solution. Everything is a positive resource; it is up to us to work out how we may use it as such.

BILL MOLLISON

HOW A FACILITATOR CAN GUIDE THE CONSENSUS PROCESS

The importance of a facilitator cannot be too strongly emphasized, says Caroline Estes, cofounder of Alpha Farm and a professional teacher and consultant on group process. This person bears the responsibility "to see that all are heard, that all ideas are incorporated if they seem to be part of the truth, and that the final decision is agreed upon by all assembled."

A facilitator can help this happen by:

- Noticing whether some information is missing—for example, because a person is too shy to speak, a helpful idea needs better articulation, or the group needs to tap nonverbal information through silence.
- Keeping the discussion from being dominated by a few and encouraging quiet members to speak.
- Constantly stating and restating the position of the meeting, while indicating the progress the group has made.
- Lightening up the discussion with appropriate humor.
- When sensing a stalemate or a poor compromise, helping the group brainstorm for dramatically new "third alternatives" that encompass everyone's views.
- Alternating between small and large group discussion formats to increase involvement and move through stuck places.
- Actively seeking out differences, disagreements, questions (even dumb ones), and irreverence to avoid "groupthink."
- Helping the group decide what to do when all are in agreement except one or two.
- Pointing out when the meeting has reached consensus and asking for confirmation.

ratifying decisions if all but one person agree. While this prevents one individual from controlling the group, some consensus advocates consider it a cop-out and no longer true consensus. Caroline Estes points out that if trust and maturity can be developed in the group, "using total consensus is well rewarded by a bonding that goes deeper than the reserve implied in consensus-minus-one." She adds, however, that in groups with loosely defined membership some compromise might be necessary or desirable. "The lesson, it seems to me, is to have lots of tools in your toolbox, and use each where it fits."

Resources

Recommended books and articles

Leadership Is an Art by Max DePree (Dell, 1989)

On Becoming a Leader by Warren Bennis (Addison-Wesley, 1989)

Why Leaders Can't Lead: The Unconscious Conspiracy Continues by Warren Bennis (Jossey-Bass, 1991)

Principle-Centered Leadership by Stephen R. Covey (Simon & Schuster, 1992)

The Fifth Discipline: The Art and Practice of the Learning Organization by Peter Senge (Currency/Doubleday, 1990)

On Leadership by John W. Gardner (The Free Press, 1990). Includes chapters on community and renewal.

Everyone Has a Piece of the Truth by Caroline Estes (forthcoming). For information on publisher and date, contact the author at Alpha Farm, Deadwood, Oregon, 97430; (503) 964-5102.

Decision Traps: The Ten Barriers to Brilliant Decision-Making and How to Overcome Them by J. Edward Russo and Paul J. H. Schoemaker (Doubleday, 1989)

The Art of Consensus Building, workbook by Michael Doyle (Michael Doyle and Associates, 906B Union Street, San Francisco, California, 94133; (415) 441-0696; 1988)

Building United Judgment: A Handbook for Consensus Decision Making (The Center for Conflict Resolution, 731 State Street, Madison, Wisconsin, 53703; (608) 255-0479; 1981)

In Context, Issue #7, Autumn 1984 on the theme of "Governance: Power, Process & New Options." Contact the magazine at P.O. Box 11470, Bainbridge Island, Washington, 98110; (206) 842-0216.

Excellent Randy Schutt articles available from the author (the number of pages is given in parentheses): "Preventing Groupthink" (1), "Organizational Structures for Cooperative Groups" (1), "Decision-Making Structures" (1), "Checklist for Consensus Process" (1), "Preparation for Meetings Checklist" (1), "Getting Unstuck: Common Problems in Meetings and Some Solutions" (7), "Group Task and Maintenance Functions" (1), "Notes on Consensus Decision-Making" (6). Send large self-addressed stamped envelope (5 pages = 1 oz) plus any donation you can afford to support this service to Randy Schutt, P.O. Box 60922, Palo Alto, California, 94306; (415) 424-8559.

Also see resources in Chapters Twelve, Fourteen, and Sixteen.

Satisfaction with decisions comes from believing that your views were heard and respected.

William R. Potapchuk

SIXTEEN

Working with Conflict

Conflict is the gadfly of thought. It stirs us to observation and memory. It instigates to invention. It shocks us out of sheeplike passivity, and sets us at noting and contriving. . . : Conflict is a sine qua non of reflection and ingenuity.

JOHN DEWEY

WHEN KAREN RETURNED HOME from work, she found the door to her bedroom blocked by two carpenters tearing out the wall above the door frame. They expressed surprise that she did not know that a window was being installed there. Hadn't the landlady told her about the renovations? they asked. The landlady? Karen looked puzzled. We don't have a landlady here, she thought. This is a shared house. Then she remembered: one of the members of the household was in fact the owner of the house, and thus legally the landlady.

For more than a year, the five members of Russell Street House had operated as equal and peaceful housemates, happy that they had found such a congenial group to live with. Now one of them, Dierdre, had chosen to exercise her legal role and order changes in the house without consulting—or even informing—Karen and two of the other housemates. This angered Karen and the downstairs housemate, Marge. The only housemate Dierdre consulted happened to be her lover, which only aggravated the situation by highlighting the power differentials in the house. The anger turned explosive when Karen and Marge learned that Dierdre had made another major decision in consultation with her lover but not the rest of the housemates. She had given notice to an upstairs housemate, Ruth, informing her that she must leave the house to make her room available to Dierdre's lover.

WELCOMING HEALTHY CONFLICT

Should you shield the canyons from the windstorms, you would never see the beauty of their carvings . . .

ELISABETH KÜBLER-ROSS

The ugly emotions that churned the once-smooth surface of this shared household shocked its members. How had they allowed their situation to degenerate into yelling and finger-pointing? They feared that this explosion of anger signaled their failure as a shared household and fledgling community. Russell Street House had yet to learn the primary lessons of conflict: first, it is inevitable in group endeavors, and second, it is not necessarily bad. In fact, when handled well, conflict can strengthen and enhance community. Indeed, a hallmark of healthy, conscious community is the willingness to acknowledge and work with conflict.

Russell Street House took a step toward rather than away from conscious community in its willingness to face conflict openly. It was making the crucial transition from the first natural phase of community, when a strong authority helps anchor the group, to the second phase, during which individual members assert more power. When members of a community suppress anger and disagreements in the name of maintaining harmony, they simply drive the unexpressed feelings underground, creating a large shadow.

People mistakenly believe that harmony means the absence of disagreement and conflict. This always results in disillusionment, because the absence of disagreement is an illusion. Even the most mature and high-minded groups are bound to disagree. People are different no matter how similar they may appear in terms of age, gender, race, sexual preference, or social class or how committed they are to a common vision. These differences contribute to the health of a community, just as diversity gives strength and stability to an ecosystem. When a community suppresses differences to avoid the pain of conflict, it deprives itself of crucial information and the collective wisdom that comes from sharing bad news as well as good.

But Karen's and Marge's outbursts of anger did not by themselves bring healing to Russell Street House. These outbursts could well have undone the household if all five members had not collectively chosen to take the further step of finding healthy solutions to the conflict. Unable to come to such solutions on their own, the warring tenants called in an outside mediator to help.

While they found the resolution process painful at times, they later acknowledged that it strengthened them as a household. They began to cooperate more on household matters. For example, the housemates helped

Dierdre select colors for a new exterior paint job, agreeing that the final decision was hers. She had not known until the blowup that they were interested in such matters. The five also began meeting regularly to hammer out a set of policies and procedures for their living together. The stickiest issue, that of Dierdre giving notice to Ruth without consulting the others, turned out to be more upsetting to Karen and Marge than to Ruth. Ruth, the member least committed to the ideal of shared living, was actually willing to move on and considered Dierdre well within her rights to ask her to do so.

If you think managing conflict and managing diversity are loaded with problems, then you haven't thought through the problems of managing sameness. I'd far rather be faced with trying to achieve harmony and goodwill among people who are at one another's throats than try to squeeze an ounce of innovation or creativity or risk out of a company full of photocopies of each other.

JIM AUTRY

In a culture that tends to leave the resolution of conflict to lawyers and law enforcement officers, few people have experienced the rewards that can come from working openly and skillfully with disagreements. And certainly the opportunity to work out conflict is not the primary reason people seek community. In fact, some may do so specifically to escape the conflict they experienced in their families of origin and are horrified when it emerges in what they had thought was a safe haven. Unable to face the scary emotions of anger, fear, pain, guilt, and shame that have begun to seep through the layers of good will, they leave. Those who either bail out at the first whiff of discord or clamp down on its expression are missing a chance to grow, by expressing more aspects of themselves, and to deepen their bonds with others. They are also losing a chance to model to the larger community a healthy, nonviolent way of working out differences.

Dierdre, the owner and initiator of Russell Street House, wanted to live cooperatively rather than perpetuate the old hierarchical social divisions, but her ideals clashed with her fear of losing control over her property. When afraid, she tended to slip into the safe, time-honored role of landlady. Karen and Marge shook her out of this trap by pointing out the discrepancy between the ideals that Dierdre espoused and her behavior. They demanded that she walk her talk. Yet Karen and Marge lacked experience in asserting themselves effectively. Fearful of power, their own and that of others, they tended to view themselves as victims and authority figures as villains. When they felt that they and Ruth were being treated unjustly, they exploded with the righteous anger of the oppressed.

By bringing in a skilled, neutral person to mediate the conflict, the members of this household not only resolved their group issues around how decisions are made and communicated, but also grew personally. Dierdre learned how to drop her defensive armor and become more receptive to others and the collective wisdom of the group. Karen and Marge became aware of their projections and discovered more effective ways of asserting themselves without turning every authority figure into a villain. All five members of the household developed their communication skills, tools that continued to serve them well outside the community as well as inside.

At its best, says psychotherapist and mediator Rosalind Diamond, the conflict resolution process "supports the development of mutual respect for the participants' differences, a sense of kinship in their similarities, and often a commitment to uphold the right of each person to have their basic needs met." It gives us greater awareness of our interdependence and "our participation together in the one whole fabric that is life."

The "nice" guy tends to create an atmosphere such that others avoid giving him honest, genuine feedback. This blocks his emotional growth.

GEORGE R. BACH AND HERB GOLDBERG

Business consultant Richard Pascale believes firmly in the value of "constructive contention" in the workplace. "Why not learn to disagree without being disagreeable?" he asks in an *Industry Week* article. "Why not develop the skills to deal with [conflict] effectively, and why not regard it as an enormous resource for keeping an organization on its toes?"

Choosing to Work It Out: A Win-Win Approach

When conflict raises its head, you have three choices in deciding how to handle it:

1. You can avoid it, pretending it does not exist. This is the most dangerous of the three options, since it will drain energy from all involved. Dr. George Bach, coauthor of *Creative Aggression*, believes that "the price of nice" is too high. The excessively polite person, who does not want to ruffle any feathers by acknowledging angry feelings, blocks feedback from others, stifling his or her own emotional growth and that of the others. No one really trusts the too-nice person.

   When groups suppress conflict, members begin to develop passive/aggressive behavior. In the workplace, for example, employees may start calling in sick more often, arriving late, stealing supplies, and wasting time. In a family or a residential community, members may neglect to keep agreements with each other. If the conflict continues unacknowledged and unresolved, the anger at its core can build up like volcanic matter until it erupts into rage. While anger can be channeled constructively, rage is merely destructive. Ultimately, unacknowledged conflict can sink a community.

2. You can argue, fight, use power plays, or take the case to court until someone "wins." This adversarial approach may seem marginally better than conflict avoidance, because at least people get some idea of where they stand with each other, even though they may not grasp the real issues. But while the "winner" may feel better for a time, the polarization has destroyed the essence of community: interdependence based on trust.
3. You can work together on resolving the conflict. This option produces a win-win situation in which all parties have a chance to get what they want, to develop their individual and group skills, and to experience interdependence at a deep level. It is an approach that can enhance community in families, schools, workplaces, friendships, neighborhoods, political structures, and international arenas.

When we get into arguments that focus and fully engage our attention, we become avid seekers of relevant information. Otherwise, we take in information passively—if we take it in at all.

CHRISTOPHER LASCH

Acknowledging the Roots of Conflict

To resolve conflict, it is important to have some understanding of where it comes from. In the majority of cases, one or both parties in a conflict feel that the other has not shown them respect. If you are angry because someone habitually keeps you waiting, your anger stems from the perception that this person does not respect your time. Karen at Russell Street House blew up at Dierdre because she considered that renovating a room without first notifying the occupant constituted a breach of respect. When one nation fails to respect another's borders, war is likely to ensue. Being discounted can cause powerful reactions.

It is important to remember, however, that the perception of being discounted is not necessarily the reality. People often base such perceptions on projection. "You're just like my mother!" a husband may shout when a conflict arises. But of course the wife is not just like her mother-in-law and may not have intended what her husband—who at that moment was seeing a picture of his mother superimposed on his wife's face—thought she had intended.

Underneath the anger that follows from lack of respect, or the perception of it, other emotions seethe. When was the last time you had an argument or fight with someone? Chances are you can recall the incident clearly, since conflict arouses such painful feelings.

One of these feelings is undoubtedly shame or embarrassment. "Oh, no, how did we get into this horrible, messy situation? I shouldn't have let it get this far." In a closely knit community where everyone is supposedly committed to common goals, conflict may seem particularly embarrassing.

Closely linked to the feelings of shame are feelings of fear—fear of separation or, conversely, of being swallowed up; fear that one's emotions may spin out of control; fear of having to give up one's position; fear that the community will disintegrate. Both parties undoubtedly feel some fear. An employer, for example, may be as frightened by a conflict with an employee as the employee is.

A community's members can fight gracefully.

FOUNDATION FOR COMMUNITY ENCOURAGEMENT

Sometimes people use conflict to cover up pain or sadness. This can be especially true of men who have trouble expressing these tender, raw feelings. "I notice that when I go into conflict with my ex-wife, I don't have to feel the pain of not being with my children," remarks one divorced father.

Not all the emotions associated with conflict are negative. I (Kristin) have noticed that, while I am frightened by conflict, I also find it exhilarating. My family suppressed disagreements and anger, so, for me, being able to get real feels liberating.

Whatever the mix of emotions, people usually experience conflict as chaotic. A culture based on control tends to view chaos as only one step away from madness. Yet chaos is a natural phase in community building, just as it is essential to any creative process. In embracing conflict, you and your group will take a step toward the co-creation of healthy, conscious community.

APPROACHES TO WORKING WITH CONFLICT

While your group or community may agree that you wish to face conflict openly, you may feel uncomfortable bringing the subject up, especially when you are not experiencing any problems. But discussing how to resolve conflicts when you are all in agreement is like making plans for medical emergencies and death when you are enjoying excellent health: it is wise to have the procedure in place before the situation arises, at which point it may be too late. Since many conflicts arise from simple misunderstandings, we recommend that your community begin by developing the kinds of communication agreements we discuss in Chapter Fourteen and back these up with conflict resolution procedures.

If you find yourself in conflict with another person, approach him or her directly and privately to discuss the problem and negotiate a resolution. If the two of you cannot work out the conflict to your mutual satisfaction, call on a third party for help. This third party can be an arbitrator, who

Four Things You Need Before Beginning a Conflict Resolution Session

1. A safe space: To minimize anxiety and stress, you need to find a place to conduct the resolution process where you and the other party will not be interrupted or distracted, and where you both will feel free to show your true feelings. If possible, meet in a neutral place that is not your or the other's personal territory. You also may wish to include a fair witness, a mediator, an arbitrator, or a group of witnesses that you and the other disputant trust.
2. Enough time: What constitutes "enough" depends on the issue, the participants involved, and the procedure used. Make sure you and the other disputant have sufficient time to express yourselves fully, and also to take a few moments periodically to experience your feelings and to understand the feelings of the other. Because conflict tends to be uncomfortable, you might be tempted to rush through the process. When that happens, something usually gets left out. Also, the slower or less articulate party may feel hurried and thus at a disadvantage.
3. Willingness to tell the truth—to the best of everyone's ability: Conflict resolution works only when all parties interact as whole, authentic persons.
4. Willingness to change: This is a tough one; almost everyone tends to become attached to his or her positions. It may help to remember the community context in which you are experiencing this conflict. Consider the relationship needs within this community as well as your individual needs and how you cannot fulfill one set in isolation from the other. Remember also that change is necessary for growth. Think about interests rather than positions and note those points at which your interests intersect with those of your disputant. Is there some way you can all get what you really need?

Stupidity is an attempt to iron out all differences, and not to use or value them creatively.

Bill Mollison

listens to both sides and then presents a solution that both parties have agreed in advance to accept; a mediator, who assists the parties in designing their own solution; or a "fair witness," who simply observes. If your community is small enough, the whole group can serve as the fair witness, gathering in a circle around the parties involved in the conflict and functioning as a safe container for its resolution.

Several residential communities have developed variations on this approach. Sirius Community has created a five-level procedure that begins with the aggrieved person visualizing the other person with clarity and love. Second, he or she approaches the other for a talk. If no solution is forthcoming, the two find a mediator—someone in the community or someone outside. The fourth step is to take the conflict to Sirius's Personnel Group, a body that deals with issues ranging from marital problems to unequal participation of members. (The Personnel Group may even initiate the meeting.) At the final level, the entire community gets involved. "Handling conflict is what makes community work or not work," declares community member Bruce Davidson. "We've made an agreement that we want to have loving, positive relationships with each other."

We cannot find personal intimacy without conflict. . . . Love and conflict are inseparable.

GIBSON WINTER

The Pathwork Communities in New York and Virginia have developed an approach that draws upon community members' mental, emotional, and spiritual resources. First, those involved clarify the facts. Second, they express feelings about the issue, following well-developed guidelines. Once they have removed the intellectual and emotional blocks, the parties meditate together, asking for guidance from within. When they sense they cannot settle the dispute by themselves, they bring in a counselor to work with them or take the issue to the larger group.

For more than 2,500 years, Buddhist monastic communities have used a reconciliation practice that involves an arbitrator rather than a mediator. Or rather, two groups of arbitrators: a committee of monks makes a decision and then asks for acceptance by the whole community. Before the decision is made, the disputants face one another in front of the community, each in turn telling the history of the conflict in every detail. A respected monk acts as a sponsor for each of the disputants to help uncover his feelings. Each disputant confesses his own part in the conflict and hears the other's confession. Both agree in advance to accept the decision of the community.

FINDING RESOURCES IN THE LARGER COMMUNITY

If your community requires the services of a mediator, you often need not look far or spend a great deal of money. An extensive network of community-based mediation organizations provides such services at low or no cost in most metropolitan areas. Organizations such as these train community members who, in turn, commit themselves to serving with the organization as volunteer mediators for their neighborhood or city. (See Resources for listings.)

The role of the mediator is a sensitive one. Mediators must care about the people involved rather than the issues. They must be aware of their personal biases and projections. They must be willing to let the participants experience their own strength rather than feel like they are being "rescued." Mediators must not, however, be so neutral that they erase themselves. A good mediator presents him- or herself as a whole human being, willing to share personal experiences and vulnerability when appropriate.

What makes disagreement destructive is not the fact of conflict itself but the addition of competition. . . . [There's a] difference between someone participating in an exchange of ideas and someone trying to score points.

ALFIE KOHN

Community Boards: Neighborhood Mediation Pioneer

After many years as a trial attorney, Raymond Shonholtz came to the conclusion that the judicial system represents one of the worst ways to solve problems. To offer more effective, less punitive, and less polarizing approaches, he founded Community Boards, the oldest and largest neighborhood conciliation program in the country. Organizations worldwide have emulated this volunteer program and adapted it to family, school, organizational, and political disputes as well as neighbor-to-neighbor conflicts.

In the neighborhood program, volunteers trained by Community Boards professionals can choose one of four roles: outreach worker who recruits others and builds respect for the program within the community, case developer, panelist, or follow-up person. Feuding neighbors can approach Community Boards together, or one can call and ask Community Boards to suggest its services to the other. After a briefing by the case developer, a panel guides the parties through the resolution process. The community at large sometimes attends the hearing.

"Having volunteers hear cases from their own community moves us away from the deaf-dumb-blind jury concept, which has actually only been used in the last sixty or seventy years," Shonholtz explains. Community cohesion increases as members take charge of their own conflicts, and the non-punitive atmosphere in which community issues can be freely articulated keeps problems from escalating.

The Community Boards process is so simple that a child could learn it. In fact, children do, through CB's school "conflict manager" program. Teachers and counselors, trained by Community Boards, show volunteer students—as young as fourth-graders—how to solve classroom and playground disputes. A pair of young conflict managers may begin by asking

In order to begin to understand our outer conflicts, we must become familiar with the inner turmoil as well.

ROSALIND DIAMOND

Communities are wise to the extent they use diversity well.

TOM ATLEE

BASIC STEPS IN A CONFLICT RESOLUTION SESSION

Before embarking on the conflict resolution process, look inside yourself. You may find an internal community of personalities waging its own battles. One part of you may feel hostile and defensive toward your partner in conflict, while another may be open-hearted and loving. You might notice a child-like part of you cowering in fear and shame while your inner rebel prepares to strike a strong blow for righteousness. Acknowledge all these parts and feelings, accept them, and recognize that the other party is probably experiencing his or her own inner struggle. Realize that you are both seeking healing or you would not have agreed to this process. Imagine an outcome that allows each of you to gain, one that enhances community for all involved.

You can adapt the following generic conflict resolution procedure for groups ranging from couples to nations. Although we have derived it from several different models, it is similar to that used by Community Boards.

Step One: Agree on goals and guidelines.

One of the agreed-upon goals should be to stay in the relationship and make it better. If one party cannot commit to this goal, the resolution cannot proceed. In such a case, all involved need to weigh the alternative, which may be going to court, to the principal's office, or to war. Clarify the purpose, stages, and expectations of the process. The stages depend on your community's established process and the preferred procedure for the mediator, if you use one. Include among your guidelines that all parties treat one another with respect. This means none of you will engage in blaming or name-calling, that each party will be open to learning from other points of view, and that everyone will listen carefully and not interrupt.

Step Two: State the initial positions.

In this step, each of you, in turn, takes a few minutes to state the way you experience the conflict. Focus on one incident or specific group of incidents and do not drag in past unresolved issues or the personal opinions of people *not* in the room (e.g., "Our neighbor Ann avoids you too because . . .") Describe behavior and include the feelings: "When you didn't keep your part of the agreement, I felt hurt and as though my time and wishes didn't count with you." Do not interpret the other person's behavior; simply report what happened. While the other person is talking, be alert for feelings. Some people are more articulate than others, and these people should allow the others time to compose their statements. Do not, at this stage, give your opinion of what should be done. If you are using a mediator, you might find it safer and more effective at this stage to talk to this third party rather than to the other disputant.

Step Three: Restate the positions.

Each party takes a minute or two to restate what the other said, highlighting the main points. Each party then says whether the restatement was complete and accurate, and makes corrections. When this step is completed, it is usually a good idea for everyone to pause, reflect, and check on what is going on inside. If one party is especially uncomfortable, he or she may be tempted to jump ahead to a solution. It is still too early for that. The important accomplishment in this step is that people recognize that they have been heard and have heard the other person.

Step Four: Continue bringing issues and feelings out into the open.

At this point, each party can take a turn speaking directly to the other. Both of you can begin identifying areas of agreement and disagreement. Keep an open heart, looking for ways to affirm the inherent goodness of the other.

Step Five: Redefine the issue and begin working on solutions.

Step back from the issues and identify the underlying assumptions, beliefs, and information sources. Brainstorm ways to meet shared interests, listing as many possibilities as possible.

Step Six: Summarize points of consensus and produce an agreement.

Make the solutions as specific as possible—"I will turn my music off at midnight" is better than "I won't play music when you need to work." If appropriate, write the agreement down and sign it. Have the mediator review it to ensure that it is doable.

Step Seven: Agree to follow up with each other at specific times.

Check on whether the solution is being followed. The solution should not be regarded as carved in stone. Since communities are fluid and dynamic, the agreement may need to be renegotiated.

We are individual designs in the fabric of life: We have our own integrity, but simultaneously we are part of the fabric, connected to and defined by the whole. Community is the human dimension of that fabric.

TOM ATLEE

the quarrelers sweetly, "Wouldn't you like us to help you resolve your problem? Because you know if you hit each other, you'll have to go to the office and your parents will have to come to school." The disputants, thus warned, generally consent. The conflict managers then ask them to abide by six rules: agree to solve the problem, be honest, no name calling, talk one at a time, speak only to the conflict managers, no interruptions.

Conflict is essential in creating and re-creating community. If there were no differences between people, there could be no community.

CARL M. MOORE

The conflict resolution process usually takes less than fifteen minutes, according to two experienced youngsters, Danay and Dong, at San Francisco's Martin Luther King, Jr., Middle School. Dong emphasizes, "We're not solving their problems—they are. Once they've tried the process, they usually don't get that close to a fight again." Danay says she applies the six rules at home, in disputes with her annoying little sister. "I always look at what I can do to avoid hitting her."

Computerized Resolution

If you have access to a computer, the outside mediator to help you resolve your neighborhood disagreements or communicate with your teenager about curfews may be as close as your keyboard. With a software program called Agree and the cooperation of the others involved in the dispute, you can all sit down in front of the computer terminal and, quite possibly, work out a quick solution. The system will prompt you all to identify core issues, points of agreement, and principles of fairness, and it will stimulate your creativity by asking you, "If you were the world's best mediator, what would you say?" It will even produce sample agreements that your family can use or modify.

Agree's developer, James Melamed, serves as executive director of the Academy of Family Mediators and teaches mediation at the University of Oregon School of Law. Jim himself belongs to an international community of conflict resolution groups that communicates by way of a computer network called ConflictNet. The electronic linkage enables these professionals to share information and resources, coordinate meetings, collaborate on projects, and even resolve their own group conflicts through the network.

HEALING A FRAGMENTED WORLD COMMUNITY

Before the disintegration of Communist rule in Eastern Europe, conflict resolution in these nations, at least at the governmental level, appeared simple: the central authority told any who disagreed with it to be silent, or else. Since many of these countries lacked democratic traditions, their decision makers possessed few non-coercive negotiating skills—that is, until the advent of Partners for Democratic Change, a nonprofit corporation funded by a consortium of foundations and the U.S. Institute of Peace. Under Partners' auspices, conflict resolution centers have been established at universities in Russia, Poland, Hungary, the Czech Republic, Slovakia, Lithuania, and Bulgaria. Western conflict resolution experts, many of them alumni of Community Boards (Ray Shonholtz was the founder of Partners), spend weeks at these centers training trainers. The computer network Conflict Net gives them access to each other.

Opposing factions—ethnic, religious, and political—now have the opportunity to talk out grievances in a fair forum of their peers and to create their own agreements. Trainees have included thousands of men and women, from Siberian miners to prime ministers. Partners for Democratic Change was instrumental in helping to enact a law in Poland, for instance, to require negotiation and mediation before strikes, and for mediating an agreement between Czech and Slovak national councils. Offspring organizations are now teaching conciliation procedures based on the same model all over the world, including Northern Ireland. Although such procedures do not always produce all the desired results, they do help the community of participants learn the skills necessary for incorporating and honoring diversity.

Empathy, in the sense of picturing myself in your situation, is not enough: The point is [for me] to see your situation from your *perspective, which is not identical with mine.*

ALFIE KOHN

The giant steps forward in the community-building process are taken by those individuals of such courage that they are able to risk speaking at a level of vulnerability and authenticity at which no one in the group has spoken before.

M. SCOTT PECK

Such skills, and the assumptions that underlie them, represent a shift in consciousness essential if human beings are to survive as a species on this planet. War, strong-arm politics, and law-and-order policies enforced in the absence of any intention to empower people simply exacerbate the polarities now tearing nations, regions, and cities apart. Unless society provides safe procedures through which warring factions can sit down together, hear each other out—including hearing one another's pain and fear—acknowledge what they both want, find areas of agreement, and work out solutions satisfying to all concerned, governments and individuals will continue to waste too much time and money on fighting one another. They will not have enough left to devote to the serious social and ecological crises that threaten to make power struggles irrelevant by destroying anything worth fighting about.

The conflict resolution procedures presented in this chapter assume that humans are all part of one living system—one body, if you will—and that each member of this body performs an important function and has access to crucial information. If a part of the body is screaming in pain, the whole body needs to welcome this pain as a danger signal, find its underlying source, and right the imbalance causing it. In social organisms, from families to neighborhoods to the world community, welcoming the pain and learning from it means respecting those on all sides of a conflict enough to listen to them and engage them in working out a solution. Only by beginning now to practice and experience the rewards of this approach to conflict, in homes and communities, will human beings find the will and the ability to implement it at national and global levels.

The current way of addressing problems through polarizing debate no longer works. We need to learn how to work together even when we disagree, listen with respect to the truth in what each other says, frame issues broadly enough to embrace conflicting perspectives, and look for the deeper truths uniting them. This new way will be the cornerstone of a sustainable culture capable of carrying our children's children into the future.

TRUDY AND PETER JOHNSON-LENZ

RESOURCES

Recommended books and articles

Getting to Yes by Roger Fisher and William Ury (Penguin, 1981)

Getting Past No by William Ury (Bantam, 1991)

Getting Together: Building Relationships As We Negotiate by R. Fisher and S. Brown (Penguin, 1988)

The Ways of Peace by Gray Cox (Paulist Press, 1986). Excellent perspectives on conflict and interconnection. Studies of Gandhian, Quaker, and "principled negotiation" approaches.

Creative Aggression by George R. Bach and Herb Goldberg (Doubleday, 1974)

Dispute Resolution Training Manual (Conciliation Forums of Oakland, 672 13th Street, Oakland, California, 94612; (510) 763-2117

The Critical Edge: How to Criticize Up and Down Your Organization and Make It Pay Off by Hendrie Weisinger, Ph.D. (Little, Brown & Co., 1989)

Breaking the Impasse: Consensual Approaches to Resolving Public Disputes by Lawrence Susskind and Jeffrey Cruikshank (Basic Books, 1987)

Win-Win Negotiating: Turning Conflict into Agreement by Fred E. Jandt with Paul Gillette (John Wiley & Sons, 1985)

The Leader as Martial Artist: Techniques and Strategies for Resolving Conflict and Creating Community by Arnold Mindell, Ph.D. (HarperCollins, 1992)

"Conflict Resolution and Democracy as a Spiritual Path" by Rosalind N. Diamond in *Creation Spirituality*, September/October 1992 (P.O. Box 19216, Oakland, California, 94619; (510) 482-4984

"Welcoming Conflict: Conflict Resolution as a Creative Process," an unpublished paper by Rosalind N. Diamond available from her at P.O. Box 8535, Berkeley, California, 94707-8535.

Organizations

The Community Boards Program, 149 Ninth Street, San Francisco, California, 94103; (415) 552-1250. Resources and training.

National Institute for Citizen Participation and Negotiation, 125 Brentwood Avenue, San Francisco, California, 94127; (415) 337-9701

National Institute for Dispute Resolution, 1901 L Street, NW, Suite 600, Washington, D.C., 20036; (202) 466-4764

Society of Professionals in Dispute Resolution (SPIDR), International Office, 815 15th Street, NW, Suite 530, Washington, D.C., 20005; (202) 833-2188

Berkeley Dispute Resolution Service, 1769 Alcatraz Avenue, Berkeley, California, 94703; (510) 428-1811. A similar service may be available in your area, possibly listed under "conciliation," "mediation," or "conflict management."

Center for Resourceful Mediation, 1158 High Street, Suite 202, Eugene, Oregon, 97401; (503) 345-1205. Source for "Agree" computer mediation program.

Also see resources for Chapters 12, 14, and 15.

There is a fantasy abroad. Simply stated, it goes like this: "If we can resolve our conflicts, then someday we shall be able to live together in community." Could it be that we have it totally backward? And that the real dream should be: "If we can live together in community, then someday we shall be able to resolve our conflicts"?

M. Scott Peck

SEVENTEEN

Celebrating and Renewing Community

What is ritual? The briefest definition I've heard is, "Ritual is anything that worked once and got repeated."

BILL KAUTH

Where there is no vision, the people perish.

PROVERBS

SHOSHANA ALEXANDER, FORTY-TWO YEARS old and eight months pregnant with her first child, looked around the living room at the more than two dozen women, men, and children gathered for her baby shower. She drank in the love pouring through her friends' eyes and felt tears welling up in her own. Inside, Shoshana sensed the familiar movements of her baby and imagined that he, also, was soaking up this love.

She could hardly believe that only a few months ago she had felt abandoned and alone. When the baby's father made it clear he had no intention of continuing to live with Shoshana or supporting the child, she had wondered how, in her financially strapped circumstances, she could responsibly bring this new life into the world. But her friends had rallied around and promised help, financial and otherwise. Now Shoshana sat in the middle of her patched-together family of friends, a community of young, old, and in-between who had brought their love along with new and used baby clothes, recycled strollers, cold hard cash, several months' worth of diaper service, and promises of babysitting, massages, and homecooked meals.

And—the hardest gift to receive or believe—they assured her that she was giving them priceless treasures in return: a child to love and the affirmation of life in a world that seemed bent on death and destruction.

As Shoshana took in these assurances, a word began to grow in her full, round belly and rise to her throat. Yes! She wanted to sing this yes, dance it, shout it. Yes, I can do this. Yes, I am not alone. She laughed and let her friends know how deeply she felt their support and how committed she was to birthing this baby with joy and strength.

Ritual affirms the value of any transition. When we celebrate life changes together, we create strong bonds of intimacy and trust that can generate new culture.

When we undergo a change uncelebrated and unmarked, that transition is devalued, rendered invisible.

STARHAWK

The ceremony that set this shower apart from most was simple. Before the traditional opening of gifts and sharing of food, the group spent a few moments in silent meditation. Shoshana told what this birth meant to her and invited others to offer wishes for her unborn child. Each person took a turn lighting a birthday candle and speaking aloud his or her wishes. Many shared more than wishes for the baby. They spoke of how, over the years, Shoshana had inspired them to give birth in one way or another in their own lives. They told how her choosing to bear this child and to call on their support enabled them to respond to life with similar courage and to remember that they, too, were not alone. This pre-birth celebration effectively countered the stereotyped notion of the unwed mother as a passive, needy victim by elevating Shoshana to the status of life-giver, the one who brings strength, joy, and hope to her community.

Although the dominant culture—unlike Shoshana's community—tends to trivialize rites and ceremony and relegate them to the fringes of life, celebrations play a central role in building and sustaining community. Properly performed, these processes transform both individuals and groups, enabling those involved to die to one identity and be born to a new one. A boy becomes a man, a girl a woman; winter dies, spring is born; a collection of separate individuals turns into a community of connected members.

Even the most powerful celebrations need not include elaborate or esoteric rituals. A genuine celebration can be as simple as sitting in a circle and taking turns sharing from the heart, as the guests at Shoshana's shower did. When members of a group intentionally step outside the flow of ordinary business and gather to acknowledge a passage or a milestone, however simply, they perceive each other with fresh eyes. They see their community or organization as a living, organic whole rather than a fragmented collection of separate parts. As members, they reaffirm their connection with one another and their identity and purpose as a group. In the truest of celebrations, they remember, as well, the larger web of relationships in which they live and the cycles of birth, growth, death, and rebirth that link them to people everywhere and to the natural world of plants, animals, and ecosystems.

If you are part of an informal circle of friends and family, you can deepen your bonds and renew yourselves each time you celebrate a birthday, a wedding, or a seasonal or religious holiday. You also may wish to create your own traditions. One group of friends retreated to a large beach house every summer for a week of play, rest, and conversation. Another generated a composite holiday that they called Thankmas. Because so many of the members celebrated Thanksgiving and Christmas with their families, the group established a date between the two holidays for their own gathering, a simple potluck enhanced with seasonal festivities.

If your community has organized itself more formally into a nonprofit group, a business, a shared living arrangement, or all three, you might develop celebrations and retreats that acknowledge and honor group anniversaries and transitions, in addition to personal and seasonal passages. Your primary celebrations may take the form of regular group retreats for renewal and recommitment. These allow you to honor your collective accomplishments, acknowledge your mistakes, agree to make changes, recreate yourselves through play, and rededicate yourselves as a group to your common vision and goals.

Formal ritual serves as a sort of transformer for powerful archetypal energy. This is the energy of transformation from one state of being to another. The most obvious in our men's work is the "rite of passage" from boyhood to manhood.

BILL KAUTH

CELEBRATING MEANS MORE THAN THROWING A PARTY

A group retreat for renewal and revisioning may not seem like a celebration in the ordinary sense of the word. People tend to equate the word "celebration" with "party," an activity they regard as fun but frivolous. This robs celebrations of their power to create community. In their deeper, more ancient meaning, celebrations are sacred acts, conducted outside ordinary time, whose primary (although not exclusive) purpose is re-creation rather than recreation.

Shoshana's shower contained the essential elements of the sacred tribal rituals that Dutch anthropologist Arnold van Gennep describes in his seminal book, *Les Rites de Passage.* According to van Gennep, such celebrations move through three major phases. In the first, which he calls the separation or preliminal phase, the participants prepare for entry into another reality by separating from the old social context and identity. In the second, labeled transition or liminal, they enter this sacred time and space and are transformed or reborn by the act of crossing the threshold. ("Liminal" comes from the Latin word limen, meaning "threshold.") Finally, in the third, called incorporation or postliminal, the participants return, changed, and are reintegrated into the social order on a new basis. Only then does the community throw a party.

Celebration Rituals for Family and Friends

A healthy community affirms itself and builds morale and motivation through ceremonies and celebrations that honor the symbols of shared identity and enable members to rededicate themselves. This doesn't mean that they suppress internal criticism or deny their flaws.

JOHN W. GARDNER

The next time you gather for a holiday feast or a reunion, pull out the photo albums or home movies and videos and let the members of your family or circle know that they can tell their own versions of the documented events.

If all members are willing, tape the stories so that every version is preserved.

Make sure everyone who wishes to gets a chance to speak. Gently draw out those who tend to keep quiet so that the story becomes truly collective and not just that of the dominant or most articulate members. At the same time, respect the choice of any who do not wish to contribute.

Look for patterns and turning points in the stories you tell. Notice how individual members and the family or circle as a whole has changed over the years. Especially acknowledge those who act against type: the quiet one who speaks up, the tough guy who shows tenderness, the non-athlete who learns a sport.

Make wishes for the year ahead, for yourselves as individuals and for your family or circle as a whole. What do you want to bring into your lives? What do you have to change or release to do that?

Shoshana's pre-birth celebration actually started when she and her friends began planning the shower. Each friend first turned within to reflect on the beginning this event symbolized and the old habits that Shoshana and her community needed to release. In welcoming her baby into the world, Shoshana was relinquishing her identity as a childless, independent woman to become a mother, dependent in new ways on the support of her community. The guests prepared for this by reflecting on their changed relationship with Shoshana, deciding what new level of commitment they felt willing to make, and choosing a gift that signified this new commitment. Once gathered in the living room, each "crossed the threshold" as he or she spoke to Shoshana, made a wish, and lit a candle. By the end of this simple ritual, the participants had transformed from a collection of separate individuals to a bonded community of support. They entered the third and final phase of the celebration when they relaxed their focused group energy, returned to ordinary reality, and began milling about, eating, drinking, and chatting, as they would at any party.

Skipping the first two phases—preparation to enter another reality and entering that reality—and just throwing the party is somewhat like presenting the Oscar awards at a gala, star-studded event without bothering to make the movies. Missing from most modern so-called celebrations is the sense of separation from the daily routine and moving into something new. In this new sacred realm of power and spirit, anything can happen. Two people can become one, a collective wound can heal, a decaying world can be reborn. The Hopi, for instance, call their winter solstice ceremony Soyal or Soyalangwul, meaning "establishing life anew for all the world."

Through stories an individual life is related to the overarching meaning of the cosmos; each individual story is linked with a Great Story.

Sara Wenger Shenk

Contemporary industrialized culture has traded this sacred, celebratory power for the mundane, workaday power of material technology. It has collapsed a multi-dimensional experience into a single factual dimension, measurable by a predictable sequence of seconds, minutes, hours, and days. In this one-dimensional culture, the work world becomes the "real" world. By discounting the sacred, this culture has reduced the ancient spiraling, cycle-based sense of time—one that expected the unexpected at each turn—to a linear arrow. A holiday now means so many days off from paid work rather than an opportunity to step into another, timeless dimension. New Year's Eve becomes not an invitation to be reborn but the mere movement of the second hand one notch on the mechanical clock face.

Renewing yourself or your community in such a linear-time culture presents a challenge. Pre-modern societies that experience time as cyclical understand that a restful phase of inner processing follows every active phase of outward production. Try explaining this to your boss, your customers, your peers, or your own inner critic who, knowing nothing of cycles, expect you to operate at peak performance at all times. These external and internal voices of the culture do not consider you or your organization successful unless you are constantly growing, moving up, and producing and earning more than the year before.

Shifting from this linear, machine-like mindset to a more cyclical, organic one means remembering that you and your community are not machines but living organisms that require regular periods of inward rather than outward focusing. These time-outs, far from being periods in which nothing happens, permit essential inner processes to take place. They function as sleep and dreaming do in daily life, allowing you to cross the threshold to another reality and return refreshed and renewed.

You can honor the cycles of life without giving up forward, or upward, progress. While you cycle through the same series of phases over and over again, you do so in a spiral, moving to a higher position with each complete cycle.

Deepening Community by Celebrating Personal Life Passages

Organizational as well as individual effectiveness requires development and renewal of all four dimensions [physical, spiritual, mental, and social-emotional] in a wise and balanced way.

Stephen R. Covey

You and your community can reinforce your shift from a mechanical, linear approach to life to an organic, spiral one by taking every opportunity to celebrate the life passages of individual members. The mere act of coming together enables your circle to recognize itself as a community and to remember and deepen connections that may have faded in the rush of daily life. In traditional cultures, religious celebrations served this function. But given the diversity in American culture today, you cannot always rely on one religious or ethnic tradition to bring you together. You can, however, develop celebrations that offer your group the chance to see itself as a whole and, if it is ready, to recommit itself to work and play together in a more conscious manner.

You can turn birthday parties, showers, weddings, funerals, even divorces into occasions for community building simply by including in these events an opportunity for risk-taking—the crossing of the threshold. This can be as mild as telling a personal story or as strong as publicly declaring intentions.

If your circle of friends is planning a birthday party for you, for instance, you might ask them to design one that will help you change in some way. If they agree, you can let them know what kind of change you wish to make in the year ahead and how they and others attending the party can help you accomplish this. Your friends, in turn, can prepare, before arriving, for this crossing of the threshold. Let's say you want to relax and play more but you feel guilty when you do so because it runs counter to the family culture in which you grew up. You need help letting go of the guilt and finding time and specific occasions in which to play. At the party, your friends might take turns telling how they have dealt with this issue. Or, they might reflect on how relaxing and having fun with you would enrich their lives as well as yours. Each might bring a gift that supports you in your intention. These need not be expensive gifts. They could be anything from tickets to a movie to a promise to walk in the park with you at least once a month. A year later, at your next birthday, you might be surprised to find out how your asking for help with your desired change has transformed and deepened your community as well.

Fran Peavey, author of *Heart Politics,* holds what she calls her "annual accounting" each year on her birthday. She invites her friends to join her for a dinner, for which she cooks something special as a thanksgiving for the support and friendship extended throughout the year. Since people come who know her but may never have met one another, Fran asks them to introduce themselves briefly. She enjoys helping people from the various parts of her multi-faceted life connect with one another. Once the food is cleared away, Fran begins her "accounting." She begins with the year in her life that has just passed, reflecting upon the accomplishments and highlights as well as the difficulties. She tries to share as openly as possible how the year has felt from the inside. Then she addresses the year ahead, speaking of the activities and challenges she foresees and the kinds of support she is going to need. Sometimes her friends ask questions or offer advice and comments. There is always a lot of laughter and goodwill.

The making of ritual is a creative act fundamental in human life.

GERTRUD MUELLER NELSON

Often, people face their most challenging passages alone because they and their society possess no rituals to acknowledge these transitions. Adolescents suffer through puberty in silence and confusion; women who miscarry or undergo an abortion find no healing from the pain because no one has supported them in grieving for such losses. Other losses go unhealed as well out of embarrassment and the lack of models: the breakup of a love relationship, losing a job, the death of a pet, the end of menstruation for women, the loss of meaning in midlife for women and men. Even when people do acknowledge communally a life passage such as a marriage or a death, they may merely show up and rely on the priest, minister, or rabbi to take care of the ceremony for them.

Picture, instead, a wedding in which the bride and groom sit down with their respective families and friends and tell how and why they decided to

make their life-long commitment, then give the guests a chance to respond. Or imagine those honoring a deceased loved one gathering in a circle to share memories of this person and, in the process, crying, laughing, and letting go. Meaningful, community-generating ceremonies need not be complicated or solemn—or laden with the trappings of a particular religion if this does not fit for the people involved.

Family rituals on religious holidays, at bedtimes or at major times of transition, like weddings and funerals, are powerful primarily because they provide the opportunity to tell the familiar stories again and again.

SARA WENGER SHENK

Most life passage celebrations in American culture acknowledge adult transitions. Few celebrate the passages young children make as they grow up. Shoshana, whose baby shower story opens this chapter, chose to correct this omission. When her son, Elias, turned three, she invited a small circle of their voluntary extended family to participate in a ritual marking his passage from babyhood to boyhood. In the ritual, Elias enacted his voluntary separation from his mother and his bonding more fully with his extended family. Before the event, Shoshana and her son discussed this passage, and Elias participated in planning his rite, including choosing the outdoor location.

The ritual began with the invited friends wrapping Elias and Shoshana in a loose paper tent to signify the intensity of the mother-son bonding for the past three years. After whispering with his mother for a while, Elias announced, "I'm ready!" and burst out of the paper wrapping. He squealed with delight as his friends tossed him on a blanket, directed them in singing special songs, listened intently as they read a fairy tale to him about a boy who becomes a man, and turned appropriately quiet and serious when the men took him off to cut his hair. The ritual "took." In the days and months that followed, Elias, who often had been reluctant to leave his mother to go on excursions with adult friends, now went off happily with his godparents and "adopted" uncles and aunts.

Seasonal, Weekly, and Daily Celebrations

Something has gone wrong when most Americans look forward to the major holiday season of the year—from Thanksgiving through New Year's Day—with dread rather than joy. For millennia, such seasonal holidays served to bind families, tribes, and cultures together and remind them of the larger stories that gave their lives purpose. Today, many families feel lucky if they survive the winter holidays intact, and those without warm family bonds tend to battle depression more at this time of year than at any other.

A combination of factors contributes to the problem. Most, at root, are connected to the culture's lack of a sense of the sacred and the honoring of natural cycles. While continuing to work just as hard at their jobs in

A New Year's Ritual

One well-known example of renewal illustrates how groups of friends can mark a turning point by reconnecting to their inner worlds. On a smaller scale, you can try this at home.

Since 1981, businessman Phil Lader and his wife Linda have celebrated New Year's by hosting a "Renaissance Weekend" on Hilton Head Island, South Carolina. Participants have included President Bill Clinton and his family as well as business executives, sports and government figures, journalists, and other achievers. During this family-oriented retreat, the participants devote long days to seminars on topics ranging from "Building an Inner Life" to world politics. They also relax, socialize, and enjoy meals together. They look forward to this annual event as a chance to mark the changing of the year by reflecting on their own lives, as well as engaging in intimate discussions with old friends.

I'm making a banner for a procession. I need a procession so that God will come down and dance with us.

THREE-YEAR-OLD ANNIKA NELSON

December as at any other time of year, people incorporate into their already overloaded schedules time for gift shopping, writing cards, decorating the house, hosting parties, taking the kids to visit Santa, and dealing with emotionally charged family interactions. All this leaves them little time or energy for contemplating the deeper meaning of the season and connecting with others in a heartfelt, renewing manner.

While no one we have met has found a totally satisfying solution to this dilemma, many are seeking quieter, more meaningful expressions of the holiday spirit. The most memorable winter holiday celebration I (Carolyn) participated in was also the simplest. On the eve of solstice, the longest night of the year, we decided to befriend the darkness for a few hours before turning on the Christmas tree lights for the first time. My husband made a blazing fire in the fireplace and, except for the votive candles we had lit to mark the beginning of the ceremony, this hearth fire provided the only light. The seven of us sat in silence for a few minutes, opening to the spirit of the winter season, then began to tell stories of our most treasured encounters with the darkness. My husband, a Dutchman who lived through Nazi occupation as a young boy, told of a winter night in wartime when his parents sent him with a lantern to the backyard shed to feed the animals. His fear turned to wonder as he felt the warm, reassuring breath of the rabbits and goats and enjoyed their gentle nuzzling. Another man spoke of a special spirit tree that helped guide him night after dark night to his cabin in the snowy woods of Canada. A woman remembered the fear and magic of a New Year's Eve alone in an isolated farm house with only candles for illumination. As the stories and our simple ceremony came to an end, we felt so warmly wrapped in the gentle robe of darkness that we could not bear to turn on either the Christmas tree or the house lights. We ate our cake by candlelight, and the tree remained dark for yet another day.

The family meal was once a primary family sacrament, where children learned the terms of civil discourse.

ROBERT N. BELLAH AND COAUTHORS

One family of four turns Hanukkah into a time for reaching out to friends and deepening the bonds of their social web. Each evening of the eight-day feast, they invite a different friend or family to their home for dinner. As the dinner hosts and guests take turns lighting the candles, they speak of what this time of year means to them, and of how, in the face of current challenges, they find hope and renew their faith.

The celebratory event that bonds your family or circle need not be seasonal or even particularly profound. One family sets Sunday morning aside for a leisurely breakfast of sourdough waffles. "It's our weekly ritual," says Ed Niehaus, "and it has become a special, almost sacrosanct time for us." Since both Ed and his wife Carol work outside the home as well as raise two children, their hectic weekday mornings leave little time for anything more than the most mundane interactions. Sunday morning waffle time represents a sharp break from routine and an opportunity to be rather than do. Parents and children relax and joke with one another and emerge, if not reborn, at least refreshed.

How Communities and Organizations Renew Themselves

"Our annual retreats have become essential to the renewal of our organization," declares Eleanor McCallie Cooper, executive director of Chattanooga Venture, the nonprofit civic group that has dedicated itself to empowering citizens to revitalize their city. "These two-day events help us recognize what we have accomplished, develop a sense of ourselves as a group, and reach agreement about our future direction."

Retreats have become a popular renewal vehicle for organizations of every size and function, from Fortune 500 companies to circles of friends. They usually consist of one or more days away from the city or the workplace at a center that provides food and lodging in a natural setting. Such retreats, often annual in frequency, provide an opportunity to tell the story of the past year (or more) and create a new one for the year ahead. Such "tribal storytelling," writes Max DePree in *Leadership Is an Art,* "preserves and revitalizes the values of the tribe." He adds that "constant renewal also readies us for the inevitable crises of corporate life."

When we asked Eleanor Cooper what might happen if her organization stopped holding such retreats, she mentioned such things as the spread of miscommunication and the buildup of tensions, but the main problem she foresaw was members "going off in our own directions." Without a regular time-out from business as usual and a chance to focus on the group's collective purpose and internal dynamics, says Eleanor, "we would not be able to build a group body."

Ceremonies of empowerment are routine in [the Goodenough] community for people taking on new responsibilities, and for people needing to clarify a new professional image and receive support for new roles.

JOHN HOFF

Chattanooga Venture's annual staff retreats produce pronounced and long-lasting effects back at the office. "After each, we work together with more humor and lightness and less tension," Eleanor reports, "and the most recent retreat reshaped our whole work. We discovered that some of our busyness was not to the point of our bigger purpose." That same retreat also shifted the way the staff and the executive committee of the board interacted. At their next meeting, they dropped the usual business agenda and instead talked about themselves as individuals, developing a deeper level of trust and appreciation for one another.

In addition to regular retreats, Rapha Community in Syracuse, New York, conducts four-hour "evaluation and visioning," or "E & V," meetings two evenings a year. A non-residential community that began in the 1960s as a house church evolving from a Methodist congregation, Rapha, now independent of any religious denomination, focuses on the spiritual and personal growth of its members and models a non-hierarchical form of shared leadership. At a recent E & V meeting, the community asked its members such questions as, "Do you feel your life is deeper than it was six months ago?" and "Has the community made a real difference in your life?" They sat with these questions in silence before launching into their evaluating and visioning. First, the members listed on a wall chart the events they had lived through since the previous E & V and discussed what worked and what did not. Then, they shifted from evaluating to visioning, exploring their current needs and what they desired, as a community, for the next six months.

Occasionally, the community realizes that it has moved so far out of balance that it cannot regain equilibrium in a single four-hour meeting. In crisis times like this, Rapha holds a full retreat to focus on the life of the community. "We reinvent ourselves at these retreats," comments longtime member Julia Ketcham, who notes that such events usually occur every four or five years. "We ask, What are we all about? Should we go on? It's like coming to a gate. It seems so scary. It feels like going through this gate will destroy the community. But actually the reverse happens. We become more deeply bonded. Going through the gate so far has seemed to be a way of opening up to a greater acceptance of our differences. We sometimes feel that not going through the gate may destroy the community." Julia adds that such retreats serve an important function for new members, giving them "a chance to buy in, to make the community their own."

If the community is lucky (and fewer and fewer are), it will have a shared history and tradition. It will have symbols of group identity, its "story," its legends, and heroes. Social cohesion will be advanced if the group's norms and values are explicit.

JOHN W. GARDNER

Whether one chooses a daily retreat or a formal sabbatical, one has access to one's soul and imagination, and one can truly reflect on experience, and learn from it, and emerge renewed and refreshed.

WARREN BENNIS

Celebrating the Phases of Your Community's Life

Celebration and renewal can help your community become more conscious by acknowledging collectively your group passages as well your individual ones. Such rites of renewal involve more than throwing a party to welcome new members, launch a new project, or celebrate a major accomplishment. If your group does not consciously acknowledge, and perhaps even grieve for, what is ending when you enter even the most positive of new phases, you may find the passage unnecessarily rocky and confusing. You may have longed to add new members, and yet, when a wave of them arrives, you feel uncomfortable and edgy even though you know these newcomers will enliven and strengthen your community. You may need to include in the process of celebrating their incorporation a collective acknowledgment of what is ending. Long-term members may lose the comfort of interacting with a small group whose members they know well and with whose styles, roles, and power dynamics they are familiar. Simply talking about this can be enough.

Another important step in incorporating the newcomers is telling them the tribal story, often called orientation in organizational terms. When my husband and I (Carolyn) joined the Shenoa Retreat and Learning Center board, we only received bits and snatches of this tribal story. Several misunderstandings later, we learned how helpful it would have been to have taken the time for a proper orientation. Shenoa has now committed itself to holding regular retreats where, among other things, this tribal story can be told.

Sometimes communities come to an end. They need to die in their present form for something new to be born. Acknowledging and celebrating these endings, however painful, can mean the difference between ex-members ready to strike out in new directions with clarity and purpose and ex-members treading water in a sea of confusion, not sure what has happened or even whether they are members or ex-members.

When Intersil, a high-tech firm in Santa Clara, California, had to close its silicon wafer plant and lay off 1,300 employees, the company rented a hotel ballroom to hold a formal wake. The firm invited former managers and employees, as well as current ones. As the highlight of the event, a New

RE-CREATING YOUR GROUP MYTHOLOGY

Every group or organization possesses some kind of mythology, even if it is only a year or two old. You can move toward deeper community by setting time aside at meetings or retreats to ask:

How did this group or organization begin? Who are the founding mothers and fathers and what motivated them?

What is our collective mythology? You might tell your history as you would a fairytale, identifying heroes, villains, seers, magicians, lost children, fairy godmothers, and such.

What does it take to succeed here? To become a hero?

What sorts of people fail, or are viewed as bad or dangerous?

What are the unwritten rules? How do certain people break these and get away with it?

What happens to people who take risks?

What kinds of comical or crazy things have happened?

What were the moments of crisis when the community and its values were tested?

What are the primary differences between the old days and the present?

Every family, every college, every corporation, every institution needs tribal storytellers. The penalty for failing to listen is to lose one's history, one's historical context, one's binding values.

MAX DEPREE

Orleans jazz band playing "The St. James Infirmary Blues" led a procession through the ballroom followed by ex-executives with black umbrellas carrying a coffin to a crepe-bedecked stage. Everyone received an address book and pen with the company logo so they could preserve their links with current and former colleagues. They also sorted through collections of old products, photos, and other memorabilia and took home what they wanted.

One former employee, who had left the division before it closed but attended the wake, commented that the ceremony not only provided a much-needed closure to an important chapter in his life, it made him feel connected to those who were involved in the plant's demise. He contrasts this feeling to his memory of another layoff, in another state, which included no formal acknowledgment. "Every time I passed that plant afterward, I got shivers up my spine."

Letting-go ceremonies need not be as elaborate as Intersil's. When a women's group began unraveling, the members held a final meeting at which each member spoke of what the group meant to her and why she did or did not wish to continue at this time. When only three women chose to continue, the group grieved together, appreciated one another, and sang a closing song. The three who chose to continue were clearly a new and different group that could—and did—redefine itself as it chose. The others knew that they had laid the original group to rest and could each strike out in a new direction with full energy.

Whatever you can do or dream you can, begin it. Boldness has genius, power, and magic in it. Begin it now.

GOETHE

We lack rituals that would allow communities to acknowledge [their] crises and to heal them.

KATY BUTLER

Unlike this group, the members of Greenvillage, which was exploring residential community, drifted apart without any clear acknowledgment of its demise. Two members worked for months developing materials for a prospectus before they realized the group had essentially died. They felt confused and hurt and had no group forum in which to express their feelings and let go of the pain. For at least one of these members, Suzanne, many more months passed before she could bring herself to continue the search for another group of people with the staying power to create community. The difficulty she felt in mourning the death of Greenvillage and moving on with her life is not unlike the problems people face in accepting the death of a loved one when no body is found.

Every powerful commitment, whether to a couple relationship or a community, requires a clear acknowledgment of its ending. This enables you to shed your old identity and freely move into a fresh commitment—either to yourself or to others—and into the new identity this generates.

Americans as a culture are releasing an old way of perceiving themselves and opening to a new one, and you are helping. As you acknowledge your yearning for community and take the risk of acting on this, you change the culture. You help others see that they need not lose their individuality by joining in community but can actually become more themselves within this larger context of challenge and support.

You may feel daunted by the task of creating community in a culture that does not value the time this takes or the processes required. But remember that each time you call a group together to reflect and celebrate, or risk greater honesty in a circle of friends or work team, you are changing the culture—and making it that much easier for others, and yourself, to build community in the future. Also remember that you are not taking these risks alone. To quote Goethe, as soon as you commit yourself, "all sorts of things occur to help one that would never otherwise have occurred."

As you join with others, even if only one or two at first, to create conscious community, you move toward the next turn of the spiral. And you enable American culture to do likewise, releasing its adolescent dream of unfettered individualism so it can commit itself to the synergy of community that honors both the individual and the group.

Resources

Recommended books and articles

Rituals for Our Times: Celebrating, Healing and Changing Our Lives and Our Relationships by Evan Imber-Black and Janine Roberts (HarperCollins, 1992)

Ceremonial Circle: Shamanic Practice, Renewal and Ritual by Sedonia Cahill and Joshua Halpern (HarperSanFrancisco, 1990)

The Art of Ritual: A Guide to Creating and Performing Your Own Ceremonies and Rituals for Growth and Change by Renée Beck and Sydney Barbara Metrick (Celestial Arts, 1990)

The Paradox of Success: When Winning at Work Means Losing at Life by John O'Neil (Tarcher/Putnam, 1993). Excellent suggestions for using personal and organizational retreats to promote renewal.

Why Not Celebrate! by Sara Wenger Shenk (Good Books, Intercourse, Pennsylvania, 17534; 1987). A collection of Christian-based celebrations useful for families, small groups, and retreats. Developed by a member of the Mennonite-inspired Reba Place Church-Community, the celebrations honor small events as well as major life passages.

To Dance with God: Family Ritual and Community Celebration by Gertrud Mueller Nelson (Paulist Press, 1986). A Christian-and-Jungian-inspired exploration of the meaning and dynamics of ritual that includes suggestions for honoring each season and major feast day of the Christian tradition.

The Magic of Ritual: Our Need for Liberating Rites that Transform Our Lives and Our Communities by Tom F. Driver (HarperSanFrancisco, 1991)

Truth or Dare: Encounters with Power, Authority, and Mystery by Starhawk (Harper & Row, 1987), especially Chapter Eleven, "Ritual to Build Community."

The Spiral Dance by Starhawk (HarperCollins, 1982)

The Rites of Passage by Arnold van Gennep, trans. Monika B. Vizedom and Gabrielle L. Caffee (University of Chicago, 1908, 1960)

The Visionary Leader: From Mission Statement to a Thriving Organization, Here's Your Blueprint for Building an Inspired, Cohesive, Customer-Oriented, Team by Bob Wall, et al. (Prima Publishing, 1992)

"Creating Our Own Holiday Rituals" by Carolyn R. Shaffer in *Yoga Journal*, November/December 1988

Visioning and Mission Development Workbook by Roger Harrison (Roger Harrison, 240 Monroe Drive, Suite 502, Mountain View, California, 94040; [415] 941-4211). A set of self-directed learning materials that groups and organizations can use to plan and execute their own vision and mission statement retreats. Also available is *On Community*, a working paper that addresses such topics as community culture, the shadow side of community, and group attunement.

Ritual affirms the common patterns, the values, the shared joys, risks, sorrows, and changes that bind a community together. Ritual links together our ancestors and descendants, those who went before with those who will come after us. It helps us face together those things that are too painful to face alone.

STARHAWK

Afterword

The Planet as Community

A human being is a part of the whole called by us universe, a part limited in time and space. He experiences himself, his thoughts and feelings as something separated from the rest, a kind of optical delusion of his consciousness. This delusion is a kind of prison for us, restricting us to our personal desires and to affection for a few persons nearest to us. Our task must be to free ourselves from this prison by widening our circle of compassion to embrace all living creatures and the whole of nature in its beauty.

ALBERT EINSTEIN

FOR MANY OF US, the loneliness that feeds our yearning for community comes from feeling cut off not only from other people but also from the rest of the natural world. Just as we need to reconnect in new ways with family, neighbors, co-workers, and those different from us if we are to survive as a species, we also need to develop a new relationship with the earth and its diverse species if we are to survive as a planetary community.

Taking on such a task may seem overwhelming. "Learning to get along with my neighbor is hard enough," you might say. "How am I also supposed to understand and respond to the needs of a river, a rainforest, or a herd of caribou, and convince my neighbor and the government to do likewise?"

There is no use pretending that building planetary community is easy. But, like creating human community, it may be simpler than you think. It begins with enlarging your sense of self and community to include the natural world. Once you have grasped that your family and your neighborhood community are systems, interdependent with the system that is your body, you can simply expand this notion to include wider communities as a single system. Our physical dependence on air, water, and food and our understanding of such planet-wide dynamics as water cycles, weather systems, and the exchange of oxygen and carbon dioxide between plants and animals helps us grasp the interdependent nature of our relationship with the earth.

You may fear that taking the earth into account in everything you do will require sacrifice and perhaps more altruism than you can muster. Shifting to a systems perspective can reassure you that, in taking a planetary view, you aren't sacrificing yourself for something outside of you or giving away your time, energy, or money with no thought of return. You are operating out of self-interest based on an expanded sense of self.

And just as the false assumption that we are not connected to the earth has led to the ecological crisis, so the equally false assumption that we are not connected to each other has led to our social crisis.

AL GORE

Activist and systems thinker Joanna Macy calls this expanded self the "ecological self." It is a sense of who we are that does not stop at our skin but includes, or is "co-extensive with," other beings and the life of the planet. In *World as Lover, World as Self,* she gives an example: "It would not occur to me to plead with you 'Oh, don't saw off your leg. That would be an act of violence.' It wouldn't occur to me because your leg is part of your body. Well, so are the trees in the Amazon rain basin. They are our external lungs. And we are beginning to realize that the world is our body." From this perspective, reducing our consumption of exotic hardwoods or fast-food hamburgers to slow the destruction of rainforests, for instance, becomes no more a sacrifice or an act of altruism than cutting down on junk food to improve our health. Of course, some habits, such as our dependence on the automobile, will be much more difficult to break. Still, the pain may be easier to take if we focus on how our changed behavior benefits both us, as individuals, and the planet in the long run.

Although creating conscious planetary community requires time and effort, you don't have to learn new skills to do it. You can use the same skills in reconnecting with the natural world that you use for building community with other humans. You simply need to apply these skills in a larger context and with beings that don't converse in human language. In a healthy community, you treat one another with respect and trust that each member holds a piece of the truth. When making a decision, you show this respect and tap the collective wisdom by communicating with those affected by the decision and including their input in the decision-making process. When your community is acting from its ecological self, you include the wisdom and needs of the natural world in your deliberations.

On a small scale, for instance, if you and your family or housemates wish to build a tool shed in the backyard, you would ask each member what would best serve his or her needs and you would also, as a group, attune to the needs of the plants and trees in the yard and the animals that travel through it. You would also consider the sun, wind, soil, and drainage factors that affect the yard and its human and non-human inhabitants. Listening to a tree to find out what it needs may sound strange and mystical, but it is no different from listening to your body to discover whether you need more rest or a different diet. Both take practice and, in some cases, training, in a culture that devalues intuition. Such an intuitive approach, however, does not preclude using your intellect. The more you have studied the tree or your body, the more informed and wiser your intuitive decision will be.

We are members of one great body, planted by nature in a mutual love, and fitted for social life. We must consider that we were born for the good of the whole.

SENECA

Joanna Macy and a colleague, John Seed, developed a process they call "The Council of All Beings." It's a simple procedure that enables groups to develop an ecological sense of the self by intuitively listening to and speaking on behalf of other species. The process, which Macy and Seed describe in *Thinking Like a Mountain*, can last anywhere from two hours to several days. It usually unfolds in three stages, beginning with participants mourning what has been lost in the natural world by sharing their stories about how this loss has affected them. The group then remembers, usually by way of a guided visualization, the evolutionary journey. The process culminates with each participant speaking formally on behalf of another life-form after having tuned into it in silence.

This Council of All Beings helps participants move beyond anthropocentrism, the chauvinistic notion deeply embedded in our culture that assumes, as Seed puts it, "that humans are the crown of creation, the source of all value, the measure of all things." Releasing this notion does not reduce humans to insignificance but instead connects us to a larger whole. "Alienation subsides," says Seed. "The human is no longer an outsider, apart."

Developing the ecological self, however, does not diminish our uniqueness. "To experience the world as an extended self and its story as our own extended story," explains Macy, "involves no surrender or eclipse of our individuality. The liver, leg, and lung that are 'mine' are highly distinct from each other, thank goodness, and each has a distinctive role to play. The larger selfness we discover today [as we sense our ecological self] is not an undifferentiated unity."

Many of us feel fear, shame, and confusion about our disconnection from nature and the ecological destruction we have wrought as a result. These feelings are natural, given the extent of the damage and the threat it poses for future generations, but they need not lead to chronic despair and paralysis. Joanna Macy has developed conscious community processes, what she calls despair and empowerment work, that help participants face and work through their painful feelings together, integrate the shadow side of their collective behavior, reconnect with nature, and empower themselves and each other. "Many of us fear that confrontation with despair will bring loneliness and isolation," she notes in *World as Lover, World as Self,* "but—on the contrary—in letting go of old defenses, truer community is found. In the synergy of sharing comes power."

A shift in perspective also can help. If we apply the phases of individual and group development to the planetary community, we can view our disconnection with the earth not as a sign of total failure as a species, but as an indicator that we are in the midst of a major transition from one phase of planetary development to another. Just as human communities must pass through several phases of development to reach maturity, perhaps the planetary community must also do so.

What pattern connects the crab to the lobster and the orchid to the primrose and all four of them to me? And me to you?

GREGORY BATESON

In this developmental model, which perceives the planetary community as a family system writ large, we have been separating from our "mother," the earth, for millennia in order to develop our own sense of identity. We have built political and religious structures, created scientific and artistic wonders, and established civilizations. And in so doing, certain cultures among us, like particularly rebellious teenagers, have turned our powerful mother and extended family, the natural world, into adversaries, fighting for autonomy and control.

From a developmental point of view, establishing a sense of autonomy is necessary to a being's full development. But the technologically developed segments of the species have chosen to push the limits. As a species, we may already have gone too far in separating from our family. Convinced of the superiority of our human powers and assuming that the natural world, like a healthy family, was inexhaustible and indestructible, we may have damaged irreparably the only place we can call home. If so, we would not be the first teenagers to destroy themselves while trying to prove something.

As in human communities, however, this period of conflict and struggle, viewed developmentally, not only signals crisis but also provides an opportunity for growth, a chance to move to the next turn of the spiral and become much more than we are now or ever have been. Cultural historian Thomas Berry likens this period in human evolution to the initiation processes, practiced by humans from the earliest times, that marked the passing of an individual from childhood to adulthood. "As the maternal bonds are broken on one level to be reestablished on another," he writes in *The Dream of the Earth,* "so the human community is being separated from the dominance of nature on one level to establish a new and more mature relationship." The earth "is insisting that we accept greater responsibility."

As we move from the autonomy to the stability phase—or, to use an ecological term, the sustainability phase—in our development as a planetary community, we humans are realizing that we are not competitors struggling against nature for control but allies with nature in a single system that has no sides. As with the members of any human community entering the stability phase, we are beginning to acknowledge our own limitations and those of the larger system and to address ourselves, in alliance with nature, to the common task of rebalancing and sustaining the planet.

We must be the change we wish to see in the world.

MOHANDAS GANDHI

According to Berry, we are moving from a technological age, in which achieving autonomy and control was our goal, to an ecological age in which we acknowledge our interdependence with nature and allow the spontaneity of the larger organism of which we are part to express itself through us. This is the dynamic process that this book describes as "synergy."

We stand at a choice point, conscious of ourselves for the first time as one planetary species among many inhabiting a single, unique watery planet with limited resources. Just as individual humans now possess the power and awareness to choose whether to participate consciously in human community, our collective human community today can choose whether to move to the next level of planetary community. "We now have extensive power," says Berry, "over the ultimate destinies of the planet, the power of life and death over many of its life systems. For the first time we can intervene directly in the genetic process. We can dissolve the ozone layer that encircles the earth and let the cosmic radiation bring about distortions in the life process." We are no longer controlled by nature, as a child by a parent. From this position of power, we can choose to rejoin our family, the planetary community, as a responsible, contributing adult member, or we can continue to pretend that we are independent rather than interdependent and destroy ourselves and much of our home.

While the stakes are high, as in any life passage, we don't have to face the challenges alone. That is the beauty of community. Once we expand our sense of self to include the planet, we can call on the immense wisdom and power inherent in the natural world, our "body," to help us make the quantum leap to a new level of planetary community. "The transformations [demanded of us] require the assistance of the entire planet," contends Berry, "not merely the forces available to the human."

We humans already have created vehicles for invoking this help. Religions and the other wisdom traditions of our heritage have long incorporated mystical and shamanic practices for expanding the self to include and communicate with the natural world. A contemporary version of this is the Council of All Beings. At the end of one council, described by Macy, the "deep-diving trout" offered its "fearlessness of the dark"; the lion, its roar, "the voice to speak out and be heard"; the rainforest, its "powers to create harmony, enabling many life-forms to live together"; and the caterpillar, its "willingness to dissolve and transform" and its courage to do so "without knowing the end result."

Many might be tempted to dismiss such ritualized communing with nature as superstitious nonsense. The Council process is certainly not the only way for people to experience their ecological selves. It may not work for some, just as certain forms of human community do not work for everybody. The challenge lies in discovering what best enables you and your community to experience your interdependence with each other and the ever-larger systems of which you are a part. By continuing to expand your awareness of who you are, however you choose to do so, you and your community will invoke help from quarters you least expect. Many religious traditions call such spontaneous assistance "grace." By opening to grace, your small community will heal and thrive. And by providing a model for others, you will also serve the planetary community, enabling it, your greater body, to heal and thrive.

As we and our land are part of one another, so all who are living as neighbors here, human and plant and animal, are part of one another, and so cannot possibly flourish alone.

WENDELL BERRY

The next time you feel overwhelmed by the magnitude of the changes we humans must make to repair our planet, give yourself some quiet time—ideally, in a supportive community setting—to feel your fear and pain and to allow these emotions to connect you with your aunts and uncles, the rivers, mountains, and forests, and your brothers and sisters, the four-legged and winged ones. Know that you are not alone in healing the damage and making the leap to a planetary community. The primary shift is one of awareness. Simply by imagining the possibility of planetary community, you have already effected change.

RESOURCES

Recommended books and periodicals

Thinking Like a Mountain: Toward a Council of All Beings by John Seed, Joanna Macy, Pat Fleming, and Arne Naess (New Society Publishers, 1988)

Simple in Means, Rich in Ends: Practicing Deep Ecology by Bill Devall (Peregrine Smith Books, 1988)

The Dream of the Earth by Thomas Berry (Sierra Club Books, 1988)

Necessary Wisdom by Charles Johnston (Institute for Creative Development, 1992)

Black Elk Speaks by John C. Neihardt (University of Nebraska Press, 1970). The life and vision of an Oglala Sioux medicine man.

World as Lover, World as Self by Joanna Macy (Parallax Press, 1991)

The Universe Story by Brian Swimme and Thomas Berry (HarperCollins, 1992)

States of Grace: The Recovery of Meaning in the Postmodern Age by Charlene Spretnak (HarperCollins, 1991)

Kinship with All Life by J. Allen Boone (Harper & Row, 1976)

Earth Prayers from Around the World edited by Elizabeth Roberts (HarperSan-Francisco, 1991)

Despair and Personal Power in the Nuclear Age by Joanna Macy (New Society Publishers, 1983)

Deep Ecology: Living as if Nature Mattered by Bill Devall (Gibbs-Smith, 1987)

Whole Earth Review (quarterly magazine, $20/year), P.O. Box 38, Sausalito, California, 94966; (415) 332-1716.

Tranet (bimonthly bulletin, $30/year) P.O. Box 567, Rangely, Maine, 04920; (207) 864-2252. Global network of transformational groups and individuals concerned with creating sustainable, humane, ecological (S.H.E.) cultures.

We need to rediscover consciously what we knew instinctively in our neolithic villages and hunter-gatherer societies: how to live in harmony with the biosphere—the co-evolving web of life, in which each species depends upon and supports the qualitative growth of all the others who share this four-billion-year-old miracle of life.

CHRISTOPHER CANFIELD

Organizations and networks

Earthstewards Network, P.O. Box 10697, Bainbridge Island, Washington, 98110; (206) 842-7986. Network circles of people discuss and act on earth- and spirituality-related topics by mail or computer or in person. The Network also conducts international environmental projects and citizen diplomacy.

The Elmwood Institute, P.O. Box 5765, Berkeley, California, 94705; (510) 845-4595. A think-tank/community/network nurturing ecological visions for a sustainable future. Quarterly newsletter, $3.

Planet Drum Foundation, Box 31251, San Francisco, California, 94131; (415) 285-6556. Proposes organizing our lives around the natural ecological and cultural communities in which we live. *Raise the Stakes* newsletter.

Institute for Deep Ecology Education, Box 2290, Boulder, Colorado, 80302; (303) 939-8398. Training and consultations on deep ecology curriculum and programs. Also deep ecology advocacy and networking.

Global Perspectives, P.O. Box 925, Sonoma, California, 95476; (800) 221-8897. A mail-order service that offers tapes and books by Thomas Berry, Miriam MacGillis, Gil Bailie, and others involved in reexamining and deepening our connections with each other, the earth, and Spirit. Provides the "Earth Literacy Start-Up Kit" for use with small groups or for personal reflection. Includes McGregor Smith's *Earth Literacy: An Ethical/Spiritual Model of Education for the Ecological Crisis.*

Workshop

Council of All Beings workshops, c/o Gateway, 6134 Chinquapin Parkway, Baltimore, Maryland, 21239; (301) 433-7873.

About the Authors

CAROLYN R. SHAFFER has been intentionally creating community since 1970, sometimes through shared-living arrangements but more often through circles of friends, personal and professional support groups, and collaborative projects. Currently, as a board member and Land Steward of Shenoa Retreat and Learning Center, she is helping to pioneer new forms of community in northern California. She is coauthor of *City Safaris: A Sierra Club Explorer's Guide to Urban Adventures for Grownups and Kids* (Sierra Club, 1987) and has contributed to several anthologies and periodicals, as well as serving as editor-in-chief of a regional weekly newspaper. With her husband and co-community-builder, Sypko Andreae, she now lives in Berkeley, California, where she conducts a private practice in clinical hypnotherapy. Through Growing Community Associates, she and her business partner, Sandra Lewis, lead workshops and consult with groups and organizations that wish to develop and maintain community. She feels fortunate to enjoy a deep sense of community with friends and family while living and working in a city.

KRISTIN ANUNDSEN has been a professional writer for more than thirty years, covering subjects ranging from technology to travel. A former editor at *Innovation* magazine and the American Management Association in New York, she now lives and works in San Francisco. She has contributed to several books, including *The Computer Entrepreneurs* (New American Library). She specializes in writing about the human side of business and the changing nature of work. Her personal community includes extended family, networks of friends, professional support groups, and social organizations.

End Note

WE HOPE YOU HAVE enjoyed this book and have found the concepts, examples, and processes discussed in it of value. If you know of communities and resources that you would like to suggest for inclusion in future editions, or, if you wish to receive information about the workshops, trainings, and consulting services offered by GCA, we welcome you to contact

Growing Community Associates
P.O. Box 5415
Berkeley, CA 94705
(510) 869-4878

Subject Index

Name Index

I Can't Believe It's Yoga for Kids!

I Can't Believe It's Yoga for Kids!

Lisa Trivell

Photography by
Peter Field Peck

Hatherleigh Press
New York
A Getfitnow.com Book

I Can't Believe It's Yoga for Kids
A GETFITNOW.com Book

Hatherleigh Press/GETFITNOW.com Books
An Affiliate of W.W. Norton & Company, Inc.
5-22 46th Avenue, Suite 200
Long Island City, NY 11101
1-800-367-2550

Visit our website: www.getfitnow.com

Disclaimer:

Before beginning any strenuous exercise program consult your physician. The author and publisher of this book and workout disclaim any liability, personal or professional, resulting from the misapplication of any of the training procedures described in this publication.

All GETFITNOW.com titles are available for bulk purchase, special promotions, and premiums. For more information, please contact the manager of our Special Sales Department at 1-800-367-2550.

Library of Congress Cataloging-in-Publication Data
TO COME

Cover design by Lisa Fyfe
Text design and composition by Dede Cummings Designs

Photographed by Peter Field Peck
with Canon® cameras and lenses on Fuji® print film
Printed in Canada on acid-free paper

10 9 8 7 6 5 4 3 2 1

I would like to dedicate this book to my two children, Amanda and Dylan, whom I love so much.

Also to all the kids pictured in the book – thanks for your participation and inspiration. I hope this book reaches many children who can start to integrate yoga into their lives.

Acknowledgements

I would like to give special thanks to Tracy Tumminello for her continued support and editing talent. She has a great sense of humor and the kids really enjoyed working with her.

For Peter Field Peck, a very talented photographer, who has a special eye for capturing kids in motion having fun.

My publisher Andrew Flach, who had faith in this project from the beginning.

And Kevin Moran, Maria Rothwell, Fleur and Len Harlin for all their generosity and support.

Special thanks to all the children who have studied yoga with me and to the kids that worked so enthusiastically on the book: Max Baez, Susannah Edelbaum, Katherine Esposito, Michael Esposito, Kinara Flagg, Liz Dankowski, Betty Dankowski, Amanda Gang, Dylan Gang, Kevin Geiger, Chris Golden, Kimberly Havlik, Annie Lee, Celina Leroy, Caroline McCann, Jami Moore, Nicholas Moore, Conner Moran, Kevin Moran Jr., Nora Moran, Tom Moran, Chris Poli, Emma Poli, Michael Poli, and Dale Sprayregen.

CONTENTS

I Can't Believe It's Yoga for Kids!

Part I
Introduction

Life can be very busy for kids these days. I have two children ages 11 and 9, and I know how their days can be so hectic and sometimes stressful. It is important for children to learn stress reduction techniques early in their lives. Between schoolwork, after-school activities and hanging out with friends, it is easy to get overwhelmed. Children and adults both need to take the time to learn the skills of relaxation. Besides being a terrific stress-reducer, yoga is a great total body workout. It stretches and tones many unused muscle groups while incorporating breathing techniques.

Yoga gives children the time they need to slow down from their busy daily activities and a chance to progress with exercises at their own pace. As one of the few non-competitive sports, yoga teaches children how to improve their strength and flexibility through practice and patience. Children will find that by studying yoga and practicing a little each day, their flexibility will increase, helping to improve athletic performance and prevent injury.

There has been research showing a strong connection between yoga and cognitive learning in children. The breathing and centering exercises in yoga enhance concentration skills and improve patience. Furthermore, yoga promotes balance through the repetition of exercises on both sides of the body. In addition to balancing the muscles and nerves, this also helps balance the right and left sides of the brain. Using both sides of the brain helps integrate a child's

creative and analytical faculties, improving his or her ability to learn on various levels. We all learn in different ways–spatially, visually, emotionally and analytically. Yoga helps us integrate and develop each of these areas of our brain.

Another, and perhaps the most important, element of yoga is that it is fun to do. Yoga can be done alone, with a friend or in a group. Kids can do the exercises when they wake-up, to stretch before sports or to just unwind at the end of the day. Yoga exercises increase energy as they release tension. Helping children feel centered, yoga can improve memory and boost self-confidence.

Success in yoga is measured by a child's progress–how one's balance improves, how far one stretches, and what new muscles groups one notices. Children will be able to take this new awareness of their bodies and minds with them throughout their lives.

PART II
WHY WE DO YOGA

Yoga is a science of movement, originating thousands of years ago in India. Yogis would meditate in the woods and carefully observe the animals and birds around them. They would tune their bodies to become supple, strong and alert, mimicking the movements they observed in nature to create yoga postures. The yogis named exercises after animals, such as the cobra, cat and dog. Other exercises were named for their surroundings, such as mountain, tree and lotus.

The yogis found that yoga increased energy and concentration by integrating stretching and strengthening exercises with synchronized breathing. Yoga is a powerful system of body and mind exercises that anyone can do. It encourages us to understand how our bodies work and

teaches us to focus from the inside out. Through exercises and conscious breath, yoga helps us get in touch with our personal energy.

Posture

Yoga helps develop good posture by balancing muscle groups throughout the body. It makes children conscious of working three dimensionally–not thinking only straight ahead but becoming aware of the sides and the back of the body. Yoga creates an awareness of how the body moves and feels by concentrating on poses that awaken various muscle groups.

Yoga also helps posture by flexing and arching the back. It stretches the torso from side to side, gently twisting the spine from bottom to top in both directions. This movement strengthens the back muscles and lengthens the spine to increase kinetic awareness. Increased kinetic awareness enables a child to remember the sensation of correct posture and apply it throughout the day.

By sitting up tall with your shoulders down, back lengthened and neck free of tension, kids are going to feel more alert and awake. The combination of body awareness and balanced muscles is the key to improved posture.

How Yoga Improves Posture

- Teaches correct deep breathing to expand the chest.
- Increases awareness of tension in the shoulders and neck and how to release it.
- Uses the internal and external abdominal muscles to help you stand or sit up tall.
- Emphasizes bending and stretching from the hip sockets rather then the lower back, helping to lengthen the spine, instead of rounding it.
- Encourages resting on the sit bones rather then the lower spine, which also can round the back.

Self Esteem

Kids between the ages of 10 and 16 need to feel good about themselves. This is a time of substantial change in their lives, both emotionally and physically. Yoga can help smooth this transition by balancing the body, improving self-confidence and releasing stress.

As children and young adults feel more relaxed and aware of the connection between their body and mind, their self-image and confidence improves. *Good posture increases self-image, and feeling good about yourself improves posture*.

Peer Pressure

What is cool? Yoga is a growing trend in our popular culture today. Kids see music stars, actors and sports figures practicing yoga and reaping the benefits. Yoga helps the musician remain limber and stay centered while touring; helps the

movie star by toning the muscles and reducing anxiety; and helps the professional athlete by increasing focus and enhancing flexibility. Adults, teenagers, and kids are now more curious than ever to experience the numerous benefits of practicing yoga. Yoga is an excellent opportunity for children to discover something new and share what they have learned with friends.

Anxiety

Yoga can help reduce performance anxiety before sports, tests and speeches. When children are in a music, theater or dance performance, they naturally experience jitters before show time. Knowing some of the basics of yoga will give them the tools to relax, center themselves and remember their lines. These days, when so much pressure is put on tests and more is demanded of kids academically, it is very important for children to learn stress management skills.

Growing Pains

As kids go through growth spurts during their childhood and adolescence, tendons and muscles can get very tight. Yoga helps stretch and loosen expanding muscles, helping to ease the discomfort of growing pains.

Appearance

Yoga can improve a child's complexion by balancing the glands, which regulate active hormones in pre-teens and teens. This can also help stabilize metabolism to regulate weight gain. Yoga exercises improve circulation, leading to healthier and clearer skin.

Benefits

- fun and creative
- teaches you exercises to do alone or in a group
- improves your flexibility
- improves body image
- increases self-confidence
- increases strength in both small and big muscle groups
- improves balance and agility
- teaches the connection between body and mind
- posture and muscle awareness
- balances the muscle groups
- enhances one's sensitivity, self-control and enjoyment in sharing

- improves athletic performance
- helps prevent injuries
- helps weight maintenance by regulating metabolism
- channels nervous energy
- helps develop self-discipline and poise
- fuels the imagination and enhances creativity
- releases tension and helps balance emotions

Part III Breathing

Breathing techniques are an important element of any yoga routine. Breathing exercises relax and invigorate as they help to center the mind. For example, a slow three-part breath can be used before and during a test or competition; fire breath is particularly beneficial in the morning or mid-afternoon when a child needs an energy boost; and punching bag breath is calming when a child feels angry or upset.

Before you begin your yoga routine, take a few minutes to focus your attention inward. Sit cross-legged and close your eyes. Feel your breath enter and exit through your nose to encourage full breathing. Envision the air passing through

your nose and sinuses, and the diaphragm muscles under your ribcage dropping to allow the lower, middle and, then, upper lungs to fill. Picture your lungs three-dimensionally as two balloons expanding with clean, fresh air. Feel the warm air exit your lungs through your nose as you exhale, relaxing your muscles. Keep your chest lifted and lengthen your spine. Breathe in energy as you exhale tension.

Our respiration and blood circulation work closely together to provide the constant supply of oxygen needed for our brain and muscles. We cannot live without oxygen, which is transferred to our bloodstream with each inhale. Our heart then pumps the blood to all areas of the body. After the blood is circulated throughout the body, it returns to the heart for oxygen. The heart pumps the blood through the lungs to restore its oxygen and circulates through the body again. This circulation process repeats itself over and over.

Do not be concerned if you have difficulty synchronizing your breathing with the exercises at first. The most important thing to remember is to not hold your breath, and to exhale completely while in each pose. The more you practice yoga, the more naturally correct breathing will come. Try to remember to inhale as you expand, exhale as you contract. It is important to breathe as you stretch because with each exhale, you can reach further into the stretch.

Breathing Exercises

Three Part Breath – Visualize the shape of your lungs as they expand three-dimensionally from the front, back and sides. Relax the diaphragm muscle, which attaches at the bottom of the rib cage. Allow the lower, middle and upper sections of your lungs to fill as you inhale and count to three.

Three Part Breath

Angel Breath – Kneel or stand with your hands in front of your chest, and your palms together with your fingers interlaced. As you inhale, lift your elbows up and your head back. Then, exhale through your mouth, slowly bringing your elbows together and your head level.

Angel Breath

Bunny Breath – On your knees with your hips resting on your heels, take two short inhales through your nose and a longer, fast exhale through the mouth.

Fire Breath – Sit cross-legged and concentrate on taking numerous quick, short breaths as you contract your stomach muscles as you exhale.

Energizer Punching Bag Breath – On your knees, make fists and breathe through your nose, exhaling as you punch in front of you.

Energizer Punching Bag Breath

Table Breath – Kneeing on all fours, lift your right arm and left leg parallel to the ground and inhale. Exhale and return to the table position. Inhale and exhale through the nose as you quicken your breath and do a set of 10 on each side.

Table Breath

PART IV
EXERCISES

Yoga exercises require the involvement of both a person's body and the mind. The stretches and isometric strength training are challenging, yet safe, while the deep breathing calms your mind and refreshes your body. The following exercises can be done in the sequence that follows, or arranged into shorter 10 or 15 minute routines such as the ones listed in Part IX.

A few things to remember when doing yoga:

- Eat very lightly one hour before and after practicing yoga. Eat a larger meal two or more hours before doing yoga.

- Have as few distractions as possible around you to make it easier to concentrate (i.e. pets, parents, loud music).

- Don't worry if you do not perform the exercise perfectly. As you continue to practice yoga, you gain more experience and can absorb more of the details.
- Perform the exercises slowly and attentively. Try to concentrate on the posture and what you are feeling.
- Never strain.
- Above all else, have fun!

Half Lotus – Sit cross-legged with one foot on top of the opposite thigh and the bottom of the foot turned up. With your back lengthened, keep your shoulders down and your neck long. Switch leg positions and repeat.

Benefit: adds flexibility to hips sockets.

Half Lotus

Full Lotus – Sit in the same position as the half lotus, but cross both feet over the opposite thighs.

Benefit: encourages correct posture and increases concentration.

Full Lotus

Seated Side Stretch

Seated Side Stretch – Sit in a comfortable cross-legged position. Drop your right hand to the floor beside you and stretch your left arm up and over your head close to your ear. Breathe in and out three times and repeat on the opposite side.

Benefit: tones the hips and torso, and encourages full breathing.

Shoulder Rolls

Shoulder Rolls – Roll your shoulders forward, up to your ears, back to your shoulder blades, and down. Repeat five times.

Benefit: relaxes and tones shoulder and neck muscles.

Neck rolls – Stretch your right ear to your right shoulder, bring your chin to chest, and stretch your left ear to left shoulder. Reverse directions and repeat three times.

Benefit: releases tension in the sides and back of the neck and jaw.

Neck rolls

Shoulder Self-Massage

Shoulder Self-Massage – While sitting up straight in a chair or cross-legged on the floor, take your right hand and reach over to your left shoulder. Squeeze your left shoulder with your right hand. Then, take your fingertips and rub a little deeper in small circles using more pressure. Try to locate and release tightness in your muscles as you take deep full breaths. Repeat on the other shoulder.

Benefit: enables you think more clearly and to release stress in your shoulders, a common place for stored tension.

Mountain Pose

Mountain Pose – Stand up straight with your feet together. Stack your body so your knees are over your ankles, your hips are over your knees, and your ribcage is over your hips. Lengthen your neck so your jaw is parallel to the ground.

Benefit: increases awareness of your posture and is a good transition pose.

Forward Bend - From the mountain pose, slowly roll down one vertebra at a time until you are bending from the hip sockets. Feel your back and neck relax and let your arms dangle to your fingertips. Bend and straighten each leg.

Benefit: relaxes the back muscles and begins to stretch the hamstrings.

Forward Bend

Swimmer's Stretch

Swimmer's Stretch – With your feet together or hips-width apart, interlace your fingers behind you and slowly roll down the back. Allow your head to drop as you keep your arms straight.

Benefit: stretches the entire back of the body as well as all the shoulder muscles.

Half Moon

Half Moon – With your feet together, interlace your hands above your head, keeping your rib cage over your hips. Stretch your arms to the right as you stretch your hips to the left and switch side. Breathe in and out and repeat three times on both sides.

Benefit: tones the waist and encourages good posture and correct full breathing.

Triangle Side Stretch

Triangle Side Stretch – Stand with your feet more than shoulder-width apart, your right foot facing forward, and your left foot turned out. Line up the heel of your left foot with the arch of your right foot. Equally balance between both feet. Stretch your arms out to the sides parallel to the ground. Stretch your left hand down to your left shin and reach your right arm over your head close to your ear. Breathe fully three times and repeat on the other side.

Benefit: tones the waist and hips, improves posture and releases tension in the spine.

Warrior

Warrior – Starting in the same position as the triangle pose, bend your left knee over your left foot. Work toward having your left thigh parallel to the floor. Hold your arms out to the sides and gaze over your left fingertips.

Benefit: increases circulation and strengthens the thighs, lower back and stomach muscles.

Triangle Spinal Twist – Start from the triangle pose with your arms out to the sides, parallel to the floor. Reach your right arm to your left shin, and your left arm behind you up to the sky. Keep your back lengthened from the tailbone through the neck as you look behind you or up to your arm. Breathe in and out three times and reverse sides.

Benefit: balances the nervous system, and the muscles up and down the spine.

Triangle Spinal Twist

Lunges

Lunges – Start in the mountain pose and drop your right leg behind you as far as possible. Keep both hands on the ground for support as you bend and straighten your left leg three times. The last time you straighten your leg, hold the pose to feel the stretch. Repeat with opposite leg.

Benefit: this is a wonderful stretch for the quadriceps, and it improves flexibility for many sports.

Down Dog

Down Dog – Press your feet and hands into the floor as you lift your hips up in the air. Concentrate on lengthening the back muscles and stretching your hamstrings. Bend and straighten your legs slowly for a deeper stretch. Take three full breaths.

Benefit: strengthens the back muscles, releases tension and activates the leg muscles.

Up Dog

Up Dog – From the down dog position, drop your pelvis to the floor and arch your back. Tighten your hip muscles as you lift your chest off the floor.

Benefit: strengthens the lower back and tones the stomach muscles.

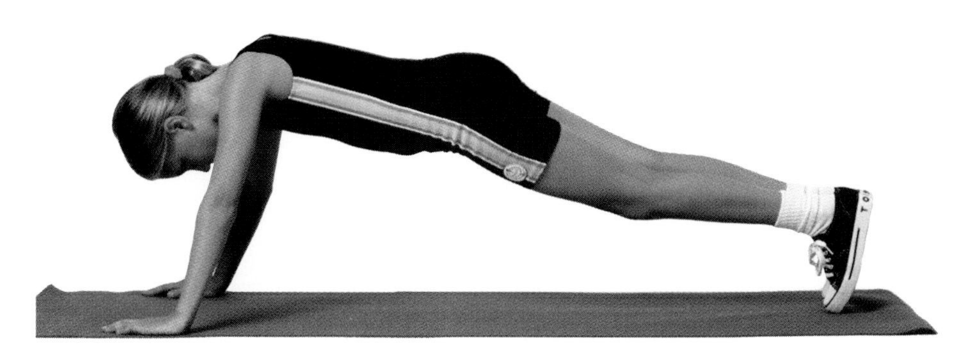

Plank

Plank – Resting on your hands and the balls of your feet, level your body so that your back and legs are straight. Tighten your buttocks and use your arm muscles to maintain the position.

Benefit: strengthens the upper back, arms and stomach muscles.

Tree

Tree – Balance on your left foot and bend your right leg, resting your right foot on your left inner thigh. Reach arms up over your head with your palms together. Focus on a stationary point in front of you to keep your balance.

Benefit: improves balance and concentration.

Dancer

Dancer – Stand with your feet a few inches apart. Shift your weight onto your right leg as you hold your left foot behind you with your left hand. Focus on a stationary point and pay attention to your breathing to help you balance. Raise your right arm over your head as you stretch your left knee and foot backward. Breathe and repeat on the opposite side.

Benefit: stretches your thigh muscles and quadriceps; and improves balance, coordination and vitality.

Flamingo – Balancing on your left leg, stretch your arms out to the sides and extend your right leg behind you. Aim to bring your torso and right leg parallel to the ground. Focus on a stationary point in front of you.

Benefit: helps to focus the mind and increase agility.

Flamingo

Cat

Cat – On your hands and knees, lengthen your back from the tailbone through the neck. Inhale as you arch your back, and exhale as you round it. Repeat five times.

Benefit: releases tension in the back and helps to balance the nervous system.

Camel

Camel – Kneel down with your legs shoulder-width apart. Slowly place your right hand on your right heel and your left hand on your left heel. As you arch your back, imagine the curve of your body is the shape of a camel's hump. Stay in the pose for a count of ten. Remember to breathe slowly and smoothly.

Benefit: strengthens the back; tones the hips and thigh muscles; trims the waist; increases flexibility in the spine; and keeps the stomach and bladder healthy by increasing circulation and toning surrounding muscles to improve digestion.

Child Pose – Starting on your knees, release your pelvis and sit on your heels. Lower your chest to your knees and stretch your arms out on the floor in front of you or down to your sides.

Benefit: a great restorative pose to release and re-energize your back.

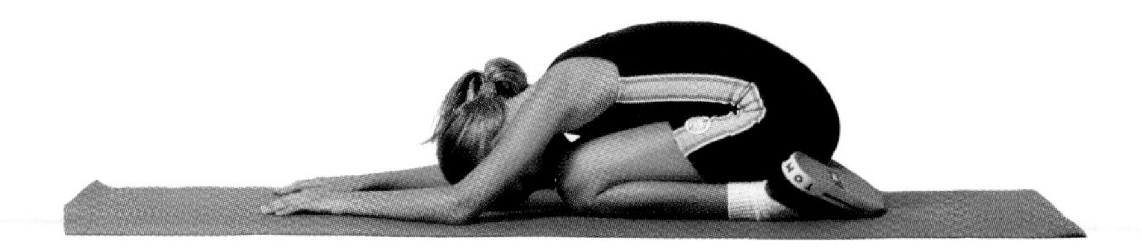

Child Pose

Cobra – Lie on your stomach with your arms resting at your sides. Breathe slowly and smoothly. With your chin on the mat and your hands under your shoulders, use your back muscles to lift your chest off the ground. Press your hands slightly into the ground as you keep your hips and legs on the floor. Slowly lower your chest and relax your head to the side.

Benefit: helps keep the spine flexible and healthy; strengthens the shoulders, elbows and wrists; and increases circulation into the digestive tract.

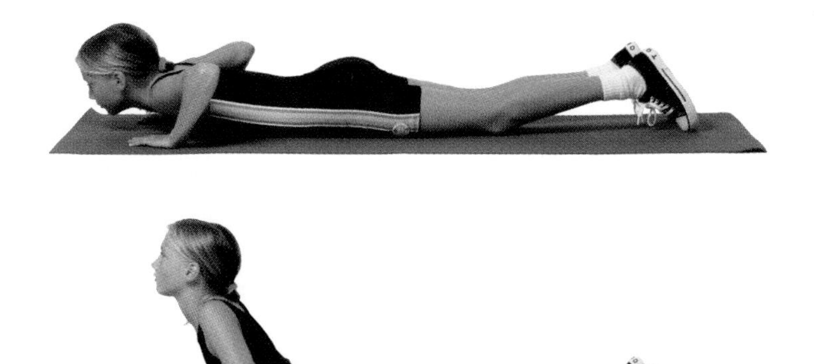

Cobra

Bow

Bow – Lie on your stomach with your legs slightly apart and arms by your sides. Bend your knees and lengthen your chest as you reach back to hold your ankles. Slowly tilt your head back and pull your feet upward. Gently rock back and forth as you breathe smoothly. Stay in the pose as long as you can, then release your arms and legs back down to the floor.

Benefit: strengthens the back muscles, increases flexibility and expands your chest to help you to breathe more deeply.

Superman

Superman – Lie on your stomach with your arms out in front of you and your chin resting on the mat. Exhale as you raise your chin, arms and legs up off the floor. Take three full breaths and relax your legs and arms. Repeat once.

Benefit: strengthens and balances the back muscles, and tones the stomach muscles.

Hurdler – Resting on your sit bones, the bottom of your hip girdle, keep your left leg straight and place your right foot against the inside of your left thigh. Be sure your left knee is facing up. Raise both arms above your head, interlace your fingers, and stretch your torso over your left leg. Reach forward to your toes for a count of three breaths, trying to stretch further with each exhale. Repeat with the opposite leg.

Benefit: lengthens the hamstring muscles and releases tightness in the back and hips.

Hurdler

Straddle

Straddle – Rest on your sit bones with your legs as far apart as you can stretch. Lift your chest and reach your arms out on the floor in front of you or to your toes. Take three full breaths, stretching further with each exhale.

Benefit: opens the hip sockets to stretch the back and hamstrings, and stretches and tones the inner thigh muscles.

Boat – Balance on your sit bones as you extend your legs and arms out in front of you. Start with your knees slightly bent and work toward straightening your legs. Continue to breathe smoothly and relax your neck muscles.

Boat

Benefit: tones abdominal muscles, transverse and oblique.

Half Bridge

Half Bridge – Lie on your back with your knees bent. Start by relaxing your back and neck into the ground and slowly lift your pelvis one vertebra at a time until you feel the weight across your shoulders. Interlace the fingers under your hips and tighten your buttocks . Hold the pose for a count of three breaths and slowly relax back down to the ground.

Benefit: increases circulation and awareness in the back, improves posture, and balances the nervous system.

Bridge – Start in the same position as the half bridge. Place your hands on the ground above your shoulders with your fingers facing you. As you exhale, push up off your hands and feet to arch your body. Hold for a count of ten breaths and slowly return back to the floor.

Benefit: a wonderful exercise for the back and stomach.

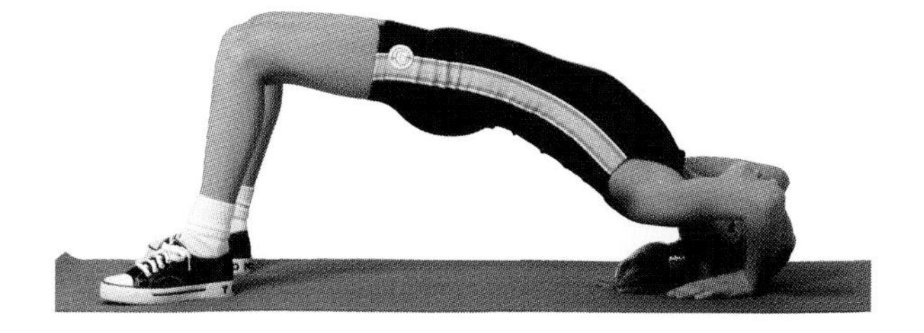

Bridge

Plow

Plow – Lie on your back and bend your knees. Roll back until your knees are over your head by your ears. Relax in this position with your head facing straight up to keep the neck aligned. Support your back with your hands and breathe smoothly. Either straighten your legs into the shoulder stand or roll down into a half bridge.

Benefit: excellent exercise for overall health, increases circulation to the skin and hair, and releases tightness in the shoulders.

Shoulder Stand – From the plow position, slowly straighten one leg up at a time until both feet are pointing upward. Gradually move your hands up your back until your body is as straight as you can hold it comfortably. Breathe smoothly and hold this position for as long as it is comfortable. Slowly lower your legs into the plow position and use your stomach muscles to roll your legs back to the ground.

Benefit: stretches the entire body and is good for balancing the thyroid gland.

Shoulder Stand

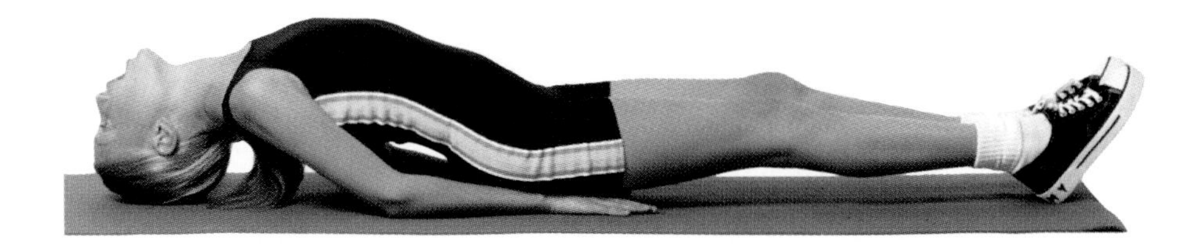

Fish

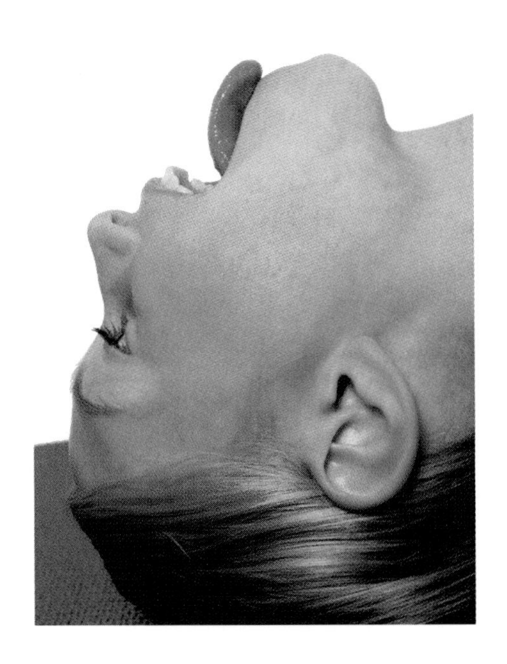

Fish – Lying on your back, arch your body from your lower back to your head. Use your back muscles to balance gently on your elbows. Stick your tongue out.

Benefit: counterbalances the shoulder stand.

Seated Spinal Twist

Seated Spinal Twist – Sit with your legs stretched out in front of you and bend your right leg over your left leg. Bend your left leg into your right hip. Reach your right arm behind you and press your left arm gently against the inside of your right thigh. Stretch your chin toward your right shoulder as you take three full breaths. Each time you inhale, lengthen your spine, and twist further on each exhale. Slowly untwist in the opposite direction. Come back to center and repeat.

Benefit: releases tension in the back, balances the spine and helps you to think more clearly.

Eye Relaxation Exercises

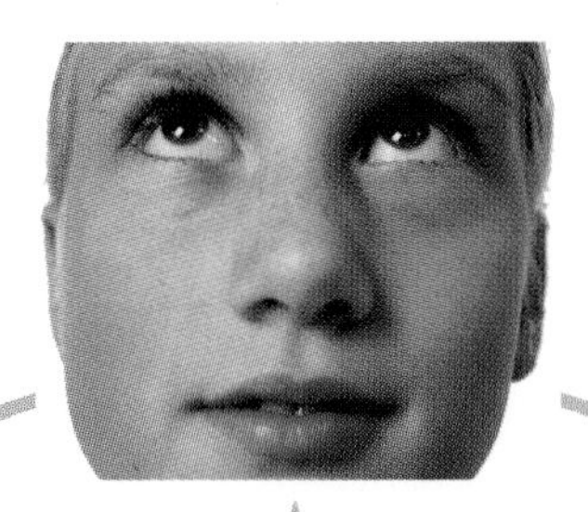

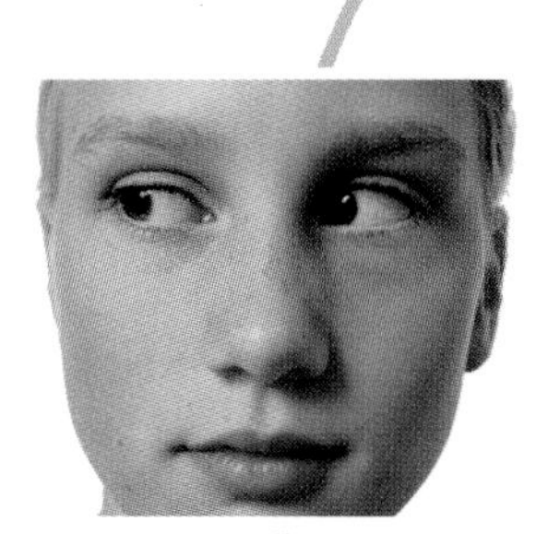

Clock – Sit or stand tall as you breathe slowly and smoothly. Imagine there is a big clock in front of you. Without your head moving, look up at 12, over to 3, down to 6, and over to 9, holding each for ten seconds. Then, roll your eyes clockwise three times. Stop and take three long breaths before rolling your eyes counter-clockwise three times.

Benefit: strengthens the eye muscles and relieves tension that can occur from reading, studying or staring at a computer screen.

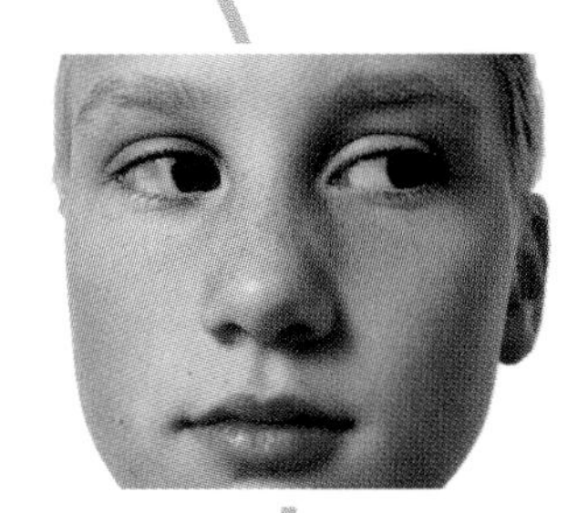

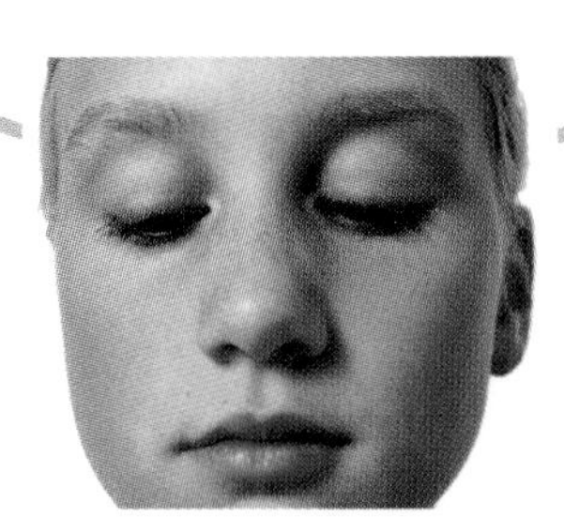

Brow Pinch

Brow Pinch – Find the ridge of the forehead above the eyes. Place your thumbs under the ridge and your index finger above it. Gently squeeze your eyebrows from the center out. Do both eyes at the same time and repeat three times.

Benefit: feels good, releases tension in the head and alleviates headaches and tired eyes.

Eye Rub – If you wear contact lenses, make sure you take them out before doing this exercise. Shake your hands out to release any tightness in them. With the index fingers, start at the corner of the eye and make tiny circles very lightly on your eyelids. Repeat in the center and to the outer corner.

Benefit: relieves eyestrain after reading or concentrating visually.

Part V
Yoga and Sports

Yoga can also be a valuable addition to any pre- or post-sport stretching routine. It encourages complete range of motion while teaching kids how to stretch properly to improve athletic performance. If muscles, tendons and ligaments are lengthened and stretched properly, the potential for injury is significantly lowered. For sports such as baseball and hockey, yoga stretches can help balance muscle groups to increase coordination; for tennis, yoga can improve agility; and for dance, yoga can be used to warm up and cool down before workouts.

Breathing

Yoga emphasizes tuning in to specific muscle groups as you stretch. The skill of concentration is essential to playing any sport well. The breathing techniques learned in yoga can be used to help children relax and focus on the game. These breathing exercises are also beneficial to aerobic endurance. Yoga helps us use our full lung capacity to improve our stamina.

Visualization

Before getting on the field or in the ring, after warming up, or on the night of a big game, practice a brief sports visualization exercise. Take three long breaths and roll your shoulders three times. Do three neck rolls in each direction as you massage the palms of your hands. Relax, close your eyes and picture yourself playing the sport with ease. If there's a particular move or play that you would like improve, picture it in your mind's eye. Feel the enjoyment that you get from playing the sport. This visualization can help relieve anxiety and improve confidence.

Improvement

At the end of a game, remember that it is not as important that you have won as it is that you have played well and to the best of your abilities. It is great to realize that you have improved your athletic ability. That is the essence of what yoga teaches us–to work from the inside out to enhance flexibility and strength. If you are involved in team sports, encourage your teammates to practice these stretches and breathing techniques before the game, instead of sitting on the bench.

Even though yoga itself is non-competitive, it can greatly enhance athletic performance. Listed are a few sports-specific yoga exercises to stretch and strengthen various muscle groups:

Running

- Lunge
- Dancer
- Hurdler

- **Sprinter's Lunge** – With your legs about three feet apart with one foot in front of the other, try to keep your back leg straight as you flex and release your front foot three times.

  Benefit: great stretch for the hamstrings and the calf muscles.

- **Side Lunge** – Lunge and stretch to the inside of your right foot as you rest your elbows on the ground.

  Benefit: releases tightness from the lower back, stretches the upper hamstrings and quadriceps.

Swimming

- Warrior
- Swimmer's Stretch
- Plow

- **Swimmer's Stretch Variation** – Standing with your legs more than shoulder-width apart, interlace the fingers behind you and roll forward, one vertebra at a time. Use your arms to increase this stretch as you lunge from one leg to the other.

  Benefit: great overall stretch for the back, lats and upper arm muscles.

Gymnastics

- Seated spinal twist
- Cobra
- Plow
- Shoulder Stand
- Bridge

- **Shoulder Stand Variation** – Once you are in the shoulder stand, reach one leg forward and one leg back. Then, reverse legs and repeat.

  Benefit: stretches all the leg muscles.

- **Side Straddle** – From the straddle pose, place your right hand or forearm on the ground near your knee. Lift your left arm up and over your head. Hold the pose for three breaths and repeat on the other side.

  Benefit: stretches and tones the torso and stomach.

Soccer

- Straddle
- Hurdler
- Lunge
- Warrior

- **Butterfly** – Sit down with the soles of your feet together. Your pinky toes should be touching and your big toes should be spread apart. Breathe deeply on each exhale as you reach your chin and chest toward your feet.

  Benefit: helps to identify and stretch your hip sockets, and is a great warm-up.

- **Rock-the-baby** – Sit in the cross-legged position and pick up your right leg. Hold and rock your leg gently from side to side.

  Benefit: stretches the hips, releases the lower back and stretches the outer thigh.

Biking

- Dancer
- Hurdler
- Forward Bend
- Lunge
- Swimmer's Stretch

- **Hybrid Stretch** – Stand in the triangle pose with your right leg turned out and your left leg pointing forward. Interlace your fingers behind your back and roll your head down to your right knee. Breathe three times slowly and roll up.

  Benefit: stretches the entire back of the body.

- **Mountain Bike Stretch** – Stand in the mountain pose, reach your arms over your head and hold your elbows. Tighten your hips, lift your chest and arch your upper back as you inhale. As you exhale, slowly roll forward. Take a full breath in and out before slowly rolling back up.

  Benefit: releases tightness in the back and hamstrings, and is good for stretching the back and shoulder muscles.

Basketball

- Hurdler
- Down Dog
- Plank Pose
- Up Dog

- **Warrior Back Stretch** – Start in the warrior pose and interlace your fingers behind you. Arch your back and feel the stretch across the front of your chest.

  Benefit: stretches the chest muscles, strengthens the leg muscles and encourages proper breathing.

- **Hoop Lunge** – With your feet three to four feet apart, bend your right knee and reach to your right foot. Take a deep breath and repeat on the opposite side.

  Benefit: loosens the hips and lower back.

Baseball

- Triangle
- Triangle Spinal Twist
- Half Moon
- Plow

- **Bench Stretch** – With your right leg up on a bench or the bleachers, reach one arm up and over your head as you inhale. On the exhale, stretch forward and reach to your toes.

  Benefit: great for stretching the hamstrings and the back.

- **Hitter's Stretch** – Stretch your right arm across your chest and gently pull your right arm toward you with your left hand. Switch arms and repeat.

  Benefit: stretches the deltoid and rotator muscles.

Tennis

- Lotus
- Shoulder Rolls
- Forward Bend
- Swimmer Stretch

- **Half Moon Arch** – Interlace your hands over your head with your palms facing the sky. Plant your feet, lift your tummy and chest, and arch your upper and mid-back.

  Benefit: releases tension between the shoulder blades and stretches the muscles throughout the arms.

- **Elbow Hold Stretch** – Stand in the mountain pose, reach your arms over your head and hold your elbows. Stretch your arms to the left and your hips to the right. Take a full breath and repeat on opposite side.

  Benefit: stretches the shoulders and upper back.

Skateboarding

- Tree Pose
- Bridge
- Plow
- Forward Fold

- **Half Pipe Bend** – With your feet hips-width apart, slowly roll down your back one vertebra at a time until your fingers reach your shins, ankles or toes, depending on your flexibility. Slowly roll back up.

  Benefit: releases stress along the entire spine and stretches the hamstrings.

- **Bow & Arrow** – Start in the warrior pose with your feet three to four feet apart and your left leg turned out. Hold your arms out to the sides and keep your legs straight. As you exhale, bend your left knee and bring your right hand together with your left hand. Bend your right elbow as you pull your right arm back across your chest. Repeat three times on each side.

  Benefit: increases coordination and balance.

Surfing

- Forward Bend
- Swimmer's Stretch
- Half Moon

- **Surfers' Back Bend** – Stand with your back to the surfboard and reach over your head to hold the top of the board. Take three full breaths. Arch your back and stretch your chest further with each breath.

  Benefit: stretches and strengthens the torso and encourages full breathing.

- **Wave Stretch** – Sit on your surf board and inhale as you reach up to the sky. Exhale as you stretch forward over your legs. Reach for your shins, ankles or toes and drop your head. Take two full breaths, stretching further each time.

  Benefit: relieves tension in the lower back and stretches the thighs and calves.

- **Lifeguard Lunge** - Place your surfboard in front of you with its tip dug into the ground. Bend your left knee and stretch the back of your right leg, pressing your right heel into the sand. Hold for a count of three breaths and switch sides.

  Benefit: strengthens the thigh and calf muscles and stretches the Achilles tendon.

Boogie Boarding

- Forward Bend
- Swimmer's Stretch
- Half Moon

- **Boogie Board Side Stretch** – Hold on to the boogie board and reach it up in the air over your head. Stretch to the right side and take a full breath. Then repeat over the left side.

Benefit: tones and stretches the torso, and is a good relaxation pose.

Hockey

- Hurdler
- Bridge
- Butterfly
- Plow

- **Hockey Stick Twist** – Hold the stick behind your head across your shoulders. Keep your lower body still and twist your shoulders to the left. Breathe and twist to the right. Let your head move with your torso.

  Benefit: warms up the back and loosens tight muscles.

- **Hat Trick Stretch** – Holding both ends of a hockey stick, reach your arms over your head. Inhale and lower your back, arms and head toward the floor. Exhale and repeat three times.

  Benefit: stretches and releases tension in the upper and middle back.

Wrestling

- Straddle
- Hurdler
- Lunge

- **Eye of the Needle** – Start on the ground in the cat pose. Reach your right arm to the sky and then down under your torso on the ground. Relax your head and rest on your right shoulder and upper arm as you lift your left arm to the sky. Take three breaths and repeat on the other side.

  Benefit: gently stretches the upper back and relieves lower back tension.

- **Wrestling Squat** – Stand with your feet a little wider then hips-width apart. Keep your knees over your feet and squat until your hips are down to the ground. Hold for three breaths, drop your head and slowly roll up.

  Benefit: releases lower back tightness and warms up hips, knees and ankles.

PART VI
DOUBLE YOGA

A great way to share what you have learned practicing yoga is to perform double yoga stretches with your friends. Double yoga is fun and can be a great way to relate to a friend in a new and creative way. While stretching with someone else, you learn to be sensitive to his or her needs. You may take the poses a little further and stretch beyond where you are accustomed to with the help of a

friend. While working with another person, a child might find it easier to concentrate and hold certain positions. Double yoga helps you center yourself while tuning in to your partner.

Double yoga is an exciting new development in the ancient art of yoga. While practicing yoga with another person, you are able to pull against your partner to stretch further and develop strength in the poses. There is often a feeling of invigoration from tuning in to the rhythm of another person. When two people hold a pose together, each partner experiences more energy then he or she contributes.

Subtle lessons in relationships are demonstrated and taught through double yoga. Each child learns to give and take, while communicating mostly non-verbally. Some verbal communication is always encouraged, especially while learning the positions.

Kids learn to literally bend over backwards to assist one another, while remaining centered and focused themselves. Double yoga gives children the opportunity to teach and help someone else. Whether a child practices with a friend or meets someone new, double yoga opens the door to friendship and fun.

Triangle – The triangle pose is the basis of many yoga positions. Start by standing back to back against your partner with your feet spread two to three feet apart. If the two of you are a different height, keep your front feet together and adjust your back leg. Your front feet should be together side to side, while your back feet should be together heel to heel. Keep your legs straight as you reach to your partner's front ankle. Stretch your opposite arm up to the sky and clasp hands. Increase your extension and try to bend from your hips, not your ribs. Be sure to keep your hips facing forward. Switch sides and repeat.

Benefit: great overall body stretch.

Tree Pose - Stand next to one another and clasp your partner's hand up in the air. Lift your outside foot and rest it against your inner thigh. Rest your outer arm on your bent leg or out to the side for balance. Stand up as straight as possible and try not to lean on your partner. Lift your chest and keep your tailbone down as you focus on a point in front of you. Hold the pose for five full breaths and repeat on the other side.

Benefit: teaches attentive stillness and strengthens the leg muscles.

The Royal Crown – Stand two to three feet apart and face one another. Clasp your hands behind your back. Lean forward, lifting your arms in the air to meet your partner's hands. Take five full breaths.

Benefit: stretches your back, hips and hamstrings.

Twisted Triangle – Facing your partner, stand about eight inches apart. From the triangle pose, bend forward from the hips and bring one arm across to your opposite shin. Lift your other arm above your head and hold your partner's hand. Twist your body and press your shoulders together. Breathe and hold for a count of five breaths. Repeat on the other side.

Benefit: stretches the leg muscles, opens the chest and shoulders, relieves tightness, and increases flexibility in the spine.

Hero – Stand next to one another with the sides of your feet together and your opposite foot turned outward. Clasp wrists as you bend your knee and stretch your arm out to the side. Be sure to keep your wrists over the ankles and gently pull away from one another. Repeat on the other side.

Benefit: strengthens the thighs, stretches the hips, and improves posture.

Suspension Bridge – Face your partner standing two to three feet apart. With your feet together and your legs straight, bend from the hips and clasp your partner's hands. Pull your hips back as you extend your spine forward.

Benefit: relieves pressure and tension along the spine, stretches the vertebra, and relieves tension in the back, hips and hamstrings.

Lotus Lion – Sit in the lotus or half lotus position about four feet apart. Sit up on your knees with your hands on the ground and your finger-tips pointing back. Support your torso as you let your hips sink down. Open your mouth as you inhale and exhale.

Benefit: opens the pelvis and increases energy.

Shooting Star - Sit side by side with the your legs straight and hips touching. Keep your inside leg straight as you place your outside foot against your inner thigh. Reach toward your straight leg, lift your back arm over your head, and hold your partner's hand. Hold the stretch for as long as you can, switch sides and repeat.

Benefit: loosens the hip sockets, stretches the inner thigh and tones the waist.

Cross Gate – Kneel side to side about six feet apart. Extend your inside leg and press the outer edge of your foot against the side of your partner's foot. Hold hands and lean sideways toward each other. Stretch your outside arm over your head and clasp your partner's hand. Hold for a count of five breaths and change sides.

Benefit: this is an intense lateral stretch that removes stiffness from the back and shoulders.

Frog Link – Squat back to back with your feet together and your heels pressed against your partner's. Spread your knees and sink your torso between your thighs. Reach back and clasp your partner's hands. Pull against your partner to feel the stretch from your tailbone to your head.

Benefit: stretches the Achilles tendon and inner thigh.

Straddle – Sit on the ground facing your partner with your legs as far apart as you can stretch. Hold hands and gently pull backward and forward.

Benefit: this pose stretches the inner thighs and pelvis.

Reclining Forward Bend – Sit back to back with your partner. Keep your legs and arms straight as you hold hands above your head. As your partner performs a forward fold, recline back and feel the stretch in your arms, back and chest. Hold this position for a count of five breaths. Return to center and slowly roll forward, stretching your partner.

Benefit: reclining partner gently stretches the rib muscles, shoulders and armpits, while the folding partner relaxes the back and promotes deep relaxation.

Warrior Diamond – Standing next to one another, start in the warrior pose with your inner feet side to side and hold hands. Reach your outside arms over your head and hold hands above you. Take three long breaths and switch sides.

Benefit: strengthens the thighs and stretches the entire side of the torso.

The Fountain – Stand facing one another with your toes together. Clasp your partner's wrists and lean back. Straighten your elbows and tighten your hips as you maintain an even pull with your partner. Communicate with each other about how far you can each bend back. Lift your chest as you hold the pose and breathe evenly. Repeat three times.

Benefit: lengthens the front of the body and corrects rounded shoulders.

The Arch – Stand about two to three feet apart back to back. Lean backward until the top of your heads touch. Reach overhead and clasp hands. Drop your tailbone and tighten your buttocks. Arch your back and take three long breaths before slowly coming out of the pose.

Benefit: increases circulation up the front of the body and strengthens the back and butt muscles.

Warrior Side Stretch – Stand back to back in the warrior pose. Lean your forearm on your bent knee and stretch the other arm over your head close to your ear. Hold the pose as you take three full breaths.

Benefit: strengthens the thigh muscles, stretches the torso and encourages full breathing and sensitivity to your partner.

Part VII
Yoga Games

An exciting way to vary your yoga routine is to incorporate yoga into some of your favorite outdoor games. Games such as Tag, Twister and Red Light, Green Light can take on another dimension when yoga is added to the fun. Whether they play in a gym, in the back yard or at the park, kids get all the benefits of yoga–stretching, twisting, and balancing–while exploring different positions. Games get children of all different ages and fitness levels together. Some children are athletic while others are not, but all kids can have a lot of fun playing yoga games.

Twister

Find your old twister game and play with as few as two or as many as four people. As you play the game, see how many yoga or yoga-like poses you can get into as you move your hands and feet around the mat. If you find yourself in an unusual position, take it to its maximum stretch and

breathe. Intertwine yourself in your friend's yoga poses. In between your turns, practice three-part breathing while holding the twister position.

Red Light Green Light, 1, 2, 3

This game is usually played outside on a lawn or at the beach. All the kids line up and one person stands a few feet in front of them. The child in front calls out "red light, green light, 1, 2, 3" and turns around. All the kids run forward toward the caller. When she turns around, everyone freezes in a yoga pose. If someone is spotted moving, they have to go back to the starting line. The first person to reach the caller is "it." Remember to breathe and be imaginative. Try to get into different poses each time you freeze.

Freeze Tag

A great game to play outdoors, one person is "it" and everyone runs around. When the person who is "it" tags someone, they freeze into a yoga pose until a team member frees them by climbing over or crawling under them.

Simon Says

The leader calls out yoga poses by saying "Simon says get in the tree pose," and everyone follows. If the leader calls out a yoga poses without starting the sentence with "Simon says," anyone who follows is out (example: "Get in the tree pose"). The last one to remain in the game is the next leader.

Shadow Yoga

Partner up with someone else. One person does a yoga pose as the other one performs the mirror image of the pose. Each person should do five poses with the partner mirroring, then switch.

Part VIII
Salutations

Salutations were named after the sun and the moon because they are especially good to do first thing in the morning to wake up or last thing at night to cool down. In the morning, I suggest warming up into salutations slowly, then increasing the tempo and intensity. In the evenings, do three salutations slowly and remember to breathe fully. This will prepare you for a sound sleep and sweet dreams. There has been a connection found between going to sleep relaxed and remembering your dreams.

Sun Salutations are perfectly balanced yoga sequences. Salutations are very efficient, reaching almost every major muscle group in the body. Salutations flow from one yoga posture to the next, connected by breathing. It is important to breathe fully and not to hold your breath. We naturally have a tendency to hold our breath when learning something new. Knowing when to inhale and exhale will come naturally with practice. The salutations are balanced workouts because they combine forward bending, backward bending, stretching side to side and twisting.

Salutation #1

1. Prayer

2. Mountain Variation

3. Half Moon Backbend

6. Down Dog

5. Lunge, right leg back

4. Forward Fold

7. Plank

8. Up Dog

9. Lunge, left leg back

13. Tree

12. Mountain Variation

11. Roll Up

10. Forward Bend

Salutations #2

1. Mountain
2. Half Moon
3. Forward Bend
4. Lunge, left leg back
5. Warrior, right leg bent
6. Triangle Spinal Twist, left hand to right leg
7. Down Dog
8. Plank
9. Up Dog
10. Lunge, right leg back
11. Warrior, left leg bent
12. Triangle Spinal Twist, right hand to left leg
13. Swimmer's Stretch
14. Mountain

Salutations #3

1. Mountain
2. Swimmer's Stretch
3. Lunge, right leg back
4. Triangle Side Stretch, stretch to the left
5. Down Dog
6. Cat Pose
7. Child Pose
8. Cobra
9. Down Dog
10. Lunge, left leg back
11. Triangle Side Stretch, stretch to the right
12. Forward Fold
13. Mountain

Part IX
Yoga Routines

Headache Eraser

Half Lotus

Seated Side Stretch

Eye Relaxation

  – Brow and Lids

Shoulder Self-Massage

Neck Rolls

Morning Wake-Up

Angel Breath

Child Pose

Butterfly

Half Bridge

Cat

Down Dog

Sun Salutation #1

Sun Salutation #2

Studying Stress Reducer

Mountain Pose
Half Moon*
Forward Bend*
Swimmer's Stretch
Fire Breath
Shoulder Rolls
Neck Rolls
Shoulder Self-Massage
(* *can also be done seated)*

Sweet Dreams

Sun Salutation #3
Half Moon
Child Pose
Camel
Straddle
Hurdler
Half Bridge
Plow
Shoulder Stand
Fish

Test Centering

Cross-Legged Position
Three-Part Breath
Angel Breaths
Eye Relaxation – Lid, Brow, and Clock
Neck Rolls
Shoulder Rolls
Shoulder Self-Massage

Part X
Relaxation

We all need to learn basic relaxation techniques to help us in our everyday lives. If taught at a young age, these techniques will always remain in a child's muscle memory. Here is a simple guided relaxation that can be read out loud to kids in a group or individually. A child can read it to a friend, or a parent can read it to a child. The relaxation should be done in a quiet place with few distractions.

Lie on your back. Tighten all the muscles in your body and then release them. Then tighten all the muscles on the right side of your body–your face, arm, hand, hip, leg, and foot–and release. Then, tighten all the muscles on the left side of your body and release. Close your eyes and feel your body sink into the floor. For the next few minutes, focus on how your body is feeling and notice how you are breathing. Feel your stomach lift as you inhale and lower as you exhale. Count five slow breaths, relaxing more with each exhale.

Follow my voice as we travel through the body to release tension, tightness and worry. Feel the back of your head relax against the ground. Let go of any fixed expression on your face. Relax the muscles around your eyes, jaw and mouth. Feel your neck release in the front, sides and back. Let go of your upper back, shoulders and chest. If you feel tension or get distracted, take a deep breath and focus on relaxing your muscles. Notice your chest expand as you inhale, filling your lungs with air.

Feel tightness and tension leave your body as you exhale. Breathe easily as you feel your stomach rise as you inhale and lower as you exhale. Take a few deep breaths. With each inhale, feel cool fresh air enter and fill your lungs. As you exhale, feel the air that has been warmed by your body exit through your nose and mouth. Feel your middle back release into the ground and the weight of your hips and legs sink into gravity. Notice your right leg, knee and foot release. Notice the left leg, knee and foot let go.

Imagine a wave of relaxation travel over the front of your body from your toes up your legs to your hips, and across your stomach, chest, neck and face. Feel this wave erase any tightness or worry from your mind and body. Feel the wave of relaxation travel from the top of your head to the heels of your feet. Now inhale slowly and feel the circulation travel up the front of your body. Exhale as you feel it travel down the back of your body. Notice this light, relaxed,

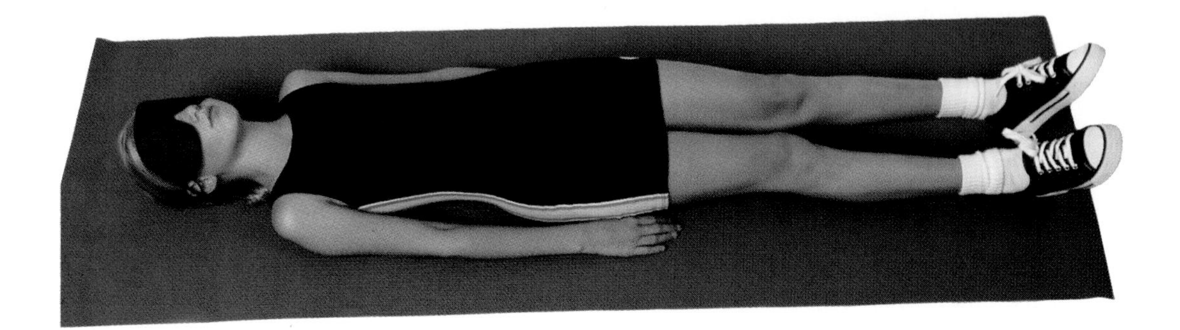

centered feeling. Open your eyes. Roll to the right side and slowly sit up into a cross-legged position.

Test-Centering Relaxation

This is a great technique for students to do on their own or for teachers to read to their classes. This relaxation is especially helpful the morning of a test day. Sit cross-legged or in a chair. Close your eyes, relax your facial muscles and drop your shoulders. Tune into the cool air coming in through your nose. Hold the air in your lungs for a few moments before slowly exhaling. Repeat and inhale for a count of three, hold, and exhale for a count of three. Relax and clear your mind. Focus on breathing as you fill yourself with confidence and clarity. Open your eyes and feel refreshed.

Travel Relaxation

Whether you are in a car, bus or plane, it is a perfect time to practice a relaxation. Take your shoes off and rotate your ankles three times in each direction. Flex and point your feet three times. Roll down your spine and slowly roll back

up. Arch and round the spine, inhaling as you arch and exhaling as you round your back three times. Do three shoulder rolls and a seated spinal twist to the left. Gain leverage with your left arm over the back of your seat and gaze over your left shoulder. Take a deep breath and repeat on the other side. Return facing forward and close your eyes. Feel a wave of relaxation travel up and down your spine. Imagine traveling to a beautiful and relaxing place. Think of what you might see, hear and feel in this paradise. Picture this place clearly in your mind's eye. Allow yourself to drift off in your imagination. As you come out of your relaxation, start to wiggle your toes. Feel the circulation spiral up your body and open your eyes. You should feel alert but relaxed.

Part XI
A Final Note

After many years of teaching yoga to adults, expanding my classes to include children was a natural progression. Yoga can be so beneficial and fun for kids to do. In my yoga classes for children, kids are always surprised that something that is so enjoyable can make them feel so good afterwards.

Yoga taps into kids' imagination and feeds their curiosity. They love hearing about the history of yoga and about poses they can do alone or with friends. Kids love learning about the fun names of yoga exercises and often enjoy naming or re-naming the poses themselves.

Whether kids want to relax, play games or participate in sports, yoga can be a valuable addition to their lives. It's a great skill to share with other kids, parents and teachers. As a full yoga workout or a stretching routine before an athletic event, kids can use I Can't Believe It's Yoga for Kids to best fit their lifestyles. Start practicing yoga now and you'll be on your way to a lifetime of better mental and physical health.

Lisa Trivell

Lisa Trivell with her daughter Amanda.

Meet the Author

Lisa Trivell is a certified exercise and yoga instructor, as well as a licensed massage therapist. For 15 years, she has taught yoga in New York City and East Hampton in corporations, schools, and her private practice. She is certified by the International Fitness Professionals Association (IFPA) and the American Aerobics Association International / International Sports Medicine Association (AAAI / ISMA).